TIPS
ON COURSEWORK

Coursework is a vital part of all GCSE Maths exams. The amount you have to do varies from exam group to exam group, and every school has its own way of organising the work. Here are some useful tips which you might find a help. Your work will be marked according to a fixed scheme, but the examiners are particularly on the look out for

TIP 1

Your overall strategy:

– Make sure that you have a good explanation of your aims at the beginning of a piece of work.
– Try and describe why you have used a particular method, and make the methods you use as clear as possible.

TIP 2

The mathematical content:

– You must use a variety of methods in any submission, and they must be appropriate to the level of entry.

TIP 3

Your accuracy:

– This really speaks for itself.
– Check your working thoroughly.

TIP 4

Your presentation:

– Although marks may not be given for neatness, you must use good diagrams if you need them.
– If your handwriting is not very good, why not use a typewriter or word processor, the results should be much easier to read.

TIP 5

Your summary:

You must try and tie up all loose ends at the end of your work: this is what a summary is. Give some general formulae if you find them. If you can't find a general formula, then state your conclusions clearly – this is what the examiner wants to see.

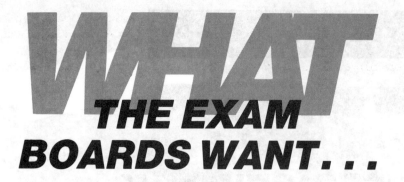

WHAT THE EXAM BOARDS WANT...

GRADE	G	F	E
AT2 NUMBER Units 1, 2, 3, 4	a) solve problems without the aid of a calculator considering the reasonableness of the answer b) demonstrate an understanding of the relationship between place values in whole numbers c) use fractions, decimals or percentages as appropriate to describe situations d) solve number problems with the aid of a calculator interpreting the display e) make sensible estimates of a range of measures in relation to everyday objects	a) use an appropriate non-calculator method to multiply or divide two numbers b) find fractions or percentages of quantities c) reline estimations by 'trial and improvement' methods d) use units in context	a) calculate with fractions, decimals, percentages or ratio as appropriate b) use estimation to check calculations
AT3 ALGEBRA Units 5, 9, 11,12	a) make general statements about patterns b) use simple formulae expressed in words c) use coordinates in the first quadrant	a) follow instructions to generate sequences b) express a simple function symbolically	a) explore number patterns using compute facilities or otherwise b) solve simple equations c) use and plot Cartesian coordinates to represent mappings
AT4 SHAPE AND SPACE Units 6, 7, 8, 9, 12, 13, 14	a) construct 2-D or 3-D shapes and know associated language b) specify location c) recognise rotational symmetry d) find perimeters, areas or volumes	a) use accurate measurement and drawing in constructing 3-D models b) use properties of shape to justify explanations c) use networks to solve problems a) use accurate measurement and drawing in constructing 3-D models d) find areas of plain shapes or volumes of simple solids	a) use 2-D representation of 3-D objects c) understand and use bearings to define direction b) transform shapes using a computer, or otherwise d) demonstrate that they know and can us the formulae for finding the area and circumference of circles
AT5 HANDLING DATA Units 4, 10, 12	a) interrogate and interpret data in a computer database b) conduct a survey on an issue of their choice c) use the mean and range of a set of data d) estimate and justify the probability of an event	a) use a computer database to draw conclusions b) design and use an observation sheet to collect data c) interpret statistical diagrams d) use an appropriate method for estimating probabilities	a) design and use a questionnaire to surve opinion b) understand and use the basic ideas of correlation c) identify all the outcomes of combining tw independent events d) know that the total probablity of all the mutually exclusive outcomes of an event i

GOOD DESIGN TO HELP YOU . . .

Notes to help you revise the facts and words you need for the exam

Useful facts fill in gaps in your knowledge with easy-to-follow summaries

Topic Choice
for full
GCSE syllabus
coverage

Every Question Graded
so you know how you're
doing

*Real Exam
Questions*
Just like you'll
meet in the exam
– you are carefully
taken through
step-by-step

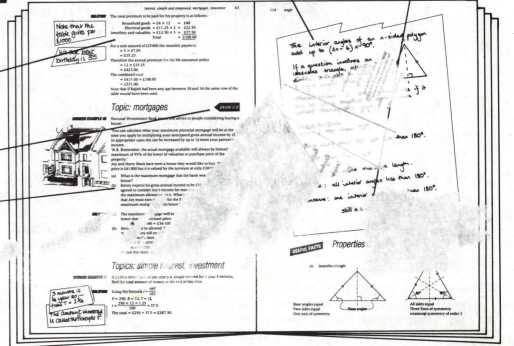

Progress Tests
4 Progress Tests to tell
you what grade to
expect: the marking
scheme tells how you
are doing and advises
points to watch and
revise further

*Hints on
Solutions*
Where you need
them to get it right
– as the question
develops

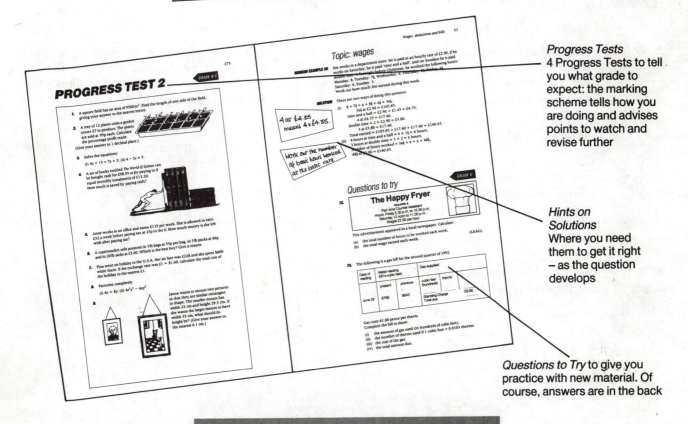

Questions to Try to give you
practice with new material. Of
course, answers are in the back

IN THIS BOOK...

Success Step by Step

S T E P 1

You have bought your copy of *Work Out Maths GCSE*.

S T E P 2

Work through the sections of the book, making sure you don't miss out any topics that you are weak at. Do not try sections that are beyond the grade you are capable of.

S T E P 3

Make full use of the three sections of Notes in each chapter: you need to be certain that you know the important words as well as the methods.

S T E P 4

Choose a selection of the Worked Examples to do – make full use of the problem solving material. Cover up the solution and check your answer against the correct one.

S T E P 5

If you find gaps in your knowledge, look at the pages headed "Useful Facts".

S T E P 6

Try the problems with answers at the back of the book. GCSE exams are much less predictable than exams used to be – you'll benefit from experience of new problems.

S T E P 7

Check your grade with a Progress Test: see where you need to do more work!

S T E P 8

You may be taking an aural or mental arithmetic test. In unit 15, you will find out how best to answer the questions. Some tests are provided for you to try. You will need someone to help read the questions to you. Take them seriously, it is important that you get the highest possible score on these tests.

All GCSE syllabuses must use the National Curriculum for the content. The grid below indicates what is required for each grade. You should work through the questions in the book up to the level you are aiming at. Twenty per cent of your marks are obtained from coursework (AT1).

You should always have access to a copy of the syllabus for your exam. Ask your teacher, or write to the exam board.

C/D	B	A	A*
multiply and divide mentally single-digit multiples of any power of 10 use a calculator efficiently when solving problems	a) calculate with numbers expressed in standard form b) evaluate formulae including the use of fractions or negative numbers c) solve numerical problems checking that the results are of the right order of magnitude	a) distinguish between rational and irrational numbers b) understand the significance of approximations	a) determine the possible effects of errors on calculations
recognise that measurement is approximate and choose the degree of accuracy appropriate for a particular purpose			
			a) use a calculator or computer to investigate sequences
use symbolic notation to express the rules of sequences solve equations or simple inequalities	a) manipulate algebraic formulae, equations or expressions b) solve inequalities	a) express general laws in symbolic form	b) manipulate algebraic expressions where necessary when saving problems
	c) interpret graphs which represent particular relationships	b) solve equations using graphical methods c) use the gradients of graphs found by constructing tangents	c) find the approximate area between a curve and the horizontal axis between two limits, and interpret the result d) sketch and compare the graphs of functions
	a) use mathematical similarity to solve problems		a) solve problems in 2-D or 3-D
use co-ordinates (x, y, z) to locate position in 3-D determine the locus of an object which is moving subject to a rule		b) use vector methods to solve problems	
use Pythagoras' theorem carry out calculations in plane and solid shapes	b) use sine, cosine or tangent in right-angled triangles c) distinguish between formulae by considering dimensions	a) carry out more complex calculations in plane or solid shapes c) use sine, cosine or tangent with angles of any size	
organise and analyse data	a) design and use a questionnaire or experiment to test a hypothesis		
	b) construct and interpret a cumulative frequency curve	a) use diagrams, graphs or computer packages to analyse a set of complex data b) use sampling to investigate a 'population'	a) describe the dispersion of a set of data b) interpret diagrams such as those used in critical path analysis or linear programming
understand and use relative frequency as an estimate of probability given the probability of exclusive events calculate the probability of a combined event	c) calculate the probability of a combined event given the probabilities of independent events	c) use conditional probabilities	c) calculate the probability of any two events happening

CONTENTS

The relevant attainment targets (AT) are noted for each chapter.

WORK OUT
MATHS GCSE

Geoff Buckwell

Illustrated by Colin Prior

Well done! You chose Work Out for its complete coverage

Acknowledgements

The author and publishers wish to thank the following for permission to use copyright material: London East Anglian Group, Midland Examining Group, Northern Examining Association comprised of Associated Lancashire Schools Examining Board, Joint Matriculation Board, North Regional Examinations Board, North West Regional Examinations Board and Yorkshire and Humberside Regional Examinations Board; Southern Examining Group and Welsh Joint Education Committee for questions from specimen and past examination papers; and Casio Electronics Co. Ltd for the illustration of their FX-85V calculator.

Every effort has been made to trace all the copyright holders, but if any have been inadvertently overlooked the publishers will be pleased to make the necessary arrangement at the first opportunity.

Editorial, design and production by Hart McLeod, Cambridge

M

NUMBER
ATTAINMENT TARGET 2 (AT2)

1 Working with numbers

TYPES OF NUMBERS:
(i) whole numbers, natural numbers, integers 1,2,3,4.....
(ii) prime numbers 2,3,5,7,11,13....
A prime number can only be divided by 1 and itself.
(1 is *not* a prime).
(iii) Square numbers 1,4,9,16,25...
(iv) triangle numbers 1,3,6,10.....

RULES.
The order in which calculations are done follows the BODMAS rule (brackets, of, divide, multiply, add, subtract).
Remember that 'of' is $\times$ (multiplication symbol), and 'share' is $\div$.

WORDS TO LEARN.
Factor: a number that divides exactly into another, 8 is a factor of 24.
Digit: a single figure number, e.g. 2 or 8
Cube: to the power 3 so 2 cubed written $2^3 =$ $2 \times 2 \times 2 = 8$.
Product: means multiply.
Multiple: The multiples of 4 are 4,8,12,16,......
Square Root: $\sqrt{}$. If you square the square root, you get back to the original number. $5^2 = 25$, so $\sqrt{25} = 5$.

Topics: multiples, H.C.F., L.C.M. ◀ GRADE G

WORKED EXAMPLE 1

(i) Find the highest common factor of 36 and 60.
(ii) Find the lowest common multiple of 12 and 14.

SOLUTION

(i) The factors of 36 are 1, 2, 3, 4, 6, 9, ⑫, 18, 36.
The factors of 60 are 1, 2, 3, 4, 5, 6, 10, ⑫, 15, 20, 30, 60.
The *highest* common factor (H.C.F.) is 12.

(ii) The multiples of 12 are 12, 24, 36, 48, 60, 72, ⑧④, 96, ...
The multiples of 14 are 14, 28, 42, 56, 70, ⑧④, 98, ...
It can be seen that the *lowest* common multiple (L.C.M.) is 84.

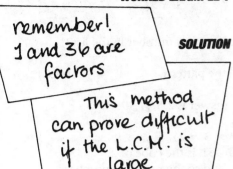

remember!
1 and 36 are
factors

This method
can prove difficult
if the L.C.M. is
large

Topics: multiples, remainders

WORKED EXAMPLE 2

A local disco is open every day of the week. Adele, Beth and Chris visit the disco together one Saturday. After that, Adele visits it every second day, Beth every third day and Chris every fifth day.

(a) After how many days will all three be at the disco together again?

(b) Which day of the week will it be?

(MEG)

SOLUTION

(a) This is actually a question about multiples. The days visited by A, B, C are as follows:
A: 2, 4, 6, 8, 10, 12, 14, 16, 18, 20, 22, 24, 26, 28, ㉚, ...
B: 3, 6, 9, 12, 15, 18, 21, 24, 27, ㉚, ...
C: 5, 10, 15, 20, 25, ㉚, ...
30 is the lowest common multiple of the three numbers 2, 3 and 5. Hence they are together again after 30 days.

(b) $30 \div 7 = 4$ remainder 2.
The day of the week is 2 days after Saturday, i.e. it is Monday.

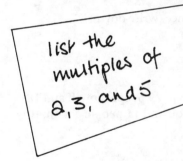

list the
multiples of
2, 3, and 5

Topic: BODMAS

◀ GRADE F

WORKED EXAMPLE 3

Find the value of:

(i) $6 \times (18 \div 2) - 3$; (ii) $(3 \times 6) \div (2 \times 6 - 3)$

SOLUTION

These questions need the BODMAS rule.

(i) Brackets first, so $6 \times (18 \div 2) - 3 = 6 \times 9 - 3$
Of and divide do not appear, so
Multiply next gives $54 - 3$.
Add does not appear.
Subtract gives the answer 51.
Hence, $6 \times (18 \div 2) - 3 = 6 \times 9 - 3 = 54 - 3 = 51$.

(ii) There are two sets of brackets here, so each one is worked out separately.
First bracket $= 3 \times 6 = 18$
Second bracket $= 2 \times 6 - 3$
(Multiply) $= 12 - 3$
(Subtract) $= 9$
Hence we have
$(3 \times 6) \div (2 \times 6 - 3)$
$= 18 \div 9 = 2$.

Topic: types of number

WORKED EXAMPLE 4   Look at this list of numbers
2, 5, 8, 11, 14, 17, 20
(a)   Which of these numbers are prime?
(b)   Which of these numbers is the cube of another number in the list?
(c)   The numbers form a pattern.
Write down the next two numbers in the pattern.   (MEG)

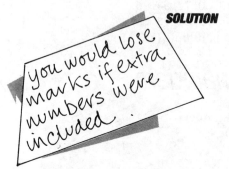

SOLUTION   (a)   Referring to a prime number list, the answer is 2,5,11,17.
(b)   The cube numbers would be given by
$1 \times 1 \times 1 = 1; 2 \times 2 \times 2 = 8; 3 \times 3 \times 3 = 27, \ldots$
You can see that the answer is 8, because it is the cube of 2.
(c)   The numbers increase by 3 each time, and so the next two numbers
will be 23, 26.

Questions to try

1.   Janet is trying to discover the factors of 570 using a calculator. She has
already discovered that 15 is a factor. To test whether the number 16 is a
factor of 570, she does the calculation $570 \div 16$
Her calculator shows

$$35.625$$

(a)   Write this calculator answer to the nearest whole number.
(b)   Is 16 a factor of 570? Give a reason for your answer.
(c)   Janet continues to look for factors.
She tests the numbers 17, 18 onwards.
What is the next factor she will find?   (NEA)

2.   Using each of the figures 2, 3, 5 and 8 only once, write down:
(i)   the largest possible four figure number;
(ii)   a multiple of 4;
(iii) a pair of 2 digit numbers that differ by 47.

3.   There were 67 people on a bus. At the first stop, 29 people got off and 18
people got on. At the next stop, 7 people got off and 11 people got on. How
many people are now on the bus?

4.

The ten tiles shown above are used in a game to make words, and the scores
shown on the tiles are added together.
For example,

scores $2 + 7 + 6 + 4 = 19$.

(a)   Calculate the score for:

(b)   A player makes the word ABODE. Calculate the score for this word.

(c)   Another player makes a five-letter word and scores a total of 23. Four of the letters in the word are A, E, L and N. What is the fifth letter?

(d)   A third player makes a six-letter word using the letters A, E, L, N and two others. All the letters in the word are different and the score for the word is 34. What are the other two letters?   (MEG)

5.

	12	14	7
	15	9	
13		8	11
16			10

(i)

2	15	9	8
14	3	5	12
7	10	16	1
11	6	4	13

(ii)

(i)   The numbers in each row, each column, and both diagonals of this number square add up to 34.
       The numbers 1, 2, 3, 4, 5 and 6 have been left out.
       Put them in their correct places.

(ii)   The number square in this part also contains many sets of four numbers which add up to 34.
       Nineteen of these sets contain the number 1.
       For example, 1 + 4 + 14 + 15.
       Find, and write down, as many sets of four numbers from this number square, which contain the number 1 and add up to 34, as you can.
                                                                              (MEG)

GRADE F

6. Using the digits 1, 5, 7 and 8 no more than once, write down:

(i)   a prime number between 10 and 30;
(ii)   a multiple of 7;
(iii) two numbers whose difference is 24;
(iv)   a number divisible by the square of 5.

2 Fractions and decimals

FRACTIONS adding or subtracting

(i) $\frac{2}{5} + \frac{1}{3} = \frac{6}{15} + \frac{5}{15} = \frac{11}{15}$

always make the bottom line the same before adding or subtracting.

multiplying (ii) $\frac{1}{4} \times \frac{2}{3} = \frac{\cancel{2}}{\cancel{12}_6} = \frac{1}{6}$

(This is called cancelling)

dividing (iii) $\frac{1}{2} \div \frac{3}{4} = \frac{1}{2} \times \frac{4}{3} = \frac{4}{6}$
$= \frac{2}{3}$ turn the second

fraction upside down and multiply.

(iv) $\frac{3}{4}$ of something means $\frac{3}{4} \times$

mixed numbers (v) $2\frac{1}{3} = \frac{7}{3}$ ← $(2 \times 3 + 1)$

This fraction is top heavy.

(vi) $2\frac{1}{4} \times 1\frac{1}{2} = \frac{9}{4} \times \frac{3}{2} = \frac{27}{8}$
$= 3\frac{3}{8}$

Always change mixed numbers to top heavy before multiplying and dividing.

DECIMALS correcting or rounding.

(i) 1.23 means $1 + \frac{2}{10} + \frac{3}{100}$

(ii) 1.463 to 2 decimal places
$= 1.46$

1.887 to 2 decimal places
$= 1.89$

1.645 to 2 decimal places
$= 1.64$ or 65.

(iii) 18.4 to 2 significant figures $= 18$

8.96 to 2 significant figures $= 9.0$

To change a fraction to a decimal, divide:
$5/7$ is $5 \div 7$

(iv) rational numbers. Any number that can be written as a fraction e.g. $\frac{3}{5}$, $1\frac{1}{4}$, 4.6 (really $4\frac{3}{5}$)

$0.\dot{1}$ means $0.1111.....$ (recurring decimal) $= \frac{1}{9}$

(v) irrational numbers. Any number that is not a rational number e.g. $\sqrt{2}$, π.

WORDS TO LEARN.
Place value: what a number actually stands
for e.g. in 36.57 the 3 stands for 30,
but the 5 stands for 5/10.
Rounding: finding the nearest (see worked example 5)
Trial and improvement: systematically working
towards an exact answer.

Topics: rounding, units

GRADE G

WORKED EXAMPLE 5   Round the following values to the accuracy stated:

    (i)   8.46 m to the nearest 10 cm;
    (ii)   a crowd of eighteen thousand seven hundred and seventy six to the nearest hundred;
    (iii) 0.00876 kg to the nearest gram;
    (iv) 8.648 cm to the nearest $\frac{1}{2}$ mm.

SOLUTION   (i)   8.46 m is 846 cm.
           Which is nearer, 840 cm or 850 cm?
           The answer is 850 cm.
    (ii)   In full, 18 776.
           The choice is between 18 700 and 18 800.
           The nearest is 18 800.
    (iii) kg to grams is × 1000.
           0.00876 × 1000 = 8.76 grams.
           The choice is between 8 and 9 grams.
           The nearest is 9 grams.
    (iv) cm to mm is × 10.
           8.648 × 10 = 86.48 mm.
           The choice is between 86 and 86½ mm.
           Clearly, 86½ is nearest.

Topic: trial and improvement

GRADE F

WORKED EXAMPLE 6   Use a trial and improvement method to find the square root of 7.63 correct to 2 decimal places. You can use a calculator only to multiply.

SOLUTION   Since 7.63 lies between 4 and 9 (both exact squares), then the square root of 7.63 lies between $\sqrt{4}$ and $\sqrt{9}$.
i.e. 2 and 3.
As a first guess take 2.5
Now 2.5 × 2.5 = 6.25   which is too low
Try 2.6 × 2.6 = 6.76   which is still too low
Try 2.7 × 2.7 = 7.29   which is still too low
Try 2.8 × 2.8 = 7.84   which is too high
Try 2.75 × 2.75 = 7.5625   which is slightly too low
Try 2.76 × 2.76 = 7.6176   this looks about the best
but try 2.77 × 2.77 = 7.6729
Hence $\sqrt{7.63}$ = 2.76 to two decimal places
To change a fraction or decimal to a percentage, multiply by 100.
To change a percentage to a fraction or decimal, divide by 100.

Topics: fractions, percentages 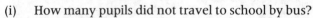 GRADE F

WORKED EXAMPLE 7   A school has 726 pupils. In a survey, it was found that $\frac{5}{6}$ of the pupils travelled to the school by bus.

(i)   How many pupils did not travel to school by bus?
(ii) What percentage of pupils did not travel by bus?

SOLUTION

(i)   Watch out for problems where you are asked the *opposite* question to the information given.
Since $\frac{5}{6}$ travel by bus, $1 - \frac{5}{6} = \frac{1}{6}$ do not travel by bus.

$$\frac{1}{6} \text{ of } 726 = \frac{1}{6} \times 726 \text{ or } 726 \div 6$$
$$= 121$$

Hence 121 pupils did not travel to school by bus.

(ii) Since $\frac{1}{6}$ do not travel by bus, we have to change $\frac{1}{6}$ to a percentage.

$$\frac{1}{6} \times \frac{100}{1} = \frac{100}{6} = 100 \div 6$$
$$= 16.7\% \text{ (to 1 dec. pl.) by calculator.}$$

Topics: decimal places, significant figures

WORKED EXAMPLE 8

(a)   Write down the following numbers correct to 2 decimal places:
(i) 8.884; (ii) 0.0907; (iii) 8.996; (iv) 3.004.

(b)   Write down the following numbers correct to 2 significant figures:
(i) 864; (ii) 0.9341; (iii) 999; (iv) 807.

SOLUTION

(a)   (i)   8.88   The 4 has no effect.
(ii) 0.09   The 0 following the 9 has no effect.
(iii) 9.00   The 6 increases the 9 by 1 which has to increase the 8 to 9.
(iv) 3.00   The 4 has no effect, but the 2 zeros *must* be included.

(b)   (i)   860   A common mistake is to write 86.
(ii) 0.93   Count significant figures from the first non-zero digit.
(iii) 1000   The 9 in the units column increases each digit by 1.
(iv) 810   The seven increases zero by 1.

Topics: fractions, decimals   GRADE E

WORKED EXAMPLE 9

(i)   Use your calculator to change $\frac{5}{8}$ into a decimal.
(ii) (a)   Write down the first 4 decimal places shown by the calculator when you change $\frac{3}{11}$ into a decimal.
(b)   Given that this decimal recurs, what digit will appear in the twenty-first decimal place?

SOLUTION

(i)   5 $\boxed{\div}$ 8 $\boxed{=}$ $\boxed{0.625}$
The answer is 0.625.

(ii) (a)   3 $\boxed{\div}$ 11 $\boxed{=}$ $\boxed{0.27272727.}$

(b)   The first 4 decimal places are 0.2727.
The pattern repeats every 2 decimal places, so
all odd numbered places are 2;
all even numbered places are 7.
The twenty-first decimal place is 2.

Topic: fractions

GRADE B

WORKED EXAMPLE 10 John receives £3.50 pocket money each week. He saves $\frac{1}{2}$ of it, and of the remainder he spends $\frac{1}{5}$ on sweets, and $\frac{1}{7}$ on his weekly sub to a youth club.

(i)   How much money is left?
(ii) What fraction of his pocket money is left (simplify your answer)?

first find how much the remainder is....

finding $\frac{1}{5}$ is the same as dividing by 5 ~

SOLUTION Always read this type of question carefully. It says he spends a certain amount of the *remainder*, not of £3.50.
Now $\frac{1}{2}$ of £3.50 is £1.75.
John has £1.75 left.
$\frac{1}{5}$ of this is £1.75 ÷ 5 = 35p.
$\frac{1}{7}$ of this is £1.75 ÷ 7 = 25p.
35p + 25p = 60p; take this from £1.75.

(i)   He has left £1.75 − 60p = £1.15.

(ii) The fraction left is $\dfrac{£1.15}{£3.50}$.

Working in pence, this is $\dfrac{115}{350} = \dfrac{\overset{23}{\cancel{115}}}{\underset{70}{\cancel{350}}} = \dfrac{23}{70}$ (cancel by 5).

23 doesn't cancel by anything, hence the answer is $\dfrac{23}{70}$.

Topic: calculations with fractions

WORKED EXAMPLE 11 Without the use of a calculator, find

(i) $2\frac{1}{3} + 3\frac{2}{5}$; (ii) $3\frac{1}{12} - 1\frac{3}{4}$.

SOLUTION (i) $2\frac{1}{3} + 3\frac{2}{5} = \dfrac{7}{3} + \dfrac{17}{5}$

$= \dfrac{35}{15} + \dfrac{51}{15} = \dfrac{86}{15} = 5\frac{11}{15}$.

(ii) $3\frac{1}{12} - 1\frac{3}{4} = \dfrac{37}{12} - \dfrac{7}{4}$

$= \dfrac{37}{12} - \dfrac{21}{12} = \dfrac{16}{12} = 1\frac{1}{3}$.

Topics: fractions, irrational and rational

WORKED EXAMPLE 12 (i) Write down a rational number between $\frac{2}{3}$ and $\frac{5}{6}$.

GRADE A

(ii) Write down an irrational number between 2 and 3.

SOLUTION (i) Rational means fractions, so can we find a fraction between $\frac{4}{6}$ and $\frac{5}{6}$?
What about $\dfrac{4\frac{1}{2}}{6}$?

× top and bottom by 2: $\dfrac{9}{12} = \dfrac{3}{4}$.

(ii) A good idea here with this sort of question is to look at the squares
$2^2 = 4$ and $3^2 = 9$.
Our irrational number can be the $\sqrt{}$ of any number between 4 and 9.
Hence $\sqrt{7}$ will do.

Questions to try

7. Write down:

GRADE G

(i)   8.465 m to the nearest cm;
(ii)   8.856 kg to the nearest gram;
(iii) 8970 to the nearest 100;
(iv)   5.87 to the nearest whole number;
(v)   8.76 to the nearest tenth;
(vi)   878494 to the nearest 10000.

8. Add eight thousand and ninety five to seven hundred and seventeen, giving your answer in figures,

GRADE F

(i) exactly; (ii) correct to 2 significant figures.

9. (a)   Write the following numbers correct to 2 significant figures:
        (i) 18.84; (ii) 8463; (iii) 999; (iv) 8.004; (v) 91.79; (vi) 84830;
        (vii) 8.994; (viii) 85.07.
    (b)   Write the following numbers correct to 1 decimal place:
        (i) 8.66; (ii) 9.03; (iii) 8.11; (iv) 18.95; (v) 9.09; (vi) 8.88; (vii) 9.99;
        (viii) 4.8812.

10. Thirty seven thousand eight hundred and nine people watched the match between Manchester United and Arsenal.

(i)   Write that number in figures.
(ii)   Write that number to the
       nearest thousand.
(iii) Write that number correct to
       1 significant figure.

11. 0.4 $\frac{2}{5}$ 0.049   0.503 $\frac{4}{7}$
From the five numbers,

GRADE E

(i)   write down the largest;
(ii)   write down the smallest;
(iii) write down the difference between the smallest and the largest, correct to 2 decimal places.

12. From the following fractions, $\frac{6}{11}$ $\frac{15}{18}$ $\frac{4}{7}$ $\frac{10}{12}$ $\frac{8}{9}$, pick out:

(i)   the smallest;
(ii)   the largest;
(iii) the two that are equal.

13. Use a trial and improvement method to find the value of $\sqrt{11.4}$ correct to one decimal place. Show all steps clearly in your working.

14. Jane is doing some painting. She uses $2\frac{1}{4}$ tins of gloss paint, $1\frac{1}{3}$ tins of
GRADE B
undercoat, and $\frac{5}{8}$ tin of primer. How many tins of paint is this altogether?

15. The sweets in a box are classed as creams, caramels, or toffees. In a box of Keely's Choice, $\frac{3}{8}$ of the contents are creams, $\frac{1}{4}$ of them are caramels and the remainder are toffees.

(a) Work out the fraction of the sweets in the box that are either creams or caramels.

(b) What fraction of the sweets in the box are toffees? (LEAG)

16. Last week, Mr McKewan worked the following hours:
Monday $7\frac{1}{4}$, Tuesday $7\frac{3}{4}$, Wednesday $8\frac{1}{2}$, Thursday $7\frac{1}{4}$, Friday 8, Saturday $3\frac{1}{2}$.
He was paid £160.55 for this work.

(i) How many hours did he work?

(ii) How much was he paid per hour?

17. Five of the numbers below are rational and five are irrational: **GRADE A**

(i) $\pi\sqrt{5}$ (ii) $\sqrt{2}+1$ (iii) $(\sqrt{2})^3$ (iv) $16^{-\frac{1}{2}}$

(v) $\dfrac{\sqrt{3}}{\sqrt{2}}$ (vi) $2^0+2^{-1}+2^{-2}$ (vii) $(\sqrt{3})^4$

(viii) $\sqrt{3}-1.732050808$ (ix) $\sqrt{3}.\sqrt{12}$ (x) 0.3

(a) Write down the five rational numbers

(b) Give an example of two different **irrational** numbers, a and b, where $\dfrac{a}{b}$ is a rational number. (LEAG)

18. For each of the following numbers, state whether it is rational or irrational.

For each rational number, write down an equivalent fraction $\dfrac{m}{n}$, where m and n are positive integers with no common factor.

(a) 0.625 (b) $\frac{1}{2}(\sqrt{3}+1)$ (c) π (d) 0.7 (e) $\sqrt{12.25}$
(MEG)

19. A calculator with a ten-digit display gives the following conversions of fractions to decimals

$$\frac{1}{17} = 0.058823529; \qquad \frac{1}{18} = 0.055555555$$

$$\frac{1}{19} = 0.052631578; \qquad \frac{1}{21} = 0.047619047$$

What can you say from these results about expressing $\dfrac{1}{17}, \dfrac{1}{18}, \dfrac{1}{19}$ and $\dfrac{1}{21}$ as recurring decimals

3 Ratio, directed numbers

RATIO : ratios can be simplified like fractions. So 16:24 is the same as 2:3 (÷ by 8).
2:3 means divide an amount into 5 parts (3+2), and then take 2 parts and 3 parts.

It is often easier to make one of the numbers 1 (called the unitary method).
So 4:50 is the same as 1:12½ (÷4)

MAP SCALES : 1:50000, means every cm on the map is 50000 cm in real distances.

But 50000 cm ÷ 100000 = 0.5 km.
Easier to use 1cm stands for 0.5 km.
Careful with areas: 1cm² represents 1cm x 1cm.
Since ½ km x ½ km = ¼ km², this means that 1cm² stands for 0.25 km².

DIRECTED NUMBERS: Used in temperature, direction, bank statements (overdrafts) etc.

Negative numbers are below zero

Positive numbers are above zero

WORDS TO LEARN.
The number line (see above)
less than : < e.g. 2 < 6
greater than : > e.g. 8 > -4

Working with directed numbers

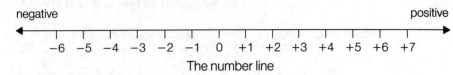

negative   positive

$$-6 \quad -5 \quad -4 \quad -3 \quad -2 \quad -1 \quad 0 \quad +1 \quad +2 \quad +3 \quad +4 \quad +5 \quad +6 \quad +7$$

The number line

To help avoid confusion, the directed numbers are circled.

(a) **Addition** $(+2) + (+5) = (+7), (+5) + (-3) = (+2), (-5) + (-7) = (-12)$

> Addition of any negative number to any other number
> always gives a *smaller* answer.
> Addition of any positive number to any other number
> always gives a *larger* answer.

This is only helpful advice, you still have to get the answer right!
The following summarises the above more accurately:

> Addition of a positive number p increases the original
> number by p (move $\rightarrow$).
> Addition of a negative number n decreases the original
> number by n (move $\leftarrow$).

Note that in the third example above, if you decrease (-5) by 7
it becomes (-12).

(b) **Subtraction** $(+2) - (+5) = (-3), (+5) - (-3) = (+8), (-5) - (-7) = (+2)$

> Subtraction of any positive number from any number
> always gives a *smaller* number.
> Subtraction of any negative number from any number
> always gives a *larger* number.

> Subtraction of a positive number p decreases the original
> number by p.
> Subtraction of a negative number n increases the original
> number by n.

Note that in the third subtraction example above, if you increase
(-5) by 7 you get $(+2)$.

(c) **Multiplication and division**

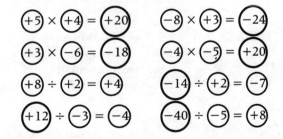

$$(+5) \times (+4) = (+20) \qquad (-8) \times (+3) = (-24)$$
$$(+3) \times (-6) = (-18) \qquad (-4) \times (-5) = (+20)$$
$$(+8) \div (+2) = (+4) \qquad (-14) \div (+2) = (-7)$$
$$(+12) \div (-3) = (-4) \qquad (-40) \div (-5) = (+8)$$

> If two positive or negative numbers are multiplied or
> divided the answer is positive.
> If a negative and a positive number are multiplied or
> divided, the answer is negative.

Topic: negative numbers

WORKED EXAMPLE 13   The temperature at midnight in Leeds on each day of a week in January is shown in the following table:

Day	Sunday	Monday	Tuesday	Wednesday	Thursday	Friday	Saturday
Temp.	−4°C	−6°C	0°C	4°C	−3°C	−4°C	−6°C

(i)   What is the range of temperatures?

(ii)   What was the average midnight temperature during the week?

SOLUTION   (i)   The highest temperature = 4°C.
The lowest temperature = −6°C.
The range = highest − lowest
$$= 4 - (-6)$$
$$= 4 + 6 = 10°C.$$

(ii)   The average
$$= (-4 + -6 + 0 + 4 + -3 + -4 + -6) \div 7$$
$$= (-23 + 4) \div 7$$
$$= -19 \div 7$$
$$= -2.7°C \text{ to 1 d.p.}$$

Topics: ratio, units

WORKED EXAMPLE 14

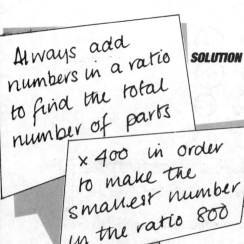

In order to dilute a bottle of orange squash, it is recommended to mix squash and water in the ratio 2:5.

(i)   How much squash should be put into a glass that holds 280 ml?

(ii)   A large jug of squash is to be made up, using a full bottle of orange that holds 0.8 litres. How much drink can be made from this bottle?

Always add numbers in a ratio to find the total number of parts

SOLUTION   (i)   2 + 5 = 7 parts in total.
280 ÷ 7 = 40 ml in 1 part.
Hence the amount of squash = 2 × 40 = 80 ml.

(ii)   0.8 litres = 0.8 × 1000 = 800 ml:
$$2 : 5$$
$$\times 400 \quad = 800 : 2000$$
The amount of water needed is 2000 ml.
Hence the amount of squash = 2000 + 800 = 2800 ml
or 2.8 litres.

× 400 in order to make the smallest number in the ratio 800

remember! 1 litre = 1000 ml.

Topics: map scales, ratio

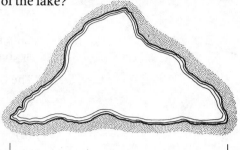

GRADE B

WORKED EXAMPLE 15   A map has been drawn to a scale of 1:50000. On the map, a lake measures 6 cm at its longest. What is this distance in km? If the area of the lake on the map is 9 cm², what is the real area of the lake?

SOLUTION $6 \times 50000 = 300000$ cm
$\div 100000 = 300000 \div 100000 = 3$ km.
The length of the lake is 3 km.
1 cm represents 50000 cm, but 50000 cm $= \frac{1}{2}$ km,
so 1 cm represents $\frac{1}{2}$ km.
Hence 1 cm² represents $\frac{1}{2}$ km $\times \frac{1}{2}$ km $= \frac{1}{4}$ km².
So 9 cm² represents $9 \times \frac{1}{4} = 2\frac{1}{4}$ km².
The real area of the lake is $2\frac{1}{4}$ km².

remember !
1 km = 100000 cm

6 cm

Questions to try

20.   What is the difference between $-6°C$ and $-12°C$?

GRADE F

21.   The temperature at Brighton changed from 4°C to −3°C overnight.

(i)   By how much did the temperature change overnight?
(ii)   If the thermometer used was reading a temperature 2°C too low, what was the real change in temperature overnight?

22.   The owner of a magazine stall estimates that he sells 5 magazines for every 15 newspapers that he sells.

(i)   In a week when he sells 85 magazines, how many newspapers did he sell?
(ii)   On another occasion, during one week he sold a total of 480 newspapers and magazines altogether. How many of these were magazines?

23.   Using numbers from the following list, complete the following statements:
7   12   18   24

(i)   The difference between ...... and ...... is 5.
(ii)   The ratio of ...... to ...... is 3:2.
(iii) The remainder when ...... is divided by ...... is 3.

24.   (i)   A motorist buys 60 litres of petrol. If one litre is approximately $1\frac{3}{4}$ pints, how many pints did he buy?
(ii)   If eight pints are equal to one gallon, how many gallons did the motorist buy?
(iii) If 25 litres of petrol cost £10.25, how much did the motorist have to pay for the petrol?
(iv)   How much per gallon was the motorist paying for the petrol?

25.

Concrete suitable for garden paths is made from a mixture of cement and aggregate. (Aggregate is made from sand and small stones.)

The cement and aggregate are mixed in the ratio of 2 to 7.

(a)   What weight of cement is needed to make up 1.8 tonnes of concrete mix?

(b)   Cement is sold in 50kg bags. How many bags of cement are needed for this amount of concrete?
(1000kg = 1 tonne)   (MEG)

26.   The table shows the maximum and minimum temperatures recorded during the year in six different towns in Great Britain.

Town	Minimum temperature	Maximum temperature
Southampton	−8°C	24°C
Plymouth	−6°C	27°C
Blackpool	−9°C	26°C
Manchester	−8°C	25°C
Aberdeen	−12°C	24°C
Swansea	−4°C	28°C

(a)   Which town had the lowest temperature?
(b)   Which town had the greatest range between the maximum and minimum temperatures?
(c)   Can you say anything about the weather in the towns from these figures?

GRADE E

27.   The number of pages in a magazine was increased from 36 to 45. The original price of 80p is increased in the same ratio. What is the new price of the magazine?

28.   An alloy is made from copper and tin in the ratio 5:7.

(i)   How much tin is there in 48kg of the alloy?
(ii)   Express the amount of copper in the alloy as a percentage.

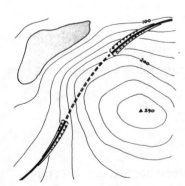

29.   A map is drawn to a scale of 1 : 20000.

GRADE B

(i)   Find the length on the map of a tunnel 3km long.
(ii)   Find the area of a lake in km², which occupies an area of 10cm² on the map.

30. A small circular wheel has teeth on the outside of its circumference. These teeth match the teeth on the outside of a larger wheel as the smaller wheel rotates around the outside of the fixed larger one.

At the start, the point marked A on the smaller wheel is alongside the point marked B on the larger wheel. The small wheel is now rotated around the outside of the larger wheel.

(a) If there are 28 teeth on the small wheel and 112 teeth on the large one, how many times will point A on the small wheel come round to touch the circumference of the large one by the time it has returned to the start position?

(b) Write down a different number of teeth for the small and large wheels so that question (a) would still have the same answer as before.

(c) Write down what you think is the rule connecting the number of teeth on the small and large wheels for this to happen.

GRADE C/D

31. The Patel family went by car from Birmingham to London to visit relatives. They travelled at an average speed of 90 km/h. On the return journey, it was misty, so they had to reduce their average speed in the ratio 2:3.

(a) What was their average speed on the return journey?

(b) They took 2 hours 12 minutes to travel to London. How long, in hours and minutes, did the return journey take?

(MEG)

CALCULATION
ATTAINMENT TARGET 2

1 The calculator, estimation and standard form

THE CALCULATOR:

If you have time, always try and check a calculation, or try to estimate the answer so that you can see if you have made an error.

Do not rush calculations; it leads to mistakes. Carry as many decimal places as you can in the calculation until the final answer, otherwise you may lose accuracy.

If you are using a calculator for trigonometry, it must be a scientific calculator. If the calculator does not have a bracket button, check that it follows BODMAS rules otherwise work out each part of the calculation separately (fortunately most calculators do).

Always show as much working as possible in an examination paper. Standard form (sometimes called scientific notation) can be used for large or small numbers

$A \times 10^{\wedge}$: must have $1 \leq A < 10$
Hence 84×10^7 is not standard form.

* Remember to check your calculator has nothing in the memory before you start any calculation. Never include too many figures in your answers: 3 significant figure accuracy is enough.

The calculator

Explanations of certain buttons

$\boxed{\%}$ percentages

$\frac{5}{8}$ as a % 5 $\boxed{\div}$ 8 $\boxed{\%}$ $\boxed{62.5}$

$\boxed{+/-}$ changes the sign

So to enter -5 5 $\boxed{+/-}$ $\boxed{-5.}$

$\boxed{\sqrt{x}}$ square root

To find $\sqrt{18}$ 18 $\boxed{\sqrt{}}$ $\boxed{4.242641}$

$\boxed{x^2}$ square

To find 12^2 12 $\boxed{x^2}$ $\boxed{144.}$

$\boxed{M+}$ adds a number to the memory*

$\boxed{MR}$ recalls the number stored in the memory*

$\boxed{x^y}$ power button*

To find 3^5 3 $\boxed{x^y}$ 5 $\boxed{=}$ $\boxed{243}$

$\boxed{\pi}$ gives a value of π $\boxed{3.141593}$

$\boxed{EXP}$ or $\boxed{EE}$ standard form

To enter 8.4×10^7

8.4 $\boxed{EXP}$ 7 $\boxed{8.4 \quad 07}$

$\boxed{\sin}$ $\boxed{\cos}$ $\boxed{\tan}$

These will be explained in unit 8.

$\boxed{(}$ $\boxed{)}$

Left and right brackets. These can be used as written.

*There are variations to this button on many calculators.

GRADE F

Topics: estimating, the calculator

WORKED EXAMPLE 16 Estimate as accurately as you can without the use of a calculator, the following:

(i) 8.6×99;
(ii) the cost of 29 pens at 62p each;
(iii) the number of pieces of wood 2.2 cm long, that can be cut from a strip of balsa wood 50 cm long;
(iv) the length of the equator in miles, if the radius of the earth is 3960 miles.

Check your answers with a calculator.

SOLUTION (i)   Choose sensible numbers near to the values given.
8.6×99 is near $9 \times 100 = 900$.
By calculator, $8.6 \times 99 = 851.4$.

(ii) 29 at 62p is near 30 at 60p = 1800p or £18.
By calculator, $29 \times 62 = 1798p = £17.98$.

(iii) 50 cm ÷ 2.2 cm is near 50 cm ÷ 2 cm = 25.
By calculator, $50 \div 2.2 = 22.7$ or 22 pieces.

(iv) We need to know the formula for the circumference $= 2\pi R$.
Hence the length $= 2 \times \pi \times 3960$.
This is near $2 \times 3 \times 4000 = 24\,000$ miles.
By calculator, $2 \times \pi \times 3960 = 24\,881$ miles.

Topic: using a calculator

GRADE E

WORKED EXAMPLE 17 Use a calculator to work out the following, and give your answers correct to 3 significant figures:

(i) $84 \times (67 + 984)$;
(ii) $85 \div (8.6 \times 11.4)$;
(iii) $2.4^2 + 1.6^2$;
(iv) $\frac{5}{7}$ as a percentage.

SOLUTION If your calculator does not have a bracket button, proceed as follows:

Check memory is empty before any calculation

(i)   67 $\boxed{+}$ 984 $\boxed{=}$ $\boxed{M+}$ 84 $\boxed{\times}$ $\boxed{MR}$ $\boxed{=}$ $\boxed{88284}$

(ii) 8.6 $\boxed{\times}$ 11.4 $\boxed{=}$ $\boxed{M+}$ 85 $\boxed{\div}$ $\boxed{MR}$ $\boxed{=}$ $\boxed{0.8669931}$

(iii) 2.4 $\boxed{\times}$ 2.4 $\boxed{M+}$ 1.6 $\boxed{\times}$ 1.6 $\boxed{=}$ $\boxed{+}$ $\boxed{MR}$ $\boxed{=}$ $\boxed{8.32}$

OR   2.4 $\boxed{x^2}$ $\boxed{+}$ 1.6 $\boxed{x^2}$ $\boxed{=}$ $\boxed{8.32}$

(iv) 5 $\boxed{\div}$ 7 $\boxed{\%}$ $\boxed{=}$ $\boxed{71.428571}$

If it does have brackets, (ii) could be done as follows:

85 $\boxed{\div}$ $\boxed{(}$ 8.6 $\boxed{\times}$ 11.4 $\boxed{)}$ $\boxed{=}$ $\boxed{0.8669931}$

Correct to 3 significant figures (i) 88300; (ii) 0.867; (iii) 8.32; (iv) 71.4.

Topic: standard form

GRADE B

WORKED EXAMPLE 18 Change into standard form,

(i) 4 860 000; (ii) 0.086.

SOLUTION (i)   Place a decimal point after the first digit (from the left)
This gives 4.860 000
$\underbrace{}$
6 figures
The answer is 4.86×10^6.

Count the numbers of figures after the point

(ii) $0.086 = 8.6 \div 100$
$= 8.6 \div 10^2$
This is changed to 8.6×10^{-2}.

0.086 $\uparrow\uparrow$ 2 zeros gives 10^{-2}

Topic: standard form calculations

WORKED EXAMPLE 19 Work out the following in standard form:

(i) $2.86 \times 10^4 + 4.3 \times 10^2$;
(ii) $(3.9 \times 10^4) \times (4.6 \times 10^5)$;
(iii) $(4.52 \times 10^5) \div (8.86 \times 10^{-2})$.

SOLUTION The working shown here assumes your calculator does not have the facility to enter numbers in standard form. If it does, then the sums can be worked out directly in standard form; see after (iii).

Take numbers out of standard form.

(i) $2.86 \times 10^4 + 4.3 \times 10^2$
$= 28\,600 + 430$
$= 29\,030$
$= 2.903 \times 10^4$.

(ii) $(3.9 \times 10^4) \times (4.6 \times 10^5)$
      $= 3.9 \times 4.6 \times 10^4 \times 10^5$
      $= 17.94 \times 10^9$.
      This is not standard form, the answer is 1.794×10^{10}.

(iii) $(4.52 \times 10^5) \div (8.86 \times 10^{-2})$

$$= \frac{4.52 \times 10^5}{8.86 \times 10^{-2}} = \frac{4.52}{8.86} \times \frac{10^5}{10^{-2}}$$
$$= 0.510 \times 10^7$$
$$= 5.1 \times 10^6.$$

Add the powers
4 + 5 = 9.

Subtract the powers
5 – –2 = 7

Convert to standard form

OR Part (i) can be done using the $\boxed{\text{EXP}}$ button as follows:

2.86 $\boxed{\text{EXP}}$ 4 $+$ 4.3 $\boxed{\text{EXP}}$ 2 $=$ $\boxed{29030}$

Questions to try

32. Use the calculator to change: **GRADE E**
   (i) $\frac{5}{8}$ into a decimal, giving 3 decimal places;
   (ii) $\frac{2}{11}$ as a percentage, giving 3 significant figures;
   (iii) the average of 8.6, 5.9, 2.7, giving 2 decimal places.

33. The following sequence is correct. What symbols are missing on the buttons?
   $8 \ \boxed{} \ 4 \ \boxed{} \ 7 \ \boxed{} \ 25$

34. Use a calculator to find: **GRADE C/D**

   (i) $64 \times (83 + 71)$; (ii) $4.1^2 + 3.6^2$; (iii) $(2.9 \div 3.7) \times 5.6$.

35. Write in standard form: **GRADE B**

   (i) 86 400; (ii) 957; (iii) 0.002; (iv) 0.0406; (v) 18×10^3; (vi) 16×10^{-3}.

36. Without the use of a calculator, estimate the value of the following calculations to 1 significant figure:

   (i) 89×58; (ii) $123 \div 18$; (iii) 0.86×0.95; (iv) $(8.9 + 11.7) \times 85$;
   (v) 293×19.

37. Work out the following, giving your answers in standard form:

   (i) $3.8 \times 10^6 + 4.2 \times 10^5$; (ii) $(2.8 \times 10^2) \times (1.2 \times 10^4)$;
   (iii) $6 \times 10^{-3} + 4 \times 10^{-2}$; (iv) 12×10^5; (v) $(6 \times 10^6)^2$; (vi) 125×10^{-3}.

38. Use your calculator to work out the following, giving your answer as a decimal to 3 decimal places:

   (i) $\frac{3}{4} \times \frac{2}{9}$; (ii) $1\frac{1}{3} + 2\frac{1}{2}$; (iii) $2\frac{1}{4} \div 1\frac{1}{3}$.

2 Percentages

PERCENTAGES : % means out of 100

To change % to fraction, ÷ by 100

So $20\% = \frac{20}{100} = \frac{1}{5}$ or 0.2

To change a fraction to %, × by 100

So $\frac{3}{8} = \frac{3}{8} \times 100 = \frac{300}{8} = 37.5\%$

Percentage 'of' : (i) To find 8% of £12

$\frac{8}{100} \times 12 = \frac{96}{100} = .96$ i.e. 96p

(ii) 80 cm as a % of 2m
(change 2m to 200cm)

$\frac{80}{200} \times 100 = \frac{8000}{200} = 40\%$

Profit and loss : % Profit (or loss) $= \frac{Profit (or loss)}{Cost} \times 100$

Changes : % change $= \frac{change}{original} \times 100$

Errors : % error $= \frac{error}{correct\ value} \times 100$

V.A.T. : value added tax, charged at 17.5% at present.

Topic: percentage

GRADE F

WORKED EXAMPLE 20   A shopkeeper can buy packets of 12 felt pens for 86p. He adds on a 'mark up' profit of 25%, and then V.A.T. has to be added on top. How much does he sell the pens for?

SOLUTION   25% of 86p is $\frac{25}{100} \times 86 = 21p$ (ignore $\frac{1}{2}$p).

This is 86 + 21 = 107p.
V.A.T. is 17.5%,

so the V.A.T. $= \frac{17.5}{100} \times 107 = 18p$.

(whole pence only)

The selling price is
107 + 18 = 125p
= £1.25.

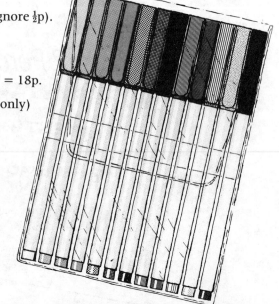

Topic: percentage differences

GRADE E

WORKED EXAMPLE 21   Joan was asked to cut $1\frac{1}{2}$m from a piece of '2 by 1' timber. When she measured the piece cut, she found it was only 145 cm long. What percentage error had she made?

SOLUTION   The difference from the correct answer

$$= 150 - 145 = 5\,\text{cm}.$$

Hence the % error $= \dfrac{5}{150} \times 100\%$

$$= 3.3\%$$

Topic: percentage changes

WORKED EXAMPLE 22   A rectangle measures 8 cm by 6 cm. The length of the longest side is increased by 10%, and the length of the shortest side is increased by 20%. Find:

(i)   the length of the sides of the larger rectangle;
(ii)   the percentage increase in the area of the rectangle.

SOLUTION
(i)   10% of 8 cm is $\dfrac{10}{100} \times 8 = 0.8\,\text{cm}$

20% of 6 cm is $\dfrac{20}{100} \times 6 = 1.2\,\text{cm}$

The new sides are $8 + 0.8 = 8.8\,\text{cm}$
$$6 + 1.2 = 7.2\,\text{cm}.$$

(ii)   The area of the small rectangle is $8 \times 6 = 48\,\text{cm}^2$.
The area of the larger rectangle is $8.8 \times 7.2 = 63.36\,\text{cm}^2$.
The increase $= 63.36 - 48 = 15.36\,\text{cm}^2$.

Hence the % increase $= \dfrac{15.36}{48} \times 100$

$$= 32\%.$$

Topic: percentage profit

WORKED EXAMPLE 23   Sam was a dealer in secondhand cars. He had bought a car recently which he sold for £1560 making a 30% profit. How much had Sam paid for the car?

SOLUTION   This is not straightforward, it is an example of working 'backwards' with percentages.

The selling price includes 30% profit.
It is $100 + 30 = 130\%$ of the cost,
hence £1560 = 130%

$\div 130 \quad = \dfrac{£1560}{130} = 1\%$

$\times 100 \quad = \dfrac{£1560}{130} \times 100 = 100\%$

£1200 = 100%

Sam paid £1200 for the car.

Questions to try

39. (i) Write down the price reduction as a fraction in its simplest form.
(ii) How much will a camera, normally priced at £90, cost while the sale lasts?

40. The following table is taken from an article in a national newspaper on employment figures for British Rail. It shows that in 1962 more than half a million people were working on the rail network, while in 1987 this figure was only 166 989.
Study the table and answer the questions below.

Changing Face of the Railway			
	December 1962	December 1963	December 1968	March 1987
Number of employees	502 703	464 286	317 478	166 989
Passenger route miles	12 915	12 631	9 471	8 912
Passenger miles travelled	19 728 m	19 575 m	17 835 m	19 150 m

(Source: *The Independent*)

(a) Express the number of employees in March 1987 as a percentage of the number of employees in December 1962. (Give your answer to 1 decimal place.)

(b) Show that in December 1962 there were about 39 employees to every passenger route mile. Obtain the corresponding figure for March 1987.

(c) Show that approximately 39 200 passenger miles were travelled per British Rail employee in December 1962, and obtain the corresponding figure for March 1987.

41. Jane earns £18 000 a year as a computer programmer. She has been offered a 7.5% pay rise. What would be her new salary after the rise?

42. A can of drink normally holds 250 ml. A special offer can is available which gives an extra 10% free. What volume does the special offer can hold?

43. The local bus company has been forced to raise its fares. An 8% increase has been agreed, and prices will be rounded to the nearest 5p.
Find the cost of the new fare, if the old fares are:

(i) 80p; (ii) 65p; (iii) £1.20.

44. Mrs Davies was looking at a television set in a shop window, which had been reduced in price from £240 to £204. The sign saying what % reduction had been given was partially hidden. She went home to try to work out the % reduction that was being offered. What answer should she get?

GRADE E

45. A vacuum cleaner sells for £104. The retailer makes a 30% profit on the sale of electrical goods. How much did he pay for the vacuum cleaner?

£104~

46. The Robinson family bought a house 12 months ago. Because of a rise in the mortgage rate, they have decided to sell the house and make a small 5% loss. If the house is sold for £79 800, how much did they pay for the house?

47. A soap film is stretched onto a rectangular shaped wire, which measures 6 cm by 5 cm. The sides of the rectangle are increased by 15%. What is the percentage increase in the area of the soap film?

3 Scales, tables

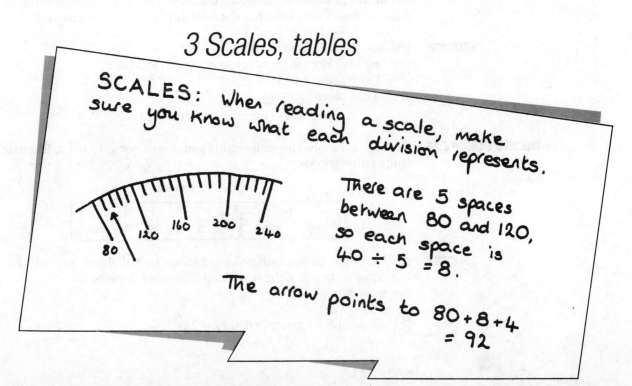

SCALES: When reading a scale, make sure you know what each division represents.

There are 5 spaces between 80 and 120, so each space is 40 ÷ 5 = 8.

The arrow points to 80 + 8 + 4 = 92

TABLE: A table is any type of information arranged in rows and columns. If a table is complicated, use a ruler to read across the required row.
You can often locate the position of a cell in a table by using coordinates, or a grid reference rather like a map.
Always check to see if there are any extra instructions alongside a table.
If asked to draw a table, make sure it has clear headings.

WORDS TO LEARN:
row = horizontal line of values
column = vertical line of values.
cell = a square in a table.
grid = vertical and horizontal lines.
data-
base = information stored in a table.

Topic: reading dials

GRADE G

WORKED EXAMPLE 24

  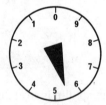  

June's reading on her electricity meter for the first quarter of the year is 82946. She has read the meter for the second quarter as shown in the diagram. How many units has she used during the second quarter?

SOLUTION The dials are read from the right (units).
They are read alternately anticlockwise and clockwise.

The reading = 84557

old reading $\underline{\quad 82946 \quad}$

1611 units have been used.

WORKED EXAMPLE 25 The diagram shows the temperature gauge on a domestic oven. Estimate the temperature shown.

Degrees Fahrenheit

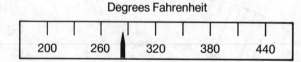

SOLUTION You have to be careful with awkward scales. Each division here is 30°F.
The arrow is about $\frac{4}{5}$ of the way along. (You may disagree.)
Better to write this as 0.8
$0.8 \times 30 = 24.$
The temperature is hence $260 + 24 = 284°F.$

Topics: reading tables, speed

WORKED EXAMPLE 26

Distances in km

Birmingham	Carlisle	Kendal	Hull	Leeds	Liverpool	Manchester	Newcastle	London
176								
236	240							
198	185	113						
175	185	115	88					
144	185	115	149	64				
126	140	123	131	104	56			
320	91	136	185	144	245	203		
176	477	405	269	304	315	296	438	

(i) How far is it from Liverpool to Carlisle?

(ii) A car rally starts at Carlisle, goes to Leeds, Hull and then back to Carlisle. How far is the circuit?

(iii) The lead car completed the course in $11\frac{1}{2}$ hours. What was its average speed (to the nearest whole number)?

SOLUTION

(i)

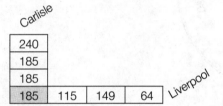

Carlisle				
240				
185				
185				
185	115	149	64	Liverpool

The cell shaded gives 185 km.

(ii) The distances for the parts of the course are 185 km + 88 km + 185 km = 458 km.

(iii) The average speed $= \dfrac{458}{11\frac{1}{2}} = 458 \div 11.5$

$\qquad\qquad\qquad\qquad = 40 \,\text{km/h}.$

Questions to try

GRADE G

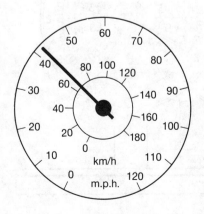

48. The diagram shows the speedometer of a saloon car.

(i) Estimate the speed the car is travelling at in km/h.

(ii) Estimate 80 m.p.h. in km/h.

49.   Estimate the readings shown on the following scales:

(i)

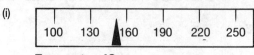

Temperature °C

(ii)

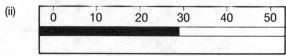

Speed km/h

(iii)

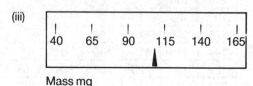

Mass mg

GRADE F

50.   The diagram represents the speedometer of a car. The speeds are given in miles per hour on the outer scale and kilometres per hour on the inner scale. There is also a fuel gauge.

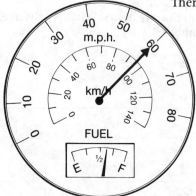

(a)   Write down the speed, in m.p.h., that is shown on the dial.
(b)   Estimate, as accurately as possible, the speed shown in km/h.
(c)   What fraction of a full tank of fuel remains in the car?

(LEAG)

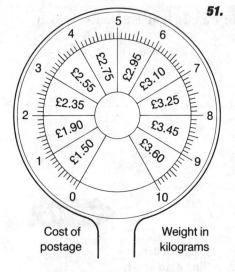

Cost of postage   Weight in kilograms

51.   The figure shows the dial of a parcel-weighing machine at a Post Office. The outer scale shows the weight of the parcel in kilograms. The inner scale shows the cost of postage. A parcel up to 1 kg in weight costs £1.50. Between 1 kg and 2 kg the cost is £1.90, and so on.
Parcel A is placed on the weighing machine. By reading the appropriate scale, write down:

(a)   the weight of parcel A;
(b)   the cost of postage for parcel A.

Parcel B weighs 4.7 kg and is to be sent to the same address. Write down:

(c)   the cost of posting parcel B;
(d)   the cost of posting parcels A and B tied together as a single parcel;
(e)   how much is saved by posting parcels A and B together as a single parcel.

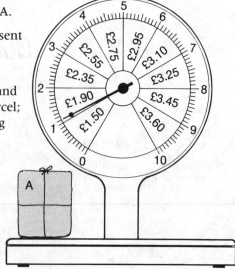

(LEAG)

52.

No. of copies	Wire 'O' Bound Price Each £	Loose Leaf Price Each £	Post and Packing £
Single	5.15	4.70	1.80
2–5	4.95	4.50	3.00
6–10	4.75	4.30	4.20
11–20	4.60	4.15	6.90
21–35	4.45	4.00	9.90
36–50	4.30	3.85	11.40
51–65	4.15	3.70	13.00
66–85	4.05	3.60	14.50
85 plus	3.95	3.50	15.50

The price list shows the cost of Wire 'O' Bound and Loose Leaf folders.
(a)   Write down the price of one Loose Leaf folder.
(b)   You buy 12 Loose Leaf folders. Write down the price of each folder.
(c)   You buy 40 Wire 'O' Bound folders.
    (i)   Find the cost of the 40 folders.
    (ii)   Write down the cost of Post and Packing for the 40 folders.
    (iii)   To the total cost of the 40 folders, including Post and Packing, 17.5% V.A.T. is added. Calculate the full cost of buying the 40 Wire 'O' Bound folders.   (LEAG)

53.

Type of Call and Charge Letter	Charge Rate Period		
	Cheap Mon–Fri 6pm–8am Sat & Sun all day	Standard Mon–Fri 8am–9am and 1pm–6pm	Peak Mon–Fri 9am–1pm
Local (L)	360	90	60
National (a)	100	34.3	25.7
National (b1)	60	30	22.5
National, calls to the Channel Islands and Isle of Man (b)	45	24	18
Calls to mobile telephones (m)	12	8	8
Irish Republic	12	8	8

The table shows the time allowed in seconds for each dialled telephone unit. The cost of each unit is 5.06p. One unit is recorded at the beginning of a telephone call. If, at the end of the time allowed for a single unit, the call is still being made, an additional unit is recorded and so on.
Calculate the cost of:

(a)   a local call at 9.00 p.m. lasting 10 minutes;
(b)   a national (b1) call at 2.00 p.m. on Wednesday lasting 6 minutes;
(c)   a national (b) call at 10.00 a.m. on Friday lasting 2 minutes.   (LEAG)

54.   A car magazine gives the following information about two models of a particular type of car.

Car model	1.1 Hatchback	1.3 Hatchback
Fuel consumption (miles per gallon)	36.9	31.8

These figures vary according to the style of driving and to the driving conditions. This table gives the relevant percentage changes.

		Driving conditions		
		Severe	Average	Easy
Driving style	Hard Average Gentle	−10% no change +10%	no change +10% +20%	+10% +20% +30%

(a) What percentage change to the fuel consumption is quoted for a car driven gently under severe conditions?

(b) Which has the better fuel consumption, a 1.1 hatchback driven hard under severe conditions or a 1.3 hatchback driven gently under severe conditions?

Show working to justify your answer.   (WJEC)

55. The table below shows the number of crimes recorded by the police for the years 1986 and 1987 and the percentage change between these years.

Recorded crimes	1986	1987	% change
Violence against the person	20308	22626	+11
Robbery	16191	18102	+12
Burglary/going equipped	157996	151359	−4
Theft/handling stolen goods	413588	392894	−5
Fraud and forgery	33687	27892	−17
Criminal damage	119918	117373	−2
Other	3002	3096	+3
TOTAL	764690	733342	−4

(a) The total number of crimes recorded in 1987 was 733342. Write this number in words.

(b) The number of burglaries recorded in 1986 was 157996. Write this number to the nearest thousand.

(c) Which recorded crime showed the greatest percentage increase between 1986 and 1987?

(d) For which crime was there the least percentage change in the figures recorded between 1986 and 1987?   (NEA)

UNITS
ATTAINMENT TARGET 2

3

1 Units, the metric system

UNITS : Most units now in use belong to the metric system (see page 38) There are some units still in use which belong to the Imperial system. Sometimes you need to convert from one to the other. This can be done by a graph see worked example 28, or otherwise worked as in example 27

CONVERSION: When changing from one set of units to another, you need to work out the conversion factor.

e.g. since 1 metre = 100 cm, then to change from cm to metres you × 100 (×100 is the conversion factor).

Since 1 yard is 90 cm approximately, then 1 cm = 1/90 yard.

Hence to change cm to yards, approximately ÷ 90

GRAPHS: A useful device for changing one quantity into another is a conversion graph.

This will be a straight line usually (but not necessarily) passing through the origin:

e.g. °C → °F would not pass through (0, 0).

USEFUL FACTS

The units most commonly used in the metric system are listed below, together with their abbreviations.

length: kilometre (km), metre (m), centimetre (cm), millimetre (mm).

1 km = 1000 m, 1 m = 100 cm, 1 m = 1000 mm.

mass: kilogram (kg), gram (g), milligram (mg).

1 kg = 1000 g, 1 g = 1000 mg.

time: seconds (s), hours (h), minutes (min).

1 h = 60 min, 1 min = 60 s.

area: square kilometres (km²), square metres (m²), square millimetres (mm²), hectare (ha).

1 km² = 1000 m × 1000 m = 1 000 000 m².

1 m² = 100 cm × 100 cm = 10 000 cm².

1 ha = 10 000 m². (This unit is commonly used in measuring land areas.)

volume: cubic metres (m³), millilitres (ml), litres (l), cubic centimetres (cm³), centilitres (cl).

1 l = 1000 cm³ or 1000 ml, since 1 cm³ = 1 ml,

1 cl = 10 ml.

1 m³ = 100 cm × 100 cm × 100 cm = 1 000 000 cm³ or 10⁶ cm³,
                                                    = 1000 l.

speed: metres per second (m/s), kilometres per hour (km/h).

There are also a number of units used in more specialised situations. A series of prefixes is available to describe these units.

mega means 1 000 000 used in megawatt or megatonne	micro means $\frac{1}{1\,000\,000} = 10^{-6}$ used in microsecond
kilo means 1000	milli means $\frac{1}{1000} = 10^{-3}$
hecto means 100	centi means $\frac{1}{100} = 10^{-2}$
deca means 10	deci means $\frac{1}{10} = 10^{-1}$

Topic: conversion of units

GRADE F

WORKED EXAMPLE 27

(i)   Change 4.7 m into mm;

(ii)   change 0.6 kg into mg;

(iii) change 686 mm into m;

(iv) change 20 m/s into km/h;

(v)   change 8 km² into hectares.

SOLUTION

(i)   4.7 × 1000 = 4700 mm.

(ii)   0.6 × 1 000 000
       = 600 000 mg
          or 6 × 10⁵ mg.

(iii) 6.86 ÷ 1000 = 0.686 m.

(iv) 20 m/s means 20 metres in 1 second.
       In 1 minute, the distance = 20 × 60 = 1200 m
       In 1 hour, the distance = 1200 × 60 = 72 000 m (÷ 1000 to give 72),
       this gives 72 km in 1 hour
       Hence the speed is 72 km/h.

(v)   1 ha = 10 000 m².
       So 1 km² = 1 000 000 ÷ 10 000 = 100 ha
       Hence 8 km² = 8 × 100 = 800 ha.

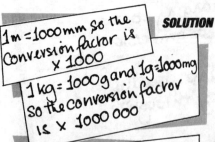

1 m = 1000 mm so the conversion factor is × 1000

1 kg = 1000 g and 1 g = 1000 mg so the conversion factor is × 1 000 000

The conversion factor is ÷ 1000 the opposite of (i)

There are 1000 m in 1 km

remember!
1 km² = 1000 m × 1000 m
       = 1 000 000 m²

Topic: conversion graphs

WORKED EXAMPLE 28   Use the fact that 0°C is the same as 32°F, and 100°C is the same as 212°F to draw a conversion graph of Celsius to Fahrenheit.

(a)   Use the graph to change (i) 80°C into Fahrenheit; (ii) 100°F into Celsius.

(b)   Can you use the graph to change 300°F into Celsius?

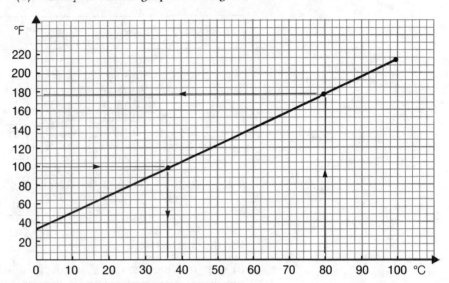

SOLUTION   First choose suitable scales to fit as much as possible of the graph paper used. Plot the 2 points that you know, and then join up with a straight line.

(a)   (i)   Follow the arrow from 80°C to give 178°F from the graph.
         (ii)   Follow the arrow from 100°F to give 36°C from the graph.
         The exact values are in fact 176°F and 37.8°C.

(b)   The graph gives 200°F as 92°C.
         Hence a rise of 100°F on the graph is 92° − 36° = 56°C.
         This means that 300°F will be 92° + 56° = 148°C.

Questions to try

56.   (i)   Convert 620 mm into cm.
         (ii)   How many cm are there in 2½ km?
         (iii)   Which is greater, 5×10^6 mg, or 2 kg?
         (iv)   Change 800 cm³ into litres.

> **GRADE F**

57.

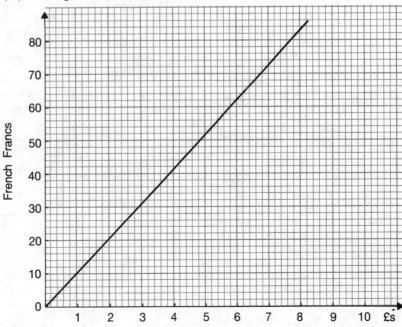

(a)   Use the graph to change:
(i) £4 to French francs; (ii) 80 francs to £ sterling.

(b)   A digital watch costs 74 francs in France. What would it cost in £ sterling?

(c)   A tourist has 63 francs left at the end of his holidays. Use your graph to find how much it would be worth if all of it was changed to £ sterling.

58.   The table shows part of a conversion chart from inches into decimals.

inches ('')		decimal	mm	inches ('')		decimal	mm
	$\frac{7}{64}$	0.1094	2.778		$\frac{39}{64}$	0.6094	15.478
$\frac{1}{8}$		0.1250	3.175	$\frac{5}{8}$		0.6250	15.875
	$\frac{9}{64}$	0.1406	3.572		$\frac{41}{64}$	0.6406	16.272
$\frac{5}{32}$		0.1563	3.969	$\frac{21}{32}$		0.6563	16.669
	$\frac{11}{64}$	0.1719	4.366		$\frac{43}{64}$	0.6719	17.066
$\frac{3}{16}$		0.1875	4.763	$\frac{11}{16}$		0.6875	17.463
	$\frac{13}{64}$	0.2031	5.159		$\frac{45}{64}$	0.7031	17.859
$\frac{7}{32}$		0.2188	5.556	$\frac{23}{32}$		0.7188	18.256
	$\frac{15}{64}$	0.2344	5.953		$\frac{47}{64}$	0.7344	18.653
$\frac{1}{4}$		0.2500	6.350	$\frac{3}{4}$		0.7500	19.050
	$\frac{17}{64}$	0.2656	6.747		$\frac{49}{64}$	0.7656	19.447

Use the chart to find:

(i) $\frac{7}{32}$'' in millimetres; (ii) $\frac{11}{16}$'' as a decimal; (iii) $\frac{1}{4}$'' in millimetres;
(iv) the nearest fraction of an inch to $17\frac{1}{2}$ mm.

59.   The current exchange rate between the Spanish peseta and the £ is £1 = 160 pesetas. On the graph below, draw a conversion graph to represent this information, and use it to find:

(i) £40 in pesetas; (ii) 500 pesetas in pounds; (iii) 2 million pesetas in pounds.

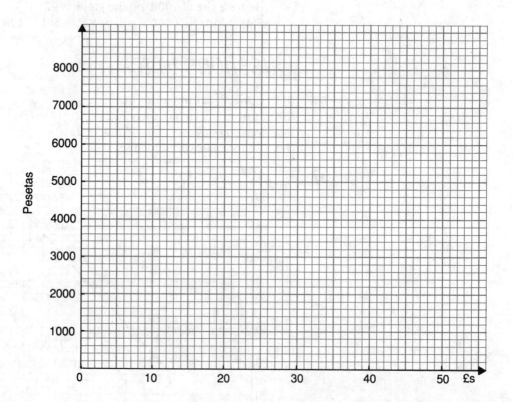

2 Time, timetables

TIME : Always remember when working with times that you are in fact working in multiples of 60.

If you are working across midnight, work out before and after times separately.

24 hour clock : To convert a time p.m. to the 24 hour clock, add 12 to the hour.

So 8.15 p.m. = (8+12).15 = 20.15h

Days in a month 30 : April, June, Sept, Nov
31 : Jan, Mar, May, July Aug, Oct, Dec.
28 : Feb (29 in a leap year)

365 days in a year (366 in a leap year)
52 weeks in a year
TIMETABLE :   A table of times used for travel information.

For bus and train timetables, make sure you read the instructions carefully. Trains often do not not stop at certain stations.

CENTURY :   100 years 1900 - 1999 is the twentieth century.

Topic: time

GRADE F

WORKED EXAMPLE 29 A train leaves London at 20.15h and arrives in Edinburgh at 01.25h the next day. How long did the journey take?

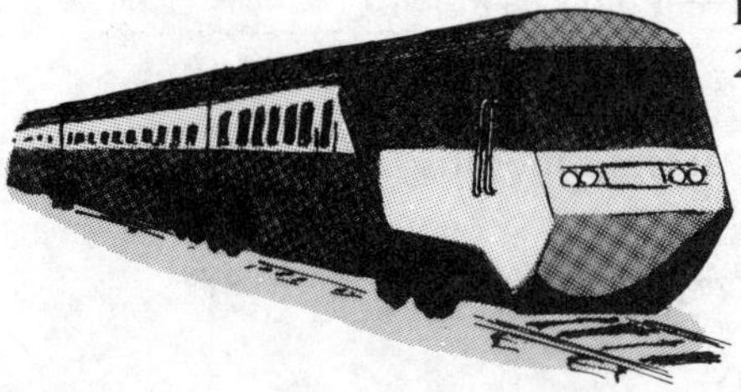

SOLUTION When calculating a time difference across midnight, it is usually safer to work with before and after midnight separately.

Hence, from 20.15h to 24.00h is 3h 45min. From 24.00h to 01.25h is 1h 25min.

The total time =

h	min
3	45
+1	25
5	10	= 5h 10min

Remember that there are only 60min in 1 hour!

Topic: timetables

WORKED EXAMPLE 30   The following questions are about the train timetable shown below.

Bristol Temple Meads	Bristol Parkway	Bath Spa	Chippenham	Swindon	Didcot	Reading	Slough	Paddington
←			departures			arrivals		→
00 35	→	00 51	→	→	→	02 18	→	03 00
03 35	→	→	→	→	→	04 59	→	05 55
03 50	→	04 08	→	04 47	→	05 24	06 32	06 15
	06 23	→	→	06 52	07 09	07 24	08 04	07 54
06 20	→	06 30	06 43	07 02	07 22	07 35	08 04	08 05
06 50	→	07 00	07 13	07 32	07 50	08 05	08 58	08 35
	07 23	→	→	07 52	→	08 19	08 58	08 50
07 15	→	07 25	07 38	07 58	08 17	→	→	08 55
	07 52	→	→	→	→	→	→	09 08
07 45	→	07 55	08 08	→	→	08 50	09 24	09 20
	08 07	→	→	→	→	→	→	09 22
				08 39	→	→	→	09 42
	08 18	→	→	08 47	09 04	09 19	10 22	09 49
	08 40	→	→	→	→	→	→	09 54
08 30	→	08 40	08 53	→	→	→	→	09 58
	09 13	→	→	→	→	10 01	10 52	10 33
09 10	→	09 20	→	→	→	10 18	→	10 54
				09 42	→	→	→	10 45
09 24	→	09 34	09 47	10 06	10 23	10 38	10 53	11 12
09 55	→	10 07	→	→	→	→	→	11 40
10 15	→	10 25	→	10 52	→	→	→	11 43
	10 37	→	→	11 06	11 35	11 52	12 09	12 30
	11 13	→	→	→	→	12 03	12 52	12 34
11 10	→	11 20	→	→	→	12 19	→	12 53
11 24	→	11 34	11 47	12 06	12 23	12 38	12 53	13 12
12 10	→	12 20	→	12 48	→	→	→	13 57
	12 37	→	→	13 06	13 23	13 38	13 53	14 12
	13 13	→	→	→	→	14 03	14 52	14 33
13 10	→	13 20	→	→	→	14 08	→	14 38
13 24	→	13 34	13 47	14 06	14 23	14 38	14 53	15 12
14 10	→	14 20	→	14 47	→	→	→	15 37
	14 37	→	→	15 06	15 23	15 38	15 53	16 12
	15 13	→	→	→	→	16 03	16 52	16 33
15 18	→	15 32	→	→	→	16 25	→	16 58
15 24	→	15 37	15 50	16 09	16 26	16 41	16 56	17 15
16 00	→	16 12	16 25	→	→	17 05	17 39	17 36

(i)   How long does the 04.47 from Swindon take to travel to Paddington?

(ii)   What is the latest time I can leave Bath Spa, if I want to arrive in London by 12.30?

(iii)   How many trains stop at Didcot between 07.00 and 09.00 inclusive?

(iv)   Are there any non-stop services between Bristol Parkway and Paddington?

SOLUTION   (i)   The 04.47 arrives at 06.15.

$$
\begin{array}{r}
5 \quad 7 \quad 5 \\
0 \quad \not{6} \quad 1 \quad \not{5} \\
- \ 0 \quad 4 \quad 4 \quad 7 \\
\hline
0 \quad 1 \quad 2 \quad 8 \\
\end{array}
$$

note that 60 is carried, making 15 into 75, since there are 60 minutes in one hour

It takes 1 hr 28 mins.

(ii)   Note: the 12.30 into Paddington does not stop at Bath Spa. The 11.43 leaves Bath Spa at 10.25.

(iii)   The 07.09, 07.22, 07.50, 08.17. There are 4 trains.

(iv)   Yes, the 07.52, 08.07 and 08.40.

Topic: the calendar

WORKED EXAMPLE 31   (i)   If January 18th is a Monday, what day of the week will January 29th be?

(ii)   If April 21st is a Sunday, what day of the week will May 7th be?

(iii)   If August 26th is a Tuesday, what will be the date on the Tuesday seven weeks after this date?

SOLUTION   (i) $29 - 18 = 11$ days, which is 1 week + 4 days.

4 days *after* a Monday is Friday.

So January 29th will be a Friday.

(ii)   This is more difficult because it goes across a month.

April has 30 days. $30 - 21 = 9$ days.

Up to May 7th will be $9 + 7 = 16$ days which is 2 weeks + 2 days.

2 days *after* a Sunday is Tuesday.

So May 7th will be a Tuesday.

(iii) 7 weeks = 7 × 7 = 49 days.
August has 31 days, so 31 − 26 = 5 days.
September has 30 days, so we have 30 + 5 = 35 days.
49 − 35 = 14 days of October.
Hence the date is October 14th.

Questions to try

GRADE G

60. Kings and queens of Great Britain in the 18th and 19th centuries.

Date	Ruler
1702–1714	Queen Anne
1714–1727	King George I
1727–1760	King George II
1760–1820	King George III
1820–1830	King George IV
1830–1837	King William IV
1837–1901	Queen Victoria

(a) How many kings began their reign in the 18th century?

(b) Which one of these kings and queens above ruled for the greatest number of years?   (NEA)

61.

GRADE F

ATHLETICS

GLASGOW MARATHON.– Men: 1 E Tirney (Dublin) 2h 19m 09s; 2 T Mitchell (Dundee) 2-19-40; 3 H Cox (Greenock) 2-19-43; 4 G New-hams (Cardiff) 2-19-55; D Watt (East Kilbride) 2-19-40; 6 A Daly (Glasgow) 2-21-00. **Women**: 1 S Catford (Leeds City) 2 h 37m 31s; 2 L Watson (London) 2-45-03; 3 P Rother (Edinburgh) 2-45-27.

How much longer did P. Rother take than S. Catford?   (LEAG)

62. (i) How long is it between 7.25 a.m. and 4.23 p.m.?

(ii) A film which lasts 1 h 46 mins starts at 6.40 p.m. What time does it finish?

(iii) A bus service runs every 12 minutes. There is one bus at 6.20 p.m. How many buses run between 4.00 p.m. and 7.00 p.m. inclusive?

(iv) How many minutes are there between 17.40 on Tuesday and 03.15 on Wednesday?

(v) How many days are there between April 14th and May 22nd inclusive?

(vi) How many hours are there in a leap year?

63. The table shows the results of the Men's Downhill Skiing at the 1988 Winter Olympics in Canada.

Position	Name	Time	Medal
1	P. Zurbriggen (Switzerland)	1 min 59.63 s	Gold
2	P. Mueller (Switzerland)	2 min 00.14 s	Silver
3	F. Picard (France)	2 min 01.24 s	Bronze

(a) What is the difference in the times recorded by the gold and silver medallists?

(b) The British entrant in the Men's Downhill, Martin Bell, took 2.86 seconds longer to ski the course than the winner. What was Martin Bell's time?

64. (i)   If March 14th is a Tuesday, what day of the week is March 27th?

(ii) If June 17th is a Friday, what day of the week will July 8th be?

(iii) If September 17th is a Wednesday, what will be the date on the Wednesday 9 weeks after this date?

65. The workers in a factory have to 'clock on' when they arrive at work. If they arrive after 9.00 a.m. they are late. Here are the 'clocking on' times of five people during a week.

(a)   On how many days was D. Maragh late for work?

	Mon	Tues	Wed	Thurs	Fri
K. Patel	8:59	9:02	9:05	9:01	9:00
F. Jones	9:07	9:01	9:14	8:57	8:55
J. Smith	9:05	9:06	9:06	8:52	9:04
D. Maragh	8:57	9:00	8:58	9:16	9:02
C. Benn	8:45	8:59	9:07	8:53	8:50

The company makes a deduction from the wages of anyone if:

(A)   they are more than 15 minutes late on any day
       OR

(B)   they are more than 20 minutes late in total.
       (Being early does not count as time off the late total.)

(b)   This is part of a page from the deductions book.
Write the name of anyone who has a deduction in the book.
Write A or B in the reason column to show which reason it was.

NAME	REASON

(MEG)

66.

ROASTING CHART		
	Cooking time	*Oven temperature*
Beef	30 min per lb plus 25 min extra	190°C
Chicken	15 min per lb plus 20 min extra	190°C
Duck	25 min per lb plus 25 min extra	190°C
Lamb	30 min per lb plus 20 min extra	190°C
Pork	35 min per lb plus 30 min extra	190°C

Jenny has bought a 3½ lb joint of beef.

(a)   She wants it to be cooked for 5.00 p.m. At what time should she put it in the oven?

(b)   Her cooker is marked in °F. Use the formula below to find the temperature, in °F, at which the beef needs to be cooked:

$$\text{Degrees F} = \frac{\text{Degrees C} \times 9}{5} + 32.$$

(NEA)

3 Speed, travel graphs

SPEED :   average speed = $\dfrac{\text{distance}}{\text{time}}$

time = $\dfrac{\text{distance}}{\text{average speed}}$

distance = average speed × time.

Make sure you do not mix units, e.g. If the speed is in km/h the time must be in hours, not minutes.

Careful with average speed:
40 km/h for 2 hours and 20 km/h for 1 hour does not give an average speed of ½ (40 + 20) = 30 km/h.

Find the total distance = 40 × 2 + 20 = 100 km.
average speed = 100 ÷ 3 = 33⅓ km/h.

TRAVEL GRAPHS :   Usually time is on the horizontal axis, and distance on the vertical axis.

The shape of the graph gives the speed.
If a vehicle travels at constant speed, the travel graph is straight.
If the graph is horizontal, the vehicle is at rest.

Topics: speed, time

WORKED EXAMPLE 32   Judy cycles to her aunt's house a distance of 9 miles away. It takes her 45 mins. What is her average speed in miles per hour? For the return journey, she averages 6 miles an hour. How long did the journey take?

SOLUTION   Average speed = $\dfrac{\text{distance}}{\text{time}}$ (or distance ÷ time),

$45 \text{ mins} = \dfrac{45}{60} = \dfrac{3}{4}$ hours (cancelling by 15).

So the average speed = $9 \div \dfrac{3}{4} = \dfrac{9}{1} \times \dfrac{4}{3} = \dfrac{36}{3} = 12$.

The average speed is 12 miles per hour.
For the return journey, we need

time taken = $\dfrac{\text{distance}}{\text{average speed}}$ = distance ÷ average speed.

So the time = 9 ÷ 6 = 1.5.
Now 1.5 hours is *not* 1 hour 5 mins,
.5 means ½ an hour = 30 mins.
The time taken = 1 h 30 mins.

you must change 45 minutes into hours.

remember!
a calculator does not work in minutes - it always gives a decimal

Topics: speed, time

WORKED EXAMPLE 33   In one of its trial flights, Concorde flew from Paris, leaving at 7.21 a.m. and returning at 9.58 p.m., having flown 12 000 miles. Calculate the average speed of the journey.

SOLUTION   9.58 p.m. is 21.58 hours.

....easier to work in the 24 hour clock.

Hence time of flight =
$$\begin{array}{r} 2158 \\ -\ 721 \\ \hline 1437 \end{array}$$

This must be changed to a decimal:

37 minutes = 37 ÷ 60 = 0.617.

Hence the time = 14.617.

You cannot divide until the minutes have been written as a decimal

$$\text{Average speed} = \frac{12\,000}{14.617} = 821 \text{ m.p.h.}$$

Topic: travel graphs

GRADE B

WORKED EXAMPLE 34   A car sets out to travel the 80 km between Alton and Barton. It leaves Alton at 11.00 a.m., and the travel graph is shown in the following diagram.

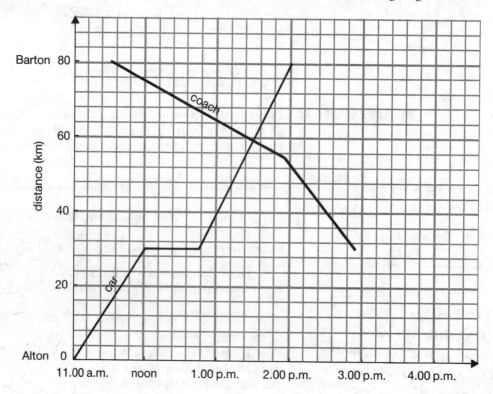

A little later, a coach leaves Barton and follows the same route in the opposite direction, to its terminus at Clapton. Its travel graph is shown on the same diagram.

(i)   How long does the car stop for on its journey?

(ii)   At what time do they pass?

(iii)   What is the average speed of the car for the journey?

(iv)   How far is Clapton from Alton?

(v)   What is the average speed of the coach on the faster part of its journey?

SOLUTION

(i)   The car is stationary when the travel graph is horizontal.
Between 12.00 and 12.45 p.m. i.e. 45 minutes.

(ii)   They pass just before 1.30 p.m.

(iii)   The car travels 80 km in 3 hours,

average speed $= \dfrac{80}{3} = 26.7$ km/h.

(iv)   Clapton is at the point where the coach travel line stops.
This is 30 km from Alton.

(v)   The faster part is where the line is steeper (the second part).
It travels 25 km in 1 hour.
The average speed = 25 km/h.

Questions to try

67.

GRADE C/D

Table 66
Birmingham and Rugby → London

Mondays to Fridays

Wolverhampton 69 d	0641	0727	0707	0757	0741	0803	0812	0827	0816	0849						
Sandwell & Dudley 69 d	0736															
Birmingham New Street 69 d	0721	0735	0748	0751	0804	0806	0818	0821	0837	0844	0848	0851	0858	0921	0937	
Adderley Park d	0725	0739		0755	0808			0825				0855		0925		
Stechford d	0729	0743		0759	0812			0829				0859		0929		
Lea Hall d	0731	0745		0801	0814			0831				0901		0931		
Marston Green d	0734	0748		0804	0817			0834				0904		0934		
Birmingham International a	0737	0752	0758	0807	0821		0828	0837	0847	0853	0858	0907	0928	0937	0937	
Birmingham International d	0737		0758	0807			0828	0837	0847	0854	0858	0907	0928	0937	0947	
Hampton-in-Arden d	0741			0811				0841				0911		0941		
Berkswell d	0745			0815				0845				0915		0945		
Tile Hill d	0749			0819				0849				0919		0949		
Canley d	0752			0822				0852				0922		0952		
Coventry a	0755	0809		0825	0839			0856	0858	0903	0909	0926	0939	0956	0958	
Coventry d	0758	0810		0826	0840			0858		0910		0940			0958	
Rugby a	0810			0839				0911							1011	
Rugby d	0811		0832	0841		0904		0911			0955				1011	
Long Buckby d	0821			0851				0921							1021	
Northampton a	0831			0901				0932							1033	
Northampton d	0836			0906				0936							1036	
Wolverton d	0850							0950							1050	
Milton Keynes Central a	0855			0923				0955				1012	1019		1055	
Milton Keynes Central d	0838	0855		0923			0925	0949	0955			1012	1020	1025	1055	
Bletchley d	0843	0900		0927			0930	1000						1030	1100	
Leighton Buzzard d	0850	0907					0937	1007						1037	1107	
Cheddington d	0855						0942							1042		
Tring d	0901					0924	0948							1048		
Berkhamsted d	0908					0931	0955	1021						1055	1121	
Hemel Hempstead d	0912					0936	0959	1025						1059	1125	
Apsley d						0939	1002							1102		
King's Langley d						0943	1006							1106		
Watford Junction 59 d	0920	0930				0948	1011	1033		1006a		1040a	1047a	1113	1135	
Bushey 59 d																
Harrow & Wealdstone 59 d	0927					0954	1017							1119		
London Euston ⊖ 59 a	0943	0953	0924	0938	1014	0956	1010	1011	1034	1035	1054	1029	1101	1112	1136	1156

I live in Rugby, which is 82 miles from London, and I have to be at a meeting in London at 10.30 a.m. It takes 15 minutes for me to walk from London Euston station to my meeting. The table is the railway timetable for the day of my meeting. Assume that all the trains run to time.

(a)   What is the departure time of the latest train that I can catch at Rugby in order to arrive at my meeting on time?

(b)   What was the average speed, to the nearest mile per hour, of that train on its journey from Rugby to London?

(c)   The meeting lasts 200 minutes. At what time does it finish?

(d)   The saver fare from Rugby to London is £8.50. Express this as a percentage of the return first class fare of £34.

           (LEAG)

68. The timetable for the evening trains between Birmingham New Street and London Euston is shown below.

Birmingham New Street	1818	1848	1953	2052	2153	2221
Birmingham International	1828	1858	2003	2103	2204	2237
Coventry	1840	1910	2015	2115	2216	2256
Watford Junction	1945	2008	2114	2213	2315	0037
London Euston	2006	2030	2136	2234	2340	0100

London Euston	1853	1910	1940	2030	2140	2315
Coventry	2003	2017	2052	2142	2247	0035
Birmingham International	2013	2028	2103	2154	2258	0048
Birmingham New Street	2029	2044	2119	2207	2315	0105

(a) Wendy wants to catch a train at Birmingham International and to get to Watford Junction by 9.30 p.m. What is the time of the latest train she should catch?

(b) Calculate the time, in hours and minutes, the 22.21 train from Birmingham New Street takes to travel to London Euston.

(c) Walid catches the 18.18 train from Birmingham New Street to go to London. He wants to be back at Birmingham New Street before midnight. What is the longest time he can spend in London?

(d) It is 18.5 km by rail from Birmingham International to Coventry. Calculate the average speed, in km/h correct to three significant figures, of the 22.37 train between these two stations.   (MEG)

69. The graph below shows Paul's journey from his home in Brighton to Portsmouth, a distance of 60 km. Paul left home at 08.00 and travelled towards Portsmouth for 40 km. He stopped at a garage to fill up with petrol before continuing his journey to Portsmouth.   **GRADE B**

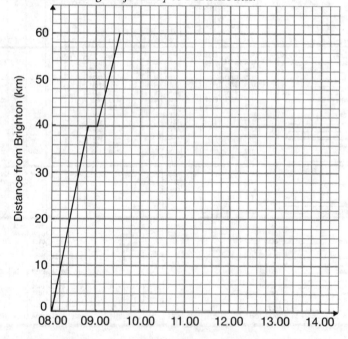

(a) What was the time when Paul stopped at the garage?
(b) How long did Paul stop at the garage?
(c) (i)   After leaving the garage, how long did it take Paul to reach Portsmouth?
   (ii)   What was Paul's speed, in kilometres per hour, during this stage of his journey?

Paul stayed in Portsmouth for 3 hours before starting his return journey to Brighton.

(d) (i)   At what time did he leave Portsmouth?
   (ii)   Draw a line on the travel graph to represent his stay in Portsmouth.

(e) Paul began driving home at an average speed of 60 kilometres per hour, but 15 minutes after starting his journey he punctured a tyre and had to stop. He took 18 minutes to change the wheel and then continued at the same average speed.

(i) Complete the travel graph to show Paul's return journey.

(ii) At what time did Paul arrive home?

70.

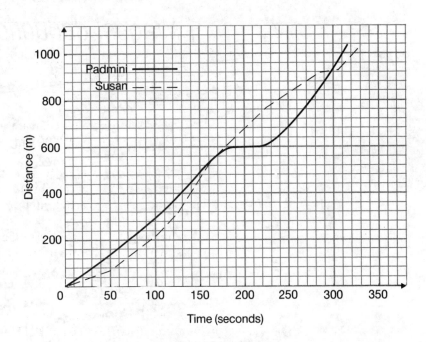

The graph illustrates a 1000 metre race between Susan and Padmini. Write a report of the race.   (NEA)

71. A car leaves Leeds and travels to London at a speed of 50 m.p.h. At the same time a car leaves London and travels to Leeds on the same route at a speed of 70 m.p.h.

On the diagram, draw the travel graph for the second car. The travel graph for the first car is already printed on the diagram.

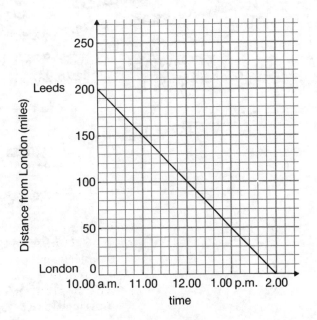

Clearly mark on your graph the point at which the two cars pass each other.

(i) At what distance from Leeds does the diagram suggest that they will pass?

(ii) How long have the cars been travelling when they pass each other? Give your answer in hours and minutes.

PERSONAL FINANCE

ATTAINMENT TARGETS 2 AND 5
1 Wages, deductions and bills

WAGES : hourly rate × number of hours worked gives the amount earned.

: salaried means an annual salary, usually averaged out over 12 months.

: overtime is often paid at 'time and a half' This means each hour is paid at 1½ × normal rate.

: piece rate means you are paid by the number of articles you make.

: commission payment by amount sold.

DEDUCTIONS : Before income tax is calculated, certain amounts are excluded from your earnings. These are called allowances. The rest is taxed at 25p in the £1 at "basic rate" or at a higher rate if you earn over a certain amount; (at present 40p in the £1). National Insurance is also removed after tax has been calculated.

The type of bills you are likely to be given are shop invoices, telephone bills, gas and electricity bills.

WORDS TO LEARN : gross pay = before any deductions

: net pay = what is left after deductions

: commission = earned by how much you sell.

: invoice = given by a shop listing the cost of items purchased.

Topics: making out a bill, V.A.T. GRADE F

WORKED EXAMPLE 35

FLOWER'S GARAGE

Phone Carmouth 2345

Main Rd.
Carmouth

£

Parts	4 spark plugs at 79p each	(a)	....
	(b) .... brake pads at £4.52 each		9.04
	4 tyres at (c) .... each		98.00
	1 only exhaust system		41.30
	Total cost of parts	(d)	....
Labour	4½ hours at £11.00 per hour	(e)	....
	Total cost of parts and labour	(f)	....
VAT at 17.5%			35.17
	TOTAL TO PAY	(g)	....

A customer received a bill from Flower's Garage. Some of the figures could not be read.

Fill in the spaces marked (a) to (g) with the correct figures.   (LEAG)

SOLUTION
(a)   4 at 79p is $4 \times 79 = 316$p = £3.16.
(b)   £9.04 ÷ £4.52 = 2 brake pads.
(c)   £98 ÷ 4 = £24.50, the cost of the tyre.
(d)   The sub-total = £3.16 + £9.04 + £98.00 + £41.30 = £151.50.
(e) $4\frac{1}{2}$ hours at £11.00 = $4\frac{1}{2} \times 11$ = £49.50.
(f)   Cost of parts and labour = £151.50 + £49.50 = £201.
(g)   This part enables you to check your working so far.

$$17.5\% \text{ of } £201 = \frac{17.5}{100} \times 201 = £35.17$$

The total to pay = £35.17 + £201 = £236.17.

Topic: reading an account

WORKED EXAMPLE 36

METER READINGS		UNITS	TARRIF	PENCE	AMOUNT	VAT
PRESENT	PREVIOUS			PER UNIT	£	%
49739E	48649	1090	D13	5.440	59.30	ZERO
		QUARTERLY CHARGE			6.27	ZERO

PLEASE ACCEPT THIS ESTIMATED BILL OR
ENTER YOUR METER READING(S) OPPOSITE
AND RETURN TO ANY NORWEB SHOP/OFFICE   * *
                                              * *
                                              * *
                                              * *

PLEASE QUOTE	PERIOD ENDED	INVOICE DATE	TOTAL NOW DUE	
213597 972	17 03 89	17 03 89	£ 65.57	
YOUR NORWEB NUMBER				

E = Estimate   C = Customer's own reading

The bill above has been estimated by the Electricity Board. The present reading should actually be 49907.

(a) (i) How many units have really been used since the last meter reading?
    (ii) Work out what the total bill should be.
    (iii) How much more is this than the estimated bill?

(b) Electricity prices are due to rise by 5%. What will be the increase in the cost of a unit?

(c) (i) The estimated bill is calculated over a quarterly period. How many weeks is this?
    (ii) From the estimated bill, find the average cost per week. (Give your answer to the nearest penny.)   (NEA)

SOLUTION

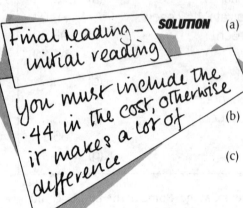

Final reading − initial reading

You must include the .44 in the cost, otherwise it makes a lot of difference

(a) (i) $49907 - 48649 = 1258$.

   (ii) $1258 \times 5.44 = £68.43$
$$+ \underline{£\ \ 6.27}$$
$$\underline{£74.70}$$

   (iii) The difference $= £74.70 - £65.57 = £9.13$.

(b) $5.440 \times \dfrac{5}{100} = 0.272$

The new price per unit $= 5.440 + 0.272 = 5.712$p.

(c) (i) A 'quarter' means $\frac{1}{4}$ of 1 year
$= \frac{1}{4}$ of 52 weeks $= 13$ weeks.

   (ii) $£65.57 \div 13 = £5.04$.

Topics: wages, deductions, income tax

WORKED EXAMPLE 37

Mr Court works at the local supermarket. He is paid at a rate of £3.80 per hour for a 35-hour week, and overtime at time and a half. At the end of the week, he pays the following deductions:
    National Insurance = £12.50,
    Pension at 6% of gross pay.
He is allowed to earn a further £55 free of tax, and the remainder is taxed at 25%. Find his net pay after working a 43 hour week.

SOLUTION

@ means at or ×

35 hours @ £3.80   = £133
8 hours @ $1\frac{1}{2}$ × £3.80 $= \dfrac{£\ \ 45.60}{£178.60}$ total earnings (gross pay).

Pension contribution $= \dfrac{6}{100} \times £178.60 = £10.72$.

His deductions before tax are $£12.50 + £10.72 + £55 = £78.22$
Taxable income $= £178.60 - £78.22 = £100.38$
Tax at 25% $= 0.25 \times £100.38 = £25.10$
Total deductions $= £12.50 + £10.72 + £25.10 = £48.32$
His net pay $= £178.60 - £48.32 = £130.28$.

Topic: wages

WORKED EXAMPLE 38

Jim works in a department store. He is paid at an hourly rate of £2.90. If he works on Saturday, he is paid 'time and a half', and on Sundays he is paid double time. A fortnight before Christmas, he worked the following hours: Monday: 8, Tuesday: $7\frac{1}{2}$, Wednesday: 6, Thursday: $8\frac{1}{2}$, Friday: $6\frac{1}{2}$, Saturday: 4, Sunday: 3.
Work out how much Jim earned during this week.

SOLUTION

There are two ways of doing this question.

4 at £4.35 means 4 × £4.35.

(i) $8 + 7\frac{1}{2} + 6 + 8\frac{1}{2} + 6\frac{1}{2} = 36\frac{1}{2}$,
       $36\frac{1}{2}$ at £2.90 = £105.85,
    time and a half = £2.90 + £1.45 = £4.35,
       4 at £4.35 = £17.40,
    double time = 2 × £2.90 = £5.80,
       3 at £5.80 = £17.40.
    Total earned = £105.85 + £17.40 + £17.40 = £140.65.

Work out the number of basic hours worked at the basic rate

(ii)   4 hours at time and a half = $4 \times 1\frac{1}{2}$ = 6 hours,
    3 hours at double time = 3 × 2 = 6 hours.
    Number of hours worked = $36\frac{1}{2} + 6 + 6 = 48\frac{1}{2}$,
    $48\frac{1}{2}$ at £2.90 = £140.65.

Questions to try

GRADE G

72.

The Happy Fryer

requires a
Part-time Counter Assistant
Hours: Friday 5.30 p.m. to 10.30 p.m.
Saturday 12 noon to 11.00 p.m.
Wages £2.50 per hour

This advertisement appeared in a local newspaper. Calculate:

(a)   the total number of hours to be worked each week;
(b)   the total wage earned each week.   (LEAG)

73. The following is a gas bill for the second quarter of 1992.

Date of reading	Meter reading (00's cubic feet)		Gas supplied		
	present	previous	cubic feet (hundreds)	therms	
June 26	8768	8643	....	....	....
			Standing Charge		£9.80
			Total due		....

Gas costs 41.00 pence per therm.
Complete the bill to show:

(i)   the amount of gas used (in hundreds of cubic feet);
(ii)   the number of therms used if 1 cubic foot = 0.0103 therms;
(iii) the cost of the gas;
(iv) the total amount due.

74. In a normal working week Jackie works from 08.30 until 16.30 each day **GRADE** from Monday to Thursday and she has a mid-morning break of ¼ hour and a lunch break of 1 hour. On Friday she works 8 hours.

(i)   How many hours does she work on each of the days from Monday to Thursday?

(ii) How many hours does she work in a normal week?

For a normal working week Jackie is paid at the rate of £3.20 per hour. Any overtime is paid at the rate of 'time and a half'. Jackie assembles clocks and she is paid a bonus of 80p for each clock assembled above 70 in a week.

(iii) Calculate the total amount earned by Jackie for the four week period shown below.

Week	1	2	3	4
Hours worked	38	36	41	45
Number of clocks assembled	68	75	81	70

75. Darren is a computer programmer. He is paid an annual salary of £38 000. His total tax free allowances come to £5800. He pays tax at 25p in the pound on the first £19 500 of taxable income, and 40p in the pound on the rest. Each month, Darren has £280 deducted for various insurances. Calculate Darren's monthly take home pay.

76. A salesman earns £90 a week.
As shown below, he also gets a commission on his sales.

Sales	Commission
Up to £5000	5%
Above £5000	5% on first £5000 10% on rest

(a)   How much actual commission would he get on sales of:

(i)   £3000;
(ii) £8500?

(b)   How much is his total weekly wage, including commission, when he sells £12 000 worth of goods in one year?

77. The rates of pay of the operatives in a small factory are given in the table below:

Class of Operative	Basic Pay (38 hr week)	Overtime Rate (per hour)	Number of Operatives
1	£120.80	£5.20	20
2	£104.40	£4.50	30

(a)   Jean is a class 1 operative. Calculate her total gross wage for a basic week and 5 hours overtime.

Owen is a class 2 operative. Over a four week period he earned a total of £512.10.

(b)   Calculate the number of hours overtime worked by Owen.

Following wage negotiations, the management agrees to pay class 1 operatives an extra 10% on their basic wage and class 2 operatives an extra $12\frac{1}{2}$% on their basic wage.

(c)   Calculate the increase in the factory's total weekly wage bill for basic pay.

(d)   Calculate the mean increase in basic pay per worker.   (LEAG)

78.

See Notes Overleaf	Payment Is Now Due	Telephone number	Date of bill (Tax point)

THWELL 8120 — 30 MAR 92

Rental / other standing charges		£ quarterly rate	£
From	1 APR	SYSTEM	13.95
to	30 JUN	APPARATUS	4.00
		TOTAL	.... (a)

Metered units (See (overleaf)	date	meter reading	units used
	22 DEC	036077	
	26 MAR	037299	.... (b)
	UNITS AT	4.40P	.... (c)

OPERATOR CONTROLLED CALLS
29 JAN £0.66
10 FEB £0.18
TOTAL OF OPERATOR CALLS .... (d)
TOTAL (EXCLUSIVE OF VAT) .... (e)
VALUE ADDED TAX AT 15.00% .... (f)
              TOTAL PAYABLE .... (g)

Tick box if receipt required

From the above telephone bill, work out:

(a)   the total cost of the system and apparatus;
(b)   the number of units used;
(c)   the cost, to the nearest penny, of the units used at 4.40p per unit;
(d)   the total cost of the two operator controlled calls;
(e)   the total of (a), (c) and (d);
(f)   the value added tax (to the nearest penny) at 17.5% charged on this total;
(g)   the total payable.

2 Credit, holidays, cars and best buys

BUYING ON CREDIT: Purchases can be made using H.P. (hire purchase This involves a deposit and regular payments) Credit or charge cards (usually no deposit), A bank loan. Holidays are often paid for by credit. You must expect to be able to read tables of flight times, and costs at different times of the year.

When going on holiday abroad, money has to be changed from sterling into foreign currency.

Study worked examples 40 and 41

RUNNING A CAR: When using a car you need to know about petrol consumption: miles per litre or km per litre: also cost of road tax, insurance and repairs.

BEST BUY: When spending money, aim at getting value for money. Find the unit cost when comparing.

WORDS TO LEARN: instalment: regular equal (usually) payment.

deposit: initial payment.

unit cost: the cost of 1 item or 1 gm or 1 oz etc.

Topic: buying on credit

GRADE F

WORKED EXAMPLE 39   Janine is going to buy herself a stereo system. It can be bought for cash at £349.99, or by paying a deposit of 10% (rounded up to the nearest £1) and the rest in equal monthly instalments of £16 over a period of 2 years.

(i)   What is the deposit she must find?
(ii)   How many instalments does she have to find?
(iii)   What is the credit purchase price?
(iv)   How much could she save by paying cash?

SOLUTION

(i)   10% of £349.99 = $\frac{10}{100}$ × £349.99 = £35 to the nearest £ rounded up.

(ii)   24.

(iii) 24 × 16 = £384
              + £ 35
              ‾‾‾‾‾
              £419 = the credit price.

(iv)   She would save £419 − £349.99 = £69.01.

2 years × 12.

Credit price − Cash price.

Topic: exchange rates

GRADE E

WORKED EXAMPLE 40   Phil and his friends were on holiday in Spain. The exchange rate at that time was 188.60 pesetas to the £1. He went into town one morning to buy a copy of his paper which normally cost him 30p. The cost of the same paper in Spain was 200 pesetas.

(i)   How much should the paper cost him if it was the same price in Spain?
(ii)   Roughly how many times more expensive was it actually?

SOLUTION   (i)   188.6 pesetas = 100 pence.

$\dfrac{188.6}{100}$ pesetas = 1 penny.

So $\dfrac{188.6}{100} \times 30$ pesetas = 30 pence.

56.58 pesetas = 30 pence.

The paper should have cost about 56 or 57 pesetas.

(ii) $200 \div 56.58 = 3.53$.

The paper was roughly $3\frac{1}{2}$ times more expensive.

WORKED EXAMPLE 41   The exchange rates for £1 sterling on the 19th February 1993 are given in the following table:

Australia	2.04 dollars	Japan	166 yen
Denmark	8.78 Kroner	South Africa	4.75 rand
Holland	2.57 guilders	Turkey	12,742 lire

Use this table to find:

(i)   the value in pence of 1 Dutch guilder;
(ii)   the number of Turkish lire you would get for 500 Danish Kroner.

SOLUTION   (i)   2.57 guilders = £1 = 100 pence
÷ by 2.57

$1 \text{ guilder} = \dfrac{100}{2.57} = 38.91$ pence

$= 39$p to the nearest penny.

(ii)   8.78 Kroner = £1,

so 1 Kroner = £$\dfrac{1}{8.78}$,

so 500 Kroner = £$\dfrac{1}{8.78} \times 500 = £56.9476$.

Now £1 = 12742 lire.
So £56.9476 = 12742×56.9476 lire
$= 725\,626$ lire.
Hence 500 Kroner = 725 626 lire.

Topic: running a car

WORKED EXAMPLE 42   Eleanor is a college student and runs an old car. She decides to estimate how much it costs each week to keep the car on the road.
Road Tax = £100 per year.
Insurance = £280 per year.
She travels about 5000 miles a year using petrol costing £2.40 per gallon, and the car averages 30 miles/gallon.
Her repair bills for the year are about £120.
How much per week does the car cost to keep on the road?

SOLUTION

Petrol costs: 5000 ÷ 30
                = 166.7 gallons
Cost = 166.7 × £2.40 = £400 petrol (to the nearest £1)
Further costs   = £100 road tax
                       = £280 insurance
                       = <u>£120</u> repairs
                         <u>£900</u> total
The weekly cost = £900 ÷ 52 = £17.31.

First find the number of gallons used

Topics: volume, best buys

WORKED EXAMPLE 43

A packet of 425 g of 'Kleenit' soap powder is in the shape of a cuboid 24 cm high, 15.5 cm long and 5 cm wide.

(a)   Calculate the volume of the packet.
(b)   This packet of 'Kleenit' contains 425 g of soap powder at a cost of 92 p. Calculate the number of grams of soap powder obtained per penny.
(c)   A larger sized packet of 'Kleenit' soap powder contains 960 g. It costs £2.03. By comparing 'grams per penny' for each packet, state which of the two packets is the better value.

SOLUTION

(a)   Volume of the box = 24 × 5 × 15.5 = 1860 cm^3.
(b)   425 g ÷ 92 will give the number of grams per penny;
      = 4.62 grams per penny.
(c)   The number of grams per penny for the larger size is 960 ÷ 203
      = 4.73 grams per penny.
      Hence the larger size gives you 'more for your money'.

Questions to try

GRADE F

79.   Alan bought a bike. He had to pay a deposit of £27.50 and the rest in equal instalments of £12.60. The total amount he paid for the bike was £203.90. How many instalments were there?

80.   Tim has 3 parcels to post. He has a large number of 15p and 19p stamps to use up. The exact postage required for each parcel is £2.72, £1.90 and 85p. What stamps should he use on each parcel so that the amount of money wasted is kept to a minimum?

81.   Hannah received a letter from her friend Raji from Calcutta. The postage on the envelope was 6.50 rupees. It cost Hannah 23p to send a letter of the same weight to Raji.
Compare the cost of sending a letter by post from Britain to Calcutta with that of sending a similar letter from Calcutta to Britain, and state which is cheaper. (£1 = 27.08 rupees.)   (NEA)

82.   The Patel family calculated that they used 13½ gallons of petrol in travelling a total distance of 586.5 miles. How many miles per gallon has the car averaged on their travels?

83. The table below shows the cost of taking either 7 days or 10 days holiday for one adult to Spain.

Departure airport		MANCHESTER	
No. of nights in hotel		7	10
Departure approx. time		0830	0830
Arrive back approx. time		14.45	14.45
First departure		14 Apr	14 Apr
Last departure		20 Oct	13 Oct
Departures on or between	14–20 Apr	£178	£216
	21 Apr–11 May	180	213
	12–18 May	178	231
	19–25 May	189	238
	26 May–8 June	182	233
	9 Jun–6 Jul	165	215
	7–27 Jul	200	248
	28 Jul–17 Aug	203	266
	18–31 Aug	196	240
	1–28 Sep	171	220
	29 Sep–12 Oct	167	209
	13–20 Oct	160	202
Children's Reductions 2–11 yrs. inc.	28 Apr–8 Jun & from 6 Oct	FREE	
	14–27 Apr, 9 Jun–27 Jul & 18 Aug–5 Oct	40%	
	28 Jul–17 Aug	20%	

(a) How much would it cost one adult for a *10 day* holiday starting on 7th July?

(b) What is the cost for two adults for a *7 day* holiday starting on 8th September?

A family of two adults and two children aged 8 years and 10 years wish to take a 7 day holiday.

(c) Give the latest date in early summer that they could leave to claim a week's free holiday for the children.

(d) If they chose a later holiday instead, leaving on 28th July for a 1 week stay, find:

    (i) the cost for one adult,

    (ii) the cost for one child (aged 10 years),

    (iii) the total cost for the four of them.

84.

Paris by SUPERSONIC CONCORDE	Tour Code	★★★ Hotel Bergere	★★★★ France et Choiseul	★★★★ Luxe Hotel Westminster
3 DAYS Depart London on Thursday by Air France A300. Return Saturday by Concorde. 9th June or 15th September only.	PS1	£365	£395	£465
3 DAYS Depart London on Saturday by Concorde. Return Monday by Air France A300. 11th June or 17th September only.	PS2	£375	£405	£475
3 DAYS Depart Manchester on Thursday by Air France 727. Return Saturday by Concorde. 22nd September only.	PS3	£385	£415	£485
3 DAYS Depart Manchester on Saturday by Concorde. Return Monday by Air France 727. 24th September only.	PS4	£395	£425	£495
3 DAYS Depart London on Thursday by Orient Express. Return Saturday by Concorde. 9th June or 15th September only.	PS5	£565	£595	£665

Prices are in £'s per person in double room according to hotel grade and travel route selected.

N.B. Single room and extra night supplements on request.

(a)   Use the above table to find the cost of a 3 day holiday in Paris for one person sharing a double room, departing on 22nd September and staying at the Hotel France et Choiseul.

(b)   Gwyn and his wife decided to take a 3 day holiday and stay at the Hotel Bergere. They departed on 24th September.

(i)   How much did they pay?

(ii)   Between them they spent about 360 francs each day. Estimate the total amount in francs that they spent during the three days.

(iii) How much is this in £, given that 10.8 francs = £1?   (WJEC)

85.   Ruth decides to buy a new radio.

Cash price   £34.60
OR
HIRE PURCHASE
Deposit £6.92 + 12 repayments of £2.95

(a)   What is the total cost of the 12 repayments?

(b)   How much is the total hire purchase price?

(c)   How much would Ruth have saved if she had paid cash rather than hire purchase?

86.   Before going to France, I am going to change £300 into francs.   ◀ **GRADE E**

(i)   At one bank, the rate of exchange is 9.4 francs to £1, and I am charged £3 commission. How many francs would I get?

(ii)   At a second bank, the rate is 9.5 francs to £1, and I am charged a 1 per cent commission on the amount changed. How many francs will I obtain at this bank?

(iii) Is it always better to go to one bank rather than the other?

87.   Using the table of exchange rates given in worked example 41 on page 57, find:

(i)   the value in pence of 1 Australian dollar;

(ii)   the number of Japanese yen you would get for £125;

(iii) the number of South African rands equivalent to 200 Danish Kroner;

(iv)   the value in Turkish lire of 1 Dutch guilder.

88.   The local supermarket sells Cox's apples in three different sizes. A packet of 4 for 65p, a packet of 6 at 90p, or a large bag containing 22 apples for £3.10.

(i)   Which packet gives the best value for money?

(ii)   Is your answer to part (i) necessarily the most sensible buy? Give a reason.

89.   WANDER crisps can be bought in 3 different sizes. A small bag weighing 1.2 oz for 18p, a larger bag weighing 2.7 oz for 38p, or a party size bag of 12 assorted flavours for £1.90. Advise somebody giving a children's party which type of crisps they should buy and why.

90. (a) Mary and Derek were organising a Valentine Disco.
   (i) Mary wanted to use 'HAM DISCO' and finish at 3.00 a.m. How much would this cost?
   (ii) Derek wanted to use 'Andys Disco', but was only prepared to pay £70. At what time would the disco have to finish?

(b) 'BaneX Disco', who also had a fixed charge with a $\frac{1}{2}$ hour rate after midnight, said that if their disco was used, they would charge £47 to finish at 2.00 a.m. or £63 to finish at 3.00 a.m. Calculate:
   (i) the $\frac{1}{2}$ hour rate after midnight;
   (ii) the fixed charge.

                                                                                         (NEA)

HAM DISCO
£25 plus
£10 each ½ hour after midnight

Andys Disco
£10 plus £12 each ½ hour after midnight

91. On a full tank of petrol of 40 litres a car completed 420 kilometres.

(i) What distance would you expect the car to complete with 22 litres of petrol in the tank?

(ii) How many litres of petrol do you need to travel 500 kilometres?

92. For every £5 I spend on petrol at my local garage I receive a gift token. If petrol costs 38.5 pence per litre, how many complete litres will I need to buy in order to obtain 1 token?

The petrol tank of my car has a capacity of 11 gallons. Using the conversion 1 gallon = 4.55 litres, determine how many tokens I would receive if I filled up with a complete tank of petrol.

If I filled up with a complete tank of petrol once a week, how long would it take me to save up for a set of cutlery worth 80 tokens?

3 Interest, simple and compound, mortgages, insurance

People invest money to earn interest, this can be in a building society, a bank, in shares etc.

Simple interest is calculated using a formula

$$I = \frac{PRT}{100}$$

I = Interest
P = amount invested.
T = time invested (in years)
$R(\%)$ is the annual interest rate.

The formula can be rearranged

$$P = \frac{100 I}{RT}, \quad T = \frac{100 I}{PR}, \quad R = \frac{100 I}{PT}$$

COMPOUND INTEREST : Usually, interest is added to the amount and interest already earned each year, this is called compound interest, see worked example 47 for more detail as to how this works.

Compound interest occurs in most financial calculations, e.g. mortgages, credit cards, bank loans.

Insurance policies are usually taken out to cover "risks". Again it involves reading tables.

WORDS TO LEARN : p.a. = per annum (each year).

GRADE E

Topics: insurance and life assurance

WORKED EXAMPLE 44   Rajish, who is 34 years old and has two children, wishes to insure his property and his life. He sees the following advertisements:

OYSTER ASSURANCE CO

Protect your Property
Competitive rates
Annual Premiums per £1000 insured:
Household goods: £4
Electrical goods: £11.25
Jewellery & valuables: £12.50

Life Assurance

Monthly Payments table for a sum assured of £5000

Age next birthday	Term (in years)			
	15	20	25	30
25	19.90	12.85	8.90	6.50
30	19.90	12.90	9.05	6.70
35	20.05	13.10	9.30	7.05
40	20.35	13.50	9.80	7.70
45	20.85	14.15	10.70	8.75
50	21.70	15.30	12.05	

Rajish assesses the value of his property as follows:

Household goods: £12000
Electrical goods: £2000
Jewellery and valuables: £3000

and he wishes to assure his life for £25000 for a period of 30 years. Calculate the total premium due in the first year.

SOLUTION

The total premium to be paid for his property is as follows:

$$
\begin{aligned}
\text{Household goods} &= £4 \times 12 &&= £48 \\
\text{Electrical goods} &= £11.25 \times 2 &&= £22.50 \\
\text{Jewellery and valuables} &= £12.50 \times 3 &&= \underline{£37.50} \\
\text{Total} & &&= \underline{£108.00}
\end{aligned}
$$

Note that the table gives per £1000

his age next birthday is 35

For a sum assured of £25 000 the monthly payment
$$= 5 \times £7.05$$
$$= £35.25.$$
Therefore the annual premium for the life assurance policy
$$= 12 \times £35.25$$
$$= £423.00.$$
The combined total
$$= £423.00 + £108.00$$
$$= £531.00.$$
Note that if Rajish had been any age between 30 and 34 the same row of the table would have been used.

Topic: mortgages

GRADE C/D

WORKED EXAMPLE 45

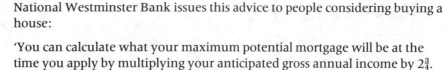

National Westminster Bank issues this advice to people considering buying a house:

'You can calculate what your maximum potential mortgage will be at the time you apply by multiplying your anticipated gross annual income by $2\frac{3}{4}$. In appropriate cases this can be increased by up to $1\frac{1}{2}$ times your partner's income.
'N.B. Remember, the actual mortgage available will always be limited to a maximum of 95% of the lower of valuation or purchase price of the property.'
Joy and Harry Black have seen a house they would like to buy. The purchase price is £41 000 but it is valued by the surveyor at only £38 000.

(a)   What is the maximum mortgage that the bank would give on this house?
(b)   Henry expects his gross annual income to be £10 200. The bank has agreed to consider Joy's income for mortgage purposes and will make the maximum allowance on it. What is the minimum gross income that Joy must earn in order for the Blacks to be able to ask for the maximum mortgage on this house?   (NEA)

SOLUTION

(a)   The maximum mortgage will be 95% of the valuation figure, which is lower than the purchase price.
$$\frac{95}{100} \times £38 000 = £36 100.$$
(b)   Henry would be allowed $2\frac{3}{4} \times £10 200 = £28 050.$
Henry and Joy still need £36 100 − £28 050 = £8050.
If Joy earns £x, then
$$x \times 1\frac{1}{2} = 8050,$$
$$\text{so } x = 8050 \div 1.5 = 5367.$$
Hence Joy needs to earn at least £5367 in a year.

Topics: simple interest, investment

WORKED EXAMPLE 46

If £250 is invested at 12 per cent p.a. simple interest for 1 year 3 months, find the total amount of money at the end of this time.

3 months is ¼ year so time T = 1¼

The amount invested is called the Principle P

SOLUTION

Using the formula $I = \dfrac{PRT}{100}$,
$$P = 250, R = 12, T = 1\frac{1}{4},$$
$$I = \frac{250 \times 12 \times 1.25}{100} = 37.5.$$
The total = £250 + 37.5 = £287.50.

Topics: compound interest, investment

WORKED EXAMPLE 47   If £800 is invested at $7\frac{1}{2}$ per cent compound interest for a period of 3 years, find the value of the investment at the end of that time.

SOLUTION   The interest for each year is added to the principal at the beginning of the next year, giving the new principal for the next year. We can proceed as follows:

First year: principal = £800,

interest $= £800 \times \dfrac{7.5}{100}$ $= £60.$

Second year: principal = £800 + 60 = £860,

interest $= £860 \times \dfrac{7.5}{100}$ $= £64.50.$

Third year: principal = £860 + 64.50 = £924.50,

interest $= £924.50 \times \dfrac{7.5}{100} = £69.34.$

The value of the investment = £924.50 + 69.34 = £993.84.
The formula:

$$\text{Total} = P\left(1 + \frac{R}{100}\right)^n$$

can be used to find the capital at the end of *n* years.
In the above example,

$$\text{Capital} = £800\left(1 + \frac{7.5}{100}\right)^3 = £993.84.$$

This formula is much easier, if you can remember it

Questions to try

93.   The Morgan family buy a house costing £25 000 with the help of a £10 000 mortgage from a building society. The table shows the monthly repayments on mortgage loans.

Mortgage	10 years	15 years	20 years	25 years
£ 1000	£ 12.95	£ 10.30	£ 9.00	£ 8.44
2000	25.90	20.60	18.00	16.88
10000	129.50	103.00	90.00	84.40
15000	194.25	154.50	135.00	126.60
20000	259.00	206.00	180.00	168.80

(a)   How many monthly payments must be made in 25 years?
(b)   What is the total amount repaid over 25 years on the £10 000 loan?

94.

LOW COST, HIGH COVER
(contribution levels of £5.90 and £6.90 also available)

YOUR AGE TODAY		£4.90 Per Month		£7.90 Per Month		£9.90 Per Month	
		Non-Smoker	Standard	Non-Smoker	Standard	Non-Smoker	Standard
		£	£	£	£	£	£
18–31	18–35	32,242	25,794	51,982	41,586	65,142	52,114
32	36	30,662	24,530	49,435	39,548	61,950	49,560
33	37	27,918	22,335	45,011	36,009	56,406	45,125
34	38	25,358	20,286	40,883	32,706	51,233	40,986
35	39	22,945	18,356	36,992	29,594	46,357	37,086
36	40	20,715	16,572	33,398	26,718	41,853	33,482
37	41	18,669	14,936	30,099	24,080	37,719	30,176
38	42	16,807	13,446	27,097	21,678	33,957	27,166
39	43	15,129	12,103	24,392	19,513	30,567	24,453
40	44	13,598	10,878	21,923	17,538	27,473	21,978
41	45	12,238	9,791	19,731	15,785	24,726	19,781
42	46	11,001	8,801	17,736	14,189	22,226	17,781
43	47	9,874	7,899	15,919	12,735	19,949	15,959
44	48	8,784	7,027	14,161	11,329	17,746	14,197
45	49	7,828	6,263	12,621	10,097	15,816	12,653
46	50	6,983	5,586	11,258	9,006	14,108	11,286
47	51	6,236	4,989	10,053	8,043	12,598	10,079
48	52	5,574	4,459	8,987	7,189	11,262	9,009
49	53	4,998	3,999	8,058	6,447	10,098	8,079
50	54	4,484	3,587	7,229	5,783	9,059	7,247
51	–	4,018	3,215	6,478	5,183	8,118	6,495
52	–	3,614	2,891	5,827	4,661	7,302	5,841
53	–	3,259	2,607	5,254	4,203	6,584	5,267
54	–	2,940	2,352	4,740	3,792	5,940	4,752

The table shows the insurance cover provided by an insurance company for different payments.
What is the value of the cover provided for a man aged 39, who does not smoke, who pays £7.90 per month?

95. Fully comprehensive insurance for my car is £500 for the year. If I am entitled to a 60% discount as a 'no claims' bonus, calculate my reduced premium. If I am entitled to a further 10% discount on this reduced premium as a mature driver and a further 7.5% discount for paying the first £100 of any claim, calculate the net balance due.

96. Using the premium rates for property offered by the OYSTER ASSURANCE CO in worked example 44, determine how much the premium would be in order to insure the following property:

	Value
Household goods:	£9500
Electrical goods:	£600
Jewellery and valuables:	£1500

97. Using the life assurance table in worked example 44, answer the following questions:

(i) A woman aged 28 next birthday takes out a £10 000 policy for 20 years. What is the annual premium?
If she decides to take out the policy for 25 years instead of 20 years, how much less will she pay?

(ii) A 39 year old man takes out a £30 000 policy for 25 years. How much does he pay altogether?
The assurance agent who sells him the policy gets a 60% commission on the first annual premium and 5% on each annual premium after that. What is it worth to the agent over the 25 years in commissions?

98. The table gives annual car insurance premiums in £. **GRADE C/D**

District	Insurance group							
	1		2		3		4	
	T	C	T	C	T	C	T	C
Rural	120	240	142	280	170	356	190	400
Town	145	287	168	340	192	400	225	462
City	168	341	190	396	228	470	264	576

T means cover for Third Party, Fire and Theft only.
C means Comprehensive cover.

(a) Jill lives in a city. Her car is in insurance group 2. How much does she pay for cover for Third Party, Fire and Theft only?

Drivers under 30 have to pay an additional premium based on age. The company adds $(90 - 3A)$ % to the basic premium, where A is the age of the driver in years.

(b) Karen is 19 years old, lives in a town and owns a Mini, which is in insurance group 1.
  (i) What percentage will the company add to the basic premium?
  (ii) How much does it cost Karen for Comprehensive cover?

(c) Because of his age, Sajid has to pay 18 per cent more than the basic premium. How old is Sajid?

(d) A 'no claims' discount is given to drivers who do not make any claims against their insurance. This discount is shown in the following table:

Number of claim-free years	1	2	3	4+
Percentage discount	30	40	50	60

Harry Driver's insurance would cost £400 but he has a 60% 'no claims' discount for 1989. One day his car skids so that he crashes into a gatepost and causes £425 worth of damage. If he claims from the insurance company he will have to pay the full £400 insurance in 1990 and gradually build up his 'no claims' discount.

(i) Copy and complete the following table:

Year	1990	1991	1992	1993	1994
Payment – no claim made	£160				
Payment – claim made	£400				

(ii) Investigate whether Harry would be better off by paying the bill for the damage himself or by claiming from the insurance company. Explain your reasoning clearly. (MEG)

GRADE B

99. A car depreciates in value by about 15% each year. If Ronald bought a car for £6800 in 1989, find its value 3 years later.

ALGEBRA
ATTAINMENT TARGET 3

1 Expressions, substitution, simplifying

Always remember when using algebra, that a letter is being used to represent a number. Do not do anything with a letter that you would not do with a number. Algebra is a form of mathematical shorthand.

$3x$ means $3 \times x$ or (3 lots of x.)

$3x + 4x = 7x$ (called: collecting like terms)

$x \times x = x^2$ (x squared or x to the power 2)

Hence $2x^2$ means 2 lots of x^2

i.e. $2 \times x^2$ or $2 \times x \times x$ [You square x before you double it.]

Removing brackets : $2(x+4) = 2x + 8$

Careful $\quad 2(x+1) + 3(x-2) = 2x + 2 + 3x - 6$
$$= 5x - 4$$

But $\quad 4(2x+1) - 2(x-1) = 8x + 4 - 2x + 2$
$$= 6x + 6$$

── is the same as +

Work carefully through the substitution examples on page 70

fractions : $\dfrac{x}{2}$ means $x \div 2$ or $\frac{1}{2}$ of x.

Topic: using formulae

WORKED EXAMPLE 48   When Diane Wales attends meetings her car expenses are worked out as follows.

For journeys of 50 miles or less,

$$\text{Amount} = £\frac{24N}{100}$$

For journeys of more than 50 miles,

$$\text{Amount} = £12 + £\frac{(N - 50)\ 12}{100}$$

N is the number of miles travelled.

(i)   How much will she be paid for a journey of 26 miles?
(ii) How much will she be paid for a journey of 75 miles?
(iii) How much will she be paid per mile for journeys of less than 50 miles?

(NEA)

SOLUTION   (i) $N = 26$, so the first formula applies:

$$\text{Amount} = £\frac{24 \times 26}{100} = £6.24.$$

(ii) $N = 75$, so the second formula applies:

$$\text{Amount} = £12 + £\frac{(75 - 50) \times 12}{100}$$
$$= £12 + £3 = £15.$$

(iii) $N = 1$, so the first formula applies:

$$\text{Amount} = £\frac{24 \times 1}{100} = £0.24$$

i.e. 24p per mile.

Topics: algebra, forming expressions

WORKED EXAMPLE 49   (i)   A number N is multiplied by 4, and 3 is subtracted from the answer. The result is then divided by 4. Write down an expression for the final answer.

(ii) Find the cost of p apples costing t pence a dozen, and q pears at 16 pence each.

(iii) A car travels at x m.p.h. for 30 minutes and then travels a further k miles for $\frac{1}{4}$ hour. Find the average speed for the journey in m.p.h.

SOLUTION   (i)   A flow chart for this is:

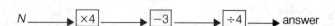

$$N \longrightarrow \boxed{\times 4} \longrightarrow \boxed{-3} \longrightarrow \boxed{\div 4} \longrightarrow \text{answer}$$

The answer is $(4N - 3) \div 4$ [You must have the brackets]

(ii) A 'dozen' is 12.

The cost of one apple is $t \div 12$

or $\dfrac{t}{12}$ pence.

The cost of p apples will be $p \times$ the cost of one apple, which is

$p \times \dfrac{t}{12}$ or $\dfrac{pt}{12}$, the cost of q pears is $16q$

$$\text{total} = \frac{pt}{12} + 16q$$

(iii)　30 minutes = $\frac{1}{2}$ hour.

Hence, distance travelled in $\frac{1}{2}$ hour = $x \times \frac{1}{2} = \frac{1}{2}x$,

total distance travelled = $\frac{1}{2}x + k$.

The total time taken = $\frac{1}{4} + \frac{1}{2} = \frac{3}{4}$ hours.

The average speed = $\dfrac{(\frac{1}{2}x + k)}{\frac{3}{4}}$

$$= (\tfrac{1}{2}x + k) \times \frac{4}{3}$$

$$= \frac{2}{3}x + \frac{4}{3}k.$$

Topic: simplifying expressions in algebra

GRADE B

WORKED EXAMPLE 50　Write the answers to the following, as simply as possible:

(i)　$2x + 1$ add $3x + 4$;

(ii)　the result of subtracting $x + 4$ from $3x + 2$;

(iii)　the average of $2x - 3$ and $4x + 1$.

SOLUTION

(i)　$(2x + 1) + (3x + 4)$

$= 2x + 1 + 3x + 4$

$= 5x + 5.$

(ii)　$(3x + 2) - (x + 4)$

$= 3x + 2 - x - 4$

$= 2x - 2.$

(iii)　$\frac{1}{2}[(2x - 3) + (4x + 1)]$

$= \frac{1}{2}[2x - 3 + 4x + 1]$

$= \frac{1}{2}[6x - 2]$

$= 3x - 1.$

Be careful with subtracting from.

Average of a and b is $\frac{1}{2}(a+b)$

Topic: simplifying powers in algebra

WORKED EXAMPLE 51　Simplify the following as much as you can:

(i) $2x^2 + 3x^2$; (ii) $p \times p^2$; (iii) $(2p)^2$; (iv) $(2x)^3 \div (3x^2)^2$.

SOLUTION

(i)　$2x^2 + 3x^2 = 5x^2.$

(ii)　$p \times p^2 = p \times p \times p = p^3.$

(iii)　$(2p)^2$ means $2p \times 2p = 4p^2.$

(iv)　$(2x)^3$ means $2x \times 2x \times 2x = 8x^3$

$(3x^2)^2$ means $3x^2 \times 3x^2 = 9x^4$

Hence $(2x)^3 \div (3x^2)^2 = 8x^3 \div 9x^4$

$$= \frac{8x^3}{9x^4}$$

$$= \frac{8}{9x}$$

Topics: simplifying expressions in algebra, perimeter

WORKED EXAMPLE 52　ABC is a right-angled triangle with $\angle C = 90°$.

$AB = (2x + 3)$ cm and $BC = (x + 1)$ cm.

(i)　If the perimeter of the triangle is 40 cm, find the length of AC in terms of x.

(ii)　If the triangle is isosceles, and $x = 4$, find the perimeter of the triangle.

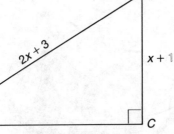

SOLUTION   (i) $40 = AB + BC + AC.$
So $40 = 2x + 3 + x + 1 + AC$
$40 = 3x + 4 + AC$
Hence $40 - 3x - 4 = AC$
$36 - 3x = AC.$

(ii)   If the triangle is isosceles, then $AC = BC$, so $AC = x + 1$
Hence the perimeter $= 2x + 3 + x + 1 + x + 1$
$= 4x + 5$
If $x = 4$, the perimeter $= (4 \times 4) + 5$
$= 21\,\text{cm}.$

WORKED EXAMPLE 53   In all of the following, $a = 2, b = -3, c = -\frac{1}{2}$. In each case find the value of x given by each formula.

(a) $x = 2a + 3b + 4c;$
(b) $x = 3a - 5b;$
(c) $x = a^2 + b^2;$
(d) $x = 2b^2 + 4c^2;$
(e) $x = \dfrac{3ac}{b};$
(f) $x = \dfrac{2}{a} + \dfrac{4}{c^2};$
(g) $x = \sqrt{\dfrac{a + b}{c}}$

SOLUTION   (a)   In full, $x = 2 \times 2 + 3 \times -3 + 4 \times -\frac{1}{2};$
with brackets, $x = (2 \times 2) + (3 \times -3) + (4 \times -\frac{1}{2})$
$= 4 + -9 + -2 = -7.$

(b)   In full, $x = 3 \times 2 - 5 \times -3;$
with brackets, $x = (3 \times 2) - (5 \times -3)$
$= 6 - -15 = 21.$

(c)   In full, $x = 2^2 + -3^2;$
with brackets, $x = (2)^2 + (-3)^2$
$= 4 + 9 = 13.$

(d)   In full, $x = 2 \times -3^2 + 4 \times -\frac{1}{2}^2$
with brackets, $x = [2 \times (-3)^2] + [4 \times (-\frac{1}{2})^2]$
$= [2 \times 9] + [4 \times \frac{1}{4}]$
$= 18 + 1 = 19.$

(e)   In full, $x = \dfrac{3 \times 2 \times -\frac{1}{2}}{-3};$
with brackets, $x = (3 \times 2 \times -\frac{1}{2}) \div -3$
$= -3 \div -3 = 1.$

(f)   In full, $f = \dfrac{2}{2} + \dfrac{4}{(-\frac{1}{2})^2}$;
with brackets, $x = [2 \div 2] + [4 \div (-\frac{1}{2})^2]$
$= 1 + [4 \div \frac{1}{4}]$
$= 1 + 16 = 17.$

(g)   In full, $x = \sqrt{\dfrac{2 + -3}{-\frac{1}{2}}}$;
with brackets, $x = \sqrt{(2 + -3) \div -\frac{1}{2}} = \sqrt{-1 \div -\frac{1}{2}} = \sqrt{2}.$

Questions to try

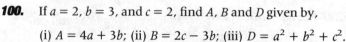   **GRADE F**

100.   If $a = 2, b = 3$, and $c = 2$, find A, B and D given by,

(i) $A = 4a + 3b;$ (ii) $B = 2c - 3b;$ (iii) $D = a^2 + b^2 + c^2.$

101.   A bowl contains n apples and p pears. David then ate an apple, and his mother emptied another 3 pears into the bowl. How many apples and pears altogether are there in the bowl?

102. If I take *F* five pound notes, and 10 ten pound notes, and change them into 50p pieces, how many coins do I get?

103. Zak earns £*e* a week, and his wife Paula earns £*E* a year. How much do they earn between them:

(i) in a year; (ii) each week?

GRADE C/D

104. Paul was good at physics, and decided to use a formula he knew to find the depth of the well in a nearby village. The formula he used was that the depth of the well *d* (metres) is given by $d = \frac{1}{2}gt^2$, where *t* is the time it takes for an object to fall to the bottom, and *g* = 10.

He timed a large stone, and it took 2.8 seconds to fall. How deep is the well?

The value he should have chosen for *g* = 9.8. What error was made?

105. The toll for vehicles to cross a bridge is 50p for cars and £1 for all other vehicles. There is no charge for people.

(a) Between 8 a.m. and 9 p.m. one morning, £365 was collected in tolls from vehicles crossing the bridge. 486 of the vehicles were cars. How many other vehicles had crossed the bridge?

(b) During each 24 hour period an average of *x* cars per hour cross the bridge and *y* other vehicles per hour.
  (i) Write in terms of *x* and *y* the total number of cars and other vehicles crossing the bridge every hour.
  (ii) Write in terms of *x* and *y* the amount, in pounds, of toll money collected every hour.

(SEG)

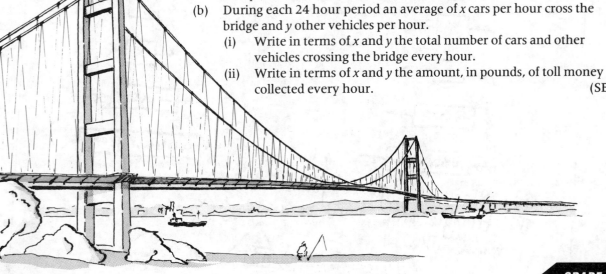

GRADE B

106. Simplify the following as much as you can

(i) $3x^2 + 4x^2$; (ii) $4x \times 3x$; (iii) $(3x)^2$; (iv) $(6x)^2 \div (2x)^2$

107. Write the answers to the following, as simply as possible

(i) The sum of $4x + 1$ and $2x - 3$; (ii) The difference between $x + 6$ and $x + 10$; (iii) The average of $6x - 5$ and $2x + 9$

2 Linear equations, re-arranging formulae

LINEAR EQUATIONS : e.g. $2x + 1 = x + 3$
$$1 - 5x = 2(x+1)$$
$$\frac{5}{x} = 6$$

Try to get x on one side.

Always do the same thing to both sides when altering an equation.
See examples on page 73

You may be asked to solve a problem that does not look at first sight like an equation.
See worked examples 54 and 55

Rearranging formulae is similar to solving an equation.
The easier questions can often be done by reversing a flow chart.

See Algebra 2 for a fuller treatment.
The triangle rule; can be used for a formula like $H = \frac{t}{D}$

Hence $t = HD$ or $D = \frac{t}{H}$

Useful in speed $= \dfrac{\text{distance}}{\text{time}}$, or trigonometry.

USEFUL FACTS

Solving linear equations

GRADE E

(a) $7x - 5 = 4x + 11$;

add 5 to each side:	$7x - 5 + 5 = 4x + 11 + 5$;
simplify:	$7x = 4x + 16$;
take $4x$ from each side:	$7x - 4x = 4x + 16 - 4x$;
simplify:	$3x = 16$;
divide each side by 3:	$x = \dfrac{16}{3}$ or $5\frac{1}{3}$.

GRADE C/D

(b) $\dfrac{6}{x} = 9$

Using the triangle rule:

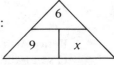

Hence $x = \dfrac{6}{9} = \frac{2}{3}$

GRADE B

(c) $4 - (3x + 1) = 2(x - 5)$;

remove brackets first:	$4 - 3x - 1 = 2x - 10$;
collect terms on the left:	$3 - 3x = 2x - 10$;
	$3 - 3x + 10 = 2x - 10 + 10$;
add 10 to each side:	$13 - 3x = 2x$;
add $3x$ to each side:	$13 = 5x$;
divide each side by 5:	$\dfrac{13}{5} = x$.

GRADE A

(d) $\dfrac{2x + 1}{4} - \dfrac{3x - 5}{2} = \dfrac{x}{3}$;

to avoid problems with signs, rewrite the equation with brackets inserted, i.e.

$$\dfrac{(2x + 1)}{4} - \dfrac{(3x - 5)}{2} = \dfrac{x}{3};$$

multiply the equation by the common denominator, i.e. the L.C.M. of 2, 3, 4, which is 12;

$$\dfrac{\overset{3}{\cancel{12}}(2x + 1)}{\underset{1}{\cancel{4}}} - \dfrac{\overset{6}{\cancel{12}}(3x - 5)}{\underset{1}{\cancel{2}}} = \overset{4}{\cancel{12}} \times \dfrac{x}{\underset{1}{\cancel{3}}}; \quad \text{cancel;}$$

So $3(2x + 1) - 6(3x - 5) = 4x$	
remove brackets:	$6x + 3 - 18x + 30 = 4x$;
collect terms:	$-12x + 33 = 4x$;
add $12x$ to each side:	$33 = 16x$;
divide each side by 16:	$\dfrac{33}{16} = x$.

GRADE E

Topic: forming and solving equations

WORKED EXAMPLE 54

Alec is asked to 'think of a number', multiply it by 4, add 3 to the answer, take away the number he first thought of, and write down the answer. He wrote down 99. What number did he think of?

SOLUTION

It is possible that you could get the answer by guessing, but the method using simple equations is much more reliable.

Let the number he thought of be N.

> Multiply it by 4 gives $4N$.
>
> Add 3 to the answer gives $4N + 3$.
>
> Take away the number he first thought of (which is N) gives
>
> $4N + 3 - N$.

His answer is 99, so

$$4N + 3 - N = 99$$

i.e. $3N + 3 = 99$

$3N = 96$

$N = 32$.

The number he thought of was 32.

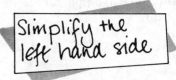

WORKED EXAMPLE 55   The sum of £61 is divided between Arthur, Brenda and Catherine. Arthur has twice as much as Brenda, and Catherine has £5 less than Arthur and Brenda together. How much do all three have?

SOLUTION   Suppose Brenda is given £M,
then Arthur is given £$2M$.
Catherine has £$M + 2M - 5 = £3M - 5$.
The total is £61,

$$\text{So } M + 2M + 3M - 5 = 61$$
$$6M - 5 = 61$$
$$6M = 66$$
$$\text{So } M = 11.$$

Hence Arthur has £22, Brenda has £11 and Catherine has £28.

Topics: flow diagrams, rearranging formulae

GRADE C/D

WORKED EXAMPLE 56   The flow chart shown below gives a way of changing temperature in degrees fahrenheit (°F) to temperature in degrees Celsius (°C).

F ⟶ $\boxed{-32}$ ⟶ $\boxed{\times 5}$ ⟶ $\boxed{\div 9}$ ⟶ C

(i)   Use the method to change 80°F into °C.
(ii)   Write down an algebraic formula for this flow chart.
(iii) Rearrange this formula to find a formula that will convert °C into °F.
(iv)   Use your formula to change 40°C into °F.

SOLUTION   (i) $80 - 32$ gives 48, × 5 gives 240, ÷ 9 = 26.7°C.
(ii) $(F - 32) \times 5 \div 9 = C$
OR $(F - 32) \times \dfrac{5}{9} = C$.

(iii)   Reverse the flow chart:

C ⟶ $\boxed{\times 9}$ ⟶ $\boxed{\div 5}$ ⟶ $\boxed{+32}$ ⟶ F

hence C × 9 gives 9C ÷ 5 gives $\dfrac{9C}{5}$ add 32 gives $F = \dfrac{9C}{5} + 32$.

(iv)   If C = 40
$$F = \frac{9 \times 40}{5} + 32 = 72 + 32$$
$$= 104$$
Hence the temperature is 104°F.

WORKED EXAMPLE 57   (i)   Write down a flow chart with x as input and H as output for the formula:

$$H = t\left(4 - \frac{p}{x}\right)$$

(ii)   By reversing the flow chart, find an expression for x.

SOLUTION   (i)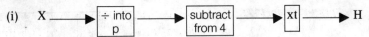

Note the use of "÷ into" and "subtract from"

(ii)   Remember that the reverse of ÷ into is also ÷ into, and the reverse of subtract from is subtract from.

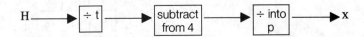

The formula will be

$$p \div \left(4 - \frac{H}{t}\right) = x$$

Questions to try   **GRADE E**

108.   Solve the equations:

(i) $2(x + 1) = 5$; (ii) $x + 7 = 3x$; (iii) $4x - 5 = 1 - x$; (iv) $3 - 5x = -12$; (v) $\frac{1}{2}(x + 6) = 9$; (vi) $\frac{1}{2}x + \frac{1}{3}x = 10$.

109.   The three sides of a triangle are of length $x + 10, x + 1$ and $3x + 2$ cm. Write down and simplify an expression for the perimeter of the triangle in terms of x.

(i)   Find x if the perimeter is 63 cm.
(ii)   Is it possible to find a value of x to make the triangle isosceles? (Give a reason.)

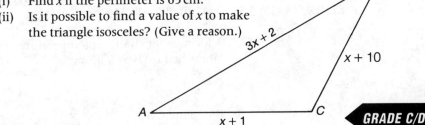

GRADE C/D

110.   Daniel is x years old. His Uncle Peter is three times as old as Daniel. In ten years' time, Peter will be twice as old as Daniel.

(i)   Write down Peter's present age in terms of x.
(ii)   Write down Peter's age in 10 years' time.
(iii)   Write down and solve an equation containing x, and hence state Daniel and Peter's ages at present.

111.   The diagram shows a number table with a sliding square that can cover any 4 numbers. The square is labelled by the number in the top right hand corner.
The one illustrated is the '21' square.

1	2	3	4	5	6	7	8
9	10	11	12	13	14	15	16
17	18	19	20	21	22	23	24
25	26	27	28	29	30	31	32
33	34	35	36	37	38	39	40

(i)   Find the total of the numbers in the '31' square.
(ii)   Write down in terms of x, the numbers in the x square.
(iii)   Show that the total of the numbers in the x square is $4x + 14$.
(iv)   Which square has a total of 118?
(v)   Why is it impossible for the total to equal 119?

112.

1	2	3	4	5	6	7	8	9
10	11	12	13	14	15	16	17	18
19	20	21	22	23	24	25	26	27
28	29	30	31	32	33	34	35	36
37	38	39	40	41	42	43	44	45
46	47	48	49	50	51	52	53	54
55	56	57	58	59	60	61	62	63
64	65	66	67	68	69	70	71	72
73	74	75	76	77	78	79	80	81

The diagram shows a number square with an outline 'T' on it. The number at the base of the outline is 20, so we say that the outline is 'based on 20'. Using a translation, the outline can be moved so that it is based on a different number, but it must always remain upright and completely within the number square.

(a) Find the total of the five numbers in the outline when it is based on 40.
(b) If the outline is based on x, write down (in terms of x) the other four numbers in the outline and show that the total of the five numbers in the outline is $5x - 63$.
(c) Find the five numbers in the outline, given that their total is 287.
(d) Explain why the total of the five numbers in the outline could not be
(i) 290; (ii) 117.

(MEG)

113. A formula for changing temperature in degrees Celsius (C) to degrees fahrenheit (F) is as follows:

$$C = \frac{5}{9}(F - 32).$$

GRADE B

(i) Find C if F = 30.
(ii) Is it possible for F and C to have the same value?
(iii) Rearrange the formula to find an expression for F.

114. Using the formula $V = 4t + q$,

(i) find q if $V = 18$ and $t = 2$;
(ii) rearrange the formula to find an expression for t;
(iii) find t, if $V = 28$ and $q = 12$.

115. Rearrange the following formulae to make x the subject.

(i) $y = 2t + kx$ (ii) $y = a(k + x)$ (iii) $y = \sqrt{\dfrac{x}{t}}$

(iv) $y = \dfrac{1}{x + 1}$ (v) $y = a + \dfrac{2t}{3x}$

3 Number patterns

A NUMBER PATTERN is a regular pattern of numbers, where you can predict numbers if the pattern is extended.
A formula can often be found to do the prediction.

The simplest type of number pattern you will probably meet is an arithmetic series
e.g.   3, 7, 11, 15, 19, ... (increase by 4)

1, 4, 7, 10, 13, ... (increase by 3)

In the first series add 1 to each number to give 4, 8, 12, 16, 20 ..... multiples of 4.

The n th number must be $4n$.
Take 1 away and the original series must have n th term $4n - 1$.

In the second series add 2 to each number to give 3, 6, 9, 12, 15, ... multiples of 3.

The n th number is $3n$
Take 2 away and the second series must have n th term $3n - 2$.

Number patterns are often associated with shapes.

Number patterns can be investigated with computers.

Triangle numbers : 1, 3, 6, 10, ...

Dot patterns : $\cdot$ $\vdots$ $\vdots\vdots$ $\vdots\vdots\vdots$

The n'th triangular number is $\dfrac{n(n+1)}{2}$

Topic: number patterns

WORKED EXAMPLE 58   Look at the following sequence of numbers:

2, 5, 11, 23, 47, . . .

(i)   Describe *two* different ways in which the numbers are calculated.
(ii)   Find the next two numbers in sequence.

SOLUTION   It is always worth looking at the difference between each number.

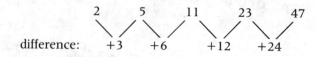

difference: +3   +6   +12   +24

(i)   One answer would be that the differences double each time, so that the next differences were +48, and +96. Finding a second way is not quite so easy. Close inspection shows if you double each number and add one, you get the next.
So $5 = 2 \times 2 + 1$, $11 = 2 \times 5 + 1$ and so on.

(ii)   The next two numbers will be
47 + 48 = 95
and 95 + 96 = 191

Topics: Number patterns, computer programs

WORKED EXAMPLE 59   The following computer program will generate a sequence of numbers

```
5 FOR X = 1 TO 10
10 PRINT X * 4 - 3
15 NEXT X
20 END
RUN
```

(i)   Write down the sequence of numbers printed out.
(ii)   How would you modify this program to get the sequence 5, 9, 13, . . . , 49

SOLUTION   (i)   Line 10 asks us to find $4x - 3$
Line 5 instructs you to use this formula for $x = 1, 2, 3, . . . , 10$

The first value $= 4 \times 1 - 3 = 1$
The second value $= 4 \times 2 - 3 = 5$
The last value $= 4 \times 10 - 3 = 37$
The sequence of numbers is 1, 5, 9, 13, . . . , 37

(ii)   You will notice that the values in the first sequence are all 3 less than the multiples of 4. In this part, they are all 1 more than the multiples of 4
Hence line 10 becomes:

```
10 PRINT X * 4 + 1
```

To get a last number of 49, you need $4 \times 12 + 1$
So line 5 becomes

```
5 FOR X = 1 TO 12
```

Topics: number patterns, re-arrangement of formulae

WORKED EXAMPLE 60   Four rods are used to make a square.

Rods are then added to make a row of 2 squares, then 3 squares and so on.

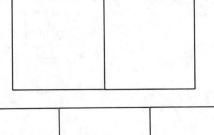

(a) How many rods are needed to make a row of,
   (i)   5 squares;
   (ii) 6 squares;
   (iii) 15 squares?
(b) Find the formula which gives the number of rods, r, needed to make a row of s squares in the form: $r = $.
(c) Use your formula to find how many squares could be made using 70 rods.
(d) Rearrange your formula in (b) into the form: $s = $.
(e) What is the greatest number of squares you can make in a row with 120 rods? How many rods will you have left over?   (WJEC)

SOLUTION   (a)   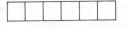   (i)   Counting gives 16 rods.

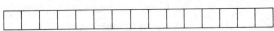   (ii)   Counting gives 19 rods.

(iii)   Counting gives 46 rods.

(b)

s	1	2	3	5	6	15
r	4	7	10	16	19	46

The r values are all 1 more than the multiples of 3.

If you multiply the number of squares by 3, and add 1 to the answer, it gives you the value of r. So $r = 3s + 1$.

(c) If $r = 70$,
$$70 = 3s + 1$$
$$69 = 3s$$
$$23 = s$$
Hence 23 squares can be made.

(d) $3s + 1 = r$

$3s = r - 1$

$s = \dfrac{r-1}{3}$ or $(r-1) \div 3$.

Using a flow chart method,

$s \longrightarrow \boxed{\times 3} \longrightarrow \boxed{+1} \longrightarrow r$

Reverse the flow chart:

$r \longrightarrow \boxed{-1} \longrightarrow \boxed{\div 3} \longrightarrow s$

Hence $s = (r - 1) \div 3$.

(e)   If $r = 120$

$s = (120 - 1) \div 3 = 119 \div 3$

$= 39$ remainder 2.

$$
\begin{array}{r}
39 \\
3\overline{)119} \\
9 \\
\overline{29} \\
27 \\
\overline{2} \quad \text{remainder}
\end{array}
$$

Hence 39 squares can be made with 2 rods left over.

Topics: number patterns, algebraic expressions

WORKED EXAMPLE 61   The diagram below shows a 'dot trapezium' with three rows.

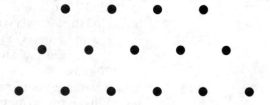

(a)   Draw a dot trapezium with three rows in which the number of dots in the top row is (i) 2; (ii) 5.

(b)   Copy and complete the following table for dot trapeziums with three rows.

Number of dots in top row	2	3	4	5	6
Total number of dots			15		

(c)   The number of dots in the top row of a dot trapezium is x. Write down the number of dots in:

(i)   the second row;
(ii)   the third row.

(d)   Use the results of part (c) to show that the total number of dots in a dot trapezium with three rows is a multiple of 3.

(e)   Show that the total number of dots in a dot trapezium with four rows is **not** a multiple of 4.

(f)   Investigate what can be said about the total number of dots in a dot trapezium with n rows,

(i)   when n is an odd number;
(i)   when n is an even number.

(MEG)

SOLUTION   (a)   (i)

(ii)

When drawing dot patterns that are triangular, some feint lines as in (ii) may help you not to miss any dots out.

(b)

Number of dots in top row	2	3	4	5	6
Total number of dots	9		15	18	

(12)   (21)

These totals are from the diagrams.
The missing values are multiples of 3, to form a pattern.

(c)   (i) $x + 1$ (one more dot than the first row).
        (ii) $x + 2$ (two more dots than the first row).

(d)   This part of the question is quite difficult.
        The total number of dots $= x + (x + 1) + (x + 2)$
$$= 3x + 3$$
$$= 3(x + 1) \text{ after putting into brackets.}$$
        It can be seen that this is a multiple of 3.

(e)   If we increase the number of rows to 4, the extra row has $x + 3$ dots.
        The total number of dots in the pattern
$$= x + (x + 1) + (x + 2) + (x + 3)$$
$$= 4x + 6 = 4x + 4 + 2$$
$$= 4(x + 1) + 2.$$
        The total is always 2 larger than a multiple of 4.

(f)   To investigate this last part, look at the total of dots in 1 row, 2 rows, 3 rows, etc.
        1 row total $= x$
        2 row total $= 2x + 1$ always odd
        3 row total $= 3x + 3 = 3(x + 1)$
        4 row total $= 4x + 6$ always even
        5 row total $= 5x + 10 = 5(x + 2)$
        6 row total $= 6x + 15$ always odd
        7 row total $= 7x + 21 = 7(x + 3)$.

        (i)   If n is an odd number, then the total is a multiple of n.
        (ii)   If n is even, the totals alternate odd and even.

Questions to try

116. (a) A sequence begins
$$1, 2, 4, 8, 16, \ldots$$
Write down a rule for continuing this sequence.

(b) A sequence of numbers begins as follows:
$$1, 3, 7, 15, \ldots$$
The rule for continuing the sequence is "every new number is obtained by doubling the last number and adding one". Write down the next number in the sequence.   (SEG)

117. (a) Here are the first four rows of a number pattern. Find the sum of the numbers in each row.

Row 1	1,
Row 2	3, 5,
Row 3	7, 9, 11,
Row 4	13, 15, 17, 19,

(b) The pattern continues in the same way. Write down the sum of the numbers in the 10th row.   (LEAG)

118. The first four terms of a sequence are:
$$6, 10, 8, 9$$
The 3rd term of the sequence is half way between the 1st and 2nd terms.
The 4th term is half way between the 2nd and 3rd terms.
The 5th term will be half way between the 3rd and 4th terms.

(a) Write down the 5th term of the sequence.
(b) Calculate the 6th term of the sequence.
(c) If the sequence had begun 10, 6 instead of 6, 10, would the further terms be the same as those in the sequence above? Give a reason for your answer.   (NEA)

119. (a) Look at this computer program

```
10 FOR NUMBER = 1 TO 6
20 PRINT NUMBER * 2 + 3
30 NEXT NUMBER
40 END
RUN
```

Write down the numbers the computer will print.

(b) Write down a similar program so that the computer will print the numbers
$$1, 4, 9, 16, 25$$ (MEG)

120. (a) Complete this table of powers of nine:
$$9^2 = \ldots\ldots\ldots\ldots\ldots\ldots$$
$$9^3 = 729$$
$$9^4 = \ldots\ldots\ldots\ldots\ldots\ldots$$
$$9^5 = \ldots\ldots\ldots\ldots\ldots\ldots$$

(b) Write down the last digit of 9^{101}.   (MEG)

121. (a) The table shows part of Pascal's Triangle and the sum of the numbers for each row. Each row starts and ends with 1 and all the remaining numbers are obtained by adding the two numbers on either side on the row above them. It follows that the middle number in row 6 is
$10 + 10 = 20$.

Row	Pascal's Triangle											Sum
0						1						1
1					1		1					2
2				1		2		1				4
3			1		3		3		1			8
4		1		4		6		4		1		16
5	1		5		10		10		5		1	32
6	1					20						

(i) Copy and complete row 6 of the Triangle.
(ii) Write down row 7.
(iii) What is the sum of the numbers in row 6?
(iv) What would be the sum of the numbers in row 10?

(b) The table below shows part of Pascal's Triangle in a rearranged form. The sum of the numbers in the diagonals is shown across the top.

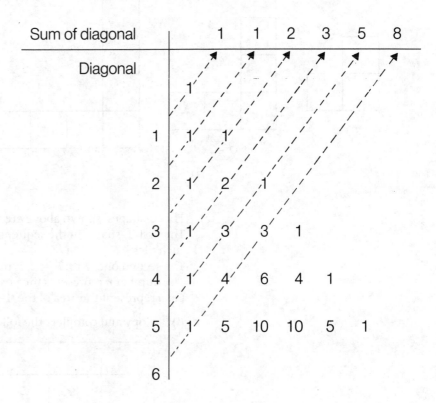

Sum of diagonal	1	1	2	3	5	8
Diagonal						
1	1					
2	1	1				
3	1	2	1			
4	1	3	3	1		
5	1	4	6	4	1	
6	1	5	10	10	5	1

(i) If the next row of the pattern were added, what would be the sum of the 7th diagonal?
(ii) Write down the sum of the 8th diagonal.
(iii) What would be the sum of the 11th diagonal? (MEG)

122. Carol and Javed did an investigation together, in which they had to count the number of intersections in a series of diagrams. They got these results:

3, 8, 15, 24.

Their teacher asked them, for homework, to see if they could find a pattern in their results. The next day the pupils returned with this:

Carol

diagram	number	pattern
1	3	1×3
2	8	2×4
3	15	3×5
4	24	4×6
5		

Javed

diagram	number	pattern
1	3	$1^2 + 2 \times 1$
2	8	$2^2 + 2 \times 2$
3	15	$3^2 + 2 \times 3$
4	24	$4^2 + 2 \times 4$
5		

(a) Their teacher asked each pupil to continue their pattern for diagram 5. Fill in what you would expect to write in the tables above.

(b) Their teacher then asked each pupil to write down a formula for the number of intersections in diagram n. Write down the two formulae that the pupils would have given.

(MEG)

123.

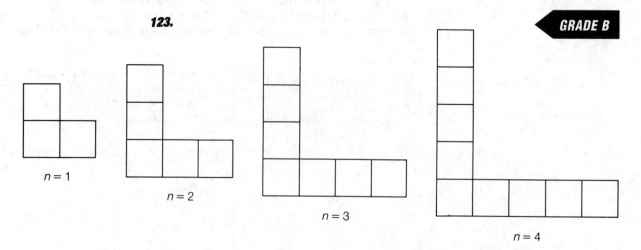

(a) The 'L-shapes' shown above are made from 1 cm square tiles.
The first 'L-shape' in the sequence, denoted by $n = 1$, is made up of 3 such tiles.
The second one, with $n = 2$, is made from 5 tiles, and so on.
The number n represents the position of the 'L-shape' in the sequence. Let a represent the area of the 'L-shape' in cm².

(i) Copy and complete the following table.

n	1	2	3	4	5	20
a	3	5				

(ii) Write down the formula connecting a and n in the form
$a =$ some expression in n.

(iii) Rearrange the formula in (ii) into the form
$n =$ some expression in a.

(b) Let the perimeter of the 'L-shapes' be denoted by p (centimetres). The perimeter of the first 'L-shape' is 8 cm and that of the second is 12 cm.

(i) Copy and complete the following table.

n	1	2	3	4	5	20
p	8	12				

(ii) Write down the formula connecting p and n in the form
p = some expression in n.

(iii) Rearrange the formula in (iii) into the form
n = some expression in p.

(iv) Use your formula in (iii) to write down the number of the
'L-shape' that has a perimeter of 80 cm. (WJEC)

124. A gardener wished to protect his seeds from the birds. He placed stakes in
the ground and joined each stake to each of the others using pieces of string.
He found that if he had 2 stakes there was 1 join, 3 stakes would need
3 joins and 4 stakes would need 6 joins.

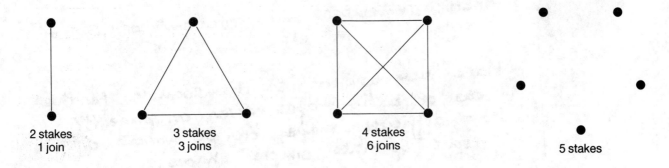

2 stakes
1 join

3 stakes
3 joins

4 stakes
6 joins

5 stakes

(a) Copy and complete the diagram for 5 stakes, showing the joins.
(b) Find how many joins there would be if he used 6 stakes.
(c) Find how many joins there would be if he used 7 stakes.
(d) Write down the first eight terms of the sequence which begins 1, 3,
6 . . ., and explain how the sequence is formed.
(e) Given that the number of stakes is n, find how many joins there will
be. (SEG)

MEASURE
ATTAINMENT TARGET 4

1 Perimeter, area, covering problems

PERIMETER: is the distance around the outside of a shape.

AREA: remember units are cm² or km² or m² etc.

Make sure you can use the formula for the areas of basic shapes, given on page 87. More difficult shapes can be worked out if split up into simple shapes.

If an area has irregular edges it can be covered with a grid of squares, and an approximate value can be found. See worked example 62

Problems about painting usually require you to find the area to be painted. If you know the area covered by 1 tin of paint, then dividing this into the area to be painted gives the number of tins required. Always round up to the nearest whole number.

To find the thickness of paint divide the volume applied by the area painted.

So thickness = volume applied (often in area painted litres)

Listed here are the areas and perimeters of basic shapes.

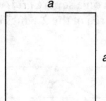

(i)   square

     area $= a^2$ perimeter $= 4a$

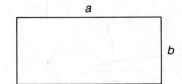

(ii)   rectangle

     area $= ab$ perimeter $= 2a + 2b$

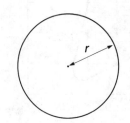

(iii)   circle

     area $= \pi r^2$ perimeter $= 2\pi r$
                        (or circumference)
                        OR $= \pi d$ (d is the diameter)

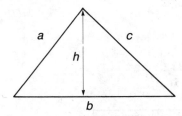

(iv)   triangle

     perimeter $= a + b + c$

     area $= \frac{1}{2}bh$

     OR $= \sqrt{s(s-a)(s-b)(s-c)}$

     where s is half the perimeter

     So s $= \frac{1}{2}(a + b + c)$

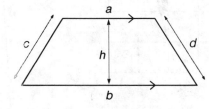

(v)   trapezium

     area $= \frac{1}{2}(a + b)h$

     perimeter $= a + b + c + d$ (remember that c and d might not be equal)

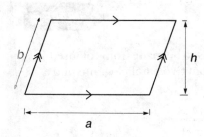

(vi)   parallelogram

     area $= ah$

     perimeter $= 2a + 2b$

Topic: area by counting squares ◀ GRADE G

WORKED EXAMPLE 62   The diagram shows a plan of a model aircraft drawn on a square grid, with each square measuring 5 cm by 5 cm. Estimate the area of the 2 wings of the model.

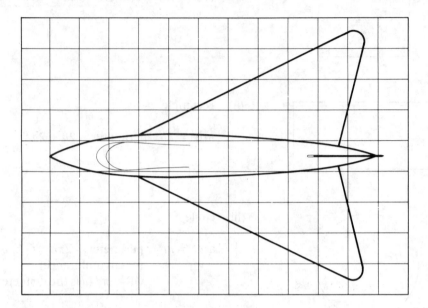

SOLUTION   The number of complete squares = 6 (shown unshaded).
There are 4 quarter squares = $4 \times \frac{1}{4} = 1$.
There are 6 three-quarter squares = $6 \times \frac{3}{4} = 4\frac{1}{2}$.
There are 2 half squares = $2 \times \frac{1}{2} = 1$.
The total number of squares = $6 + 1 + 4\frac{1}{2} + 1 = 12\frac{1}{2}$.
Now each square is 5 cm × 5 cm = 25 cm².
Hence 12 squares have an area = $12\frac{1}{2} \times 25 = 312.5$ cm².
The total area of the 2 wings is 2 × 312.5 = 625 cm².

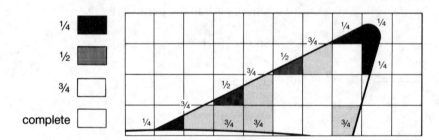

Topic: area of rectangle and parallelogram   ◀ GRADE E

WORKED EXAMPLE 63   The diagram shows a direction arrow which is to be made from coloured perspex. Assuming the shape can be made from two parallelograms and a rectangle, calculate the area of perspex used.

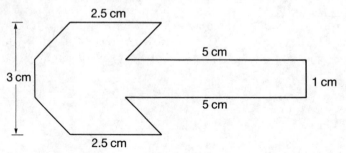

SOLUTION   The arrow is split up as shown.

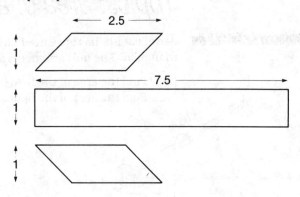

Each parallelogram has an area $= 1 \times 2.5 = 2.5 \, \text{cm}^2$.
The rectangle has an area $= 1 \times 7.5 = 7.5 \, \text{cm}^2$.
The total area $= (2 \times 2.5) + 7.5 = 12.5 \, \text{cm}^2$.

Topics: area, painting, volume

WORKED EXAMPLE 64   Mrs Davies is going to emulsion her dining room. The walls are rectangular, and the lengths of the walls are 4.2 m and 3.6 m. The height of each wall is 2.8 m. There is a door which measures 2.2 m by 0.8 m, and a window which measures 1.6 m by 1.2 m.

(a)   Calculate the total area of the walls to be painted.

A 1 litre tin of paint covers an area of 14 m².

(b)   How many tins of paint does Mrs Davies need to buy?

(c)   Assuming that the paint goes on in a uniformly thick layer, find the thickness of the paint in cm, giving your answer in standard form.

SOLUTION   (a)   There are 2 walls $4.2 \times 2.8 \;=\; 11.76 \, \text{m}^2$
$11.76 \, \text{m}^2$

There are 2 walls $3.6 \times 2.8 \;=\; 10.08 \, \text{m}^2$
$\underline{10.08 \, \text{m}^2}$
$\underline{43.68 \, \text{m}^2}$

Areas not painted are:
the door $2.2 \times 0.8 \;=\; 1.76 \, \text{m}^2$
the window $1.6 \times 1.2 \;=\; \underline{1.92 \, \text{m}^2}$
$\underline{3.68 \, \text{m}^2}$

The area to be painted $= 43.68 - 3.68 = 40 \, \text{m}^2$.

(b) $40 \div 14 = 2.86$.
She must buy 3 tins of paint.

(c)   The volume in 1 tin $= 1000 \, \text{cm}^3$.
Now $14 \, \text{m}^2 = 14 \times 100 \times 100 = 140\,000 \, \text{cm}^2$.
The thickness of paint $= 1000 \div 140\,000$
$= 0.007 \, \text{cm}$
$= 7 \times 10^{-3} \, \text{cm}$.

Topics: area of a triangle, units

WORKED EXAMPLE 65   Farmer Jones has measured one of his fields, which can be assumed to be triangular. The measurements are shown in the diagram.

(i)   Find the area of the field in m².
(ii)   Find the area of the field in hectares (assume 1 hectare = 10 000 m²).

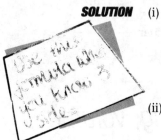

SOLUTION   (i)   The perimeter of the field = 65 + 85 + 120 = 270 m.
The semi-perimeter $s = \frac{1}{2} \times 270 = 135$ m.
Using the formula area $= \sqrt{s(s-a)(s-b)(s-c)}$
$$= \sqrt{135(135-120)(135-85)(135-65)}$$
$$= \sqrt{135 \times 15 \times 50 \times 70}$$
$$= 2662 \text{ m}^2.$$

(ii)   2662 ÷ 10 000 = 0.2662 hectares.
He would probably say the area of the field is about $\frac{1}{4}$ hectare.

Questions to try

GRADE F

125.   Stamp collectors use a unit called a 'perf' to describe the size of perforations around a stamp. A 'perf' is the number of perforations in 2 cm along one edge of a stamp. The answer is given to the nearest $\frac{1}{2}$.

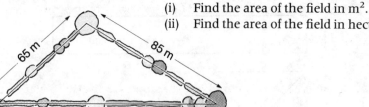

(i)   What is the 'perf' of a stamp 3.8 cm long with 28 perforations along that side?
(ii)   Estimate the 'perf' of the stamp shown in the picture.
(iii) A stamp has one side measuring 2.5 cm, and is described as perf 11. How many perforations does it have along that side?

126.   Mr Brown laid rectangular paving stones to form a patio. Each paving stone measured 90 cm by 60 cm. Three sides of the patio are to be edged by a lawn. The shaded part of the figure shows the paving stones Mr Brown laid on the first day.

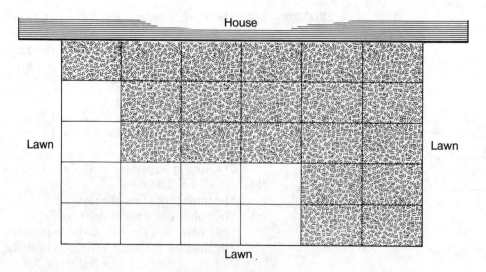

Find:

(a)   the perimeter of the part to be edged by lawn;
(b)   the number of paving stones still to be laid.

Mr Brown worked for 6 hours on the first day to lay the paving stones.

(c)   Estimate the time needed to complete the patio the next day assuming that Mr Brown worked at the same rate.

Each paving stone weighs 50 kg.

(d)   Calculate the total weight of the paving stones in the completed patio
    (i)   in kilograms,
    (ii)   in tonnes.

The paving stones cost £2.32 each.

(e)   Calculate the total cost of the paving stones in the completed patio.
(LEAG)

127.

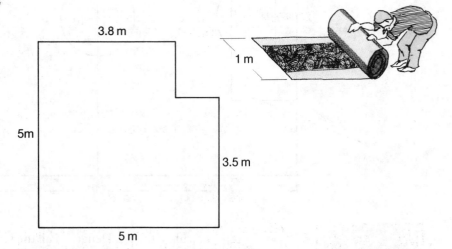

The figure represents the floor of the living room of a house and a roll of carpet.

(a)   Calculate the perimeter of the room in metres.
(b)   Calculate the area of the floor of the room in square metres.
(c)   The carpet is sold in strips, 1 m wide, to any required length.
    (i)   Draw lines on the figure to show how you would completely cover the floor of the room with carpet, using as few strips of carpet as possible.
    (ii)   Calculate the total length of carpet you would use. Any part width strips must be counted as full width.
(LEAG)

GRADE E

128.   A 5 litre can of emulsion paint can cover 85 m² on a non-porous surface, but only 60 m² on a porous surface.

    (i)   How many cans do you need to buy to cover an area of 350 m² of a porous surface?
    (ii)   If the walls are coated with a sealant, the surface becomes non-porous.
       How many tins would you then need to buy?

129.   The diagram (**which is not to scale**) shows the markings and dimensions of a soccer pitch. All lengths are in yards. All curves are circles or arcs of circles. The markings are usually done with white lines.

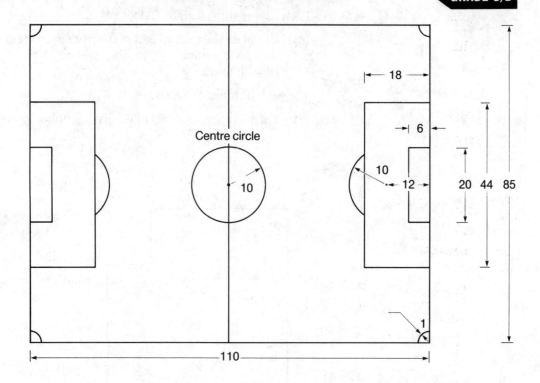

(a)   Calculate the total length of all the straight lines in the pitch.

(b)   Calculate the total length of the circumference of the centre circle and the four corner arcs.

(c)

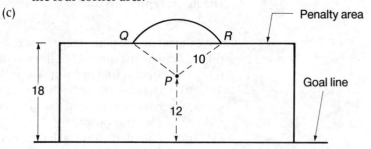

The diagram shows more detail of part of the penalty area markings. The penalty spot, *P*, is 12 yards from the goal line. The arc *QR* has centre *P* and radius 10 yards. Find the length of the arc *QR*.

(d)   Calculate the total length of all the markings (to the nearest yard).

(NEA)

2 Nets, surface area

NET : A net is a flat shape that will fold up into a 3-dimensional shape.

In mathematical problems, a net is usually drawn without tabs to glue the shape together.

The area of the surface of a solid (its surface area) can usually be found more easily from the net, which often consists of rectangles and triangles.

Problems about dice often require you to realise that the sum of the dots on opposite faces is always 7.

You can be asked which points on the net join up when the solid is formed. It is helpful to label the corners as in the diagrams on page 94

These questions often involve scale drawing

WORDS TO LEARN : vertex = a corner (or point)

: tetrahedron = a solid with 4 triangular faces.

: edge = straight line between two faces.

: face = flat surface on a solid.

USEFUL FACTS

Here are some nets which can be used to construct some well known solids. They are not unique. Look for others (flaps have been omitted).

(i)   Cube

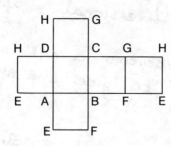   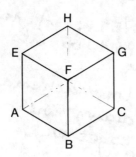

(ii)   Cuboid

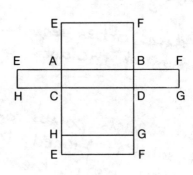   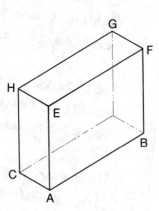

(iii)   Triangular prism

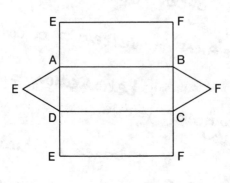   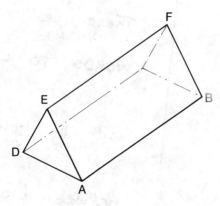

(iv)   Regular tetrahedron

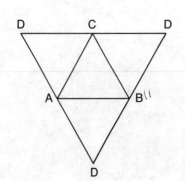   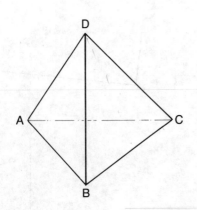

(v) Square based pyramid

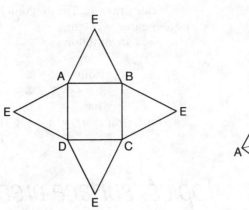

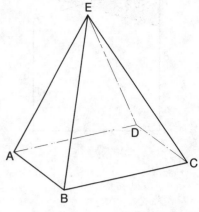

(vi) Cylinder

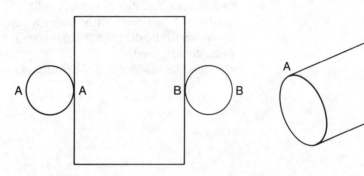

Topics: nets, surface area, scale drawing

GRADE E

WORKED EXAMPLE 66 The diagram shows a sketch of a gift box that Joe is making in a CDT project. All measurements are in cm.

(i)   Which measurement has he got wrong?
(ii) What is x?
(iii) Draw a sketch to show what the box looks like.
(iv) What is the surface area of the box?

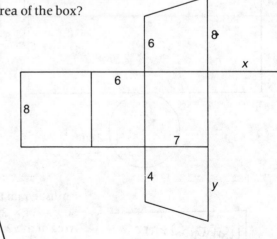

SOLUTION

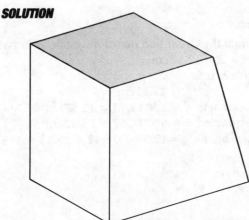

(i)   The 2 trapeziums must be identical, so the 4 is incorrect, it should be 6.
(ii) $x = 8$.
(iii) The finished box looks like this.

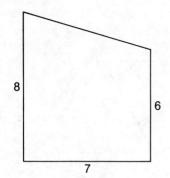

(iv) To find the surface area, it is necessary to find the length of the sloping side. This could be done using trigonometry, but it is just as easy to do it by scale drawing. The diagram has been drawn half size. The sloping edge measures 7.3 cm.

The areas are as follows:

$$
\begin{aligned}
\text{top} &= 8 \times 7.3 & &= 58.4\,\text{cm}^2 \\
\text{front} &= 6 \times 8 & &= 48\,\text{cm}^2 \\
\text{back} &= 8 \times 8 & &= 64\,\text{cm}^2 \\
\text{base} &= 7 \times 8 & &= 56\,\text{cm}^2 \\
\text{Two ends (trapezia)} &= 2 \times \tfrac{1}{2} \times 7(6 + 8) & &= 98\,\text{cm}^2 \\
& & \text{Total} &= 324.4\,\text{cm}^2
\end{aligned}
$$

GRADE C/D

Topics: surface area, nets of solids

WORKED EXAMPLE 67   A perfume container is made from strong cardboard in the shape of a cylinder of radius 2 cm, and height 6 cm. A tight-fitting lid 1 cm deep is fitted over the top, as shown in the diagram. Find the area of cardboard used.
(Neglect the thickness of the cardboard.)

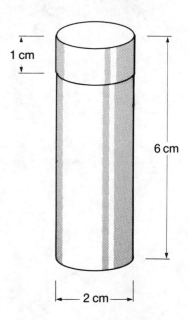

SOLUTION   This question is much easier to visualise if you draw the nets involved.

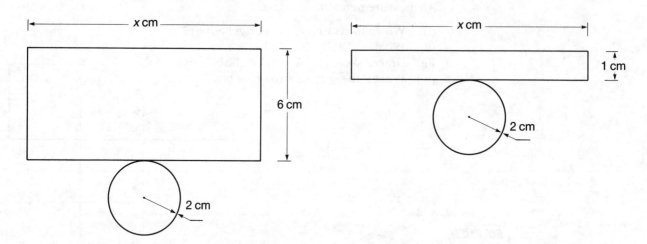

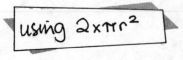

x must equal the circumference of the circle, otherwise it will not fit.
So $x = 2\pi \times 2 = 12.57$ cm.
Area of the 2 circles $= 2 \times \pi \times 2^2$
$\qquad\qquad\qquad\quad = 25.13\,\text{cm}^2.$
Smaller rectangle $\quad = 1 \times 12.57 = 12.57\,\text{cm}^2.$
Larger rectangle $\quad\;\; = 6 \times 12.57 = 75.42\,\text{cm}^2.$
The surface area $\quad\;\; = 12.57 + 75.42 + 25.13 = 113.12\,\text{cm}^2.$

Topic: nets

WORKED EXAMPLE 68 A fly is at one corner X of a wooden cube of side 8 cm. If it walks along the surface of the cube to the corner Y that is furthest from X, what is the shortest distance it would have to walk?

SOLUTION The net has been drawn to scale alongside. You may have been tempted to say on the real cube that the shortest distance is XDY, which is 19.3 cm. However, if you look at the net, the path $XNY = 17.9$ cm is the shortest. The diagram below shows the point N that the fly has to aim at.

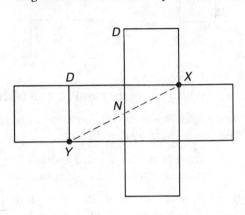

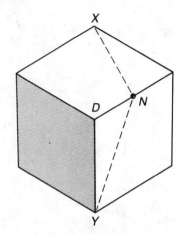

Questions to try

GRADE G

130. (a) Diagram (i) represents a view of a cubical die. The number of dots on opposite faces add up to seven. Write down the number of dots on the back face and the bottom face, as indicated in the diagram.

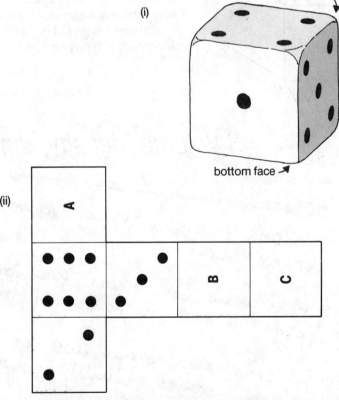

(b) Diagram (ii) represents the net of another die. As before, the number of dots on opposite faces add up to seven. Write down the number of dots that would appear on each of the faces marked as A, B and C, respectively.

(MEG)

131.

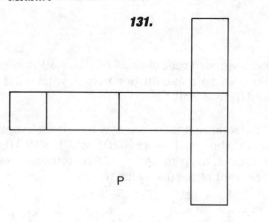
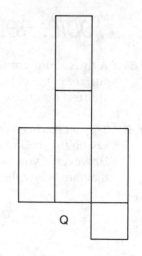
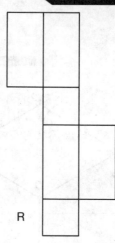

P   Q   R

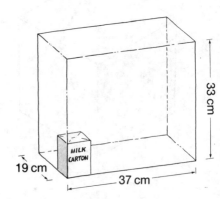

33 cm

19 cm

37 cm

(a)   Which one of the nets P, Q or R is *not* the net of a cuboid?

Longlife milk is packed in cuboid cardboard cartons. Each milk carton measures 16 cm by 6 cm by 9 cm.

(b)   What area of cardboard is needed to make one milk carton (ignore any extra cardboard needed for overlap)?

Longlife milk cartons are delivered to shops in containers which are cuboids measuring 19 cm by 33 cm by 37 cm.

(c)   Cartons are packed in containers as shown in the diagram. What is the maximum number of cartons each container can hold?

132.

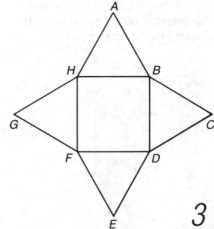

(a)   Which points will coincide with A when the net is folded up to make the solid?

(b)   Describe the symmetry of:
    (i)   the net;
    (ii)   the solid.

(c)   How many faces, edges and vertices has the solid?

(d)   A new solid is to be formed from a modification of this net. *HGF*, *BCD* and *HBDF* are unaltered but *ABH* is replaced by a square. Describe the shape which must replace *FED*.

3 Volume, density, dimensions

VOLUME : the units of volume are cm³, m³ or km³ etc.

Make sure you know the formulae given on page 100 and the names of the shapes.

A complicated shape must be split up into simple shapes, usually cuboids.

Packaging problems usually involve dividing a shape into layers, and finding how many items fit into each layer. See worked example 69!

Make sure units are consistent; many mistakes occur with circular wires, where the lengths are very long and the widths very small! Choose a sensible common unit.

Density: Density $D = \dfrac{Mass (M)}{Volume (V)}$;

$$D \times V = M \quad or \quad V = \frac{M}{D}$$

Units :   gm per cm^3 or   kg per m^3 etc.

WORDS TO LEARN : prism = any solid which has the <u>same</u> cross section throughout.
: rate in filling problems is usually litres/sec or similar!

Dimensions: A formula can be checked for mistakes by looking at its dimensions:
Area must contain <u>two</u> lengths multiplied (ignoring multiples) e.g. πr^2, $2\pi rh$, $6ab$, $bc + 4\pi r^2$.

Volume must contain three lengths multiplied together.

e.g. $\dfrac{4\pi r^3}{3}$, $\pi r^2 h$, $6abc$, $ab^2 + 4\pi r^2 h$.

See worked example 72

USEFUL FACTS

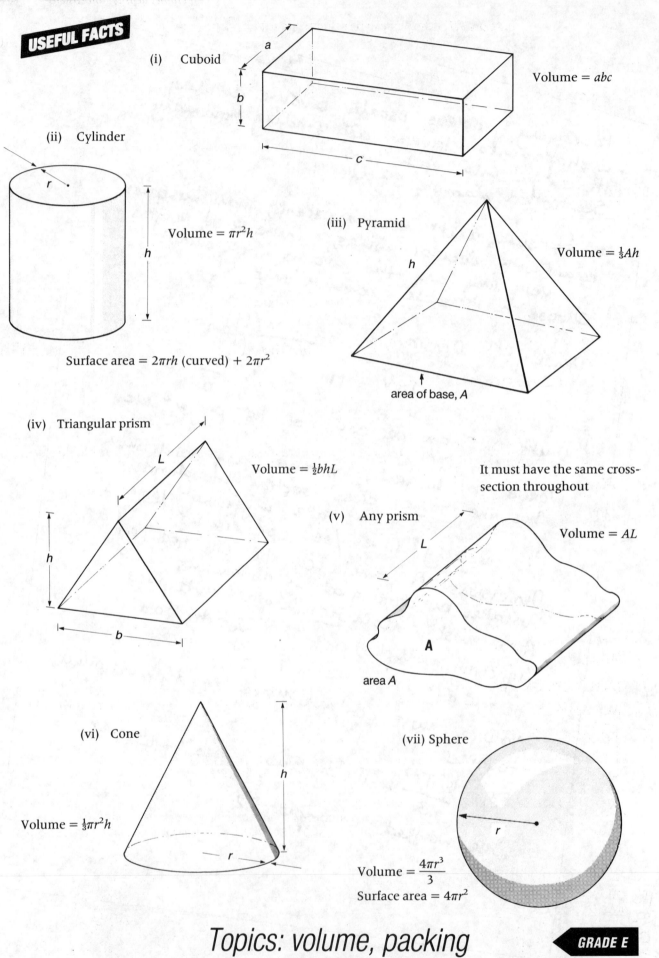

(i)   Cuboid

Volume $= abc$

(ii) Cylinder

Volume $= \pi r^2 h$

Surface area $= 2\pi rh$ (curved) $+ 2\pi r^2$

(iii) Pyramid

Volume $= \frac{1}{3}Ah$

area of base, A

(iv) Triangular prism

Volume $= \frac{1}{2}bhL$

It must have the same cross-section throughout

(v)   Any prism

Volume $= AL$

area A

(vi) Cone

Volume $= \frac{1}{3}\pi r^2 h$

(vii) Sphere

Volume $= \dfrac{4\pi r^3}{3}$

Surface area $= 4\pi r^2$

Topics: volume, packing

GRADE E

WORKED EXAMPLE 69   A cardboard box with internal dimensions of 80 cm by 54 cm by 45 cm, is filled with packets of margarine that measure 10 cm by 6 cm by 9 cm. How many packets of margarine can be put into the box?

SOLUTION   The box can be split up into a grid.
$80 \div 10 = 8$
$54 \div 6 = 9$
$45 \div 9 = 5$
The number of packets = $8 \times 9 \times 5 = 360$.

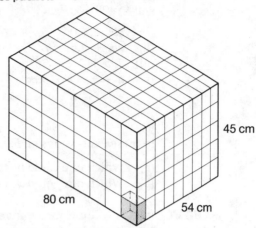

45 cm

80 cm

54 cm

Topics: volume, rate

GRADE C/D

WORKED EXAMPLE 70   A water trough has a rectangular cross-section measuring 62 cm by 46 cm, and is $2\frac{1}{2}$ m long.

(i)   Find the volume of water the tank holds when full in cm^3.
(ii)   What is this volume in litres?
(iii)   If water empties into the tank from a tap at a rate of $1\frac{3}{4}$ litres per minute, how long does it take to half fill the tank?

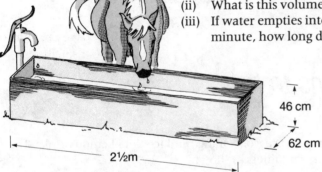

46 cm

62 cm

2½m

SOLUTION   (i)   The tank measures $62\,cm \times 46\,cm \times 250\,cm = 713\,000\,cm^3$.
(ii)   Since 1 litre = $1000\,cm^3$, volume = 713 litres.
(iii)   Half full = $713 \div 2$
            = 356.5 litres.
Time taken = $356.5 \div 1\frac{3}{4}$
            = $356.5 \div 1.75 = 204$ minutes (to the nearest minute).
This is better written as 3 hours 24 minutes.

Change all the measurements to the same units....

divide the volume by the rate.

Topics: volume, density

WORKED EXAMPLE 71   A roll of copper wire is made of wire 200 m long with a circular cross-section of diameter 1.2 mm. Calculate the volume of the coil in cm^3.
If the density of copper is 8.8 g/cm^3, calculate the mass of the copper wire in kilograms.

The piece of wire is a very long cylinder

watch out for units...

200 m = 20000 cm.

radius = 0.6 mm = 0.06 cm

1 kg = 1000 g

SOLUTION   Volume = $\pi r^2 h$
            = $\pi \times 0.06^2 \times 20000$
            = $226\,cm^3$.
Using $M = D \times V$
   Mass = $8.8 \times 226 = 1989\,g$
   $\div 1000$ to give 1.989 kg.

Topic: dimensions in formulae

GRADE B

WORKED EXAMPLE 72   The diagram shows a sketch design for a torch. Look at the following expressions:

(i) $abc + 6\pi r^2$
(ii) $abc + 9.5\pi r^2 h$
(iii) $2ab + 2bc + 7\pi r^2$
(iv) $a + b + c + 5\pi r^2$

In these expressions, a, b, c, r and h are various measurements on the shape.

(a)   Which one could be the volume of the shape?
(b)   Which one could be the surface area of the shape?

SOLUTION

(a)   A volume always involves three lengths (dimensions) multiplied together. Only in part (ii) does each part involve three lengths i.e. $a \times b \times c$ and $r \times r \times h$

(b)   Area always involves two lengths (dimensions) multiplied together. This only occurs in (iii) i.e. $a \times b$ and $b \times c$ and $r \times r$

Note: You will notice that you do not need to know what the letters a, b, r etc. stand for, only that they represent lengths.

Questions to try

GRADE F

133.   Birtles Snack Bar sells Ice Cold Orange and Ice Cold Lemon drinks. The drinks are kept in containers as shown.

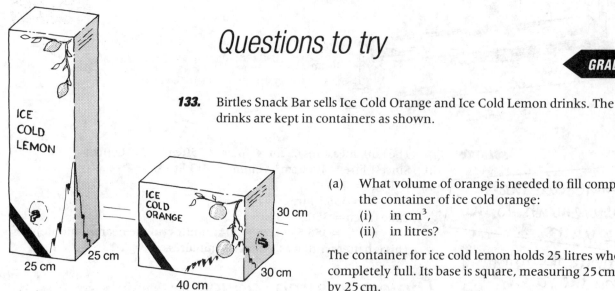

(a)   What volume of orange is needed to fill completely the container of ice cold orange:
  (i)   in cm³,
  (ii)   in litres?

The container for ice cold lemon holds 25 litres when completely full. Its base is square, measuring 25 cm by 25 cm.

(b)   (i)   Work out the height of the lemon container.
      (ii) Work out the number of 20 cl glasses that can be filled from the full container of lemon.

134. The diagram shows a ridge tent of length 3 m. Each end is an isosceles triangle with base 2.4 m, and height 1.6 m.
Calculate:

(a) in m² the area of the end *ABC* of the tent;
(b) the length of *AC*;
(c) the area of the sloping side *ADEC* in m²;
(d) the volume of the tent, in m³.

3 m

1.6 m

B

2.4 m

135. The drawing to the left shows a ridge tent of length 2.5 m. Each end is an isosceles triangle with base 1.5 m and height 1.6 m.

(a) Calculate, in m², the area of the end, *ABC*, of the tent.
(b) Calculate, in m³, the volume of the tent.

1.6 m

2.5 m

B — 1.5 m — *C*

3.6 cm

P   *A*

1.6 m

Two wooden poles support the tent. Each pole is a cylinder with diameter 3.6 cm and height 1.6 m.

(c) Taking π to be 3.142, calculate, in cm³, the volume of a tent pole. Give your answer correct to three significant figures.
(d) A groundsheet, which covers the base of the tent exactly, is made of material weighing 0.7 kg/m². Calculate, in kg, the weight of the groundsheet.
(e) The tent canvas weighs 5.75 kg and each tent pole weighs 850 g. Calculate, in kg, the total weight of the tent and groundsheet.

(MEG)

136. The diameter of a table tennis ball is 4 cm and its volume is 33.5 cm³. The balls are sold in cylindrical plastic tubes, each containing six balls tightly packed together.

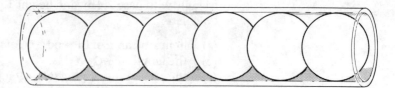

Calculate:

(a)   the radius of the tube;
(b)   the length of the tube;
(c)   the total volume inside the tube which is not occupied by the balls (to the nearest cm³).
(d)   Sketch the net of the cylinder showing all measurements.
(e)   Calculate the total area of plastic used to make one tube (including both ends).

The distribution company considers packing the balls in cardboard cartons in the shape of a cuboid with a square end:

(f)   If the balls are again tightly packed, calculate the total area of cardboard needed to make one container.
(g)   The company decides to double the dimensions of its tubes and cartons to increase the number of balls contained in each. By considering drawings of cross-section, or otherwise, estimate the number of balls that could be packed:
(i)   in a tube with dimensions doubled;
(ii)   in a carton with dimensions doubled.   (SEG)

137. The diagram shows a glue stick in the shape of a cylinder. If 90% of the volume is actually the glue, find the volume of glue in the stick.

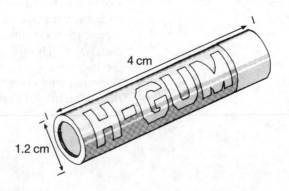

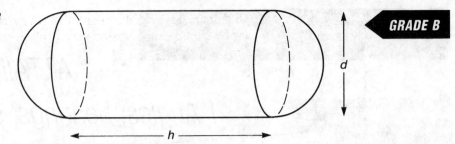

138

An expression for the volume and an expression for the surface area of the capsule shown in the diagram are contained in the following list.

$$\pi d \quad + 2h$$
$$\pi d^2 + \tfrac{1}{4}\pi d^2 h$$
$$\pi d^2 + \pi dh$$
$$\tfrac{1}{6}\pi d^3 + \tfrac{1}{4}\pi d^2 h$$
$$\tfrac{1}{6}\pi d^3 + \pi dh$$

(a)   (i)   Write down the expression for the volume.
      (ii)   Give a reason for your choice.
(b)   Write down the expression for the surface area.   (MEG)

139.   (i)   A lead fishing weight has a volume of $41\,\text{cm}^3$. If the density of lead is $2.7\,\text{g/cm}^3$, how much does it weigh? If its weight is to be increased to $120\,\text{g}$, what volume of lead must be added to the weight?

     (ii)   A cannister of hydrogen holds 1000 litres of the gas. The gas weighs $90\,\text{g}$. Find the density of hydrogen in g/cm^3. Give your answer in standard form.

Make sure you can recognise the simple relationships that exist between angles that occur in parallel lines and triangles.

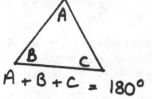

$A + B + C = 180°$

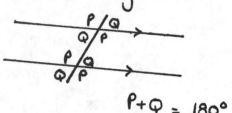

$P + Q = 180°$

In any quadrilateral
$A + B + C + D = 360°$

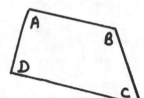

Watch out for isosceles triangles, and regular polygons (all sides equal).
It is always easier to work with external angles of shapes.

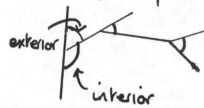

The external angles always add up to 360°

exterior angle + interior angle = 180°
A bearing is always measured from the North in a clockwise direction.
SCALE DRAWING: Always state clearly the scale you use. Check that the question allows you to use scale drawing!
If it says calculate you cannot draw it.
Map scales such as 1:50000 means 1cm is 50 000 cm.
But since 100 000 cm = 1km, then 1cm is really ½ km.
* IMPORTANT : $1cm^2 = \frac{1}{2}km \times \frac{1}{2}km = \frac{1}{4}km^2$.

Topics: angles, parallel lines

GRADE F

WORKED EXAMPLE 73   In the diagram find angles *a* and *b*.

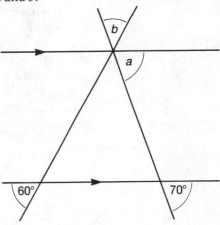

SOLUTION $a = 70°$. (They are called *corresponding* angles, because they are in the same position.) It can be seen that $60 + b + 70 = 180$.
Hence $b = 50°$.

Put in the 60° angle, and also b opposite b

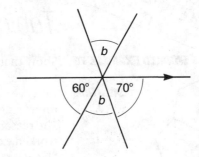

GRADE E

Topics: polygons, interior angles

WORKED EXAMPLE 74   *ABCDE* is a regular pentagon.
Find the interior angles of the pentagon.

SOLUTION   Let each *exterior* angle = *x*.
The exterior angles add up to 360°.
So $5x = 360°$.
Hence $x = 72°$.
The interior angle
$= 180° - 72°$
$= 108°$.

It is always easier to work with the exterior angles

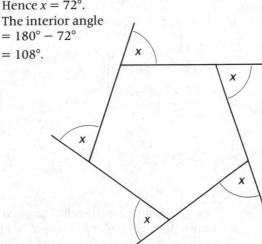

Topics: angles, polygons

WORKED EXAMPLE 75   *ABCDEF* is a hexagon which has only two lines of symmetry. These lines are shown on the diagram as *XX'* and *YY'*. Angle $q = 115°$. Find the size of angle p.

(MEG)

SOLUTION   Angle B is the same as angle q,
     so $B = 115°$.
CF is parallel to *BA*
     so angle $B + p = 180°$
     $115° + p = 180°$
Hence $p = 65°$.

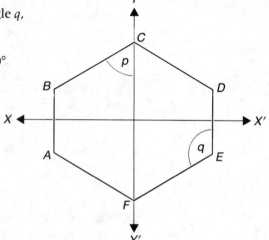

A very dangerous approach is a rough diagram, shown alongside, which suggests it is possible —

Topics: polygons, tessellations

WORKED EXAMPLE 76   Show that it is not possible to tessellate the plane with a regular pentagon.

SOLUTION   However, look at the accurate diagram shown below, and it can be seen that there is a gap.
The reason for this is that the interior angle of a pentagon is 108°, see worked example 74.
So at O, $3 × 108° = 324°$. This must leave $360° - 324° = 36°$ as a gap.
Clearly this is not enough to insert another pentagon.

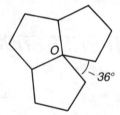

Topics: angles, bearings

WORKED EXAMPLE 77   The bearing of a boat X from a lighthouse Y is 068°. Find the bearing of the lighthouse from the boat.

SOLUTION

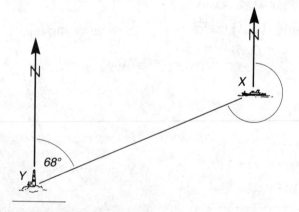

The angle required is the reflex angle at X.
The obtuse angle at X is $180° - 68° = 112°$.
Hence the bearing $= 360° - 112° = 248°$.

Topics: scale drawing, bearings, area of a triangle

WORKED EXAMPLE 78   In the diagram, P, Q and R represent the positions of three towns. R is 18 km due south of P, and Q is 13 km from R on a bearing of 040°.

Using a scale of 1 cm to 2 km, make an accurate scale drawing of the triangle PQR.

From the diagram, find:

(i)   the distance between P and Q;
(ii)   the angle RPQ;
(iii)   the bearing of Q from P;
(iv)   the area of the triangle PQR.

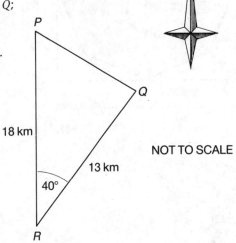

18 km   13 km

40°

NOT TO SCALE

SOLUTION   Since 1 cm = 2 km, scale lengths of PR and RQ must be 9 cm and 6.5 cm.

(i) PQ = 5.9 cm on the drawing.
     The distance PQ = 5.9 × 2 = 11.8 km.
(ii) $\angle RPQ$ = 45°.
(iii)   The bearing of Q from P = 180° − 45° = 135°.
(iv)   Draw NQ perpendicular to PR; this will be the height of the triangle PQR, and PR is the base.
     NQ = 4.2 cm on the drawing.
     The distance NQ = 4.2 × 2 = 8.4 km.
     The area of the triangle = $\frac{1}{2}$ × 18 × 8.4 = 75.6 km².

Scale 1 cm to 2 km

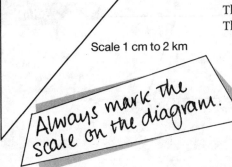

Always mark the scale on the diagram.

Topics: scale drawing, maps

GRADE B

WORKED EXAMPLE 79   A map is drawn to a scale of 1:20 000. Find:

(i)   the distance representing 8 km on the map;
(ii)   the area of a lake which has an area of 4 cm² on the map.

Always interpret what 1:n means

SOLUTION   1:20 000 means 1 cm represents 20 000 cm
       20 000 ÷ 100 000 = 0.2 km
So 1 cm represents 0.2 km.

(i)   8 ÷ 0.2 = 40
     So the distance is 40 cm.
(ii)   1 cm represents 0.2 km
     So 1 cm² represents 0.2 × 0.2 = 0.04 km².
     So 4 cm² represents 4 × 0.04 = 0.16 km².

Questions to try

GRADE F

140. Part of a shop display is being made in the shape of an octagonal design from 8 identical isosceles triangles. These are joined together as shown in the diagram.

(i)   Make an accurate scale drawing of the shape, using a scale of 1 cm to 10 cm.

(ii) By making suitable measurements, find the area of one of the triangles.

(iii) What is the perimeter of the octagon?

|← ——— 160 cm ——— →|

141. The diagrams have not been drawn to scale.

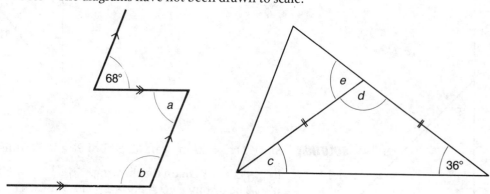

(i)   Calculate the size of the angles *a* and *b*.
      There are two pairs of parallel lines.

(ii) Calculate the size of the angles *c*, *d* and *e*.
      There are two sides marked equal.

142.

GRADE E

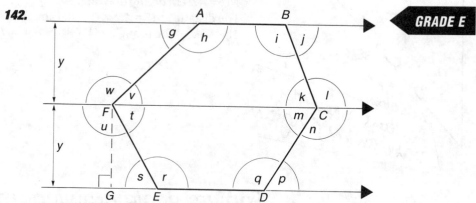

ABCDEF is an irregular hexagon. *AB, FC* and *ED* are parallel.

(a) Give one angle that is equal to,
    (i)   angle *g*;
    (ii) angle *n*.

(b) How many degrees is:
    (i)   *g* + *h*;
    (ii) *h* + *i* + *k* + *v*;
    (iii) *h* + *i* + *k* + *m* + *q* + *r* + *t* + *v*?

Given that angle *s* = 70° and angle *m* = 60°, the length of *FE* = 5 cm and the length of *ED* = 6 cm, calculate:

(c) the height *y* of the trapezium *FCDE*;
(d) the length of *GE*;
(e) the length of *FC*.

(SEG)

143. This sketch shows three posts *A*, *B* and *C* on a building site. It also shows some lengths and some bearings.

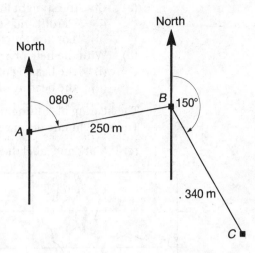

(a) Using the distances and bearings shown on the diagram make a scale drawing to show the positions of *A*, *B* and *C*. Use a scale of 1 cm to represent 50 m.

(b) (i) Join *AC* and measure its length to the nearest millimetre.
 (ii) What is the distance, on the building site, between the two posts *A* and *C*?

(c) (i) Measure and write down the size of angle *BAC*.
 (ii) What is the bearing of *C* from *A*?
 (iii) What is the bearing of *A* from *C*?

(d) By drawing further lines on your scale drawing, find how far the post *C* is east of the post *A*.

144. The diagram represents a strip of sticky tape of uniform width laid across a sheet of card near to one corner of the sheet which is right-angled. The strip is then neatly folded under the sheet and pressed to the sheet, such that angle *PAQ* = angle *BAC*, as shown in (b). Similarly, the tape is folded at *B* so that equal angles are formed with the edge of the card.

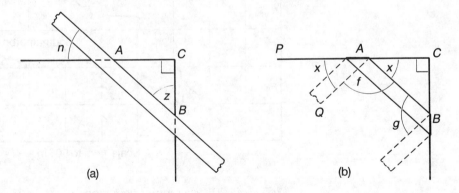

(a) (i)

(a) If *x* = 37°, calculate the sizes of the angles:
 (i) *n*; (ii) *z*; (iii) *f*; (iv) *g*.

(b) (i) Find a formula for *f* in terms of *x*;
 (ii) Find a formula for *g* in terms of *x*;
 (iii) For what values of *x* are the folded parts of the tape parallel?

145.   The diagram shows part of a map of the British Isles, drawn to a scale of 1 cm to 50 km.

(a)   Give the straight line distance, in km, between,
    (i)   Cardiff and Southampton;
    (ii)   London and Birmingham.

(b)   With the help of a protractor, find:
    (i)   the bearing of Newcastle from Dublin;
    (ii)   the bearing of Liverpool from Birmingham.

The bearing of Nottingham from Cardiff is 040°.
The straight line distance of Nottingham from Cardiff is 225 km.

(c)   Mark and label the position of Nottingham on the map.   (LEAG)

Scale 1 cm to 50 km

146.   *ABCDE* is a regular pentagon.
    (i)   Write down the values of *x*, *y* and *z*.
    (ii)   Show, giving reasons, that *ED*
        is parallel to *AC*.

GRADE C/D

147. The diagram for a job on a lathe is shown below.

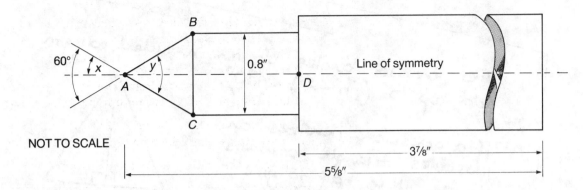

NOT TO SCALE

The dotted line is the line of symmetry of the diagram.

(a) (i) Find the sizes of the angles x and y.
(ii) What type of triangle is triangle ABC?
(b) What is the distance between points A and D?
(c) The rotation speed (revolutions per minute) at which the lathe is to be set is given by the formula:

$$\text{rotation speed} = \frac{12 \times \text{cutting speed}}{3.14 \times \text{diameter}},$$ where the cutting speed is

measured in ft/min, and the diameter in inches.
Calculate the rotation speed for the above job when the cutting speed is 170 ft/min and the diameter is 0.8 inches.

(NEA)

148. A map is drawn to a scale of 1:20 000. Find: **GRADE B**

(i) the distance represented by 6 cm on the map;
(ii) the distance on the map which represents 8 km;
(iii) the area on the map of a lake which has an area of 5 km².

2 Shapes, polygons, tessellations

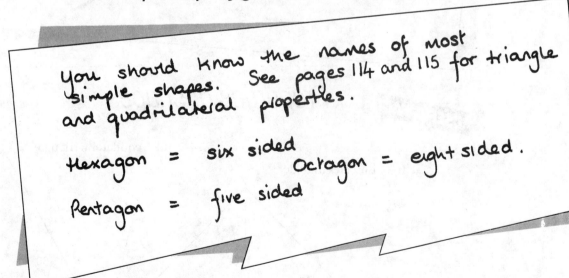

You should know the names of most simple shapes. See pages 114 and 115 for triangle and quadrilateral properties.

Hexagon = six sided   Octagon = eight sided.

Pentagon = five sided

The interior angles of an n-sided polygon add up to $(n-2) \times 180°$.

If a question involves an isosceles triangle, always divide it in half to give 2 right angled triangles.

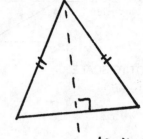

Tessellations: A shape tessellates if it can be fitted together to cover an area without leaving any gaps.

WORDS TO LEARN
acute : less than 90°,

obtuse: more than 90°, but less than 180°.

Reflex : more than 180°.

Regular: all sides the same length and all angles equal.

Convex : all interior angles less than 180°.

Concave: one interior angle more than 180°.

still a hexagon. →

USEFUL FACTS   *Properties of shapes*

(i)   isosceles triangle

Base angles equal
Two sides equal
One axis of symmetry
— Base angles —

(ii)   equilateral triangle

60°
60°   60°

All sides equal
Three lines of symmetry
rotational symmetry of order 3

(iii) square

4 lines of
symmetry

rotational symmetry
of order 4

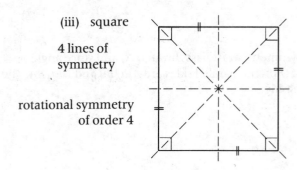

(iv) rectangle

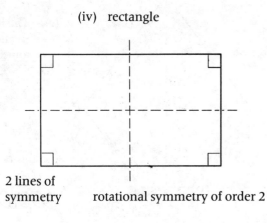

2 lines of
symmetry   rotational symmetry of order 2

(v) parallelogram

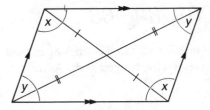

Opposite sides parallel
Diagonals cross in the middle

rotational symmetry of order 2

(vi) rhombus

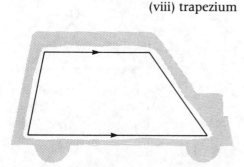

Diagonals cross in the middle at right angles

rotational symmetry of order 2

(vii) kite

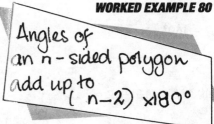

Diagonals perpendicular
One axis of symmetry
Two pairs of adjacent sides equal

(viii) trapezium

Two opposite sides parallel
No symmetry in general

Topics: polygons, symmetry   ◄ GRADE E

WORKED EXAMPLE 80

In the pentagon *ABCDE*, angle *B* = angle *E* = 144° and angle *C* = angle *D* = 108°.

(a) Calculate the size of angle *A*.
(b) Prove that *AB* is parallel to *ED*.
(c) Sketch the pentagon *ABCDE* given that it has one line of symmetry. Indicate clearly the pairs of sides of the pentagon which are parallel.

(MEG)

Angles of an n – sided polygon add up to
$(n-2) \times 180°$

SOLUTION

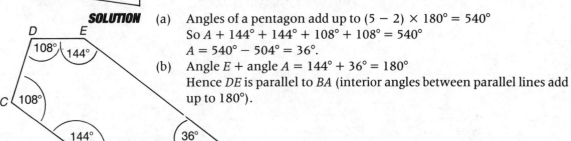

(a) Angles of a pentagon add up to $(5 - 2) \times 180° = 540°$
So $A + 144° + 144° + 108° + 108° = 540°$
$A = 540° - 504° = 36°$.

(b) Angle *E* + angle *A* = 144° + 36° = 180°
Hence *DE* is parallel to *BA* (interior angles between parallel lines add up to 180°).

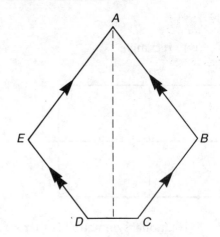

(c)   The line of symmetry must pass through A, and since angle *A* + angle *B* = 180°, the parallel sides are *AE*//*BC* and *DE*//*BA*. The sketch appears alongside.

Topics: polygons, angles

WORKED EXAMPLE 81   The diagram shows the side view of a folding clothes airer made out of several straight pieces of covered wire, hinged at the joints.

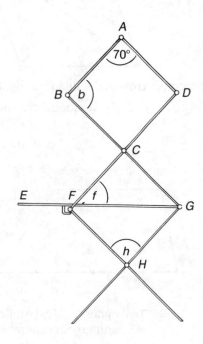

(a)   What type of quadrilateral is *ABCD*?
(b)   State the size of angles *b*, *h* and *f*.
(c)   The length *EG* is exactly the same as the length *BG*. Given that *AD* = 26 cm, find the length of *EG*.

(NEA)

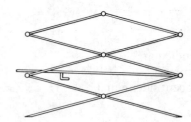

SOLUTION   You would assume that all the pieces of wire are the same length.

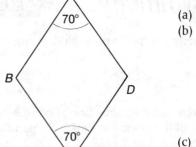

(a)   So the quadrilateral *ABCD* has four equal sides. It is a *rhombus*.
(b)   angle *C* = 70°
      angle *B* = angle *D*
      angle *A* + angle *B* + angle *C* + angle *D* = 360°
      Hence *b* = (360° − 140°) ÷ 2
            = 110°.
      h = angle *C* = 70°.
      The sliding piece *EG* cuts angle *F* in half, so *f* = 110° ÷ 2 = 55°.
(c)   Since *AD* = 26 cm, *BC* = 26 cm,
      so *EG* = 2 × 26 cm = 52 cm.

Properties of tessellations

A shape tessellates if it covers a surface without leaving any gaps.

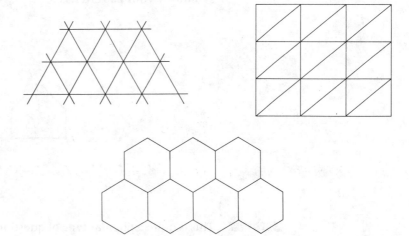

COMBINED OR MODIFIED POLYGONS

(a)   Combines together 5 squares.

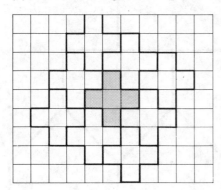

(b)   Modifies the equilateral triangle.

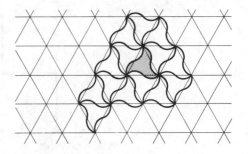

(c)   Combines together 2 hexagons.

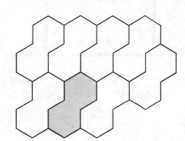

SEMI-REGULAR TESSELLATIONS   These are based on two or more different regular polygons.

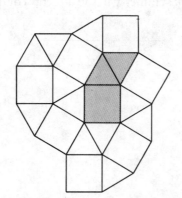

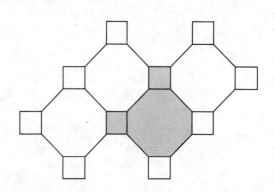

Topic: tessellations

WORKED EXAMPLE 82   On the grid provided, show how the shape shown alongside can be used to tessellate the plane. At least eight shapes should be drawn. Describe any symmetry your pattern has.

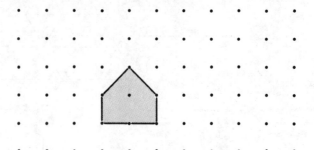

SOLUTION   This is quite a popular type of question, and often there is more than one solution. A possible arrangement is shown below.

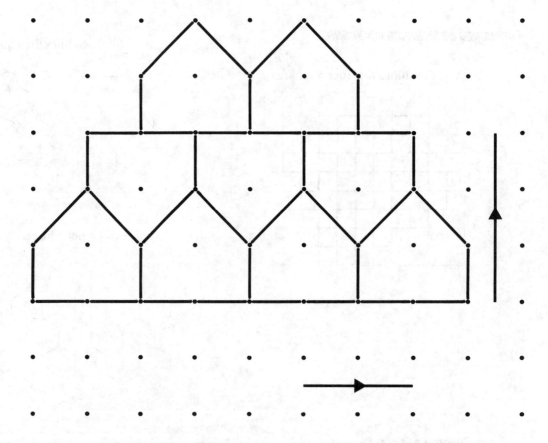

The pattern has *line* symmetry about any vertical line through a column of dots, and *translation* symmetry in the direction of the arrows.

Questions to try

149. On the grid below are 4 quadrilaterals. One diagonal has been drawn in each shape.

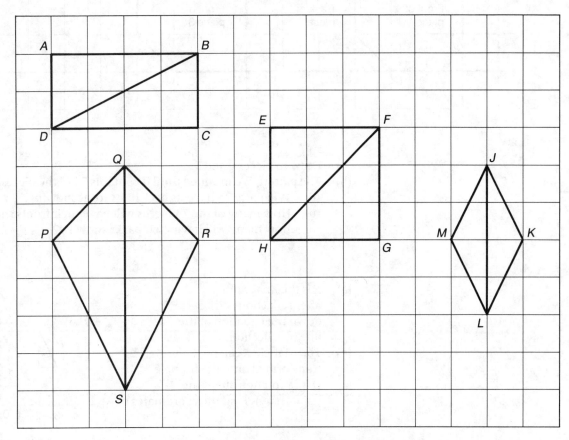

(a) What is the special name given to the quadrilateral *PQRS*?

(b) What is the special name given to the triangle *ABD*?

(c) In which shapes does the diagonal divide the quadrilateral into two isosceles triangles?

(d) In the shape *JKLM*, angle *JML* is 126°. Calculate, showing your method, the size of angle *MJK*.

150. A coloured tile is in the shape of a right-angled triangle with sides of length 8 cm and 3 cm. How many of these tiles are needed to cover a rectangular shaped area, which measures 120 cm by 45 cm?

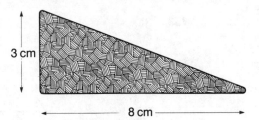

3 cm

8 cm

151. A pattern is made up of cardboard pieces like the one shown alongside. To make the pattern some pieces are placed with their fronts showing and some with their backs showing.

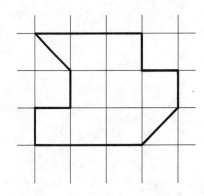

Front of
piece 1

Back of
piece 2

Front of
piece 3

(a) Draw in pieces 4 and 5.
(b) The pattern is continued until it contains 73 of the pieces.
   (i) Will piece 25 have its back or its front showing?
   (ii) How many of the 73 pieces will have their fronts showing and how many will have their backs showing?

GRADE E

152. (a) *R* is the image of *P* after reflection. Write down the equation of the line of reflection.

(b) The triangle *R* can be transformed onto the triangle *Q* by a rotation about the point *A(x,y)*. Find the coordinates of A.

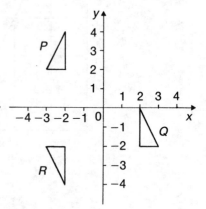

(c) Draw the image of triangle *P* after an enlargement, scale factor ½, using (0,0) as the centre of the enlargement. Label the triangle *S*.   (SEG)

153. (a)

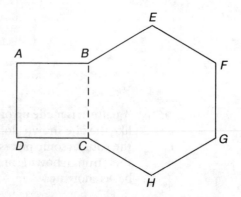

The tile *ABEFGHCD* is made up of a square *ABCD* attached to a regular hexagon *BEFGHC* along their common side *BC*.
What is the size of (i) ∠ *ABC*; (ii) ∠ *EBC*; (iii) ∠ *ABE*?

(b)   Tiles of the same shape as *ABEFGHCD* are placed in the pattern shown below.

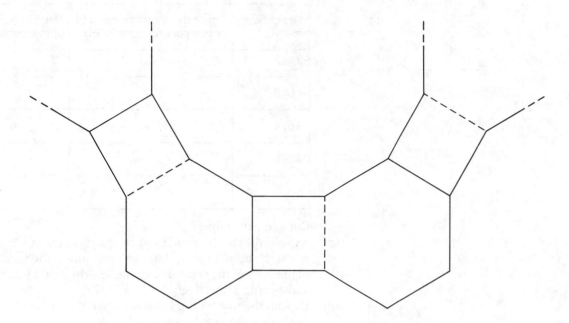

(i)   Without drawing the completed figure, explain why the tiles will form a closed shape if the pattern is continued.

(ii)   The completed shape encloses a regular polygon.
How many sides has this polygon?   (WJEC)

154. Elin has some rectangular cards measuring 3 cm by 2 cm. They have an arrow painted on them which points in a direction parallel to the longer side. She places some of these cards on the table with their longer edges together and the arrows pointing to the RIGHT, as shown in (i).

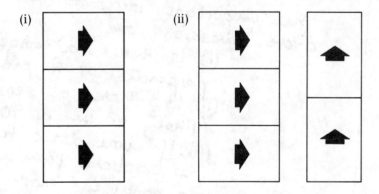

She then places some cards alongside with their shorter edges together and the arrows pointing UP as shown in (ii).
The column of cards with arrows pointing to the RIGHT and the column of cards with arrows pointing UP have a matching height when they contain 3 and 2 cards, respectively, as shown in (ii). This is the smallest number of cards necessary for such a match.

(a)   Robert has some rectangular cards like Elin's, but they measure 4 cm by 3 cm. He places them on a table in the same way and looks for the same kind of match as Elin found.
What is the smallest possible number of cards he must place in each column to make such a match?
Draw a sketch of Robert's cards in this matching position.

(b)   Elin then tries rectangular cards of size 6 cm by 4 cm and finds that the smallest number of cards with arrows pointing to the right and up are the same as for the 3 cm by 2 cm cards.

They both experiment with other sized cards and enter their results in a table.

Size of card in cm	Smallest number of cards with arrows pointing to the RIGHT	Smallest number of cards with arrows pointing UP
3 by 2	3	2
4 by 3		
6 by 4	3	2
9 by 6		
5 by 3		

Complete the table.

(c) Explain the rule by which you can predict that a match will occur when the number of cards in both columns is the same as the lengths of the sides of the cards. For example – the 3 cm by 2 cm cards need 3 and 2 cards, respectively.

(d) Explain the rule for the situation when this does not happen. For example – the 6 cm by 4 cm cards.

3 The circle

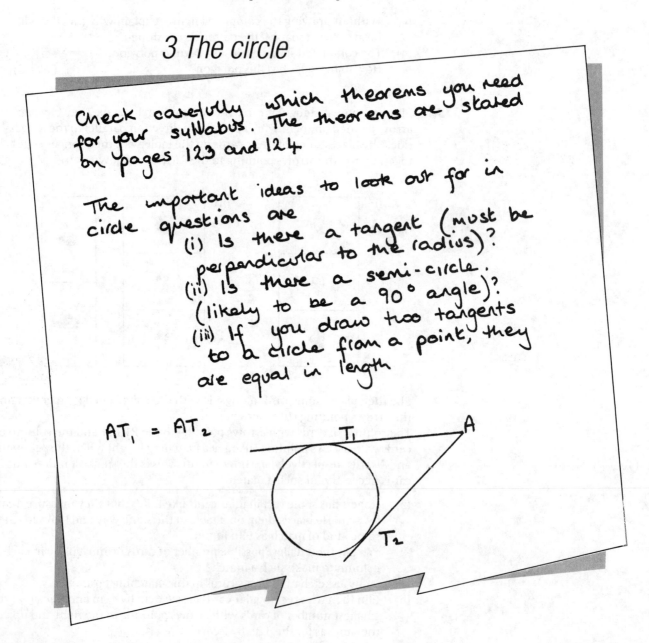

Check carefully which theorems you need for your syllabus. The theorems are stated on pages 123 and 124

The important ideas to look out for in circle questions are
(i) Is there a tangent (must be perpendicular to the radius)?
(ii) Is there a semi-circle. (likely to be a 90° angle)?
(iii) If you draw two tangents to a circle from a point, they are equal in length

$AT_1 = AT_2$

(iv) You always get an isosceles triangle from the centre of a circle, because of equal radii.

OAB is an isosceles △

WORDS TO LEARN: sector, segment, chord Look at the diagrams on this page.
cyclic quadrilateral: four points on a circle.
Supplementary: add up to 180°
tangent to a circle: a line that touches a circle at one point.

Properties of the circle

USEFUL FACTS

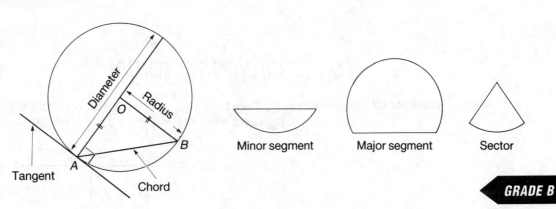

Tangent   Chord

Minor segment   Major segment   Sector

THEOREMS   (i)   The angle between a tangent and radius = 90°.

GRADE B

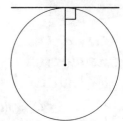

(ii)   The angle in a semi-circle is 90°.

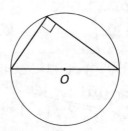

(iii)

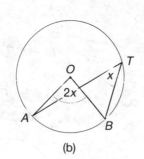
(a)

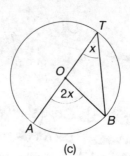
(b)

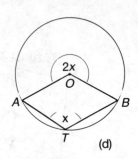
(c)

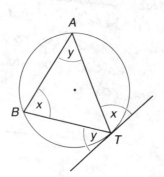
(d)

(iii)   The angle at the centre is twice the angle at the circumference.

GRADE A

(iv)   Opposite angles of a cyclic
quadrilateral add up to 180°.

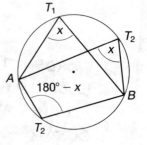

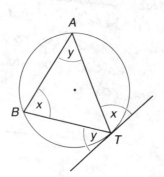

(v)   Angle between tangent and chord
= angle in alternate segment.

Topic: circle theorems

GRADE A

WORKED EXAMPLE 83   In the diagram, AT is a tangent to the circle, AOR is a straight line with O at the centre of the circle. Find angles a and b if $\angle TAO = 28°$.

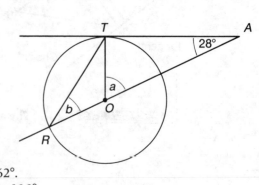

remember!
a tangent is
perpendicular to a
radius

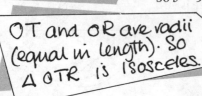
Angles of a
triangle add up to
180°

SOLUTION $\angle ATO = 90°$
So $a + 90° + 28° = 180°$
$a + 118° = 180°$
Hence $a = 180° - 118° = 62°$.
Now $\angle TOR = 180° - 62° = 118°$
So $b + b + 118° = 180°$
$2b = 62°$
So $b = 31°$.

OT and OR are radii
(equal in length). So
$\triangle OTR$ is isosceles.

Topic: circle theorems

WORKED EXAMPLE 84

A cyclic quadrilateral *PQRS* has *PQ* = *PS*. The diagonal *QS* = *QR*.
If $\angle QSR = 52°$, find $\angle PQR$.

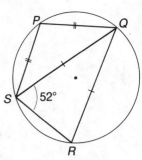

SOLUTION

Since $\triangle SQR$ is isosceles, $\angle QRS = 52°$
So $\angle SQR = 180° - 2 \times 52° = 76°$
$\angle SPQ$ and $\angle SRQ$ are opposite angles in a cyclic quadrilateral.
So $\angle SPQ + \angle SRQ = 180°$
$\angle SPQ + 52° = 180°$.
Hence $\angle SPQ = 128°$.
$\triangle SPQ$ is isosceles
Hence $\angle PQS = \frac{1}{2}(180° - 128°) = 26°$
So $\angle PQR = 26° + 76° = 102°$.

Topics: circle theorems, algebra

WORKED EXAMPLE 85

POQR is a straight line, where *O* is the centre of the circle, and *P* and *Q* are on the circle. *TR* is a tangent to the circle at *T*, and $\angle TPO = x°$.
Find, in terms of *x*:

(i) $\angle PTO$; (ii) $\angle TQP$; (iii) $\angle TRO$.

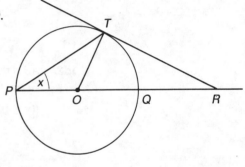

SOLUTION

(i) $\angle PTO = \angle TPO = x°$.
(ii)   Since $\angle PTQ = 90°$,
     $\angle TPO + \angle TQP = 90°$
     Hence $\angle TQP = 90° - x°$.
(iii) $\angle TOQ = 2x$
     $\angle OTR = 90°$
     $\angle TRO = 90° - \angle TOR$
        $= 90° - 2x°$.

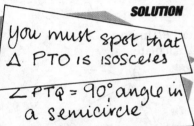

you must spot that △ PTO is isosceles

∠ PTQ = 90° angle in a semicircle

∠TOQ = 2∠TPO angle at centre is twice angle at circumference

Questions to try

GRADE A/B

155. Find the angles marked with a letter in the following diagrams.
All lines drawn through a point *T* are tangents, and *O* is the centre.

(i)

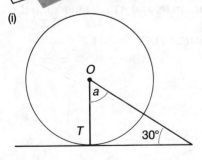

(ii)

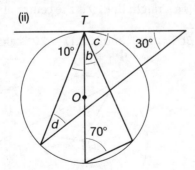

(iii)

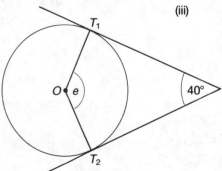

(iv)

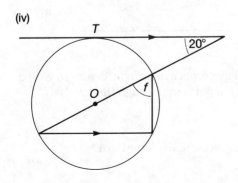

(v)

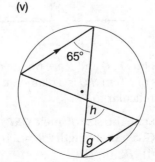

(vi)

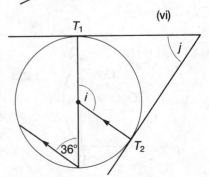

156.

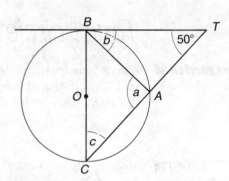

A, B and C are three points on the circumference of a circle with centre O. BOC is the diameter of the circle and BT is a tangent to the circle. Write down the values of a, b and c.

157. In the diagram, TA and TB are tangents to a circle centre O, TOC is a straight line and ∠ATB = 60°. Calculate:

(i) ∠ABT; (ii) ∠AOB (reflex); (iii) ∠BCO.

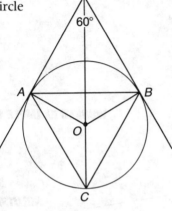

158. AC is the diameter of the circle and the chord BD intersects AC at X. Given that ∠BCA = 26° and ∠CAD = 47°, calculate:

(i) ∠BAC; (ii) ∠AXD.

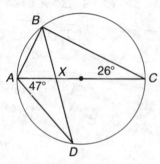

159. ABC is a straight line, O is the centre of the circle, and AT is a tangent to the circle.
If ∠BOT = 100° and ∠BAT = 20°, calculate ∠TOC (obtuse).

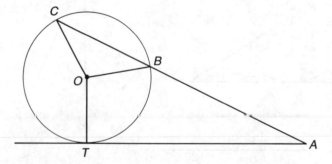

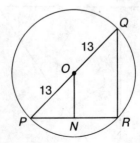

160. The points P, Q and R are on the circumference of a circle, centre O, with a radius of 13 cm. PQ is a diameter. N is a point on PR such that ON is perpendicular to PR.

(a) State the size of angle QRP.
(b) Given that length PR = 24 cm, calculate the lengths of
(i) NR; (ii) ON.

(SEG)

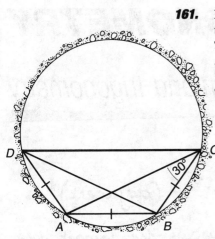

161. In this question you must give valid reasons for your answers. Numbers on their own will not be sufficient.
The diagram shows the cross-section of a tunnel. The tunnel is circular with a platform *DC* in it. The platform is held by five rods *AB, BC, BD, AD, AC*.
Rods *AB, AD* and *BC* are all the same length.
The angle between *AC* and *BC* is 30°.

    (a)   Find:
         (i) $\widehat{ADB}$; (ii) $\widehat{ABD}$; (iii) $\widehat{DBC}$; (iv) $\widehat{BDC}$.

    (b)   (i)   Explain how you know that platform *DC* must be parallel to rod *AB*.
         (ii)   What does the answer to (a) (iii) tell you about *DC*?

                                                  (WJEC)

162. Calculate the size of the angles *f*, *g* and *h*. *O* indicates the centre of the circle.

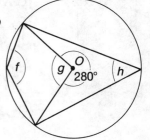

163. Calculate the size of the angles *i* and *j*. *O* indicates the centre of the circle.

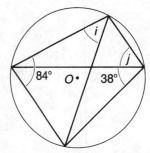

164. In the diagram, *O* is the centre of the circle. The straight line *AOBC* meets the circle at *A* and *B*. The straight line *ETC* is a tangent to the circle at *T*. Angle *ABT* = *x*°.
Find, in terms of *x*,
    (a)   angle *BAT*;
    (b)   angle *AOT*;
    (c)   angle *BCT*.

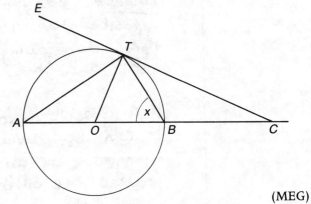

                                                  (MEG)

TRIGONOMETRY

1 Pythagoras' theorem and trigonometry

PYTHAGORAS'S THEOREM.

$$(\text{hypotenuse})^2 = (\text{opposite})^2 + (\text{adjacent})^2$$

Remember hypotenuse is always the longest side. If a diagram contains angles <u>and</u> lengths, and uses the word <u>calculate</u>, it usually requires trig ratios.

Remember $\sin x = \dfrac{\text{opposite}}{\text{hypotenuse}}$

$\cos x = \dfrac{\text{adjacent}}{\text{hypotenuse}}$

$\tan x = \dfrac{\text{opposite}}{\text{adjacent}}$

The hypotenuse is the longest side, and is opposite the right angle. The opposite is the side facing the angle you are working with, and the remaining side is the adjacent.

If a question contains an isosceles triangle, it can be divided into 2 right-angled triangles, by using the line of symmetry (called the altitude).

These methods only work if the question can be phrased to involve a right-angled triangle.

Topics: Pythagoras, tangent ratio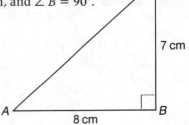

WORKED EXAMPLE 86 In the diagram, $AB = 8$ cm, $BC = 7$ cm, and $\angle B = 90°$.
Find:

(i) AC; (ii) angle A.

SOLUTION (i) No angles are involved, so use Pythagoras' theorem.
$(AC)^2 = (AB)^2 + (CB)^2$
So $(AC)^2 = 8^2 + 7^2 = 64 + 49 = 113$
Hence $AC = \sqrt{113}$
$\quad\quad = 10.6$ (3 significant figures).

You always know 2 quantities apart from the right angle

(ii) An angle is involved, so name the sides before choosing the correct ratio.

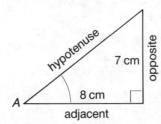

Opposite and adjacent is tangent.
So $\tan A = \dfrac{7}{8}$.

This is solved with the calculator as follows:

7 ÷ 8 = inv tan   41.185925

Hence $\angle A = 41.2°$.

Topics: Pythagoras, cosine ratio

WORKED EXAMPLE 87 In the diagram, $QR = 7.8$ cm, $PR = 8.3$ cm, and $\angle Q = 90°$.
Find:

(i) PQ; (ii) angle R.

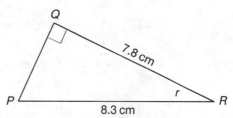

SOLUTION (i) No angles are involved, so use Pythagoras.
$(PR)^2 = (PQ)^2 + (QR)^2$
So $8.3^2 = (PQ)^2 + 7.8^2$
$68.89 = (PQ)^2 + 60.84$
$68.89 - 60.84 = (PQ)^2$
So $PQ = \sqrt{8.05}$
$\quad\quad = 2.84$ (3 significant figures).

If you are finding one of the shorter sides you have to subtract squares.

(ii) Adjacent and hypotenuse give cosine.
So $\cos R = \dfrac{7.8}{8.3}$

Hence 7.8 ÷ 8.3 = inv cos   19.988871

So $\angle R = 20°$ (3 significant figures).

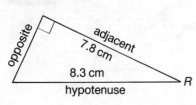

Topics: trigonometry, area

WORKED EXAMPLE 88 The diagram shows part of a bridge structure, made from five girders *AD*, *DC*, *BC*, *AB*, *DB*. Find:

(i) the total length of the girders needed;
(ii) the area of the figure *ABCD*.

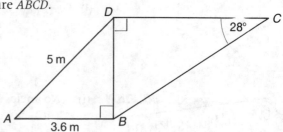

SOLUTION (i) To find *DB*:
$$(AD)^2 = (DB)^2 + (AB)^2$$
$$5^2 = (DB)^2 + (3.6)^2$$
Hence $(DB)^2 = 25 - 12.96 = 12.04$.
So $DB = 3.47$ m.

In $\triangle BDC$, $\sin 28° = \dfrac{DB}{BC} = \dfrac{3.47}{BC}$

Hence $BC = \dfrac{3.47}{\sin 28°} = 7.39$ m.

This last calculation can be done on the calculator as follows:

3.47 $\boxed{÷}$ 28 $\boxed{\sin}$ $\boxed{=}$ $\boxed{7.391289}$

To find *DC*:
$$(BC)^2 = (BD)^2 + (DC)^2$$
So $7.39^2 = (3.47)^2 + (DC)^2$
Hence $(DC)^2 = 54.61 - 12.04 = 42.57$.
Therefore $DC = 6.52$ m.
The total length of girder $= 3.47 + 5 + 3.6 + 7.39 + 6.52$
$\qquad\qquad\qquad\qquad\qquad = 26$ m (3 sig. figures).

(ii) The shape is a trapezium:
area $= \frac{1}{2} \times 3.47 \times (3.6 + 6.52) = 17.6$ m^2.

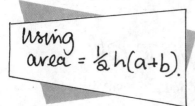

You need to find DB before you can work in △ BDC

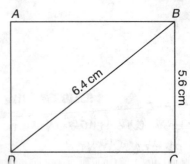

using area = ½ h(a+b).

Questions to try

165. In the diagram, *DB* is the diagonal of a rectangle *ABCD*. Find

(i) *AB*; (ii) the area of *ABCD*.

GRADE C/D

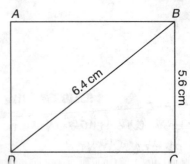

166. Find all sides and angles marked *a*, *b*, *c*, . . . in the following diagrams. Give your answers correct to 3 significant figures.

GRADE B

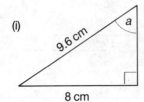

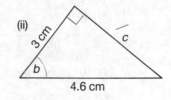

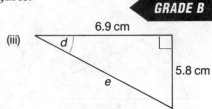

(iv)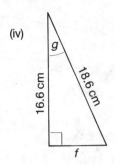

(v)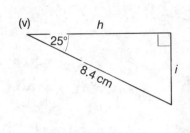

(vi)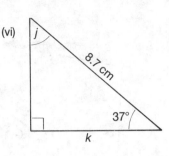

167. The diagram shows the cross-section of a factory roof. *EDB* is vertical and *ABC* is horizontal.

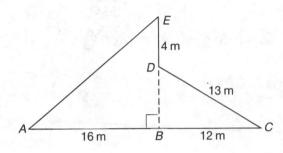

$AB = 16\,\text{m}$, $BC = 12\,\text{m}$, $CD = 13\,\text{m}$ and $ED = 4\,\text{m}$.

Calculate:

(a) the length, in metres, of *BD*;
(b) the size, correct to the nearest degree, of angle *EAB*;
(c) the total area, in square metres, of the cross-section. (MEG)

2 Problem situations, sections of circles

Very often, you need to realise that a diagram does contain a right-angled triangle. Always draw a clear lettered diagram before starting to use trigonometry.

You may need to use bearings.

If using 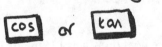 button

press button first if you are trying

to find the angle
If you know the angle, just press the relevant button.

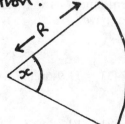

A sector of a circle is a fraction of a circle.

$$\text{Area} = \pi R^2 \times \frac{x}{360}$$

$$\text{Length of arc} = 2\pi R \times \frac{x}{360}$$

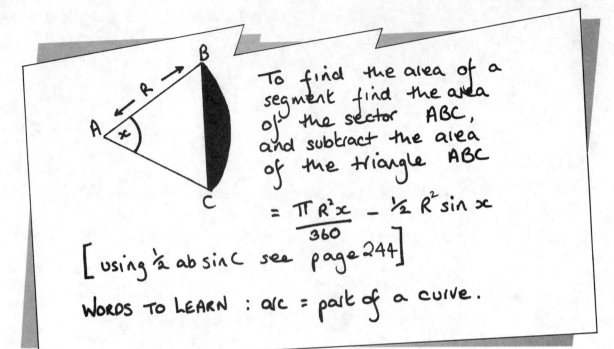

To find the area of a segment find the area of the sector ABC, and subtract the area of the triangle ABC

$$= \frac{\pi R^2 x}{360} - \frac{1}{2} R^2 \sin x$$

[using $\frac{1}{2} ab \sin C$ see page 244]

WORDS TO LEARN : arc = part of a curve.

Topics: trigonometry, bearings, speed

WORKED EXAMPLE 89   The diagram shows the route taken by a boat on a fishing trip.   **GRADE B**
The boat starts from port A and sails 16 km on a bearing of 042° to its first
stop at the point B. In the diagram, N is the point which is due North of A
and due West of B.

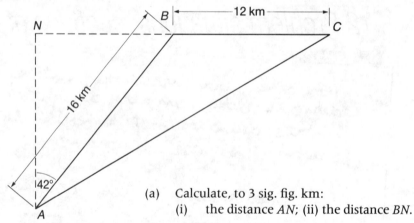

(a)   Calculate, to 3 sig. fig. km:
(i)   the distance AN; (ii) the distance BN.

The boat then sails 12 km due East to its second stop at the point C.

(b)   Calculate:
(i)   the distance AC, in km, to the nearest 0.01 km;
(ii)   the bearing of C from A, to the nearest degree.
(c)   What is the bearing of A from C?
The boat travels at 6.4 km/h.
(d)   Find the time it takes to return directly to A from C.   (LEAG)

SOLUTION   This question is typical of the problem situations, in that a number of ideas
are involved, including bearings and speed.

Note: that ANB=90°
because—
AN is due North
NB is due East

(a)   (i) $\frac{AN}{16} = \cos 42° = 0.7431$.

Therefore $AN = 16 \times 0.7431 = 11.9$ km (3 s.f.).

(ii) $\frac{BN}{16} = \sin 42° = 0.6691$.

Therefore $BN = 16 \times 0.6691 = 10.7$ km (3 s.f.).

(b)   Note *ANC* is a right-angled triangle.
  (i)   So $(AC)^2 = (AN)^2 + (NC)^2$
    $= (11.9)^2 + (10.7 + 12)^2 = 656.9$.
    Hence $AC = \sqrt{656.9} = 25.6\,\mathrm{km}$ (3 s.f.).
  (ii) $\tan N\hat{A}C = \dfrac{NC}{NA} = \dfrac{(10.7 + 12)}{11.9} = \dfrac{22.7}{11.9}$
    $= 1.908$.
    Hence $\angle\, NAC = 62°$ (nearest degree).
    The bearing $= 062°$.

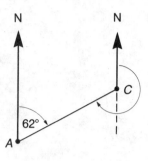

Bearings are always measured clockwise.

(c)   The bearing of *A* from *C* is $180° + 62° = 242°$.
(d)   The distance $AC = 25.6\,\mathrm{km}$.
  The speed $= 6.4\,\mathrm{km/h}$.
  Using time $= \dfrac{\text{distance}}{\text{speed}} = \dfrac{25.6}{6.4} = 4$ hours

Topics: sectors, area, perimeter   ◄ GRADE A

WORKED EXAMPLE 90   A cardboard name tag is in the shape of a sector of a circle of radius 6 cm, and an angle of 40°. Find:

(i)   the area of the name tag;
(ii)   the perimeter of the name tag.

SOLUTION   (i)   A full circle has area
    $= \pi r^2 = \pi \times 6^2$
    $= 113\,\mathrm{cm}^2$ (3 s.f.).
    We only have $\dfrac{40}{360} = \dfrac{1}{9}$ of a circle.
    So $\dfrac{1}{9} \times 113 = \dfrac{113}{9} = 12.6\,\mathrm{cm}^2$.

(ii)   The perimeter of a circle (i.e. the circumference)
    $= 2\pi r = 2\pi \times 6$
    $= 37.7\,\mathrm{cm}$.

    The length of the curved edge of the tag is
    $\dfrac{1}{9}$ of $37.7 = \dfrac{37.7}{9} = 4.19\,\mathrm{cm}$.
    The perimeter of the tag $= 6 + 6 + 4.19 = 16.19\,\mathrm{cm}$.

Topics: trigonometry, sectors, percentages

WORKED EXAMPLE 91

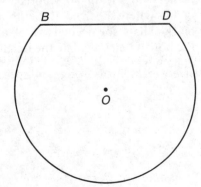

The shape of the top of a table in a cafe is shown by the part of the circle, centre *O*. The angle $BOD = 90°$ and $BO = OD = 50\,\mathrm{cm}$.

The top of the table is made of laminate and a thin metal strip is fixed to its perimeter.

(a)   Calculate:
    (i)   the length of the metal strip;
    (ii)   the area of the laminate surface.

(b)   If the table top is to be cut from a square of laminate of area $1\,m^2$, what percentage of laminate is wasted?

(SEG)

SOLUTION   (a)   (i)   The perimeter of the table is found in two parts, the straight part BD, and the arc of a circle. Since triangle BOD is right-angled, Pythagoras' theorem states:
$$BD^2 = BO^2 + OD^2$$
Hence $BD^2 = 50^2 + 50^2 = 2500 + 2500 = 5000$
So $BD = 70.7\,cm$.
The arc of the circle corresponds to 270°, hence its length is given by:
$$\text{arc} = 2 \times \pi \times 50 \times \frac{270}{360} = 235.6\,cm.$$
Length of metal strip $= 235.6 + 70.7 = 306.3\,cm$.

    (ii)   The area of the triangle $BOD = \frac{1}{2} \times 50 \times 50 = 1250\,cm^2$.
The area of the rest $= \pi \times 50^2 \times \frac{270}{360} = 5890\,cm^2$.
The area of the laminate $= 1250 + 5890 = 7140\,cm^2$.

(b) $1\,m^2 = 100 \times 100 = 10\,000\,cm^2$.
Amount of laminate wasted $= 10\,000 - 7140 = 2860\,cm^2$.
The percentage wasted $= \dfrac{2860}{10\,000} \times 100 = 28.6\%$.

Questions to try

GRADE B

168.   A man, 1.85 m tall, casts a shadow 2.46 m long on flat horizontal ground. Calculate the angle of elevation of the sun.
If the length of the shadow increases at about 0.6 m/h, estimate the length of his shadow 30 minutes later.

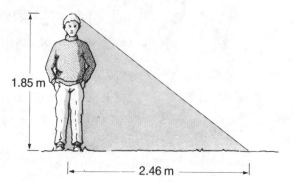

1.85 m

2.46 m

169.

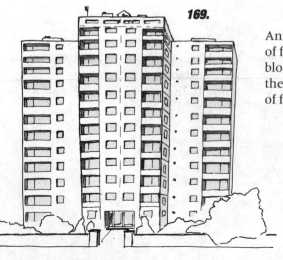

Anne, who is 1.5 m tall, wanted to calculate the height of the block of flats where she lived. If she stood 10 m away from the foot of the block of flats, she needed to look up to the roof at an angle of 80° to the horizontal. Calculate the height Anne would give for the block of flats.

170. The foot of a ladder 12.5 ft long rests on level ground a distance of 3.5 ft from the base of a vertical wall.

(i) Calculate the height *d* ft of the top of the ladder above the ground.
(ii) Calculate the angle *x*° which the ladder makes with the ground.

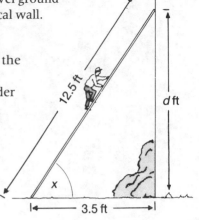

171. *ABCD* represents part of the cross-section of a circus tent with *BC* and *AD* being vertical poles. *FECD* is level ground and *AF* and *BE* are guy-ropes to support the tent.

$AF = 39$ m, $BE = 9$ m, $EC = 3.8$ m and $\angle AFE = 40°$. Calculate:

(a) the height of the tent *AD*;
(b) the size of $\angle BEC$.

(WJEC)

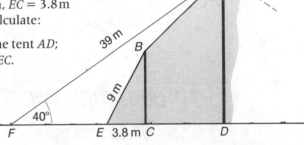

GRADE A

172. *ABC* is a sector of a circle of radius 10 cm, and arc length 8 cm. Find:

(i) the angle *BAC*;
(ii) the area of the sector.

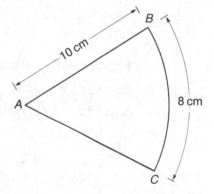

173. A flat metal component is to be made in the shape shown in the figure. The curves *AB* and *DC* are both arcs of circles with centre *O*. The radius of the arc *AB* is *r*, the radius of the arc *DC* is *R*. The angle $AOB = 60°$.

(a) (i) Write down a formula for the area of sector *ODC* in terms of *R*.
(ii) Show that the area of the shaded region *ABCD* is $\frac{1}{6}\pi(R^2 - r^2)$.

The unshaded ends of the shape are both semicircles.

(b) (i) Write down the length of the diameter *BC* in terms of *R* and *r*.
(ii) Find the total area of the two semicircles in terms of *R* and *r*.

(LEAG)

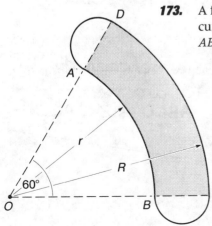

174. (a) *XYZ* is an isosceles triangle with *XY* = 18 cm and *YZ* = 10 cm.
Calculate:
   (i)   the perpendicular height *XD*;
   (ii) the size of the angle *XYD*.

  (b) *C* is the centre of the circle that touches
the three sides of the triangle.
   (i)   Write down angle *CYD*;
   (ii) Find the radius of the circle.

GRADE A*

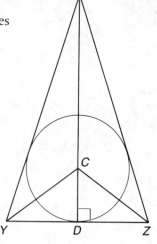

3 Three dimensional problems, angles of elevation

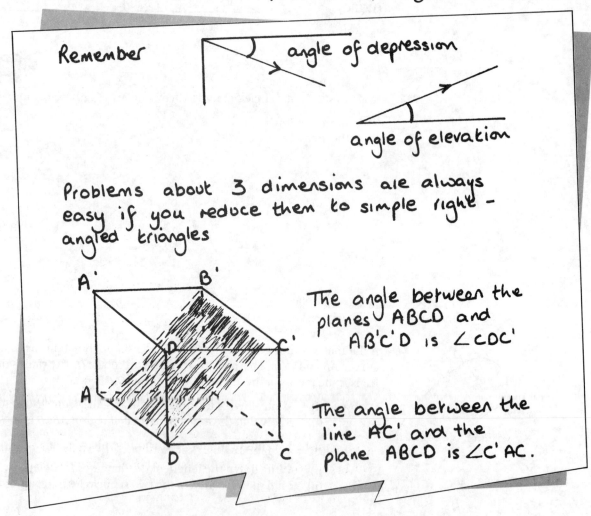

Often useful to draw a cross-section through a solid.

Trigonometry questions often involve volume, particularly a prism.

Remember Volume of a prism = length × area of cross-section.

GRADE B

Topic: angle of elevation

WORKED EXAMPLE 92   From a first floor window, the top of a lamp-post is seen at an angle of elevation of 21.8°. If the height of the window above the ground is 4 m and the distance of the window from the lamp-post is 20 m, calculate the height of the lamp-post.

SOLUTION   The situation is represented by the diagram shown alongside.

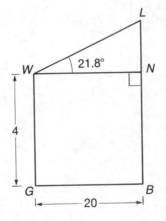

$WN = 20$,

so $\dfrac{LN}{WN} = \tan 21.8° = 0.4.$

$LN = 20 \times 0.4 = 8\,\text{m}.$

The height of the lamp-post $= 4 + 8 = 12\,\text{m}.$

Topics: angles of elevation, speed

WORKED EXAMPLE 93   Heather is in a boat which has broken down. She looks up at the base of a lighthouse on a cliff 180 m high, and estimates the angle of elevation as 15°. The boat is drifting towards the shore. About 5 minutes later, she looks up again, and reckons the angle of elevation is 20°. How fast in m/s is the boat drifting?

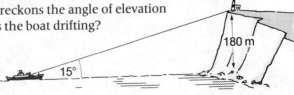

SOLUTION   The diagram is a good representation of the problem.

In $\triangle ALC$ $\tan 15° = \dfrac{LC}{AC}$

Be careful with the rearrangement of this

so $0.2679 = \dfrac{180}{AC}$

Hence $AC = \dfrac{180}{0.2679} = 672$ m.

In $\triangle LBC$ $\tan 20° = \dfrac{180}{BC}$

so $BC = \dfrac{180}{0.364} = 495$ m.

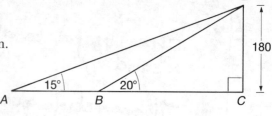

The distance the boat drifts $= AC - BC$
$$= 672 - 495 = 177 \text{ m}.$$
Now 5 minutes $= 5 \times 60 = 300$ seconds.

Speed = $\dfrac{\text{distance}}{\text{time}}$.

The speed $= \dfrac{177}{300} = 0.59$ m/s.

GRADE A

Topic: 3 dimensional trigonometry

WORKED EXAMPLE 94

The diagram shows a vertical pole AD supported by two ropes AB and AC. The base BDC is a triangle with $\angle BDC = 90°$, $BC = 20$ m and $DC = 16$ m. If $\angle ABD = 32°$, find the height of the pole.

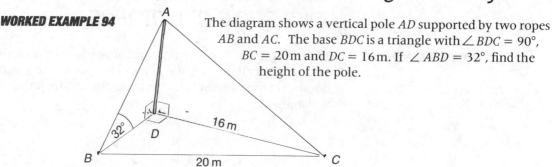

SOLUTION   In $\triangle BDC$, $20^2 = (BD)^2 + 16^2$
$$400 - 256 = (BD)^2$$
$$144 = (BD)^2$$
$$\text{so } BD = 12.$$

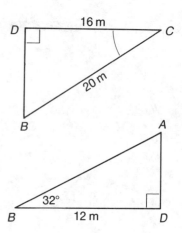

$\dfrac{AD}{12} = \tan 32°$

$AD = 12 \times 0.6249$

so $AD = 7.5$ (3 s.f.).
The height of the pole is 7.5 m.

WORKED EXAMPLE 95   The diagram shows a box 10 cm deep, with a square base measuring 4 cm by 4 cm. A pencil is placed in the box. What is the longest pencil that can be put into the box?

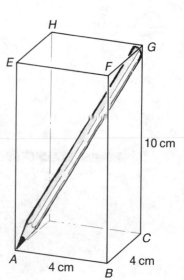

SOLUTION Diagram (i) shows a vertical slice through the box. You cannot find the
length AG until you find AC.
Diagram (ii) is looking down from the top of the box.
$(AC)^2 = 4^2 + 4^2 = 32$
so $AC = \sqrt{32} = 5.66 \text{cm}^2$.
Referring back to diagram (i)
$(AG)^2 = 10^2 + 5.66^2$
$\qquad = 100 + 32 = 132$
so $AG = 11.5 \text{cm}$ (3 s.f.).
The length of the longest pencil is about $11\frac{1}{2}$ cm.

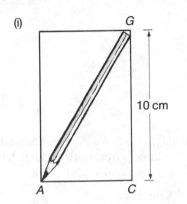
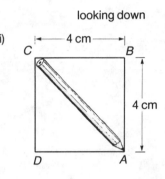

Questions to try

GRADE A/B

175. The diagram shows a wedge of cheese bought at a local supermarket.

(i) Calculate the height h of the wedge of cheese.
(ii) Calculate the area of cross-section of the
wedge of cheese.
(iii) What is the volume of the piece
of cheese?

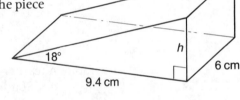

176.

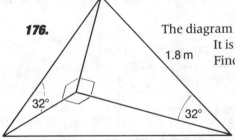

The diagram shows a proposed design for a new windbreak.
It is made from 3 triangular sections.
Find the area of material that is needed to make it.

177. (i) A, B and C are three points on level ground. B is due East of A, C is due
North of A, and the distance AC is 160 m. The angles of elevation from
A and B to the top of a vertical mast whose base is at C are, respectively,
30° and 28°. Calculate:

(a) the distance BC;
(b) the bearing of C from B;

(ii) The points O, P, Q and T lie in a horizontal plane, but, because of an
obstruction, the point T is not visible from the point O. The bearings of
the points P and Q from O are 029° and 062°, respectively; $OP = 0.8$ km
and $OQ = 1.2$ km. The bearing of T from P is 126° and the bearing of T
from Q is 160°.
Using a scale of 10 cm to 1 km, draw a diagram showing the points O, P,
Q and T. From your diagram, obtain the bearing and distance of T from
O.

178. The diagram shows a storage shed on a building site.

    (a)   Calculate the angle of inclination of the roof to the horizontal.

    (b)   Calculate the length of the longest rod that can be stored in the shed.

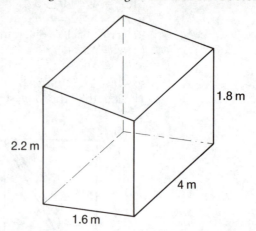

179. In the diagram, O, A and B represent three positions on level ground. A is 2 km due South-west of O, and B is 18 km South-east of O. At O is a vertical tower of height 130 m. Calculate:

    (i)   the distance AB;

    (ii)   the bearing of B from A;

    (iii)   the angle of elevation of the top of the tower from A.

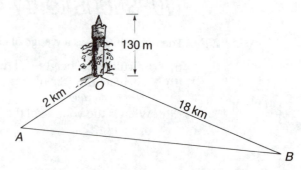

180. A teacher set up an orienteering course. She started at a point A and walked due South, a distance of 900 m to a point P. The table of her final course plan is as follows.

From	To	Bearing	Distance (m)
A	P	180°	900
P	Q	035°	560
Q	R	290°	770
R	A		

    (a)   Using this table, draw to scale the route taken by the teacher from A to R, assuming that all the points are joined by straight lines.

    (b)   Measure and write down:

        (i)   the distance RA, in metres;

        (ii)   the bearing from A to R.

A class of pupils walked the course in groups of three. One group walked at an average speed of 4 km/h and they left A at 1120 hours.

    (c)   Calculate the time of day when they arrived back at A.

When the pupils reached the point R they saw a radio aerial. They knew that the aerial was standing on ground at the same horizontal height as R and that the aerial was 35 m high. They measured the angle of elevation of the top of the aerial from R and found that it was 6°.

    (d)   Calculate the horizontal distance from R to the bottom of the aerial.

                                                                     (SEG)

181. A right pyramid stands on a horizontal square base, *ABCD*, and *V* is the vertex of the pyramid. The diagonals of the base of the pyramid intersect at *N* and the midpoint of *AB* is *X*. Given that *AB* = 10 cm and the angle *VXN* = 39°, calculate, correct to 3 significant figures,

(a) the length, in cm, of *VN*;
(b) the volume, in cm³, of the pyramid;
(c) the length, in cm, of *VX*;
(d) the length, in cm, of *AV*;
(e) the size of the angle *AVB*, by considering the triangles *AVX* and *AVB*.

(LEAG)

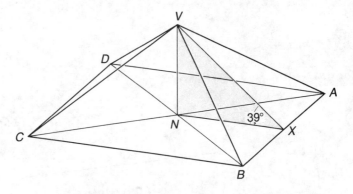

182. The diagram shows a pyramid whose horizontal base is a square *ABCD*. The vertex *V* is vertically above *N*, the centre of the base.

(a) Given that the base has an area of 50 cm², find the length of a diagonal of the square *ABCD*.

(b) Given also that each slant edge of the pyramid is 13 cm, find the volume of the pyramid.

183. The diagram shows a ridge of land. The ridge is in the path of a motorway which is being built. The ridge has a uniform vertical cross-section, *ABC*. *CF* is at right-angles to this cross-section. The distance *AB* is 17.3 m and *AB* slopes at 22.3° to the horizontal. Angle *ABC* is 90°. *A* and *C* are at the same horizontal level. Calculate:

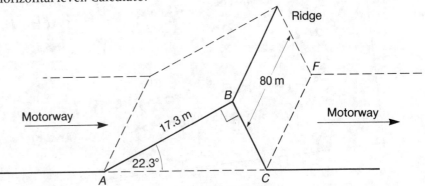

(a) the length *BC*;
(b) the approximate area of triangle *ABC*.

A length of 80 m of the ridge has to be levelled. The earth removed will be taken away in lorries, each of which has a capacity of 12 m³.

(c) How many lorry loads will be needed for this task?

COORDINATES

ATTAINMENT TARGETS 3 AND 4

9

1 Straight line graphs

Use of straight line graphs covers many situations.
Conversion graphs, exchanging money, working out bills.
These can lead to a formula. See Worked Example 96
Always make sure you read the scales correctly. A graph will often be drawn with different scales on the x and y axes.

Always label the axes. (The scale does not have to be the same on each axis)
You are often required to draw a conversion graph from a simple piece of information, such as £1 = $1.58

This requires using the fact that £0 = $0, and drawing a straight line through the origin.

See worked example 97.
Travel graphs: covered in unit 3

Topic: straight line graphs

GRADE C/D

WORKED EXAMPLE 96 To hire a ladder from Strong's costs £10 basic charge plus £2 for each day you keep the ladder.

(a)   Fill in the spaces in this table showing the cost for the different numbers of days.

Number of days	1	2	4	6	8	11
Cost in pounds	12	14		22		32

(b)   Gale's also hires out ladders. The graph below can be used to find the cost of hiring a ladder from Gale's for various numbers of days.

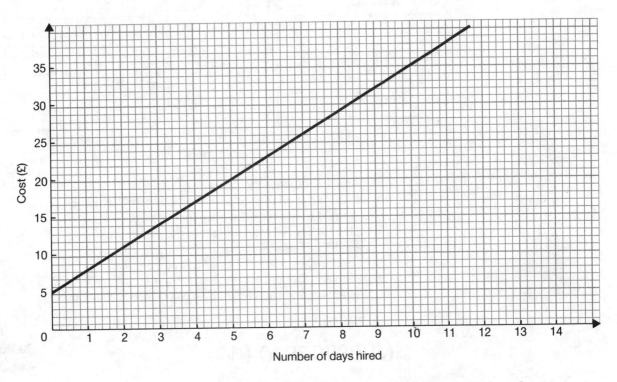

Number of days hired

How much does it cost to hire a ladder from Gale's for 4 days?

(c)   Jacki wants a ladder for 6 days. How much more will it cost her to hire it from Gale's instead of Strong's?

(d)   What formula does Gale use to work out his costs?   (WJEC)

SOLUTION   (a)   4 days will cost £10 + 4 × £2 = £18.
8 days will cost £10 + 8 × £2 = £26.

(b)   Reading up from 4 and across gives £17.

(c)   6 days from Gale's is £23.
6 days from Strong's is £22.
Hence it will cost £1 more.

(d)   The cost rises £3 per day, with a basic charge of £5. Hence $C = 3D + 5$.

Topic: conversion graphs

WORKED EXAMPLE 97   Use the fact that 1 inch = 2.54 cm to draw a conversion graph for 0–20 cm. Use the graph to change:

(i)   9 cm into inches;

(ii)   45 cm into inches;

(iii)   2 ft 3 inches into cm;

(iv)   8 ft into mm.

SOLUTION   Remember that 0 inches = 0 cm. The two points can be plotted, and a straight line drawn as shown.

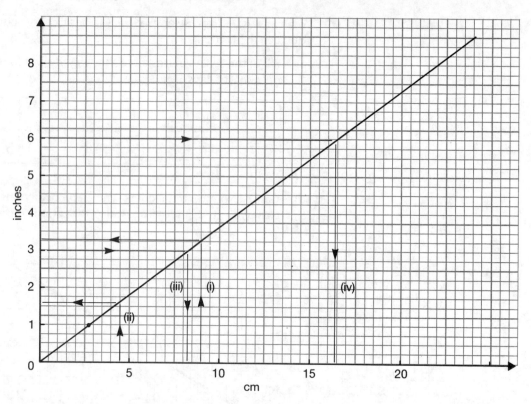

(i)   9 cm is 3.3 inches.
(ii)   45 cm is not on the scale, so read 4.5 cm = 1.6 inches.
        Hence 45 cm is 10 × 1.6 = 16 inches.
(iii)   2 ft 3 inches = 27 inches (again not on the scale).
        Read 3 inches = 8.25 cm.
        So 27 inches = 9 × 8.25 = 74.25 cm.
(iv)   Read 6 inches = 16.4 cm.
        So 8 ft = 16 × 16.4 cm = 262.4 cm, which is 2624 mm.

Questions to try

GRADE C/D

184. The removal firm of W. E. Shiftham hires out vans at a basic charge of £20 plus a further cost of 30p per kilometre. Some of the charges for given distances are shown in Table 1.

Dist. (x km)	0	100	200	300
Charge (£C)	20			110

Table 1

(a)   Complete Table 1.
(b)   Use the values from Table 1 to draw a graph to show the charges up to a distance of 300 km.

Another firm, D.I.Y. Transport, hires out vans at a basic charge of £35 plus a further cost of 20p per kilometre.

Dist. (x km)	0	100	200	300
Charge (£C)				

Table 2

(c)   Complete Table 2 for D.I.Y. Transport charges.

(d)   Using the same axes as in part (b), draw a graph to show the charges of D.I.Y. Transport up to a distance of 300 km.

(e)   For what distance do both firms charge the same amount?

(f)   (i)   Which firm is the cheaper for a journey of 180 km?
      (ii)   What is the difference in charges between the firms for a journey of 180 km?

(g)   For D.I.Y. Transport, write down a formula giving the value of C in terms of x.   (LEAG)

185.   A machinist in a clothing factory is paid a weekly wage consisting of a fixed sum of money plus a bonus for each skirt made. The table shows the weekly wage earned for different numbers of skirts made.

Number of skirts made	10	20	30	40	50	60
Wage earned in £	40	55	70	85	100	115

(a)   Using a scale of 2 cm for 10 units on each axis, draw clearly labelled axes on the grid opposite. Plot the points for the values given in the table. Draw a straight line through these points.

(b)   Use your graph to find:
      (i)   the weekly wage earned when the machinist made 34 skirts;
      (ii)   the smallest number of skirts to be made in one week to earn more than £95;
      (iii)   the fixed sum of money paid each week.

In the first week at work, a machinist made 30 skirts. During the next week the machinist's output increased by 20%.

(c)   Find:
      (i)   the number of skirts made in the second week;
      (ii)   how much more the machinist earned in the second week than in the first week.   (LEAG)

186.   The graph enables you to convert petrol consumption in miles per gallon to kilometres per litre.

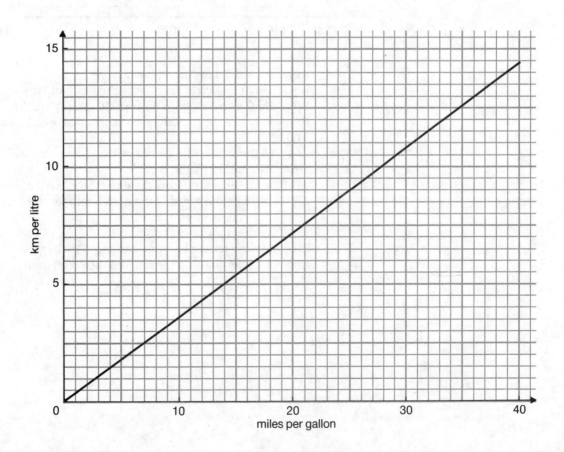

(a) At a steady speed of 40 miles per hour, a British car travels 35 miles per gallon of petrol.
  (i) Express the petrol consumption in kilometres per litre.
  (ii) How much petrol, in gallons, will this car use if it is driven at 40 miles per hour for 2½ hours?

(b) A foreign car, driven at 80 kilometres per hour, has a petrol consumption of 12 kilometres per litre. Express this petrol consumption in miles per gallon.

(c) Can this graph be used to compare the economy of the two cars?

GRADE B

187. An electric train sets off at 10.00 a.m. from Axeter travelling towards Besley. A diesel train sets off from Camford travelling towards Besley. The graph shows the distance of each train from Axeter.

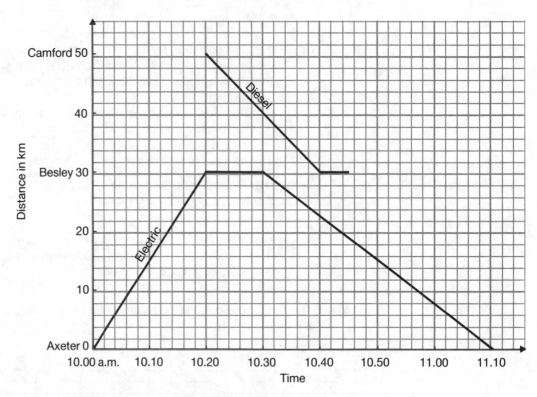

(a) At what time did the diesel start?

(b) How many kilometres apart were the trains at 10.30?

(c) What did the electric train do at (i) 10.20; (ii) 10.30?

(d) How many kilometres did the electric train travel between 10.30 and 11.10?

(e) At 10.45 the diesel train continued its journey towards Axeter and arrived 30 minutes later.
  (i) On the diagram, draw the line for this part of the journey.
  (ii) Calculate the speed of the diesel train for this part of the journey. Give your answer in km/h.

(f) (i) Did the trains meet at Besley?
  (ii) Give the reason for your answer to (f)(i).

(g) How long after the electric train did the diesel train arrive at Axeter?

(SEG)

2 Algebraic graphs and curved graphs

For a straight line $y = mx + c$.

m is the gradient, c is where the line crosses the y-axis.

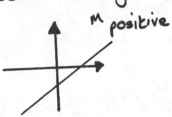

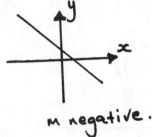

If the equation is given in any other way it must be rearranged.

(i) $3y = 2x + 6$ becomes $y = \frac{2}{3}x + 2$.

(ii) $y + 2x = 5$ becomes $y = -2x + 5$.

Curve lines worth knowing.

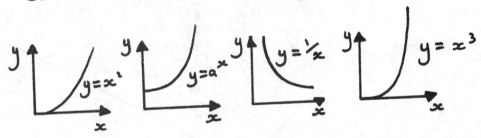

lines $x = 3$, $x = -1$, etc. are parallel to the y-axis.

lines $y = 4$, $y = -2$, etc. are parallel to the x-axis.

To plot $4x + 6y = 30$, let $x = 0$ so $0 + 6y = 30$ $y = 5$. This gives the point $(0,5)$. Now let $y = 0$, so $4x + 0 = 30$, $x = 7\frac{1}{2}$ giving the point $(7\frac{1}{2}, 0)$. The line can now be drawn.

Topic: $y = mx + c$

GRADE B

WORKED EXAMPLE 98 For each of the following equations, find the gradient of the line, and where the line cuts the y-axis. Draw a sketch to show the positions of each line.

(i) $y = 3x + 2$; (ii) $y + 5x = 7$; (iii) $2y + x = 4$.

SOLUTION   All of these involve $y = mx + c$.

(i) $m = 3$, the gradient is 3.
  $c = 2$, the line crosses the y-axis at 2.

(ii) $y + 5x = 7$, so $y = -5x + 7$.
  $m = -5$, the gradient is -5.
  $c = 7$, the line crosses the y-axis at 7.

(iii) $2y + x = 4$, so $2y = -x + 4$
  $y = -\frac{1}{2}x + 2$.
  $m = -\frac{1}{2}$, the gradient is $-\frac{1}{2}$.
  $c = 2$, the line crosses the y-axis at 2.

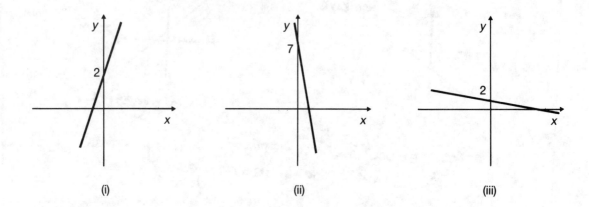

(i)   (ii)   (iii)

Topics: coordinates, straight lines

WORKED EXAMPLE 99   The diagram shows two lines labelled l and m.

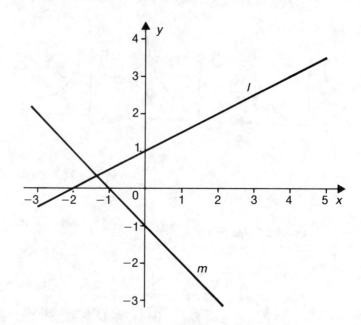

(i)   Write down the equation of l.

(ii)   If the line l was extended to $x = 10$, what would be the value of y on the line at this point?

(iii)   Write down the equation of line m.

(iv)   What is the equation of the reflection of m in the x-axis?

SOLUTION   (i)   The gradient of the line is $\frac{1}{2}$. The intercept on the y-axis is 1.
  So $y = \frac{1}{2}x + 1$.

(ii)   Since $x = 10$, $y = \frac{1}{2} \times 10 + 1 = 6$.

(iii)   The gradient of this line is -1. The intercept on the y-axis is -1.
  So $y = -x - 1$.

(iv)   If m is reflected in the x-axis it passes through $(-1,0)$ and $(0,1)$,
  its equation is $y = x + 1$.

Topic: equation of a straight line

WORKED EXAMPLE 100 On graph paper, plot the lines $x = 2$, $y = -1$ and $4y - 3x = 12$. Use values of x from -6 to 3 and values of y from -2 to 5. Write down the coordinates of the vertices of the triangle formed by these lines. How many points *inside* the triangle have coordinates that are whole numbers?

SOLUTION For the equation $4y - 3x = 12$.
If $x = 0$ $4y - 0 = 12$, so $y = 3$. This gives the point $(0,3)$.
For $y = 0$ $0 - 3x = 12$, so $x = -4$. This gives the point $(-4,0)$.
The lines can now be drawn as shown in the diagram.
The vertices of the triangle are $(2,4\frac{1}{2})$, $(2,-1)$ and $(-5\frac{1}{3},-1)$.
The points with integer coordinates are marked with crosses.
There are 13 points.

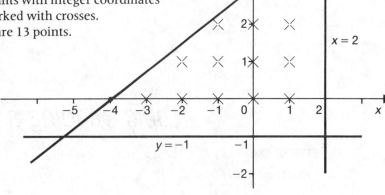

Topic: plotting curved lines

WORKED EXAMPLE 101 Complete the table below, for the equation $y = 2x^2 - 3x + 1$.
Draw the graph of this equation.

x	-3	-2	-1	0	$\frac{1}{2}$	1	2	3
y		15				0		

Use your graph to find:

(i) y when $x = 1.5$;
(ii) x when $y = 8$;
(iii) the smallest value of y.

SOLUTION It is safer with this type of problem to expand the table.

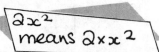

$2x^2$ means $2 \times x^2$

x	-3	-2	-1	0	$\frac{1}{2}$	1	2	3
x^2	9	4	1	0	$\frac{1}{4}$	1	4	9
$2x^2$	18	8	2	0	$\frac{1}{2}$	2	8	18
$-3x$	9	6	3	0	$-1\frac{1}{2}$	-3	-6	-9
$+1$	$+1$	$+1$	$+1$	$+1$	$+1$	$+1$	$+1$	$+1$
y	28	15	6	1	0	0	3	10

(a)   Clearly the scale on the y-axis cannot be the same as the scale on the x-axis.

(b)   You must not join AB with a straight line, the curve goes just below the x-axis.

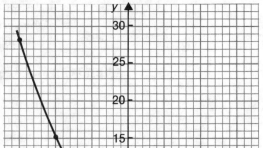
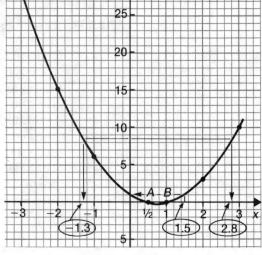

(i) $x = 1.5$ gives $y = 1$.

(ii) $y = 8$ has two values of x: $x = 2.8, -1.3$.

(ii)   Difficult to see, but estimate $y = -0.2$.

Topic: reading a curved graph

WORKED EXAMPLE 102   The diagram shows a graph of the relation $y = x^2$ for values of x from $x = 0$ to $x = 6$.

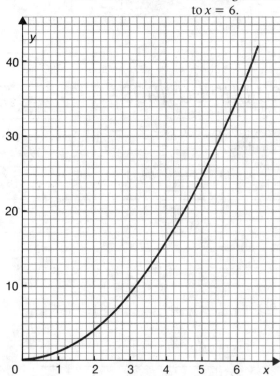

(a)   Use the graph to find an approximate value for $(3.6)^2$.

(b)   Use the graph to find an approximate value for $\sqrt{28}$.

(c)   Use the graph to find an approximate value for $\sqrt{600}$.

SOLUTION   (a)   This means $x = 3.6$.
The sketch shows how this is done, $y = 13$, so $(3.6)^2 = 13$.

(b)   Since $y = x^2$, $x = \sqrt{y}$.
So $y = 28$, this gives $x = 5.2$.
Hence $\sqrt{28} = 5.2$.

(c)   600 is not on the y-axis,
but $600 = 6 \times 100$, so $\sqrt{600} = \sqrt{6} \times \sqrt{100}$
$= 10 \times \sqrt{6}$.
$\sqrt{6} = 2.4$ from the graph.
Hence $\sqrt{600} = 10 \times 2.4 = 24$.

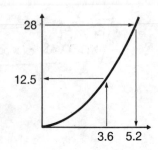

Questions to try

188. Referring to the diagram alongside,

(i) What are the coordinates of A?

(ii) The *x*-axis is a line of symmetry of triangle *OAB*. What is the name we give to this type of triangle?

(iii) What are the coordinates of *B*?

(iv) What is the equation of the straight line which passes through *O* and *B*?

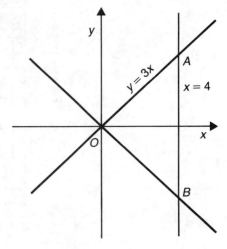

189. Midland Motors hire out lorries at a basic charge of £60, plus a further charge of 60p per km travelled.

(a) If £*C* is the total hire charge when the lorry travels *x*km, copy and complete the following table of values:

x(km)	0	50	100	150	200	250	300
C(£)	60		120	150			240

(b) Using a scale of 2 cm to represent 50 units on the *x*-axis and 2 cm to represent 20 units on the *C*-axis, draw a graph to show how *C* varies with *x*.

(c) Use your graph to find the distance travelled by a lorry for which the hire charge was £192.

(d) Write down a formula for *C* in terms of *x*.

190. Corresponding shoe sizes in Britain and Europe are shown in the table below.

British shoe size (x)	4	7	10
European shoe size (y)	37	41	45

(a) On the axes below, plot points to represent this information and connect them with a straight line.

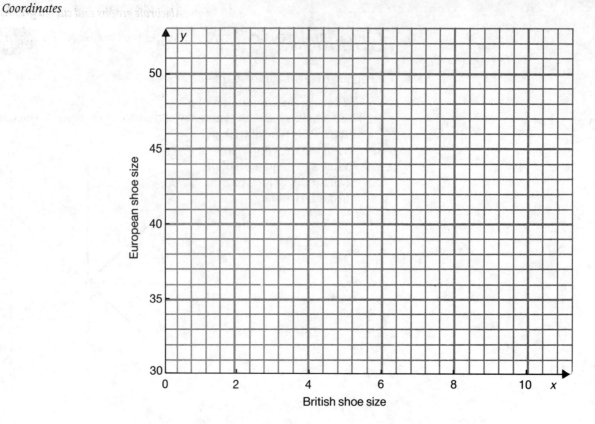

(b) Read off the graph, correct to the nearest whole number,
   (i)   the European size corresponding to British size 8;
   (ii) the British size corresponding to European size 34.
(c) What is the gradient of the line?
(d) Find the equation of the line in the form $y = mx + c$.   (MEG)

191. Match these equations to the graphs shown below:

$$y = 3x; \quad y = 3^x; \quad y = \frac{3}{x}.$$

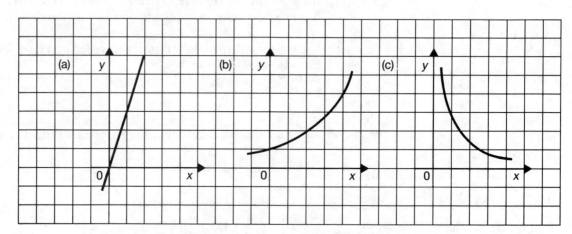

192. A container has a capacity of 2 litres. Water is poured into the container at a rate of 125 ml per second.

(a) How many seconds will it take to fill the container?

(b) The container has a height of 18 cm.

On the axes below, sketch graphs to show how the depth of water increases with time

(i) when the container is cylindrical (label the graph I),

(ii) when the container is an inverted cone (label the graph II).

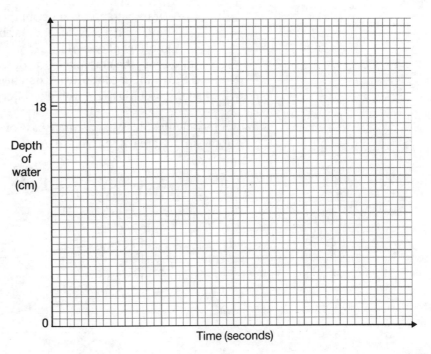

18

Depth
of
water
(cm)

0

Time (seconds)

(MEG)

193. (a) A rectangular water tank with a capacity of 62.5 m³ has a square base of side 5 m.
Find the depth of water in the tank when it is full.

(b) A firm manufactures a range of rectangular water tanks of height 4 m with square bases. The volume, V m³, of a tank with a square base of side x metres is given by the formula $V = 4x^2$.

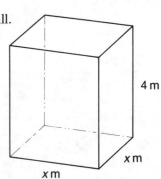

4 m

Not to scale

x m

x m

(i)   Copy and complete the following table to calculate the values of V for the given values of x.

x	0	1	2	3	3.5
V				36	

(ii)   Using a horizontal scale of 2 cm to represent 0.5 m and a vertical scale of 2 cm to represent 5 m^3, plot these values and draw a smooth curve through your points.

(iii)   Use your graph to estimate:
   (a)   the volume, in m^3, of a tank with a square base of side 1.5 m;
   (b)   the length of the side of the base of a tank of volume 25 m^3.

(MEG)

194.   The number of bacteria in a colony doubles every 30 minutes.

(a)   Complete the table to show the number of bacteria for the first four hours. The colony starts with 25 bacteria.

Time (hours)	0	$\frac{1}{2}$	1	$1\frac{1}{2}$	2	$2\frac{1}{2}$	3	$3\frac{1}{2}$	4
Number of bacteria	25	50							

(b)   (i)   Draw a graph to represent these figures, joining the points with a smooth curve. (You should choose a suitable scale for the number of bacteria.)
   (ii)   From the graph, find the time when there will be 2500 bacteria.
(c)   If the number continued to double every 30 minutes, *calculate* how many bacteria there would be after 10 hours.   (MEG)

195.   A rectangular block has a square base of side x cm and a height of h cm. The total surface area of the block is 72 cm^2.

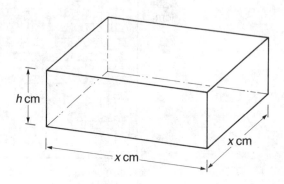

(a)   Express h in terms of x.
(b)   Show that the volume, V cm^3, of the block is given by $V = 18x - \frac{1}{2}x^3$.
(c)   Copy and complete the following table to show corresponding values of x and V.

x	0	1	2	3	4	5	6
V	0			40.5	40		0

(d)   Using a scale of 2 cm to represent 1 unit on the x-axis and 2 cm to represent 10 units on the V-axis, draw the graph of $V = 18x - \frac{1}{2}x^3$ for values of x from 0 to 6 inclusive.
(e)   A block of this type has a volume of 30 cm^3. Given that $h > x$, find the dimensions of the block.

(MEG)

196.

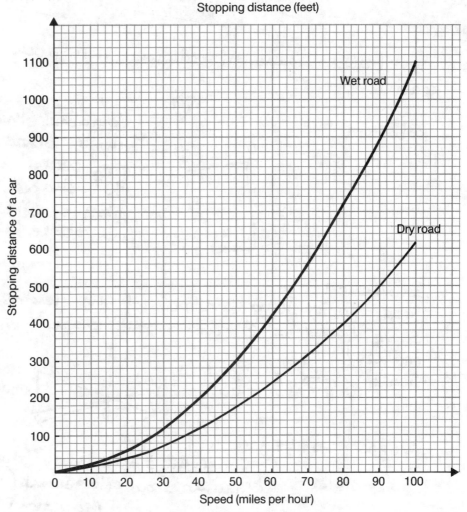

The graph shows the stopping distance, in feet, of a car travelling at various speeds on both a wet road and a dry road. From the graph, find:

(a) the stopping distance on a dry road at 60 miles per hour;
(b) the maximum safe speed 100 feet before a zebra crossing on a wet road;
(c) the difference between the stopping distances of a car travelling at 70 miles per hour on a wet road and 70 miles per hour on a dry road.

(LEAG)

3 Transformations and three dimensions

The main transformations are reflection: you must give the mirror line; rotation: you must give the centre of rotation and the angle (clockwise or anticlockwise); translation: is a slide in a straight line best represented by a vector $\binom{a}{b}$.

Use tracing paper if allowed, it is much easier.

Rotation:

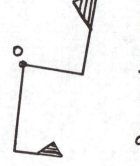

Imagine the shape joined to the centre by a 90° shaped piece of wire, and rotate this.

Enlargement:
Scale factor is a multiple of the lengths.
Scale factor = ½ means the shape is reduced.
Scale factor = -2

object   image

WORDS TO LEARN
Congruent = the same shape.
Similar = an enlargement (or reduction)

Three dimensions (solid as opposed to flat)
The ideas encountered in two dimensions (xy plane) can be extended to three dimensions, using coordinates (x, y, z) See worked example 105

Topics: coordinates, transformations

WORKED EXAMPLE 103   Describe fully the simple transformation that maps *ABCDE* to ◀ **GRADE E**

(i) $A'B'C'D'E'$;

(ii) $A''B''C''D''E''$;

(iii) $A'''B'''C'''D'''E'''$.

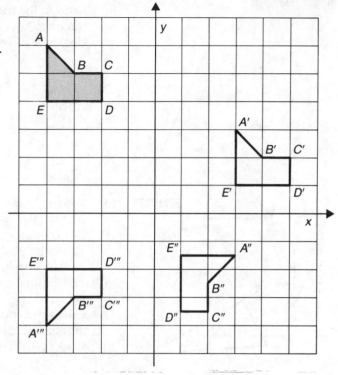

SOLUTION   (i) $ABCDE \rightarrow A'B'C'D'E'$ by sliding in a straight line (translation). It can be

expressed using vectors as 7 'along' and 3 'down', i.e. $\begin{pmatrix} 7 \\ -3 \end{pmatrix}$

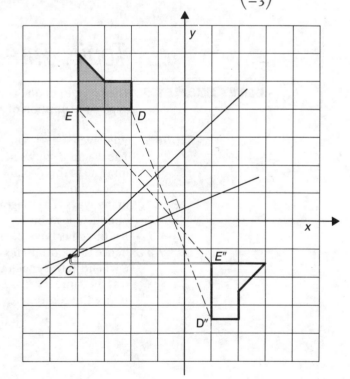

(ii) $ABCDE \rightarrow A''B''C''D''E''$ certainly by a rotation of 90° clockwise. The
problem is finding the centre.
Join EE'' and bisect.
Join DD'' and bisect.
The bisectors meet at C $(-4\frac{1}{2}, -1\frac{1}{2})$.
The centre of rotation is $(-4\frac{1}{2}, -1\frac{1}{2})$.

(iii) $ABCDE \rightarrow A'''B'''C'''D'''E'''$ by a reflection in a line parallel to the *x*-axis.
It must be half-way between ED and $E'''D'''$, i.e. $y = 1$.

Very often tracing paper can be helpful.

Topic: transformations

WORKED EXAMPLE 104
(i) Describe the transformation that maps triangle *T* on to triangle *Q*.
(ii) Draw in the triangle *R* obtained by rotating *T* by 120° about *O* in a clockwise direction.

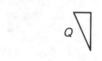

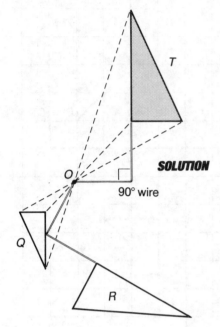

SOLUTION
(i) You might not easily spot that this part is a reduction.
Draw in the dotted lines as shown (joining corresponding points).
$T \to Q$ by an enlargement scale factor $-\frac{1}{2}$, centre *O*.
The negative sign indicates that the centre is between the object (*T*) and the image (*Q*).

(ii) 120° is not a nice angle. If you are allowed, it is better to use tracing paper.
Otherwise, join the shape *T* to the centre of rotation by an imaginary 90° shaped wire. Then rotate the wire by 120°. The shape remains stuck on the end of the wire, and its position is located.

GRADE C/D

Topic: Three dimensional coordinates

WORKED EXAMPLE 105
The position of one vertex A of a cube is (3, 1, 0). If the length of the side is 3, give the position of any two other vertices.

SOLUTION
We have $x = 3, y = 1, z = 0$.
The diagram shows that the point must lie in the *xy* plane. The cube can of course be drawn in many ways. The diagram shows one such position.
B is directly above *A*, and $AB = 3$, hence the coordinates of *B* are (3,1,3)
C will lie in the *yz* plane, with *C* at the same level as *B*.
Hence the coordinates of *C* are (0,4,3).

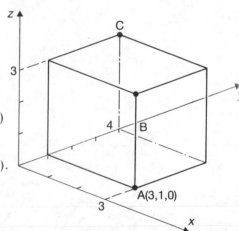

Questions to try

197.

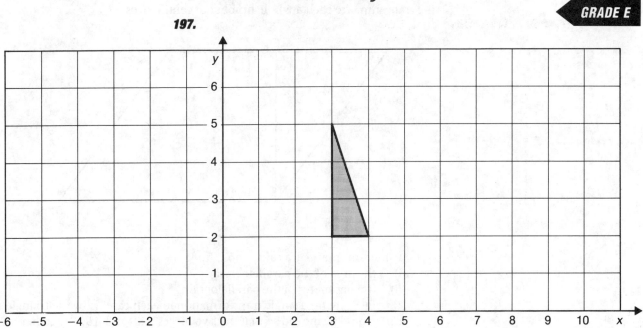

Triangle T has vertices (3,2), (4,2), 3,5), as shown in the diagram.

Triangle T is translated using the vector $\begin{pmatrix} 3 \\ 2 \end{pmatrix}$ to triangle T_1.

(a)   Show T_1 on the diagram.

Triangle T_1 is reflected in the line $x = 3$ to triangle T_2.

(b) Show T_2 on the diagram.

Triangle T_2 is reflected in the line $x = 0$ to triangle T_3.

(c)   Show T_3 on the diagram.

(d)   What is the vector of the translation that will take triangle T_3 to triangle T?

198.   (i)   Draw the position of T after reflection in m. Label it T_1.

       (ii)   Draw the position of T after an enlargement scale factor 2, centre A. Label it T_2.

       (iii)   Draw the position of T after an anticlockwise rotation of 90° about B.

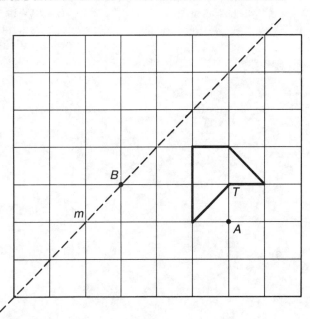

199. The diagram shows a parallelogram *ABCD* which is made up of a right-angled triangle *AED* and a trapezium *ABCE*. The sides of the triangle and of the trapezium are each a whole number of centimetres.

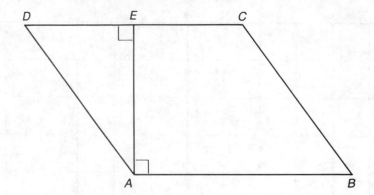

(a) By measurement and calculation, find:
   (i)   the area of the parallelogram;
   (ii) the perimeter of the parallelogram.
(b) Describe fully (as a single transformation in each case) how the triangle *AED* should be moved so that the two pieces *AED* and *ABCE* together form:
   (i)   a rectangle;
   (ii) a right-angled triangle.
(c) Find the perimeter of:
   (i)   the rectangle formed in part (b)(i);
   (ii) the right-angled triangle formed in part (b)(ii).

GRADE C/D

200. Four of the vertices of a cuboid are at the points (1,0,0), (4,0,0), (1,5,0) and (1,0,2). Write down the coordinates of the other four vertices of this cuboid.
(MEG)

201. (a) The distance between the point *P*(3,4,0) and the point *Q*(3,4,12) is 12 units.
   (i)   Write down the coordinates of three other points which are 12 units from *Q*.
   (ii) Describe fully the geometrical figure formed by the set of points which are 12 units from *Q*.
(b) (i) Calculate the length of the line from the origin *O*(0,0,0) to the point *Q*(3,4,12).
   (ii) Write down the coordinates of the point *R* on the positive *z*-axis such that *RQ* = *OQ*.
   (iii) Calculate the size of angle *OQR*.
(MEG)

STATISTICS
ATTAINMENT TARGET 5

1 Probability

PROBABILITY is written as a fraction. The probability is _zero_ if something is impossible, and _one_ if it is certain.

Always find how many outcomes N are possible. If the number of favourable outcomes is x, then the probability $= \frac{x}{N}$.

The probability that something doesn't happen, is 1 − the probability it does happen.

If more than one event is happening, then a tree diagram is the best way to represent the problem.

For example a coin is spun and a die is rolled can be represented by 2 trees:

The probabilities are marked on the 'branches' of the trees.

As you travel along a path of the tree you multiply probabilities.

In fact if events are <u>independent</u>, then the probability of <u>A and B</u> is $P(A) \times P(B)$

If two events are <u>mutually exclusive</u>,

Then the probability of <u>A or B</u> is

$$P(A) + P(B)$$

Topics: probability, expectation   GRADE E

WORKED EXAMPLE 106   Two coins are spun and the result is written down after each go.

   (i)   Find the probability of obtaining two heads.
   (ii)   Find the probability of the coins showing different sides.
   (iii) If it is repeated 100 times, roughly how many times would you expect to see two tails?

SOLUTION   There are *four* outcomes:

(H) (H)   (H) (T)

(T) (H)   (T) (T)

   (i)   The probability of two heads $= \frac{1}{4}$.

   (ii)   The probability of being different $= \frac{2}{4} = \frac{1}{2}$.

   (iii) Since the probability of both tails is $\frac{1}{4}$, this means that $\frac{1}{4}$ of 100 will be both tails, i.e. 25 times.

Topics: probabilities, types of number

WORKED EXAMPLE 107   Toby is asked to think of a number between 15 and 30 inclusive. What is the probability that the number he thinks of is:

   (i)   divisible by 4;
   (ii)   a prime number;
   (iii) a multiple of 3 or 5?

SOLUTION   15–30 inclusive is *16* numbers listed as follows:
        15, 16, 17, 18, 19, 20, 21, 22, 23, 24, 25, 26, 27, 28, 29, 30.

   (i)   Divisible by 4 are
           16, 20, 24, 28, i.e. 4 numbers
        The probability $= \frac{4}{16} = \frac{1}{4}$.

   (ii)   The prime numbers are
           17, 19, 23, 29, i.e. 4 numbers.
        The probability $= \frac{4}{16} = \frac{1}{4}$.

   (iii) The multiples of 3 *or* 5 are
           15, 18, 20, 21, 24, 25, 27, 30, i.e. 8 numbers.
        The probability $= \frac{8}{16} = \frac{1}{2}$.

Note: you cannot use the addition of probabilities here, because multiples of 3 and multiples of 5 have numbers in common.

The multiples of 3 are 15, 18, 21, 24, 27, 30, i.e. 6 numbers.

$$\text{The probability} = \frac{6}{16} = \frac{3}{8}.$$

The multiples of 5 are 15, 20, 25, 30, i.e. 4 numbers.

$$\text{The probability} = \frac{4}{16} = \frac{1}{4}.$$

Hence $\frac{3}{8} + \frac{1}{4} = \frac{5}{8} \neq \frac{1}{2}$, i.e. it gives the *wrong* answer.

GRADE C/D

Topic: probability, mutually exclusive

WORKED EXAMPLE 108

Judy has a bag containing 8 red sweets, 6 blue sweets, 5 green sweets and 6 yellow sweets.

If she removes a sweet from the bag, what is the probability that it is:

(i) red; (ii) not green; (iii) either blue or yellow?

SOLUTION

The total number of sweets = 8 + 6 + 5 + 6 = 25.

(i) Probability of red $= \frac{8}{25}$.

(ii) EITHER Probability of green $= \frac{5}{25} = \frac{1}{5}$.

   So probability of not green $= 1 - \frac{1}{5} = \frac{4}{5}$.

   OR The number of non-green sweets $= 25 - 5 = 20$.

   The probability of not green $= \frac{20}{25} = \frac{4}{5}$.

(iii) EITHER The number of sweets that are blue or yellow is 6 + 6 = 12.

   The probability of either $= \frac{12}{25}$.

   OR Since blue sweets and yellow sweets have nothing in common

   Probability of blue $= \frac{6}{25}$.

   Probability of yellow $= \frac{6}{25}$.

   Probability of either $= \frac{6}{25} + \frac{6}{25} = \frac{12}{25}$.

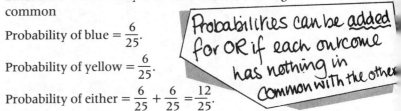

Probabilities can be added for OR if each outcome has nothing in common with the other

Topic: estimating probabilities

WORKED EXAMPLE 109

The drinks machine in the sixth form common room serves four types of drink. The sales during a morning break are given in the following table:

Drink	Coffee	Tea	Soup	Coke
Number sold	12	8	10	5

The probabilities here are all based on what happens in one break; they may not be typical This is why the question says estimate.

(a) Estimate the probability that the next drink sold will be:
   (i) coffee; (ii) not soup; (iii) hot.

(b) How many cokes do you think were sold in a week where the total number of drinks sold was 420?

SOLUTION

(a) The total number of drinks sold = 12 + 8 + 10 + 5 = 35.

(i) The probability of coffee $= \frac{12}{35}$.

(ii) The number of drinks that are not soup is $35 - 10 = 25$.

The probability of soup $= \frac{25}{35} = \frac{5}{7}$.

(iii) Assuming coffee, tea and soup are sold hot!
The number of hot drinks $= 12 + 8 + 10 = 30$.

The probability $= \frac{30}{35} = \frac{6}{7}$.

(b) The probability of a coke $= \frac{5}{35} = \frac{1}{7}$.

This means also that one seventh of the drinks are cokes.

$\frac{1}{7}$ of $420 = 420 \div 7 = 60$.

Hence 60 cokes were sold.

Topics: probability, tree diagrams, independent events

GRADE B

WORKED EXAMPLE 110   The Post Office have stated that approximately 90% of all first class letters are delivered the next day. Jason posts 2 letters on Tuesday. What is the probability that:

(i)   both letters are delivered on Wednesday;
(ii) neither letter is delivered on Wednesday;
(iii) at least one letter is delivered on Wednesday?

SOLUTION   This type of question is best answered by means of a tree diagram.

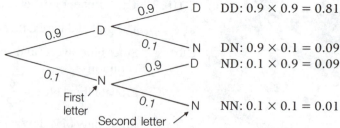

Note probabilities are multiplied as you travel along the branches.

(i)   Both letters delivered is DD, i.e. 0.81.
(ii) Neither letter delivered is NN, i.e. 0.01.
(iii) At least one letter delivered is DN or ND or DD,
i.e. $0.09 + 0.09 + 0.81 = 0.99$.
This can also be found by finding: $1 - \text{Prob (neither letter is delivered)}$
$= 1 - 0.01 = 0.99$.

Topic: probability, dependent events

GRADE A

WORKED EXAMPLE 111   A bag contains 6 red balls and 4 blue balls. Nadine removes two balls from the bag without replacing the first. What is the probability that (i) both balls are red; (ii) the balls are of different colours.

SOLUTION   Because the first ball is not replaced, there are only 9 balls left when the second is removed. The probabilities for the second ball are calculated out of 9. (They are dependent on the first draw.)

The tree is as follows:

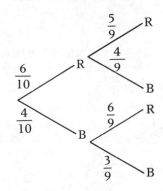

RR: $\dfrac{6}{10} \times \dfrac{5}{9} = \dfrac{30}{90} = \dfrac{1}{3}$

RB: $\dfrac{6}{10} \times \dfrac{4}{9} = \dfrac{24}{90} = \dfrac{8}{30}$

BR: $\dfrac{4}{10} \times \dfrac{6}{9} = \dfrac{24}{90} = \dfrac{8}{30}$

BB: $\dfrac{4}{10} \times \dfrac{3}{9} = \dfrac{12}{90} = \dfrac{4}{30}$

(i)   RR: the probability is $\dfrac{1}{3}$

(ii) RB or BR: the probability is $\dfrac{8}{30} + \dfrac{8}{30} = \dfrac{8}{15}$

Questions to try

GRADE G

202.   Christine was given a second-hand computer for her birthday. Unfortunately there were no instructions with it.

The leads A and B from the cassette player plugged into two of the sockets **P, Q** or **R**, but she did not know which.

List all the possible ways of plugging in A and B.

Two have already been done, AB–, A–B.

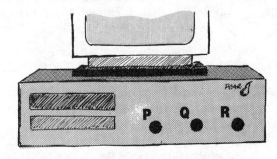

Socket		
P	Q	R
A	B	
A		B

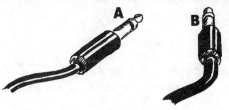

(MEG)

203. A coin is spun three times, and on each occasion it lands 'tails'. If the coin is spun once more, what is the probability that it lands tails again?

204. A die is biased (loaded) towards a 5 so that the probability of getting 5 is $\frac{1}{4}$. The probabilities of the other scores are all equal. If the die is rolled, what is the probability of:

(i)   not getting a 5;
(ii) getting a 3;
(iii) getting a 2 or a 5.

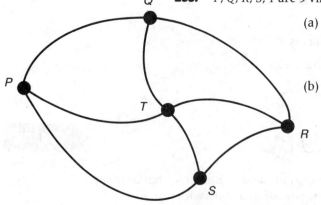

205. *P, Q, R, S, T* are 5 villages linked by country roads.

(a)   In how many ways can a person travel from *P* to *R* without going through any village more than once on each journey?
(List your routes: *PQR*, *PTQR*, etc.)

(b)   What is the probability that a random route from *P* to *R* would pass through *T*?

206. Matthew has 6 tapes, each of which can record 60 minutes of music. The amount of time already used on the 6 tapes is 30 minutes, 48 minutes, 20 minutes, 40 minutes, 25 minutes, 32 minutes. Matthew is in a hurry to record a programme which lasts for 25 minutes. If he picks a tape at random, what is the probability that there is enough space on the tape? What is the average time recorded on these 6 tapes?

207. In a game of darts, the probabilities of three players Ann, Brian and Chetan scoring a double are $\frac{1}{2}$, $\frac{3}{4}$ and $\frac{2}{5}$, respectively.
Each of the players throws one dart. Calculate the probability that:

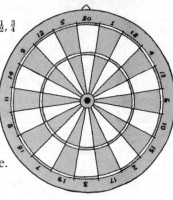

(a)   all three players will score a double;
(b)   only Ann will score a double;
(c)   only one of the three players will score a double.

(LEAG)

208. Mr Jones travels to work by car on five days each week. He has to cross three busy junctions. He finds that he is delayed by 2 minutes at the first junction three times a week. At the second junction there is a longer delay of 3 minutes, but only twice a week. Once a week, he is delayed for 4 minutes at the third junction. A delay at one junction does not affect a delay at any other junction.

(a)   Copy and complete the tree diagram, using D for delay and N for no delay in the Outcome column.

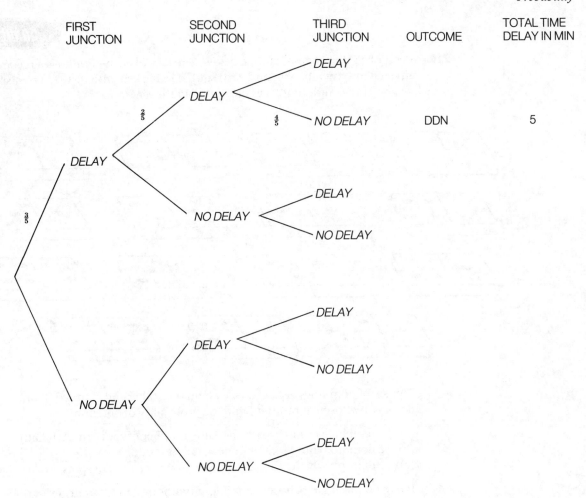

FIRST JUNCTION   SECOND JUNCTION   THIRD JUNCTION   OUTCOME   TOTAL TIME DELAY IN MIN

(b) Find the probability that, on any morning, he will arrive at work without being delayed.

(c) Find the probability that, on any morning, he will be delayed at only *one* of the three junctions.

Mr Jones leaves for work at 8.30 a.m. each day. The journey takes him 25 minutes when he has no delays. He is due into work at 9.00 a.m.

(d) Find the probability that, on any morning, he will be late for work.

(LEAG)

209. Said and Nathan work at the local newsagent. The probability that Said arrives late for work is $\frac{1}{6}$, and the probability that Nathan arrives late for work is $\frac{1}{5}$. Assuming that each travels to work independently, calculate the probabilities that on any day:

(i) Nathan arrives on time;

(ii) both arrive on time;

(iii) at least one of them is late.

GRADE A

210. A set of 15 dominoes is shown below. The face of each domino is a rectangle divided into two squares and each square is marked with 0, 1, 2, 3 or 4 spots to give the 15 different faces illustrated in the diagram.

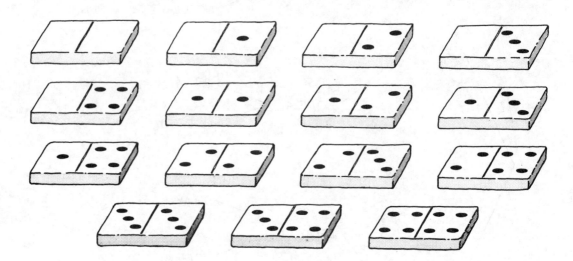

This set of dominoes is placed face down on a table and shuffled. If one domino is chosen at random, find the probability of obtaining:

(a) a double (a domino with the same number of spots on each half);
(b) a domino whose total number of spots is odd;
(c) a domino which either is a double or whose total of spots is odd.

If two dominoes are chosen at random (without replacement) from the complete set, find the probability of obtaining:

(d) two doubles;
(e) only one double;
(f) two dominoes which together have a total of 3 spots.

If three dominoes are chosen at random (without replacement) from the complete set, find the probability of obtaining at least one double.

(NISEC)

2 Averages

The main averages used are the mean (usually called the average):
Total of values ÷ no of values;
the mode: the value that occurs most often;
the median: the middle value by position if arranged in order of size.

The range is sometimes used. This is the difference between the largest and the smallest value.

Careful with the median:

2, 5, 8, 11, 12   3, 4, 5, 8, 12, 15,

median ↑ is 8   median is ↑ $\dfrac{5+8}{2}$ = 6.5

The median is least affected by extreme values. Useful in shoe sizes.
The average is badly affected by extreme cases, dangerous if quoting average salaries.
The mode is often useful because it gives the most common value.

Frequency table

value x	a	b	c	d
frequency	p	q	r	s

To find mean. $\dfrac{p \times a + q \times b + r \times c + s \times d}{p + q + r + s}$

often forgotten

Topics: mean, range

GRADE G

WORKED EXAMPLE 112

Jasmin and Julie were comparing the marks they had been given for French homework. They wrote the results down in a table as follows:

Jasmin	8	9	10	4	3	7	6	2	5	10
Julie	7	7	7	5	7	6	5	8	6	6

(i) Calculate the average mark for each girl.
(ii) State the range of each set of marks.
(iii) Can you comment on which girl was better at French?

SOLUTION

(i) The total of Jasmin's marks = 64.
Her average = 64 ÷ 10 = 6.4.
The average for Julie is 64 ÷ 10 = 6.4.

(ii) The range of Jasmin's marks = 10 − 2 = 8 marks.
The range of Julie's marks = 8 − 5 = 3 marks.

(iii) Although the average marks are the same, Julie's work is much more consistent; however, Jasmin has scored one or two very high marks, which means that Jasmin may be better than Julie, but the evidence is not conclusive.

Topics: mean, median, mode

WORKED EXAMPLE 113   Six people were asked to guess the length in cm of a piece of wood. Their answers are shown in the following table:

Person	1	2	3	4	5	6
Guess	80	82	78	71	73	78

For these guesses, find; (i) the mode; (ii) the mean; (iii) the median.

SOLUTION   (i) The mode is 78 cm.

(ii) $\dfrac{80 + 82 + 78 + 71 + 73 + 78}{6} = \dfrac{462}{6} = 77.$

The mean is 77 cm.

(iii) Arranging in order of size

$$71 \qquad 73 \qquad 78 \qquad 78 \qquad 80 \qquad 82$$

middle

Because the middle is between 78 and 78, the median is the average of 78 and 78, which is of course 78.
The median = 78 cm.

Topic: frequency tables

WORKED EXAMPLE 114   Josie carried out a survey on her class to see how many nights each week they spent doing homework. The results are shown in the following table:

Number of evenings doing homework	0	1	2	3	4	5	6	7
Frequency	2	2	4	8	12	2	1	1

Find (i) the mode; (ii) the mean; (iii) the median of the data.

SOLUTION   (i) The mode is 4 evenings.

(ii) $\dfrac{2\times0 + 2\times1 + 4\times2 + 8\times3 + 12\times4 + 2\times5 + 1\times6 + 1\times7}{2 + 2 + 4 + 8 + 12 + 2 + 1 + 1}$

$= \dfrac{0 + 2 + 8 + 24 + 48 + 10 + 6 + 7}{32} = \dfrac{105}{32}$

$= 3.3$

The mean is 3.3 evenings.

(iii) Put 32 values in order gives

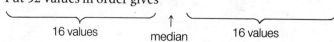

16 values   median   16 values

The median is the average of the 16th and 17th values. Counting the frequencies from the left of the table, 2 + 2 + 4 + 8 is 16.
Hence the 16th value is 3 evenings.
The 17th value must be 4 evenings.

Hence the median $= \dfrac{3 + 4}{2} = 3.5$.

The median is $3\frac{1}{2}$ evenings.

Topics: statistical averages, frequency tables, tally charts

WORKED EXAMPLE 115   The marks obtained out of 10 in a single multiple-choice test by 20 students were 8, 6, 5, 0, 1, 4, 3, 4, 6, 7, 6, 5, 5, 6, 3, 4, 7, 6, 9, 10. Calculate (i) the mean score; (ii) the median score; and (iii) the mode, by using a frequency table.

SOLUTION A tally is made of the number of 0s, 1s, 2s etc. in the following table. Note that 5 is 卌.

Score	Tally	Frequency	Score × Frequency
0	I	1	0
1	I	1	1
2		0	0
3	II	2	6
4	III	3	12
5	III*	3	15
6	卌*	5	30
7	II	2	14
8	I	1	8
9	I	1	9
10	I	1	10
	Total	20	105

A common mistake here is to divide by 10 or 11 because there are digits 0–10

(i) The mean is found by dividing the sum of (score × frequency) by the total number of students, which is 20.

Hence the mean $= \dfrac{105}{20} = 5.25$.

(ii) The median will be the average of the 10th and 11th numbers shown by * in the table.

Median $= \dfrac{5 + 6}{2} = 5.5$.

(iii) The mode is clearly 6.

Topic: averages from grouped frequencies

WORKED EXAMPLE 116 The heights of 30 children are represented in the following table:

Height (cm)	90–99	100–109	110–119	120–129	130–139	140–149
Frequency	2	5	7	10	5	1

Calculate the mean height.

SOLUTION
(1) You will find it easier to write the figures downwards.
(2) The middle value column is obtained from the average of the extremes of the group.
So $94.5 = (90 + 99) \div 2$.

Height (cm)	Frequency	Middle value	Frequency × middle value
90–99	2	94.5	189.0
100–109	5	104.5	522.5
110–119	7	114.5	801.5
120–129	10	124.5	1245.0
130–139	5	134.5	672.5
140–149	1	144.5	144.5
	Total 30		3575.0

The average height $= \dfrac{\text{sum of (frequency} \times \text{middle value)}}{\text{total number of children}}$

$= \dfrac{3575}{30} = 119.2 \, \text{cm}.$

Topic: averages

WORKED EXAMPLE 117   The average age of the pupils in Tim's class is 14 years. The average age of the pupils in Alan's class is 15 years. If there are 20 pupils in Tim's class, and 25 pupils in Alan's class, what is the average age of the pupils in the two classes?

SOLUTION   The total age of the pupils in Tim's class = 20 × 14 = 280 years.
The total age of the pupils in Alan's class = 25 × 15 = 375 years.
The total age of all the pupils = 280 + 375 = 655 years.
There are 45 pupils altogether, so the average age = 655 ÷ 45 = 14.56 years.
This should be written in years and months.
Now 0.56 years = 0.56 × 12 months = 7 (nearest whole number)
The average age is 14 years 7 months.

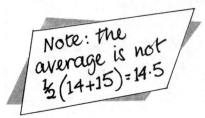

Note: the average is not ½(14+15)=14·5

Questions to try

GRADE C/D

211.   The statement "Average contents 48" is printed on a box of Bryan's matches.

The contents of 50 boxes are counted.

This is the distribution of the number of matches in each box.

Number of matches per box	Number of boxes
44	1
45	2
46	8
47	9
48	8
49	21
50	1

(a)   What is the range?
(b)   State (i) the mode,
      (ii) the median.
(c)   Calculate the mean.
(d)   Is the claim "Average contents 48" true?
      Give reasons for your answer.
(e)   What is the probability of buying a box of Bryan's matches with less than 48 matches in it?

(MEG)

212.   The table below shows the results when a square spinner was spun 100 times.

Score	Frequency
1	17
2	31
3	24
4	28

(a)   What is the mode of the 100 scores?
(b)   Calculate the mean of these scores.

(MEG)

213. A shop manager records the sales of blouses on a computer. The sales for a certain week are shown in the table.

Price (£)	12.99	13.99	14.99	15.99	16.99
Number sold	2	7	23	20	17

For all the blouses sold during the week,

(a) calculate the mean price;
(b) calculate the median price;
(c) calculate the modal price.

The manager records all of these averages. He later accidentally deletes the original sales figures. He wishes to calculate the total amount of money received for the blouses during that week.

(d) (i) Which of the three averages should he use?
    (ii) Give the reason for your answer.

(e) What other single piece of information must he also have in order to calculate the total amount of money received for blouses during that week?

214. At a public library, books can be borrowed for three weeks free of charge. For example, books borrowed on May 6 have to be returned by May 27. A fine has to be paid on any book kept for more than three weeks. The scale of fines is shown below.

Period overdue	Fine per book
1 to 7 days	10p
8 to 14 days	25p
15 to 21 days	40p
22 to 35 days	55p
36 to 42 days	70p
43 to 49 days	85p

(a) Mr Khan borrowed books from the library on May 6 and returned them on June 13.
    (i) How many days were the books overdue?
    (ii) Mr Khan borrowed four books. What fine did he have to pay?

(b) On one particular day, the fines collected at the library were as shown in the table below.

Fine	10p	25p	40p	55p	70p	85p
Number of books	70	45	15	10	3	2

(i) On how many books were fines paid?
(ii) Calculate the total of the fines paid on these books.
(iii) Calculate, to the nearest penny, the mean of the fines paid on these books.
(iv) On graph paper, draw a bar chart to represent the information in the table.

(MEG)

215. (In this question all the weights are given to the nearest gram.)
Bars of chocolate are made to a minimum weight of 250 g. Helen finds that the weights of 25 of these bars are:

```
251   255   252   250   255
251   254   253   253   252
250   255   250   256   253
250   254   254   250   252
252   253   250   252   254
```

(a)   Complete the frequency table for these weights.

Mass	Tally	Frequency
250		
251		
252		
253		
254		
255		
256		

(b)   Find the median weight.

Helen selects one of the 25 bars at random.

(c)   Find the probability that the bar she selects,
    (i)   will weigh 251 g;
    (ii)   will weigh more than the median weight.
                                  (LEAG)

216.   The average of 3 numbers is 14, the average of a different group of 7 numbers is 20. What is the average of all 10 numbers?

217.   The average height of 6 boys is 1.8 m and the average height of 9 girls is 1.5 m. What is the average height of all the children?

218.   What number must be added to the set {1,8,15,9,11,18,15} to increase the average from 11 to 13?

219.   Given that 9 is the average of 2, x, 10, 12 and 15, find x.

3 Statistical diagrams, sampling, correlation

There are 3 main types of diagram:

(i) BAR CHART;   (ii) PIE CHART   (iii) PICTOGRAM.

A bar chart is the most accurate if drawn on graph paper.
A pie chart is the most difficult to draw and read, but it gives a clear visual comparison of fractions or percentages.
A pictogram is often not very accurate but again it gives a good visual comparison, and can be read quickly.

When drawing a diagram, make sure it is clearly labelled. There may be marks awarded for the labelling.

Line graphs will be illustrated in unit 12. A Histogram is not a bar chart. See page 218

Sometimes a statistical diagram can be misleading because it has unequal scales on the horizontal and vertical axes. Always read a diagram's values, don't just look at what it looks like.

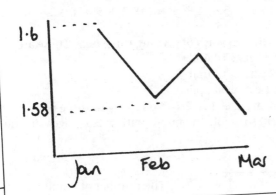

So a reading the £ falls dramatically for this is totally misleading.
It has only dropped from £1·60 to £1·58.

Words to learn

<u>Data</u> is collected by <u>sampling</u>, which may be by questionaire, or from a <u>data base</u>.

In a <u>random</u> sample every item must have an equal chance of being selected.

<u>Correlation</u> is measured using scatter diagrams

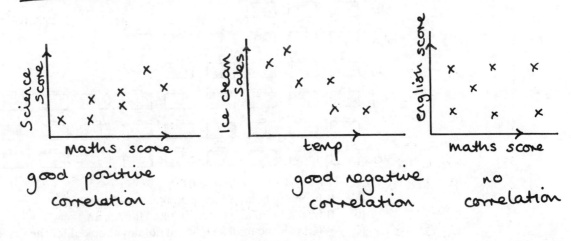

good positive correlation   good negative correlation   no correlation

Topic: reading a database

GRADE F

WORKED EXAMPLE 118   The table gives the results of a survey on how many cats and dogs the children in class 5X owned (e.g. 5 children owned 1 dog and 1 cat).

CATS

		0	1	2	3
	0	3	4	4	1
DOGS	1	2	5	1	2
	2	1	2	0	1

Use this information to find:

(i)   How many children there are in the class
(ii) How many children owned three pets
(iii) How many children owned at least two pets

SOLUTION   (i)   Assuming all the children are represented, each child can only be in one category
Hence the total $= 3 + 4 + 4 + 1 + 2 + 5 + 1 + 2 + 1 + 2 + 0 + 1$
$= 26$

(ii) There are different ways of owning three pets. These are:
0 dogs and 3 cats : 1 Pupil
1 dog and 2 cats : 1 Pupil
2 dogs and 1 cat : 2 Pupils
Hence there are $1 + 1 + 2 = 4$ pupils with three pets.

(iii) If we circle in the table the pupils with at least two pets the table is as follows:

	0	1	2	3
0	3	4	④	①
1	2	⑤	①	②
2	①	②	⓪	①

The number of pupils is:
$4 + 1 + 5 + 1 + 2 + 1 + 2 + 0 + 1$
$= 17$

Topic: interpreting data (pictogram)

WORKED EXAMPLE 119   The pictogram illustrates the numbers of holidays booked through a travel agency for each of the first 8 months of a year.

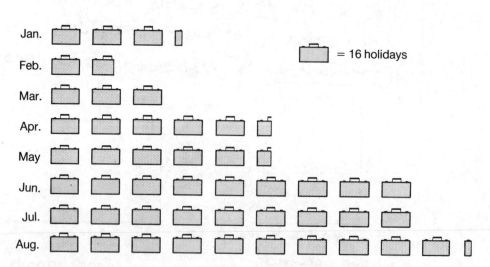

(a)   How many holidays were booked for March?
(b)   How many holidays were booked for April?
(c)   What was the total number of holidays booked for the first three months of the year?
(d)   122 holidays were booked for September. On squared paper draw the line of symbols that should be added to the diagram for September.

SOLUTION (a) $3 \times 16 = 48$.

(b) ▣ is 8 holidays (as near as you can guess).
The number of holidays = $5 \times 16 + 8 = 88$.

(c) There are 7 complete motifs = $7 \times 16 = 112$.
There is a '$\frac{3}{4}$', which gives 12.
There is a '$\frac{1}{4}$' which gives 4.
The total = $112 + 12 + 4 = 128$.

(d) $122 \div 16 = 7.625$. This is just over $7\frac{1}{2}$ cases, i.e.

Topic: interpreting data (pie chart) ◄ GRADE E

WORKED EXAMPLE 120   Trumpton police investigated the cause of 900 accidents within the county and displayed their findings in the form of a pie chart.

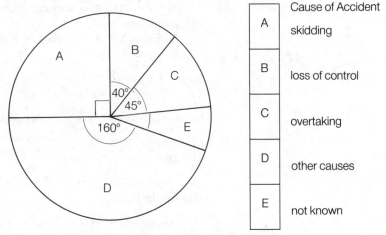

(i) How many accidents were due to loss of control?

(ii) In how many accidents was the cause unknown? (Comment on your answer.)

SOLUTION (i) Sector B is 40°.

As a fraction of the total, this is $\dfrac{40}{360}$

$= \dfrac{1}{9}$.

$\frac{1}{9}$ of 900 = $900 \div 9 = 100$ accidents.

(ii) Sector E has an unknown angle.
The angles must add up to 360°,
so angle E = $360° - (90° + 40° + 160° + 45°) = 25°$.

As a fraction of the total, this is $\dfrac{25}{360} = \dfrac{5}{72}$.

$\dfrac{5}{72} \times 900 = \dfrac{4500}{72} = 62.5$. Either 62 or 63 accidents.

The answer 62.5 suggests the pie chart is not completely accurate.

Topic: drawing statistical diagrams

WORKED EXAMPLE 121   A survey was carried out of the morning newspapers read by the inhabitants of Steyning. The results were as follows:

Daily Mail	270	*Sun*	340
Guardian	139	*Daily Express*	240
The Times	61	*Daily Mirror*	200
Daily Telegraph	150	*Morning Star*	40

Illustrate this information, using (a) a bar chart; (b) a pie chart; (c) a pictogram.

SOLUTION   (a)   A bar chart needs a clearly labelled vertical scale.

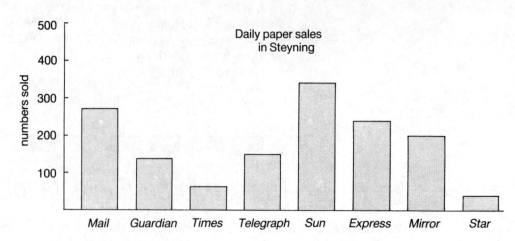

(b)   When constructing a pie chart, first of all calculate the total number being represented.

$$\text{Total} = 270 + 139 + 61 + 150 + 340 + 240 + 200 + 40$$
$$= 1440.$$

Method 1:
This is being represented by 360°,

hence each degree is $\dfrac{1440}{360} = 4$ people,

or each person is $\frac{1}{4}°$.
The angles are as follows:

$$Mail = 270 \times \tfrac{1}{4} = 67.5°,$$
and similarly,

$$Guardian = 34.75°, Times = 15.25°, Telegraph = 37.5°, Sun = 85°,$$
$$Express = 60°, Mirror = 50°, Star = 10°.$$

Method 2:
The angles can be found in a more routine method using the following formula:

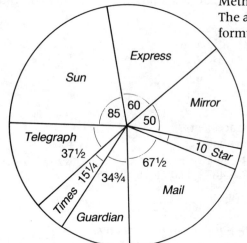

$$\text{angle for quantity } Q = \frac{\text{quantity } Q}{\text{total}} \times 360.$$

For example, that for the *Mirror* would be:

$$\text{angle for } Mirror = \frac{200}{1440} \times 360 = 50°.$$

The pie chart can now be drawn. If the angles are not drawn on the pie chart, this is a very difficult diagram to read.

(c)   When drawing a pictogram, first choose a motif to represent a certain unit. In this case, we will use ⚛ to represent 50 people.

The pictogram can now be drawn.

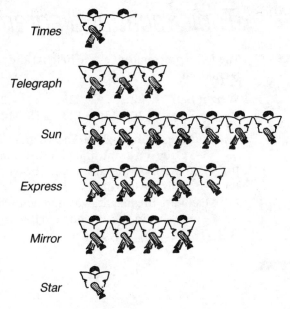

Times

Telegraph

Sun

Express

Mirror

Star

Accuracy again is limited, although it is better than the pie chart to read.

Topic: interpreting data (bar chart)

WORKED EXAMPLE 122 The diagram shows the number of goals scored in a season by the Vikings ladies' football team. From the diagram, find:

> **GRADE C/D**

(i) the number of matches played in the season;

(ii) the average number of goals scored per match;

(iii) the number of occasions the number of goals scored was greater than the median.

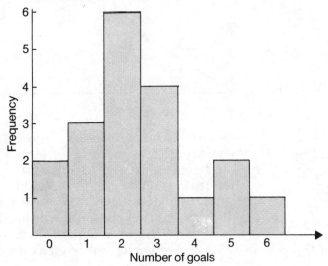

SOLUTION

(i) The sum of the frequencies = 2 + 3 + 6 + 4 + 1 + 2 + 1
$$= 19.$$
Hence 19 matches were played.

(ii) The average $= \dfrac{2 \times 0 + 3 \times 1 + 6 \times 2 + 4 \times 3 + 1 \times 4 + 2 \times 5 + 1 \times 6}{19}$

$$= \dfrac{0 + 3 + 12 + 12 + 4 + 10 + 6}{19}$$

$$= \dfrac{47}{19}$$

The average = 2.5 goals (1 decimal place).

(iii) There are 19 values, hence the median is the 10th value.
Adding the frequencies 2 + 3 + 6 = 11
Hence the median is 2 goals.
The number of times they scored more than twice = 4 + 1 + 2 + 1
$$= 8 \text{ occasions.}$$

Topic: scatter diagrams

WORKED EXAMPLE 123   The following table gives the heights and corresponding weights of
8 children

Weight (kg)	22	29	23	20	24	30	27	27
Height (cm)	120	130	123	118	128	134	132	125

(a)   On axes with height from 118cm to 140cm and weight from 20kg to
32kg, draw a graph and plot this data.

(b)   Comment on the correlation shown.

(c)   Draw in the line of best fit.

(d)   Estimate the height of a child whose weight is 26kg

(e)   Could the line be extended to find the height of a child of weight
(i) 32kg; (ii) 5kg. Give reasons.

SOLUTION   (a)

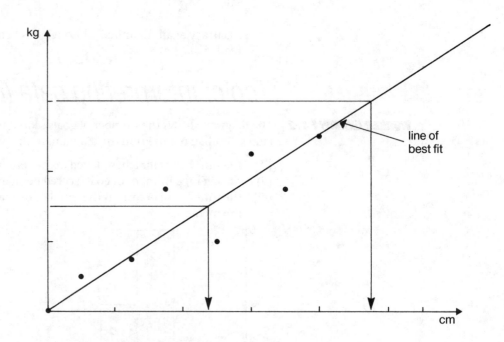

(b)   The data shows good positive correlation.

(c)   See diagram.

(d)   From the graph 127.5cm.

(e)   (i)   From the graph 137cm. Although it is just outside the given data,
the answer is probably a reasonable guess.

   (ii)   You must be very careful in extending a line of best fit. A weight
of 5kg means the child hasn't been born. Although the graph
would give an answer if extended, it clearly would have no
meaning.

Questions to try

220. The Governors of a school decided that they wanted to change the colour of the school uniform.
Two boys carried out a survey to find out which colour pupils would like.
They asked their friends and people in their classes.
A page from their notebook is shown below: (NEA)

Black	Red	Grey
Red	Grey	Green
Blue	Blue	Brown
Black	Green	Black
Blue	Red	Black
Green	Blue	
Red	Red	
Blue		

(a)   In the space below, show a better way of collecting the information.
(b)   When the boys had completed their survey, they realised that their results might not be very useful.
    (i)   Explain why this may be so.
    (ii)   Suggest a way in which they could improve their survey. (NEA)

221. The table shows the number of cars and the number of bicycles owned by a group of families (e.g. 5 families owned neither a bicycle nor a car).

		CARS			
		0	1	2	3
BICYCLES	0	5	2	1	0
	1	2	6	1	0
	2	0	0	1	1

Using the information from the table find

(i)   how many families owned two cars,

....

(ii)   how many families had at least one bicycle. (NEA)

222. A teacher thinks that the nearer her pupils sit to the front of the class, the higher their test results will be. The scatter diagrams show the results for her second and fourth year classes.

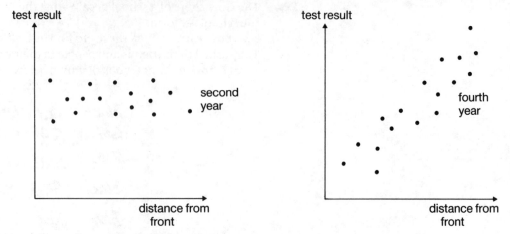

For each class, say whether the teacher's ideas are right or wrong. If she is wrong, describe what conclusions you could come to about that class.

Second year ....

Fourth year ....

(MEG)

223. A survey of 120 families was carried out. It was found that 76 had a video recorder, 37 had Prestel on their television but no video recorder, and the rest had neither. If this information is represented using a pie chart, what would be the angle for the sector representing Prestel users?

224. Rohan carried out a survey of 50 households in his district to find the number of occupants per house. The results are illustrated alongside.

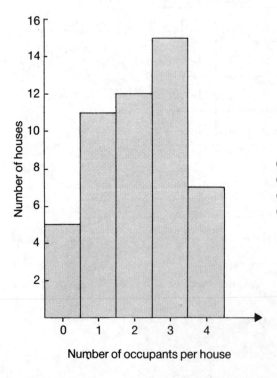

(i)   State the mode and median number of occupants per house.
(ii)   How many occupants in total live in the 50 houses surveyed?
(iii) Calculate the mean number of occupants per house.
(iv)   What is the probability that a house chosen at random from the houses surveyed will have at least one occupant?

225.   The pie chart represents the number of homes in a village that are heated by either coal, gas or electricity.

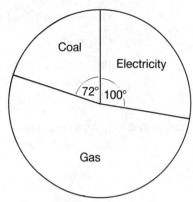

(a)   2000 homes are heated by electricity. Calculate the number of homes that are heated by (i) coal; (ii) gas.

(b)   What percentage of homes are heated by coal?   (WJEC)

226.   In the diagram, ▭ represents 20 Awayday rail tickets to London sold at Oakwood Station during a typical week.

Sun ▭

Mon ▭ ▭ ▭ ▭

Tue ▭ ▭

Wed ▭ ▭ ▭ ▭

Thu ▭ ▭ ▭ ▭ ▭ ▭ ▭

Fri ▭ ▭ ▭ ▭

Sat ▭ ▭ ▭ ▭ ▭ ▭ ▭ ▭ ▭ ▭

(a)   Calculate the total number of tickets sold during the week.

(b)   If the Awayday fare is £4.70 on Saturday and Sunday and £6.40 on all other days, calculate the total amount received by British Rail during the week for these tickets.

(c)   It is decided that the same fare will be charged on all days. What should that fare be if, with the same number of people travelling, British Rail wishes to receive the same total amount of money? (Give your answer to the nearest penny.)

(d)   Which day of the week do you think is early closing day in Oakwood? Give a reason for your answer.

227.

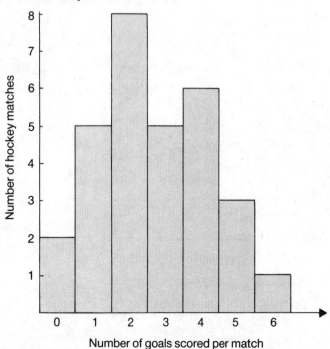

The bar chart shows the goals scored per match in league hockey matches on a certain Saturday.

(a)   Write down the number of matches in which 2 goals were scored.

Calculate:

(b)   the number of matches played;
(c)   the number of goals scored altogether;
(d)   the mean number of goals scored per match.   (WJEC)

228.   In 1986 the Khan family had a weekly income of £180. They spent the money as follows.

	Expenditure
Mortgage	£40
Fuel	£26
Food	£70
Clothing	£14
HP repayments	£12
Other expenses	£18

(a)   A pie chart is to be drawn to represent this information. Copy and complete the table below showing the angles required for this pie chart.

	Expenditure	Angle
Mortgage	£40	
Fuel	£26	52°
Food	£70	
Clothing	£14	
Credit repayments	£12	
Other expenses	£18	
Total	£180	

(b)   Represent the information on a pie chart of radius 6 cm, labelling each sector clearly.
(c)   In 1987 the family income rose to £192 per week.
   (i)   Calculate the percentage increase in the family income.
   (ii)   In 1987 the credit repayments remained at £12 per week. What angle would be needed to represent the repayments on a pie chart for 1987? (Do not draw the pie chart.)
   (iii) Between 1986 and 1987, the family spending on food increased in the ratio 9:8. How much did the family spend on food in 1987?
                                                                    (MEG)

229. The scatter diagram below represents the number of road deaths per 100 000 population (*y*) and the number of vehicles per 100 population (*x*) in ten countries.

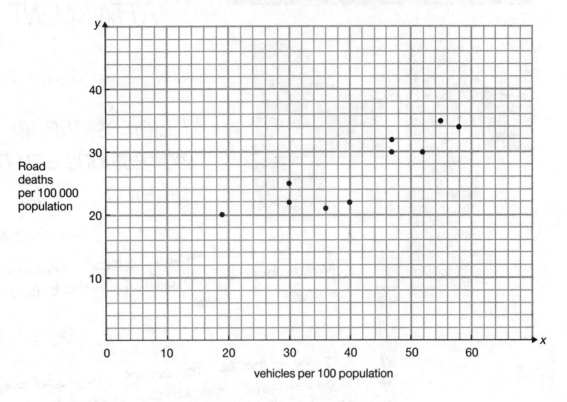

(a) On the diagram, draw the line of best fit.

(b) Find the equation of the line of best fit.   (MEG)

230. The marks obtained by 15 students in their Mathematics and Physics examinations are shown in the table below.

Spirit	A	B	C	D	E	F	G	H	I	J	K	L	M	N	O
Mathematics	36	50	17	53	42	38	66	30	60	48	26	45	74	15	44
Physics	49	68	34	64	55	56	80	46	73	63	39	61	88	30	58

(a) On graph paper, draw a scatter diagram to represent the marks obtained by these 15 students in Mathematics and Physics.

(b) On the scatter diagram, draw the line of best fit.

(c) Another student in the class, who was absent for the Mathematics examination, scored 52 marks in Physics. Estimate the mark this student might have obtained in Mathematics.

(d) Complete the following statement:

"The marks of these students in _____ are about _____ marks higher than their marks in _____ ."

(e) Considering the marks of the 15 students in Physics, which student's mark in Mathematics was rather surprising? Give a reason for your answer.   (MEG)

ALGEBRA 2
ATTAINMENT TARGET 3

1 Indices, further equations, expressions and number patterns

Learn the rules about indices on page 187. Remember, in particular, that a negative power means '1 over'.

$$2^{-3} = \frac{1}{2^3} = \frac{1}{8}.$$

If you have to solve a quadratic equation, don't waste too much time trying to factorise if you are not good at factorising but use the formula

$$x = \frac{-b \pm \sqrt{b^2 - 4ac}}{2a} \quad \text{instead}$$

They can also be solved by trial and improvement see worked example 12b.

When changing the subject of a formula do <u>not</u> take short cuts, follow the rules given on page 191.

If a question contains <u>two</u> unknowns, it will probably involve <u>simultaneous</u> equations. It may be possible to solve these using a graph, similar to earlier chapter.

Number patterns: but worth learning 1, 3, 6, 10, ... triangular numbers, the nth number is $\frac{n(n+1)}{2}$.

WORDS TO LEARN

factorise = put brackets into an expression

Simplify = collect together as many terms as possible.

USEFUL FACTS

The next few pages cover all the algebraic techniques you are likely to require.

Indices

(1) $a^m \times a^n = a^{m+n}$

(2) $a^m \div a^n = a^{m-n}$

(3) $(a^m)^n = a^{mn}$

(4) $a^{1/p} = \sqrt[p]{a}$

(5) $a^{q/p} = (\sqrt[p]{a})^q$ or $\sqrt[p]{a^q}$

(6) $a^0 = 1$

(7) $a^{-n} = \dfrac{1}{a^n}$

(8) $(ab)^n = a^n b^n$

GRADE C/D

GRADE A

WORKED EXAMPLE 124   Simplify the following:

(a) $(2^3)^2 \div 2^{-4}$; (b) $(49^{\frac{1}{4}})^{\frac{3}{2}}$; (c) $16^{-\frac{3}{4}}$; (d) $(a^2b)^3 \div 4ab^3$.

SOLUTION

(a) $\quad (2^3)^2 \div 2^{-4} = 2^6 \div 2^{-4}$ Rule 3
$\qquad\qquad\qquad\quad = 2^{10}.$ Rule 2

(b) $\quad (49^{\frac{1}{4}})^{\frac{3}{2}} \qquad = 49^{\frac{1}{2}}$ Rule 3
$\qquad\qquad\qquad\quad = 7.$ Rule 4

(c) $\quad 16^{-\frac{3}{4}} \qquad = \dfrac{1}{16^{\frac{3}{4}}}$ Rule 7

$\qquad\qquad\qquad = \dfrac{1}{(16^{\frac{1}{4}})^3}$ Rule 5

$\qquad\qquad\qquad = \dfrac{1}{2^3}$ Rule 4

$\qquad\qquad\qquad = \dfrac{1}{8}.$

(d) $\quad (a^2b)^3 \div 4ab^3 = a^6b^3 \div 4ab^3$ Rule 8

$\qquad\qquad\qquad\quad = \dfrac{a^6b^3}{4ab^3} \quad = \dfrac{a^5b^0}{4}$ Rule 2

$\qquad\qquad\qquad\quad = \dfrac{a^5}{4}.$ Rule 6

A useful trick when working with indices is always to get rid of negative powers first if possible.

Brackets

Reminder. Brackets can be removed in the following way:

(a) $\quad 4x(a + x) + 3a(x + a)$
$\quad = 4xa + 4x^2 + 3ax + 3a^2$
$\quad = 4x^2 + 7ax + 3a^2.$
(*Note:* $4xa$ and $3ax$ are *like* terms.)

(b) $\quad 2y(x - y) - 3x(y - x)$

> *Subtraction of a negative quantity is the same as addition*

$\quad = 2yx - 2y^2 - 3xy \oplus 3x^2 = 3x^2 - xy - 2y^2.$

(c) $\quad (2x - 1)(3x + 1)$
$\quad = (2x \times 3x) + (2x \times 1) - (1 \times 3x) - (1 \times 1)$
$\quad = 6x^2 + 2x - 3x - 1 = 6x^2 - x - 1.$

Factors

The reverse process of putting brackets back into an algebraic expression is called *factorising*.

(A) TWO TERMS   Look for the *highest* factor that can be taken out.

GRADE B

(i) $\quad 8x + 16y = 8(x + 2y).$
(ii) $\quad 4p^2 + 8pq = 4p(p + 2q).$

> $p(4p + 8p)$ is correct but not completely factorised

(B) FOUR TERMS

Note:
this is negative
because
$-b \times -3 = +3b$

(i) $6a + 12 + 4ab + 8b$
$= 6(a + 2) + 4b(a + 2)$
$= (6 + 4b)(a + 2)$
$= 2(3 + 2b)(a + 2).$

(ii) $a^2 - 3a - ab + 3b$
$= a(a - 3) - b(a - 3)$
$= (a - b)(a - 3).$

GRADE A

(C) THREE TERMS (QUADRATIC)

It is shown on page 187 that
$(2x - 1)(3x + 1) = 6x^2 - x - 1;$
the expression $6x^2 - x - 1$ is called a *quadratic* expression.
The process of factorising a quadratic is not easy and will be considered in stages.

(i) $x^2 + 5x + 6 = x^2 + 2x + 3x + 6$
$= x(x + 2) + 3(x + 2)$
$= (x + 3)(x + 2).$

(ii) $x^2 + x - 6 = x^2 + 3x - 2x - 6$
$= x(x + 3) - 2(x + 3)$
$= (x - 2)(x + 3).$

(iii) $x^2 - 7x + 10 = x^2 - 5x - 2x + 10$
$= x(x - 5) - 2(x - 5)$
$= (x - 2)(x - 5).$

The process is really trial and error, and practice makes perfect.

(iv) $2x^2 - x - 6 = 2x^2 + 3x - 4x - 6$
$= x(2x + 3) - 2(2x + 3)$
$= (x - 2)(2x + 3).$

(v) $18x^2 + 45x - 8 = 18x^2 + 48x - 3x - 8$
$= 6x(3x + 8) - (3x + 8)$
$= (6x - 1)(3x + 8).$

When splitting up into four terms, notice that the product of the two middle terms equals the product of the two outside terms, e.g.:

(i) $x^2 \times 6 = 2x \times 3x = 6x^2;$
(iii) $x^2 \times 10 = -5x \times -2x = 10x^2;$
(v) $18x^2 \times -8 = 48x \times -3x = -144x^2.$

> It is not always possible to put a quadratic expression into brackets; the following rule can save you a lot of time.
> For the expression $ax^2 + bx + c$, work out $b^2 - 4ac$.
> If it is a perfect square it factorises, if not it doesn't.

For example:

(i) $x^2 + 6x + 8$ $a = 1, b = 6, c = 8;$
$b^2 - 4ac = 36 - 32 = 4$, which *is* a perfect square.
In fact $x^2 + 6x + 8 = (x + 4)(x + 2).$

(ii) $x^2 - 4x - 12$ $a = 1, b = -4, c = -12;$
$b^2 - 4ac = 16 + 48 = 64$, which *is* a perfect square.

The alternative method, which also involves trial and error, is illustrated as follows:

Factorise $6x^2 + 19x - 20.$

↑   ↑
Consider   Consider
this   this number
number   second.
first.

$6x^2$ suggests $3x \times 2x$.

-20 suggests 5×-4 or 2×-10.

Try $(3x + 5)(2x - 4)$ $= 6x^2 + 10x - 12x - 20$
$= 6x^2 - 2x - 20$. ✗

Try $(2x - 10)(3x + 2) = 6x^2 + 4x - 30x - 20$
$= 6x^2 - 26x - 20$. ✗

There are many possibilities.

In fact, $(6x - 5)(x + 4) = 6x^2 - 5x + 24x - 20$
$= 6x^2 + 19x - 20$. ✓

(D) $a^2 - b^2$ This expression is known as a *difference of two squares*.
$a^2 - b^2 = (a - b)(a + b)$.
Example: $16x^2 - 25y^2 = (4x^2) - (5y^2) = (4x - 5y)(4x + 5y)$.

(E) $a^2 \pm 2ab + b^2$ This expression is a *perfect square*.
$a^2 + 2ab + b^2 = (a + b)(a + b) = (a + b)^2$.
$a^2 - 2ab + b^2 = (a - b)^2$.

LCM and HCF

`GRADE C/D`

The lowest common multiple (LCM) of two numbers is the smallest number that both numbers divide into exactly. It can be found by first expressing each number as the product of its prime factors. Consider the following example.

To find the LCM of 48 and 84:

2)	48
2)	24
2)	12
2)	6
3)	3
	1

2)	84
2)	42
3)	21
7)	7
	1

So $48 = 2^4 \times 3$ and $84 = 2^2 \times 3 \times 7$.

Take the highest power of every prime number occurring in the two products and multiply these powers together. Hence,

$$\text{LCM} = 2^4 \times 3 \times 7 = 336.$$

The highest common factor (HCF) is the largest number that divides exactly into each number.

To find the HCF of these numbers, take the lowest power of each prime number occurring in both numbers, and multiply them together. Hence,

$$\text{HCF} = 2^2 \times 3 = 12.$$

LCM and HCF in algebra

`GRADE B`

The method is slightly easier in algebra, because most of the work is done already.

For example, the LCM of $4a^3bc$ and $6a^2b^4c^2$ is:

$$12 \times a^3 \times b^4 \times c^2 = 12a^3b^4c^2.$$

The HCF is $2 \times a^2 \times b \times c = 2a^2bc$.

Algebraic fractions

(i)   Addition or subtraction.

$$\frac{x+1}{2} + \frac{x-1}{4} = \frac{2\,(x+1) + (x-1)}{4}$$

$$= \frac{2x+2+x-1}{4} = \frac{3x+1}{4}.$$

$$\frac{1}{a} + \frac{1}{2a^2} = \frac{2a}{2a^2} + \frac{1}{2a^2} = \frac{2a+1}{2a^2}$$

(ii)   Multiplication.

cancel
x

$$\frac{x}{y} \times \frac{4}{x} = \frac{4\overset{1}{x}}{\overset{}{x}y} = \frac{4}{y}.$$

(iii)   Division.

turn second fraction upside-down and multiply

$$\frac{x^2}{4} \div \frac{x}{2} = \frac{x^2}{4} \times \frac{2}{x} = \frac{\overset{1}{2}x^2}{\underset{2}{4}x} = \frac{x}{2}.$$

Quadratic equations

(A) BY FACTORS

Consider $x^2 - 5x + 6 = 0$.
Hence $(x - 3)(x - 2) = 0$,
either $x - 3 = 0$, or $x - 2 = 0$.
We get two solutions: $x = 3$ or $x = 2$.

A further example: $6x^2 - x - 2 = 0$;
factorising, $(2x + 1)(3x - 2) = 0$
$2x + 1 = 0$ or $3x - 2 = 0$,
$\quad\;\; 2x = -1$ or $3x = 2$,
$\quad\quad\; x = -\frac{1}{2}$ or $x = \frac{2}{3}$.

(B) BY FORMULA

The equation $x^2 + x - 1 = 0$ cannot be solved by factors, because it
does not factorise. The following formula can be used. A proof is given.
    Consider the equation $ax^2 + bx + c = 0$.

Divide by a: $x^2 + \dfrac{bx}{a} + \dfrac{c}{a} = 0$.

Add $\dfrac{b^2}{4a^2}$ to both sides. This is part of the technique

of completing the square.

$$x^2 + \frac{bx}{a} + \frac{b^2}{4a^2} + \frac{c}{a} = \frac{b^2}{4a^2},$$

$$\left(x + \frac{b}{2a}\right)^2 = \frac{b^2}{4a^2} - \frac{c}{a} = \frac{b^2}{4a^2} - \frac{4ac}{4a^2}$$

check by squaring out the bracket

$$= \frac{b^2 - 4ac}{4a^2}.$$

Take the square root of each side, remembering that it could be
positive or negative:

$$x + \frac{b}{2a} = \pm \frac{\sqrt{b^2 - 4ac}}{2a}.$$

Subtract $\dfrac{b}{2a}$ from both sides:

$$x = \frac{-b \pm \sqrt{b^2 - 4ac}}{2a}.$$

In the equation $x^2 + x - 1 = 0$, $a = 1, b = 1, c = -1$.

$$x = \frac{-1 \pm \sqrt{1+4}}{2} = \frac{-1 \pm \sqrt{5}}{2}.$$

Hence, $x = 0.618$ or -1.618.

Simultaneous equations

GRADE C/D

(a)   Solve

$$3x + 4y = 10 \quad (1)$$
$$5x + 3y = 13 \quad (2)$$

Multiply (1) by 5: $15x + 20y = 50 \quad (3)$
multiply (2) by 3: $15x + 9y = 39 \quad (4)$

Each equation has the same number of x's. The equations can be subtracted:

$(3) - (4)$: $11y = 11, y = 1$.

Substitute this value into any of the equations, e.g. (1):
$$3x + 4 = 10 \qquad 3x = 10 - 4 = 6 \qquad x = 2.$$

The solution to the equations is $x = 2$, $y = 1$.

(b)   A slightly harder example:

$$5x - 4y = 14 \quad (1)$$
$$7x + 9y = 18. \quad (2)$$

Multiply (1) by 9: $45x - 36y = 126 \quad (3)$
multiply (2) by 4: $28x + 36y = 72. \quad (4)$

This time, y can be eliminated by adding the equations:
$(3) + (4)$: $73x = 198, \qquad x = \frac{198}{73} = 2.71$ (2 d.p.).

Substitute in (2):

$$18.97 + 9y = 18, \qquad 9y = -0.97, \qquad y = -0.11.$$

The solution is $x = 2.71, y = -0.11$.

Notes:
(1)   It may be possible to eliminate x or y without multiplying either equation (see the following example).
(2)   It doesn't matter which variable is eliminated.

(c)   Solve

$$4x = 5 + 3y, \quad (1)$$
$$3y - 5x = -4. \quad (2)$$

These are rewritten as $4x - 3y = 5 \quad (1)$
$-5x + 3y = -4 \quad (2)$
$(1) + (2)$ $-x = 1$, so $x = -1$.

Substitute in (2): $5 + 3y = -4$
so $3y = -9$.

Hence $y = -3$.

Changing the subject of formulae

In each of the following examples, try to make x the new subject of the formula.

It is important to realise that the following solutions are not the only ones, but are an attempt at a systematic approach. Short cuts are often possible with experience, you may like to use flow charts.

(a)

$$t = ax + b.$$

Subtract b from each side: $t - b = ax.$

$\div a$: $\therefore \dfrac{t - b}{a} = x,$

or, better, $x = \dfrac{(t - b)}{a}.$

GRADE B

(b)

$$t = a(x + b).$$

Remove brackets: $t = ax + ab.$

Subtract ab from each side: $t - ab = ax.$

$\div a$: $\therefore x = \dfrac{(t - ab)}{a}.$

(c)

$$t = 2a\sqrt{x+y}.$$

Square both sides
(remember to square $2a$): $t^2 = 4a^2(x + y).$
Remove brackets: $t^2 = 4a^2x + 4a^2y.$
Subtract $4a^2y$ from each side: $t^2 - 4a^2y = 4a^2x.$

$\div 4a^2$: $\therefore x = \dfrac{(t^2 - 4a^2y)}{4a^2}.$

(d)

$$y = \frac{1}{t}(ax - k).$$

Remove brackets: $y = \dfrac{ax}{t} - \dfrac{k}{t}.$

$\times t$: $yt = ax - k.$
$+ k$ each side: $yt + k = ax.$

$\div a$: $\therefore x = \dfrac{(yt + k)}{a}.$

(e)

$$y = \frac{2t}{1 + x}.$$

$\times$ common denominator
$(1 + x)$: $y(1 + x) = 2t.$
Remove brackets: $y + xy = 2t.$
$- y$ each side: $xy = 2t - y.$

$\div y$: $\therefore x = \dfrac{(2t - y)}{y}.$

GRADE A

(f)

$$p = a\sqrt{x} + \frac{q}{t}.$$

$- \dfrac{q}{t}$ each side: $p - \dfrac{q}{t} = a\sqrt{x}.$

Square both sides:

$$\left(p - \frac{q}{t}\right)^2 = a^2x.$$

Remove brackets: $p^2 + \dfrac{q^2}{t^2} - \dfrac{2pq}{t} = a^2x$

$\times$ common denominator t^2: $p^2t^2 + q^2 - 2pqt = a^2t^2x.$

$\div a^2t^2$: $\therefore x = \dfrac{(p^2t^2 + q^2 - 2pqt)}{a^2t^2}.$

(g)

$$y = \frac{ax + b}{cx + d}.$$

Common denominator $cx + d$, so $y(cx + d) = ax + b.$
Remove brackets: $ycx + yd = ax + b.$
  So $y(cx+d) = ax+b.$

Factorise side containing
new subject x: $x(yc - a) = b - yd.$

$\div (yc - a)$: $\therefore x = \dfrac{b - yd}{yc - a}.$

(h)

$$y = \frac{t}{1 - x^2}.$$

Common denominator
$(1 - x^2)$, $y(1 - x^2) = t.$
Remove brackets: $y - yx^2 = t,$
                      $y - t = yx^2$

$\div y$: $x^2 = \frac{y - t}{y}.$

Take square root:

$$\therefore \quad x = \sqrt{\frac{y - t}{y}}$$

Further number patterns

GRADE A/B

In chapter 5, we looked at number patterns that were linear in that they increased by a constant difference. For example, 2, 5, 8, 11, . . . We now look at number patterns that are quadratic in nature.

Already we have looked at the triangle numbers T, given by

      T : 1   3   6   10   15   21 . . .

The formula for predicting the n'th term is

$$T_n = \frac{n(n + 1)}{2} = \frac{1n^2}{2} + \frac{1n}{2}$$

In order to recognise a quadratic sequence, look at the differences. These will increase by a constant amount.

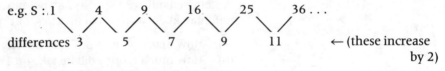

e.g. S : 1   4   9   16   25   36 . . .

differences   3   5   7   9   11   ← (these increase by 2)

Subtract the triangle numbers from S

       S : 1   4   9   16   25 . . .
       T : 1   3   6   10   15 . . .
S − T : 0   1   3   6   10 . . .

S − T is still not linear, so we subtract T again

      S − T − T : − 1   − 2   − 3   − 4   − 5 . . .

This number pattern is predicted by $-n$
      Hence S − T − T : $-n$
      i.e.   S − 2T : $-n$
$\therefore$ S : $-n + 2T$
But T (the triangular numbers) are predicted by $\frac{n(n + 1)}{2}$
$\therefore$ S: $-n + 2 \times \frac{n(n + 1)}{2}$
     $= -n + n(n + 1) = -n + n^2 + n$
     $= n^2$

Hence the number sequence S is predicted by the formula n^2. In fact, if we look at the sequence again, we have
      S : 1^2 2^2 3^2 4^2 5^2 . . .
And so we could have found the n'th term quite easily. This method, however, will work for any quadratic type sequence.

Topic: problem leading to simultaneous equations

WORKED EXAMPLE 125

GRADE C/D

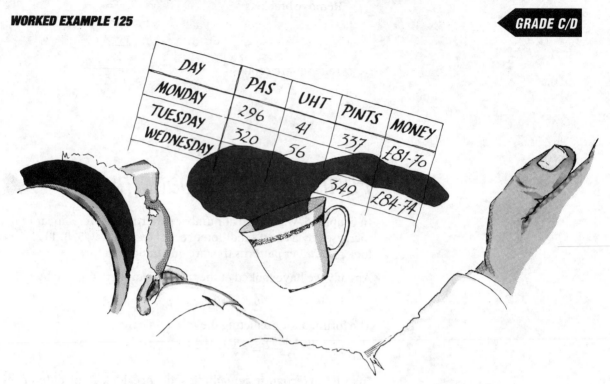

DAY	PAS	UHT	PINTS	MONEY
MONDAY	296	41	337	
TUESDAY	320	56		£81·70
WEDNESDAY			349	£84·74

Pasteurised milk (PAS) costs 24p per pint and UHT milk costs 26p per pint. A milkman keeps a record of his sales, but spills coffee on his record book.

(a)   How many pints of milk did he sell on Tuesday?
(b)   How much money did he take on Tuesday?
(c)   How many pints of each type did he sell on Wednesday?   (WJEC)

SOLUTION

(a)   He sold 320 + 56 = 376 pints.

(b)   320 × 24p + 56 × 26p = £76.80 + £14.56
$$= £91.36.$$

(c)   If P is the number of pints of PAS, and U the number of pints of UHT, then: the total cost of the PAS = $24P$ pence
    the total cost of the UHT = $26U$ pence
The total takings = £84.74, i.e. 8474 pence
So $24P + 26U = 8474$ (1)
But $P + U = 349$ (2) (the number of pints sold)
(2) × 24: $24P + 24U = 8376$ (3)
(1) − (3): $2U = 98$
So $U = 49$
Using (2), $P = 300$
Hence the milkman sells 300 pints of pasteurised milk, and 49 pints of UHT milk.

There are two missing numbers suggesting simultaneous equations

Topics: quadratic equations, trial and improvement

GRADE C/D

WORKED EXAMPLE 126 Use trial and improvement to find the solution of the equation $x^2 + 17x + 11 = 0$ which is near to $x = -1$, correct to 1 decimal place.

SOLUTION Try $x = -1$ in the equation:
$$(-1)^2 + 17(-1) + 11 = 1 - 17 + 11 = -5.$$
Try $x = 0$ in the equation:
$$0^2 + 17 \times 0 + 11 = 11.$$
The answer has *changed sign*, so the solution must be between 0 and -1.
Try $x = -0.5$:
$$(-0.5)^2 + (17 \times -0.5) + 11 = 2.75.$$
The answer is positive, hence the solution lies between -0.5 and -1.
Try $x = -0.75$:
$$(-0.75)^2 + (17 \times -0.75) + 11 = -1.1875.$$
This is negative, hence the solution lies between -0.5 and -0.75.
Try $x = -0.625$:
$$(-0.625)^2 + (17 \times -0.625) + 11 = 0.765625.$$
Now try half-way between -0.625 and -0.75
$$= \frac{-(0.625 + 0.75)}{2} = -0.69 \text{ (2 dec. places)}$$
$$(-0.69)^2 + (17 \times -0.69) + 11 = -0.2539.$$
Now try half-way between -0.69 and $-0.625 = -0.66$:
$$(-0.66)^2 + (17 \times -0.66) + 11 = 0.2156.$$
The answer is between -0.69 and -0.66, which is -0.7 correct to 1 decimal place.

Topic: problems leading to quadratic equations

GRADE A

WORKED EXAMPLE 127 A machine produces two types of bolt. Bolt A is produced at the rate of x per minute, and bolt B is produced at the rate of $(x - 6)$ per minute.

(a) Write down an expression in seconds for the time taken to produce each bolt.

(b) If it takes $\frac{5}{6}$ seconds longer to produce bolt B than bolt A, write down an equation in x and solve it.

SOLUTION (a) If x of bolt A are produced in 60 seconds, then one is produced in $\frac{60}{x}$ seconds.

Similarly, one of B is produced in $\frac{60}{x-6}$ seconds.

(c) Seeing that the difference is $\frac{5}{6}$ seconds, and $\frac{60}{x-6}$ is larger than

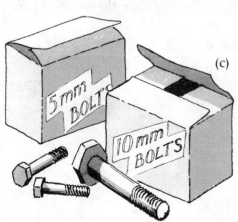

$\frac{60}{x}$ (because less bolts are produced per minute), it follows that:
$$\frac{60}{x-6} = \frac{60}{x} + \frac{5}{6};$$
multiply by common denominator $6x(x-6)$:
$$360x = 360(x - 6) + 5x(x - 6)$$
$$360x = 360x - 2160 + 5x^2 - 30x$$
rearranging: $5x^2 - 30x - 2160 = 0$
or $x^2 - 6x - 432 = 0$
$$(x + 18)(x - 24) = 0.$$
x cannot be -18, so $x = 24$.

Questions to try

231. Simplify the following, expressing your answer by using a power of a single number.

(i) $2^2 \times 2^3$; (ii) $3^4 \div 3^2$; (iii) $(2^2)^2$; (iv) $(3^4)^2$; (v) $2^{10} \div (2^2)^2$;
(vi) $(4^2)^3 \times (4^3)^2$

232. Remove brackets from the following and simplify

(i) $2(x + 1) + 3(x + 2)$; (ii) $4(t - 1) + 2(2t + 1)$;
(iii) $6(2k - 1) - 3(k + 1)$; (iv) $2(x + 3) - 2(x - 1)$;
(v) $a(b + 2) + b(2a + 1)$

233. Solve the following simultaneous equations:

(i) $x + y = 7$,
      $2x - y = 8$.

(ii) $3x - 2y = 4$,
      $5x - 2y = 0$.

(iii) $2x + y = 8$,
      $5x - y = 6$.

(iv) $x + 3y = 2$,
      $2x - 4y = 1$.

(v) $3x + 2y = 17$,
      $4y - x = -8$.

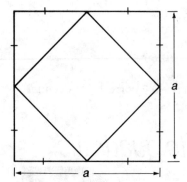

234. The drawing shows a square of side a and a second square formed by joining the midpoints of its sides. The area of the outer square is A_1. The area of the inner square is A_2.

(a) State, in terms of a, the area A_2.
(b) Find, in terms of a, the area A_3 of a third square, formed by joining the midpoints of the sides of the second square.
(c) Find, in terms of a and n, an expression for the area A_n of the nth square.   (NEA)

235. (a) Susan wants to find, correct to one decimal place, a solution of the equation
$$2x^2 = 5.$$

She tries by guessing values of x that might satisfy the equation.

First she tries $x = 1.2$ and gets the result 2.88 for $2x^2$.

Then she tries $x = 1.9$ and gets the result 7.22 for $2x^2$.

By trying other values of x and showing your working clearly, find a solution of the equation correct to one decimal place.

(b) Susan now has to find, correct to one decimal place, the solution of the equation.

$$x^2 + x = 1.$$

By trying values of x and showing your working clearly, find a solution to Susan's equation.   (NEA)

236.

	A	**B**	**C**	**D**
1	x	x cubed	x	x cubed
2	1	1	3	27
3	2	8	3.1	29.791
4	3	27	3.2	32.768
5	4	64	3.3	35.937
6	5	125	3.4	39.304
7			3.5	42.875
8			3.6	46.656
9			3.7	50.653
10			3.8	54.872
11			3.9	59.319
12			4	64

This spreadsheet calculates the values of x^3 for some values of x.

(a) Use columns A and B to explain why there is a solution to the equation $x^3 = 50$ between $x = 3$ and $x = 4$.

(b) Use columns C and D to find a solution to the equation $x^3 = 50$ correct to 1 decimal place.

(c) Use trial and improvement and a calculator to find the solution correct to 2 decimal places. Show your working clearly. (MEG)

237. Factorise completely

(i) $4x + 8y$; (ii) $x^2 + xy$; (iii) $4xy - 2xt$; (iv) $3x^2 + 9x$; (v) $25x - 15y$; (vi) $pq^2 + p^2q$

238.

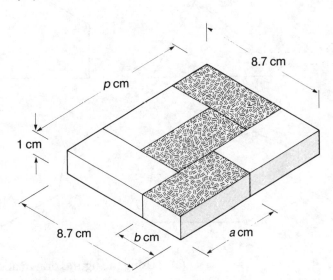

The drawing shows six identically shaped rectangular blocks of modelling clay – it is not drawn to scale. The length of each block is a and its width is b. Find the width b and hence the values of a and p. (NEA)

239.   A bill of £445 was paid using £5 notes and £20 notes. If 35 notes were used altogether, find how many of each were used.

240.   The design shown in the figure below is formed by repeatedly circumscribing a square with a circle and then circumscribing the circle with a square. The squares and circles are lettered $S_1, S_2, S_3 \ldots$ and $C_1, C_2 \ldots$, respectively, from the inside, as shown. The inner square S_1 has an area of 4 square units.

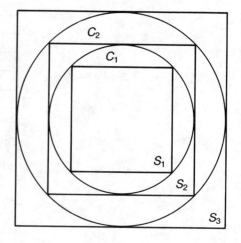

(a)   What is the radius of circle C_1?
(b)   What is the area of square S_2?
(c)   What is the area of square S_3?
(d)   What is the area of square S_{10}?
(e)   What is the area of square S_n?

241.

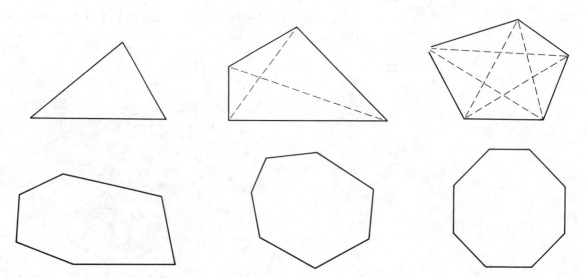

(a)   Using the figures drawn above, or otherwise, find the number of diagonals in each polygon, and then complete the table below.

Number of sides of polygon (n)	3	4	5	6	7	8
Number of diagonals (d)	0	2	5			

(b)   By considering the pattern of the numbers in this table, find:
(i)   the number of diagonals in a polygon with twelve sides;
(ii)   the number of sides of a polygon in which there are forty-four diagonals.

(c)   The formula $d = an^2 + bn$, where a and b are constants, gives the number of diagonals, d, in terms of the number of sides, n, of a polygon.

Using the information above, write down two simultaneous equations in a and b and, by solving them, find the exact relationship that exists between d and n.

242.

0	1	2	3	4	5	6	7	8	9
10	11	12	13	14	15	16	17	18	19
20	21	22	23	24	25	26	27	28	29
30	31	32	33	34	35	36	37	38	39
40	41	42	43	....					

Look at this number pattern. 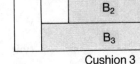 'This is called the **I2L** because **12** is the middle number.

To find the value of **12L** you multiply the end numbers and add the middle number, as follows: $(2 \times 13) + 12$

Therefore the value of **12L** is 38.

(a) What is the value of the **27L**?

(b)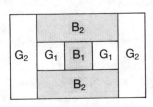
   (i) Write the numbers missing from this **L** in terms of x.
   (ii) Find the value of this **L** in terms of x.

(c) Which **L** has a value of 998?   (WJEC)

243. A regular polygon has exterior angles of $x°$. Find, in terms of x,

(a) the interior angle;
(b) the number of sides;
(c) the number of lines of symmetry;
(d) the order of rotational symmetry of the polygon.   (WJEC)

244.

Cushion 2

Cushion 3

A craft shop sells a range of cushions of different sizes whose fronts are made from strips of blue (B) and green (G) ribbon, each 5 cm wide. Cushions 2 and 3 are shown in the diagram, and the lengths of the strips are given in the table below.

Strip	B_1	B_2	B_3	G_1	G_2	G_3
Length (cm)	10	20	30	5	15	25

The pattern is extended for cushions 4, 5, 6, etc.

(a) (i) State the lengths of strips B_4, B_5 and G_4, G_5.
    (ii) State, in terms of n, the lengths of strips B_n and G_n used in cushion n. Find n if cushion n measures 85 cm by 100 cm.

(b) (i) Find the total length of the green strips used in cushion 3.
    (ii) The total length, R cm, of the green strips in cushion n is given by the formula
$$R = 10n^2.$$
Show that this is true for cushion 3.
    (iii) 280 cm each of green and blue ribbon are available to make a cushion front. Making no allowance for joins, find the largest possible value of n.   (LEAG)

245. Simplify the following:

(i) $\sqrt{10^4}$; (ii) $\sqrt[3]{27^2}$; (iii) $(0.09)^{1/2}$; (iv) $125^{-2/3}$; (v) $27^{-1/3}$; (vi) $(2^{1/5})^{10}$;
(vii) $(3^{2/3})^0$; (viii) $49^{1/2}$; (ix) $32^{2/5}$; (x) $625^{-1/2}$; (xi) $4x^5 \div 2x^2$; (xii) $5p^{-3} \div 4p^5$;
(xiii) $3x^{-2} \times 4x^{-4}$; (xiv) $(3-m)^3$; (xv) $\sqrt[3]{27x^6}$; (xvi) $\sqrt{25y^{16}}$; (xvii) $(8q^2)^{2/3}$;

(xviii) $\left(\dfrac{1}{y^{-2}}\right)^{1/2}$; (xix) $\left(-\dfrac{1}{3y^2}\right)^{-2}$; (xx) $1 \div (\frac{4}{9})^{-3/2}$.

246. Factorise if possible the following:

(i) $ay + 4y^2$; (ii) $3t^3 + 2t^2 + 5t$; (iii) $p^2q^3 - q^2p^3$; (iv) $7(p-2) - 3(p-2)$;
(v) $p(y-z) - q(z-y)$; (vi) $qr + rs - ps - pq$; (vii) $t^2 - 3t - tp + 3p$;
(viii) $ax + bx + cx - ay - by - cy$; (ix) $x^2 - 11x + 24$; (x) $x^2 + 2x - 3$;
(xi) $x^2 + 11x - 26$; (xii) $x^2 - 7x + 8$; (xiii) $2x^2 + 13x + 15$;
(xiv) $4x^2 + 8x + 3$; (xv) $6x^2 - 5x + 1$; (xvi) $9x^2 - 7x - 2$;
(xvii) $4x^4 - 3x^2 - 1$; (xviii) $4x^2 - 25$; (xix) $1 - x^2$; (xx) $\pi R^2 - \pi r^2$;
(xxi) $(x-3)^2 - 9$; (xxii) $121x^2y^2 - 4$; (xxiii) $4x^2 - 12xy + 9y^2$;
(xxiv) $25x^2 - 10xy + y^2$; (xxv) $25 - 10b + b^2$.

247. Work out and simplify:

(i) $\dfrac{1}{x} + \dfrac{1}{x^2}$;

(ii) $\dfrac{2}{a} + \dfrac{3}{ab}$;

(iii) $\dfrac{x}{2} + \dfrac{x}{3} + \dfrac{x}{4}$;

(iv) $\dfrac{4}{y} - \dfrac{2}{3y} + \dfrac{5}{y}$;

(v) $4x + \dfrac{1}{x}$;

(vi) $\dfrac{2a + 5b}{4} + \dfrac{3a + 2b}{8}$;

(vii) $\dfrac{x+2}{3} - \dfrac{5}{6}$;

(viii) $\dfrac{x}{y} \times \dfrac{2y}{x}$;

(ix) $\dfrac{pq}{t} \times \dfrac{t^2}{q}$;

(x) $\dfrac{a}{b} \div \dfrac{1}{2}$;

(xi) $\dfrac{b}{c} \div \dfrac{c}{b}$;

(xii) $\dfrac{x}{y} \times \dfrac{2y}{x} \times \dfrac{4x}{5y}$;

(xiii) $\dfrac{pq}{r} \div \dfrac{3p}{2r}$.

248. Solve, where possible:

(i) $x^2 - 2x - 3 = 0$; (ii) $x^2 - 10x + 16 = 0$; (iii) $2x^2 + x - 1 = 0$;
(iv) $3x^2 - 10x + 3 = 0$; (v) $x^2 + 3x - 9 = 0$;

(vi) $x + \dfrac{1}{3x} = 2$.

249. Simplify (a) $2x^4 \times 4x^{-3}$; (b) $8x^2y \div 4x^4$; (c) $x^{0.5} \times x^{2.5}$; (d) $(x^{1/2})^{-4}$;

(e) $\dfrac{1}{2x} - \dfrac{1}{2x+1}$

(MEG)

2 Functions and graphs

$f(x)$ means that f depends on the value of x, or f is a function of x. $y = x^2 + 2$ can be written $f(x) = x^2 + 2$.

$f(2)$ means put $x = 2$, so $f(2) = 2^2 + 2 = 6$

$fg(2)$ means put $x = 2$ into g, and then put the answer into f. It is called the composite function of f and g.
Alternative notation $fx \to x^2 + 2$ sometimes called a mapping.
Often used in abstract questions, see worked examples 129 and 130
When plotting the graph of a curved line, always split the table up. So to plot $y = 3x^2 + 2x + 5$, allow a line for $3x^2, 2x, +5$.
If you are asked to draw two graphs on the same diagram, they can be used to solve equations.
$y = x^3 + 1$ and $y = 2x + 4$ can be used to solve $x^3 + 1 = 2x + 4$.

The values of x used in plotting are the domain of the function.

WORDS TO LEARN: gradient of a curve; draw a tangent and find the slope of the tangent, see worked example 128. Sometimes you may be asked to find the inverse of a function f^{-1} This means find the rule that takes you back from y to x.

Using graphs to solve equations   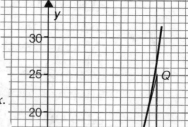 GRADE A

WORKED EXAMPLE 128 (i) Solve by a graphical method the equation $x^3 = 2x + 1$. Without too much extra work, how could you solve the equation $2x^3 - 3 = 4x$?

(ii) Find the gradient of $y = x^3$ at $x = 2.5$.

SOLUTION (i) To solve $x^3 = 2x + 1$ is fairly easy. If you plot $y = x^3$ and $y = 2x + 1$, when the lines cross, the two y values are equal, hence $x^3 = 2x + 1$. The values of x where the curves cross will be the solution of the equation.

The most difficult part of this is plotting $y = x^3$. It is worth seeing if this can be used again.

Consider $2x^3 - 3 = 4x$;

$$2x^3 = 4x + 3; \text{ so } x^3 = 2x + \frac{3}{2}.$$

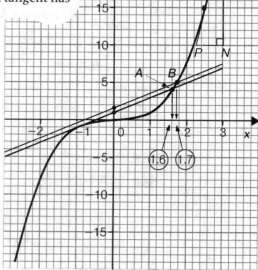

The diagram is plotted alongside.
At A, $x = 1.6$.
Hence $x = 1.6$ is a solution of $x^3 = 2x + 1$.
At B, $x = 1.7$.
Hence $x = 1.7$ is a solution of $2x^3 - 3 = 4x$.

(ii) At the point $(2.5, 15.6)$ a tangent has been drawn.

The gradient of the
$$\text{tangent} = \frac{QN}{PN} = \frac{15}{0.8}$$
$$= 18.8$$

Topic: function notation   GRADE A*

WORKED EXAMPLE 129 If $g(x)$ denotes the sum of all the prime numbers which are less than x, find:

(a) $g(16)$;
(b) a value of x such that $g(x) = 77$;
(c) the solution of the equation $g(x) = g(10)$.

SOLUTION (a) $g(16) = 2 + 3 + 5 + 7 + 11 + 13 = 41$.

(b) This is basically trial and error.
Since $2 + 3 + 5 + 7 + 11 + 13 + 17 + 19 = 77$, then any number greater than 19 and less than or equal to the next prime number, which is 23, works.
Hence $x = 20$ will do.

(c) If $g(x) = g(10)$, then $x = 10$ is an obvious solution.
However, $g(10) = 2 + 3 + 5 + 7 = 17$, also $g(8) = 17$, $g(9) = 17$ and $g(11) = 17$.
Hence the solution is $\{8, 9, 10, 11\}$.

WORKED EXAMPLE 130   For any positive integer n, T (n) is defined as the smallest multiple of 3 which is larger than or equal to n, e.g. $T(5) = 6$.

(a)   Write down the value of T(9) and that of T(10).

(b)   Give the solution set of the equation $T(n) = 12$.

(c)   State whether each of the following equations is satisfied by all values of n, by some values of n, or by no values of n. Give the solution set of each equation which is satisfied by some values of n.

    (i) $T(n + 1) = T(n) + 1$;

    (ii) $T(n + 3) = T(n) + 3$;

    (iii) $T(2n) = 2T(n)$.

SOLUTION   This example illustrates a function which cannot easily be represented by formulae.

(a) $T(9) = 9$, $T(10) = 12$.

(b)   **Try to express in words what this says:** the smallest multiple of 3 which is larger than or equal to n is 12. Hence $n = 10$, 11 or 12. The solution set is 10,11,12.

(c)   (i)   Since $T(n)$ is a multiple of 3, $T(n) + 1$ is not a multiple of 3, therefore it cannot be $T(n + 1)$. Therefore (i) is not satisfied by any values of n.

    (ii)   This is true for all values of n. (Convince yourself with a few examples.)

    (iii)   This is not always true, since $T(10) = 2T(5)$ but $T(14) \neq 2T(7)$. It is true, however, unless $n \in \{1,4,7,10,...\}$.

Topics: composite and inverse functions

WORKED EXAMPLE 131   If $f: x \rightarrow 3x + 5$, and $g: x \rightarrow x^2 + 5$, find:

(i) $f(2)$; (ii) $fg(2)$; (iii) $gg(0)$; (iv) $f^{-1}(4)$; (v) $fg(x)$.

SOLUTION   (i) $f(2) = 3 \times 2 + 5 = 11$.

(ii)   To find $fg(2)$, find $g(2)$ first.
$g(2) = 2^2 + 5 = 9$.
Now find $f(9) = 3 \times 9 + 5 = 32$,
so $fg(2) = 32$.

(iii)   To find $gg(0)$, find $g(0)$ first.
$g(0) = 0^2 + 5 = 5$.
Now find $g(5)$:
$g(5) = 5^2 + 5 = 30$,
so $gg(0) = 30$.

(iv)   The flow chart for f is,

Now reverse this:

Hence $f^{-1}: x \rightarrow (x - 5) \div 3$
so $f^{-1}(4) = (4 - 5) \div 3$
$= -\frac{1}{3}$.

(v)   g turns x into $x^2 + 5$,
f will multiply by 3 and add 5.
So $fg(x) = 3 \times (x^2 + 5) + 5 = 3x^2 + 15 + 5 = 3x^2 + 20$.

Questions to try

250. (a) Given that $y = (x - 1)^2$, copy and complete the table.   **GRADE C/D**

x	−1	−0.5	0	0.5	1	1.5	2	2.5	3
y		2.25	1	0.25		0.25	1		4

(b) (i) Using a scale of 4 cm to represent 1 unit on each axis, draw the graph of $y = (x - 1)^2$ for values of x from −1 to 3 inclusive.

(ii) By drawing a tangent, estimate the gradient of the graph $y = (x - 1)^2$ at the point (2,1).

(c) Use your graph to find the values of x for which $(x - 1)^2 = 3$.   (MEG)

251. The following information on stopping distances is reproduced from the Highway Code.

Shortest stopping distances

At 30 mile/h

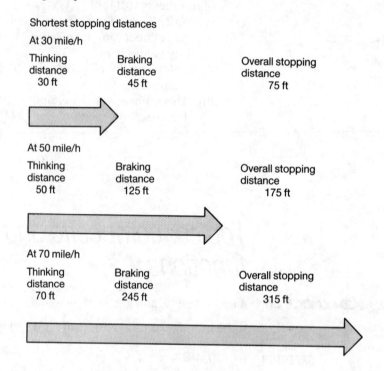

| Thinking distance 30 ft | Braking distance 45 ft | Overall stopping distance 75 ft |

At 50 mile/h

| Thinking distance 50 ft | Braking distance 125 ft | Overall stopping distance 175 ft |

At 70 mile/h

| Thinking distance 70 ft | Braking distance 245 ft | Overall stopping distance 315 ft |

It is known that the overall stopping distance d and the speed v are related by the formula $d = av + bv^2$, where a and b are constants.

(a) Complete the table showing values of d and v.

v (mile/h)	30	50	70
d (feet)	75		

(b) Use your completed table to show that the formula relating d and v is
$$d = v + \frac{v^2}{20}.$$

(c) On graph paper draw the graph of d against v, for values of v from 10 to 90.

If the road surface is wet then twice the normal overall stopping distance should be allowed. Use your completed graph to estimate the maximum speed at which a car should travel if visibility is limited to 150 feet,

(d) on a dry road,

(e) on a wet road.

(NISEC)

252. A function is defined by

GRADE A*

$$y = \begin{cases} (2-x) \text{ if } 0 \leqslant x \leqslant 1 \\ x \text{ if } 1 < x < 3 \\ \frac{1}{4}(15-x) \text{ if } 3 \leqslant x \leqslant 7 \end{cases}$$

On the grid below, draw a graph of the function.

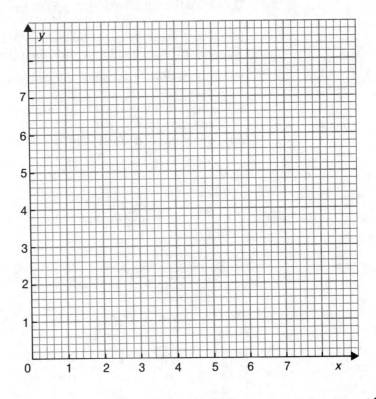

GRADE B

253. A group of students went to play a game of rounders in the park. During play, one of the windows of a nearby building was broken. The students, agreeing that they should admit to the breakage, discussed who should pay for the new window. They realised that the more of them who were prepared to contribute, the less it would cost per person. It worked out that if 10 of them were to contribute, the cost per person would be £6.

(a) What would be the cost per person if 15 of them were prepared to contribute?

(b) What would be the cost per person if 8 of them were to contribute?

(c) Find the formula relating c, the cost in pounds per person, and n, the number of students.

(d) Which one of the following sketch-graphs labelled A, B, C, represents this relation?

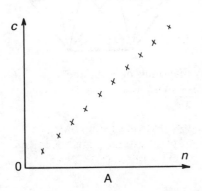

A

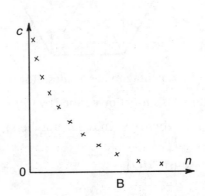

B

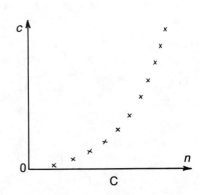

C

(e) Draw a sketch-graph of the relation between c and $\frac{1}{n}$.   (WJEC)

254. Two students were attempting to find the relationship between the variables y and x from the data given in the table.

x	2	4	5
y	4	1	0.2

They tried the equation $y = ax + \dfrac{b}{x}$.

(a) Using values from the table, form two equations in a and b.

(b) Solve these equations to find the values of a and b.

(c) Check that these values of a and b in $y = ax + \dfrac{b}{x}$ fit all three pairs of data.

(d) Given that $y = 4$, use your answers to part (b) to form a quadratic equation in x.

(e) Solve this equation to find the other value of x which will give $y = 4$.

(LEAG)

GRADE A*

255. The tables below give the output for various inputs to the two functions f and g.

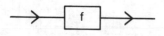 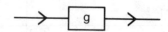

Input	Output	Input	Output
3.6	−3.6	1.8	2
−2.8	2.8	3.4	3
10	−10	0.4	0
−5.0	5.0	−0.8	−1
36.2	−36.2	−2.2	−2

(a) The function g rounds the input to the nearest whole number. Describe in your own words what the function f does.

(b) Find (i) g(−6.8); (ii) fg(6.8); (iii) gf(6.8).

(c) Describe the inverse function of f.

(WJEC)

256. (a) A hexagon has 6 sides and 9 diagonals. A heptagon has 7 sides and 14 diagonals.

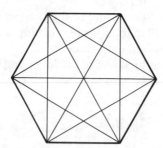 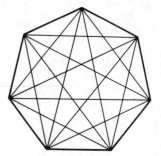

A pentagon has 5 sides. How many diagonals does it have?

(b) f is a function defined by $f(n) = \dfrac{n(n-3)}{2}$,

where $n \in \{\text{positive numbers}\}$,
Find:

(i) f(2);

(ii) f(6);

(iii) f(7).

(iv) Draw the graph of f(n) for values of n from 0 up to 8.

(v) What is the value of n if f(n) = 10?

(c)   The formula $d = \dfrac{n(n-3)}{2}$ can be used to find the number of

diagonals (d) in a polygon with n sides.

Give a domain for f such that f(n) will give the number of diagonals of a polygon with n sides.   (WJEC)

257. $\sigma(n)$, for a positive number n, is defined as the sum of the factors of n.

For example, $\sigma(6) = 1 + 2 + 3 + 6 = 12$

t is a power of 2.

(a)   Find and write down an expression for $\sigma(t)$ in terms of t.

p is a prime number.

(b)   (i)   Show that $\sigma(p) = p + 1$.
      (ii)   Find $\sigma(p^2)$.
      (iii)   Find $\sigma(p^n)$.   (LEAG)

258.   (a)   Factorise $x^2 - 5x + 6$.
(b)   Solve the equation $x^2 - 5x + 6 = 0$.
(c)   The figure below shows the graph of $y = x^2 - 5x + 6$.
Write down the coordinates of the points marked A, B and C.

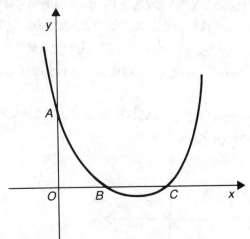

(d)   Find the values of p and q in the equation $y = x^2 + px + q$ of the quadratic curve shown below.   (WJEC)

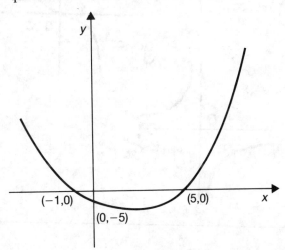

259. $f(x) = x^2$ and $g(x) = x^2 - 2x + 3$.

(a) $g(x) = f(x - a) + b$, where a and b are constants. Find the values of a and b.
(b)   Hence sketch the graphs of f and g, indicating clearly the relationship between the two graphs.   (MEG)

260.   If $f(x) = (2x - 1)^2$ (i) Find $f(-2)$; (ii) Find the possible values of t if $f(t) = 16$; (iii) sketch the graph of (a) $y = f(x)$ (b) $y = 2f(x) + 1$.

3 Variation, proportion and similar figures

VARIATION, PROPORTION.

If A is proportional to B,

$A \propto B$ means $A = kB$ (k is a constant).

If A is proportional to B^2, $A = kB^2$

If A is inversely proportional. to B,

$A = \dfrac{k}{B}$

Always find k from the information given.

If two shapes are similar, then all lengths are multiplied by a scale factor F;
All areas are multiplied by F^2;
All volumes are multiplied by F^3.

If you are asked to sketch a graph showing proportion:

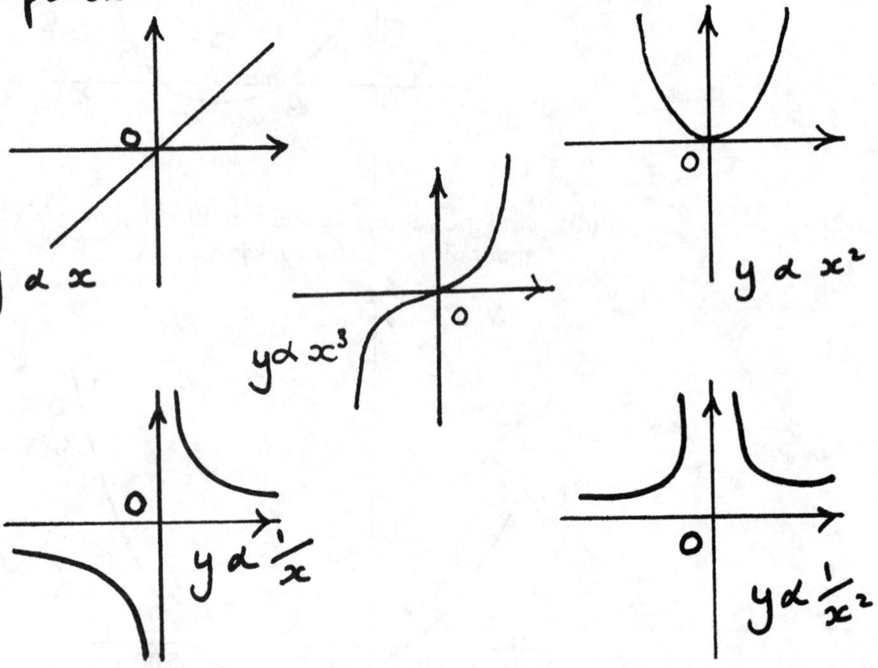

$y \propto x$

$y \propto x^3$

$y \propto x^2$

$y \propto \dfrac{1}{x}$

$y \propto \dfrac{1}{x^2}$

Topic: variation

GRADE B

WORKED EXAMPLE 132   The lift, L, produced by the wing of an aircraft varies directly according to its area, A, and the square of the airspeed, V.
For a certain wing, $L = 1200$ when $A = 15$ and $V = 200$.

(a)   Find an equation connecting L, A and V.
(b)   If, for the same wing, the airspeed is increased by ten per cent, find the corresponding percentage increase in lift.

SOLUTION (a) If L varies directly with A, and with the square of V, then
$L = kAV^2$.
$L = 1200$ when $A = 15$, $V = 200$,
hence $1200 = k \times 15 \times (200)^2$,
i.e. $k = \dfrac{1200}{15 \times 40\,000} = \dfrac{1}{500}$,
so $L = \dfrac{AV^2}{500}$.

(b) If V increases by 10 per cent, then $V = 220$.

Therefore $L = \dfrac{15 \times (220)^2}{500} = 1452$.

The percentage increase $= \dfrac{\text{increase}}{\text{original}} \times 100$

$= \dfrac{252}{1200} \times 100 = 21\%$.

WORKED EXAMPLE 133 A cylinder has a volume of $100\,\text{cm}^3$. If another cylinder of the same material is made with half the radius, and three times the height of the original cylinder, find the volume of the second cylinder.

SOLUTION In this problem, it would appear that there are two unknowns, the height and radius of the original cylinder. Also, we are not given a value for π.
Let $R\,$cm be the radius of the first cylinder.
Let $H\,$cm be the height of the first cylinder.
The volume of a cylinder is given by the formula $V = \pi r^2 h$,
so $100 = \pi R^2 H$. (1)
For the new cylinder, $r = \frac{1}{2}R$ and $h = 3H$.
The new volume $V = \pi(\frac{1}{2}R)^2(3H) = \dfrac{3\pi R^2 H}{4}$. (2)

Using equation (1), $V = \frac{3}{4} \times 100 = 75$.
The new volume is $75\,\text{cm}^3$.

Questions to try

GRADE B

261. A bath can be filled using only the hot tap, in 8 minutes. Using the cold tap only, it takes only 5 minutes. If the bath holds 160 litres of water,

(i) find the rate in litres/minute of the water coming from the hot and cold taps;

(ii) how long would it take to fill the bath if both taps are full on?

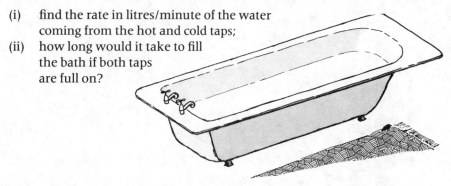

262. (i) If y is proportional to the square of x, and $y = 2$ when $x = 4$, find y when $x = 3$.

(ii) If p varies inversely as the square of q, and $p = 4$ when $q = 2$, find p when $q = 6$.

(iii) If y varies as the square of x, and inversely as the cube of H, and $y = 4$ when $H = 6$ and $x = 2$, find y when $H = 4$ and $x = 6$.

263. The pressure needed to blow up a balloon varies as to the cube of its radius. When the radius is 5 cm, the pressure needed is 80 g/cm^2.

(a)   What pressure is required when the radius is 15 cm?

(b)   What is the radius of the balloon when the pressure needed is 640 g/cm^2?

(WJEC)

264. The following table shows some values of the variables x and y which are linked by the equation $y = 8x^n$.

x	$\frac{1}{4}$	1	16
y	16	8	2

(a)   Find the value of n.

(b)   Find y when $x = 36$.

(c)   Find x when $y = 20$.

(d)   Express x in terms of y.

(WJEC)

GRAPHS

ATTAINMENT TARGETS 3, 4 AND 5

1 Venn diagrams, flow charts and iteration

A VENN DIAGRAM is a useful device for classifying information.

Sometimes a diagram involves unknown values leading to equations, see worked example 135

Remember A∪B is set A and B taken together; A∩B is where A and B overlap; A' means outside A. ℰ is the universal set under consideration.

A FLOW CHART is another device for classifying information in the form of instructions. Usually a path along a flow chart is marked with arrows.

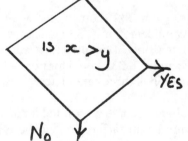

This is a decision box. The exit depends on the answer to the question.

AN ITERATION formula is a repeating process.

e.g. $x_{n+1} = x_n + \frac{1}{x_n}$ Set up a starting value, usually x_0 e.g. $x_0 = 1$

So $x_1 = 1 + \frac{1}{1} = 2$, then $x_2 = 2 + \frac{1}{2} = 2.5$, etc.

Topic: reading a Venn diagram GRADE A*

WORKED EXAMPLE 134   Some of the results of a survey amongst 70 fifth-year pupils are shown in the Venn diagram.

$\in$ = {pupils questioned in the survey},
C = {pupils who went to the cinema},
T = {pupils who went to the theatre},
P = {pupils who went to a pop concert}.

Calculate the number of pupils:

(a)   who had been to the cinema;
(b)   in $C \cup P$;
(c)   in $C \cap T$, explaining the meaning of your answer;
(d)   in $P \cup (C \cap T)$;
(e)   in $(C \cup T \cup P)'$, explaining the meaning of your answer.

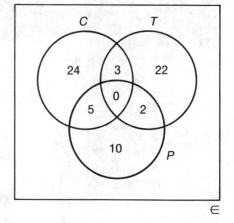

SOLUTION   (a) $24 + 3 + 0 + 5 = 32$ pupils.
(b) $24 + 3 + 0 + 2 + 10 + 5 = 44$ pupils.
(c)   3 pupils.
This means that 3 pupils went to the cinema and the theatre.
(d) $3 + 0 + 2 + 10 + 5 = 20$ pupils.
(e)   In the three sets taken together, there are
$24 + 3 + 22 + 5 + 0 + 2 + 10 = 66$.
$(C \cup T \cup P)'$ means outside $C \cup T \cup P$.
The number $= 70 - 66 = 4$ pupils.
This means that 4 pupils did not go to any of the three activities.

Topic: problem solving with Venn diagrams

WORKED EXAMPLE 135   In a local election, 3325 constituents voted for a number of candidates. 800 voted for candidate A only, 850 voted for candidate B only, and 630 voted for candidate C only. 425 voted for A and B, 120 voted for A and C, and 157 voted for B and C. If 537 voted for none of the candidates A, B and C, how many voted for all three candidates?

SOLUTION   If the number of people who voted for all three candidates is denoted by x, then the number in each region will be as in the following Venn diagram.

Since the total number of people represented in the diagram is 3325, then

$800 + (425 - x) + 850 + (120 - x) + x + (157 - x) + 630 + 537 = 3325$.
$3519 - 2x = 3325$.
Hence $x = 97$.
97 people voted for all three candidates.

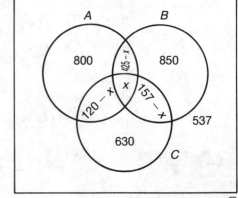

Topic: flow charts, solving equations

WORKED EXAMPLE 136   Follow the flow chart shown alongside.

(a)   What number does the flow chart give?

(b)   How can you alter it to give $\frac{1}{3}$?

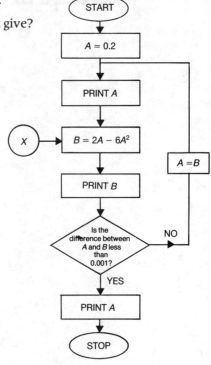

SOLUTION   *Notes:*

(a)   PRINT *A* means only print the value of *A* at that part of the loop.

(b)   *A* = *B* means change *A* to whatever value *B* has.

(c)   The values calculated are shown in the table below.

A	B
0.2	0.16
0.16	0.1664
0.1664	0.1667
0.1667	0.1667
0.1667	

This flow chart, which continually uses the same formula $B = 2A - 6A^2$, is called an *iteration*.

Since eventually *A* and *B* are equal, it must solve the equation

$$A = 2A - 6A^2;$$

i.e. $$6A^2 - A = 0, \; A(6A - 1) = 0$$

Hence $$A = 0 \text{ or } A = \tfrac{1}{6}.$$

As a decimal, $\frac{1}{6} = 0.1666$.

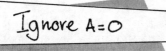

Ignore A = 0

(a)   The flow chart gives $\frac{1}{6}$ as a decimal.

(b)   In order to give a value of $\frac{1}{3}$, we need to change box *X* to

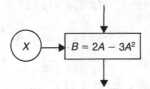

Topic: algebra, iteration formulae

WORKED EXAMPLE 137

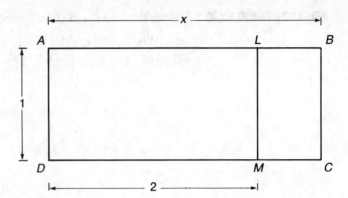

The rectangle $ABCD$ is divided into two smaller rectangles by the line LM.
$AD = 1$, $DM = 2$, $AB = x$.

(a)   Write down MC in terms of x.

(b)   Rectangles $ABCD$ and $BCML$ are similar. Use this fact to write down two expressions that must necessarily be equal to each other and show that $x^2 - 2x - 1 = 0$.

(c)   Show that the equation $x^2 - 2x - 1 = 0$ can be written in the form

$x = 2 + \dfrac{1}{x}$.

With $x_0 = 3$, use $x_{n+1} = 2 + \dfrac{1}{x_n}$ to calculate x_1 and x_2.

Write down all the figures shown by your calculator.

(d)   Continue the iteration and find a solution of the equation $x^2 - 2x - 1 = 0$, correct to three significant figures.   (LEAG)

SOLUTION   (a) $MC = x - 2$.

(b) $\dfrac{BC}{AB} = \dfrac{MC}{BC}$.

So $BC^2 = MC \times AB$

$1 = (x - 2)x = x^2 - 2x$

$x^2 - 2x - 1 = 0$.

(c)   Equation (1) can be written $x^2 = 2x + 1$.

Divide each side by x: $x = \dfrac{2x}{x} + \dfrac{1}{x}$

i.e. $x = 2 + \dfrac{1}{x}$.

Change this into an iteration formula:

$x_{n+1} = 2 + \dfrac{1}{x_n}$.

$x_0 = 3$,

$x_1 = 2 + \frac{1}{3} = 2.333\,333\,333$,

$x_2 = 2 + \dfrac{1}{2.333\,333\,333} = 2.428\,571\,429$.

(d)   The change from x_1 to x_2 is too much to give an answer, so try again:

$x_3 = 2 + \dfrac{1}{2.428\,571\,429} = 2.411\,764\,706$,

$x_4 = 2 + \dfrac{1}{2.411\,764\,706} = 2.414\,634\,146$,

$x_5 = 2 + \dfrac{1}{2.414\,634\,146} = 2.414\,141\,414$.

Hence $x = 2.41$ (3 s.f.).

Questions to try

GRADE A*

265. In a survey of 149 households about an evening's television viewing, 25 watched BBC1 and ITV only, 53 watched BBC2 and BBC1 only, 26 watched BBC2 only and 27 watched ITV only. If 8 had not watched the television, and nobody watched all three, how many had watched ITV? Assume nobody had watched BBC1 only.

266. Of the 125 members of a youth club, 46 like table tennis (T), 38 like darts (D) and 63 like snooker (S). 13 like table tennis and darts, 12 like darts and snooker and 16 like table tennis and snooker. All members like at least one of the three sports. Illustrate this information in a Venn diagram and find:

(a)   the number of members who like all three;
(b)   the number of members who like only darts.

267. (a)   In a survey of shoppers it was found that 60 per cent were pensioners and 30 per cent were male. If 60 per cent of the pensioners were female, what percentage of the shoppers were female non-pensioners? Show the information on a Venn diagram.

(b)   A survey of cars in a car-park revealed that the most popular optional extras were radios, clocks and sunroofs. 6 of the cars had radios and sunroofs, 14 had radios and clocks and 5 had clocks and sunroofs but did not have radios. 20 had sunroofs, 60 had radios and 22 had clocks but neither radios nor sunroofs.

(i)   If x cars had clocks, radios and sunroofs, complete a Venn diagram showing all the above information.

(ii)   If there were 120 cars in the car-park, write down, on the Venn diagram, how many cars had none of these optional extras (answer in terms of x).

(iii)   If 19 cars had exactly 2 of these optional extras, write down an equation and solve it to find x.

268. A sequence is defined by $u_n = \frac{1}{2}n(n + 1)$.

(a)   Work out u_0, u_1, u_2, u_3 and u_4.
(b)   Work out $u_1 - u_0$, $u_2 - u_1$, $u_3 - u_2$ and $u_4 - u_3$.
(c)   Write down u_{n-1}, and simplify $u_n - u_{n-1}$.
(d)   Hence show that $1 + 2 + 3 + \ldots + n = u_n$.
(e)   If the sum of the first n positive integers is 4950, show that $n^2 + n - 9900 = 0$, and hence find the value of n.   (MEG)

269. (a)   If p is the largest whole number which is a perfect square and which is also less than or equal to n, find p when:

(i) $n = 4.9$;
(ii) $n = 49$;
(iii) $n = 490$.

(b)   The flow diagram below can be used to find the approximate square root of 20, after first choosing an appropriate whole number x as an estimate of $\sqrt{20}$.
Start with $x = 4$ and make out a table like the one here to show every stage in finding $\sqrt{20}$ to 7 significant figures. Show all the figures on your calculator at each stage.

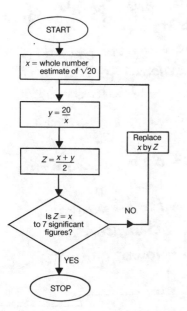

x	y	Z	Difference between x and Z
4.0 4.5 4.4722222 etc.	5.0 4.4444444	4.5	0.5

(SEG)

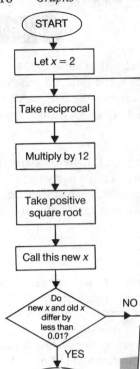

270. (a) The flow chart below will solve a certain equation by an iterative method.
   (i) Work through the flow chart, writing down each value of *x*. State the final value to the appropriate degree of accuracy.
   (ii) Find and simplify the equation which the flow chart solves.
 (b) (i) Show algebraically that the iteration

$$u_{n+1} = \sqrt{\sqrt{12u_n}}$$

   also solves the same equation.
   (ii) Use this iteration, starting again with *x* = 2, to find the root to the same degree of accuracy.
 (c) Comment on your results.

2 Further statistics

A histogram is often misunderstood to be a bar chart.

In a bar chart the height is all that matters. In a histogram, it is the <u>area</u> that measures quantity.

They are only the same, if all bars are the same width.
See worked example 139, for unequal widths.
The horizontal axis must have a continuous scale.
For a grouped frequency table, a cumulative frequency diagram is often the best graph for problem solving.

When plotting cumulative frequency points, they must be plotted at the end points of each group, not the mid-points.
A cumulative frequency diagram is usually a curve. You may lose accuracy if you join with straight lines.

WORDS TO LEARN:
   median = 50% mark on a cumulative frequency curve.
   quartiles = 25% and 75% marks on a cumulative frequency diagram.
interquartile range = upper quartile − lower quartile

Standard deviation.

The spread of data can also be described using the standard deviation. Defined as $S.D = \sqrt{\dfrac{\sum x^2}{n} - \left(\dfrac{\sum x}{n}\right)^2}$ $\begin{bmatrix}\sum \text{means} \\ \text{sum}\end{bmatrix}$

For a frequency table

$$S.D = \sqrt{\dfrac{\sum fx^2}{n} - \left(\dfrac{\sum fx}{n}\right)^2}$$

See worked example 140

Normal distribution

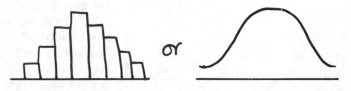 or

Topic: cumulative frequency
GRADE B

WORKED EXAMPLE 138

The heights of a group of 30 children are measured to the nearest centimetre. The results are given in the following table:

Height (cm)	90–99	100–109	110–119	120–129	130–139	140–149
Frequency	2	5	7	10	5	1

Draw up a cumulative frequency table, and hence plot the cumulative frequency curve.
Use your graph to find:

(i) the median height; (ii) the semi-interquartile range.

SOLUTION

The cumulative (or running totals) are given in the following table:

Height (cm)	<100	<110	<120	<130	<140	<150
Cumulative frequency	2	7	14	24	29	30

When plotting the graph of these figures, since the values are given to the nearest cm, the points are plotted at 99.5 cm, 109.5 cm, etc. The cumulative frequency curve (or ogive) can then be plotted.

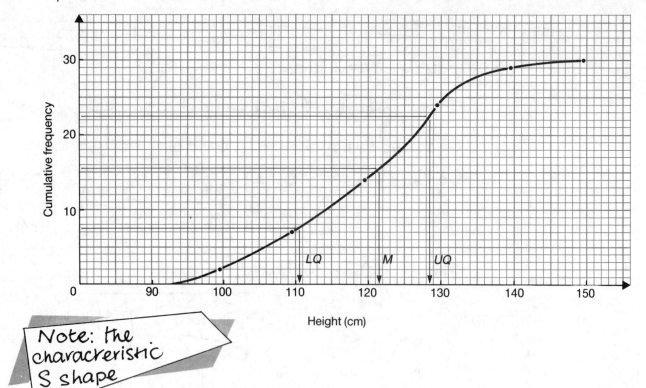

Note: the characteristic S shape

(i)   The median of 30 values is half-way between the 15th and the 16th values. Reading across, 15.5 gives the median = 121.5 cm.
(ii) The quartiles divide the 30 values into 4 equal parts. Although not exactly true, read across $\frac{1}{4}$ of 30 = 7.5.
      This is called the lower quartile = 110.5.
      Read across $\frac{3}{4}$ of 30 = 22.5.
      This is called the upper quartile = 128.5.
      The interquartile range = 128.5 − 110.5
      $$= 18\,\text{cm}$$
      The semi-interquartile range = $\dfrac{18}{2} = 9\,\text{cm}$.

Topic: histogram

GRADE A

WORKED EXAMPLE 139   The following table gives the distribution of the number of employees in the 50 factories in Stenworth:

Number of employees	0–39	40–59	60–79	80–99	100–139
Number of factories	5	15	13	10	7

Construct a histogram to show the distribution.

SOLUTION   The widths of the five class intervals are
                    40   20   20   20   40

Referring to the histogram, we see that as the widths of the first and last intervals are twice the width of the other three, the heights of the rectangles are reduced in proportion: i.e. if the height of the second rectangle is 15 units, the height of the first rectangle is $\frac{5}{2} = 2\frac{1}{2}$ units and the height of the last rectangle is $\frac{7}{2} = 3\frac{1}{2}$ units.

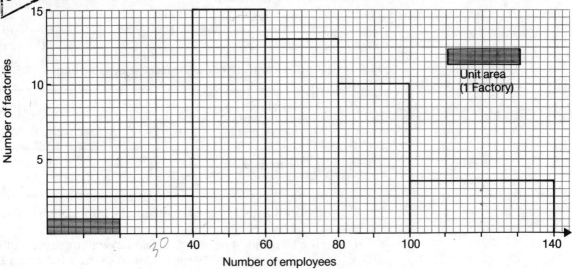

bars should strictly speaking be plotted at 39.5, 59.5 etc.

Topic: standard deviation

GRADE A*

WORKED EXAMPLE 140 Ten students answered a multiple choice test containing 12 questions. The scores of the students were as follows:

$$7, 8, 6, 3, 9, 11, 12, 4, 6, 7$$

For these students, calculate

(i) the mean score
(ii) the standard deviation

A second group of twelve students took the test. On analysis of the results, the mean score for this group was 6.6, and the standard deviation was 1.8.

(iii) calculate the mean score of all twenty-two students
(iv) Compare the results of the two groups.

SOLUTION (i) the mean $= (7 + 8 + 6 + 3 + 9 + 11 + 12 + 4 + 6 + 7) \div 10$
$$= 73 \div 10 = 7.3$$

(ii) Use the formula

$$\text{Standard Deviation} = \sqrt{\frac{\Sigma x^2}{n} - \left(\frac{\Sigma x}{n}\right)^2}$$

$$= \sqrt{\frac{(7^2 + 8^2 + 6^2 + 3^2 + \ldots + 7^2)}{10} - 7.3^2}$$

$$= \sqrt{\frac{605}{10} - 53.29} = \sqrt{7.21}$$

$$= 2.69$$

(iii) To find the average for all the pupils, you must find the total mark of all pupils first.

The total mark $= 10 \times 7.3 + 12 \times 6.6$
$$= 152.2$$
The average $= 152.2 \div 22 = 6.9$

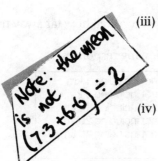

Note: the mean is not $(7.3 + 6.6) \div 2$

(iv) Although the average score for the second group was lower, the fact that the standard deviation was lower means that the scores of the pupils in the second group were close together, whereas in the first group one or two pupils did very well.

Questions to try

271. A student asked 30 people arriving at a football ground how long, to the nearest minute, it had taken them to reach the ground. The times they gave (in minutes) are listed below:

35	41	22	15	31	19	12	12	23	30
30	38	36	24	14	20	20	16	15	22
34	28	25	13	19	9	27	17	21	25

(a) (i) Copy and complete the frequency table here.

Time taken in minutes (to nearest minute)	8–12	13–17	18–22	23–27	28–32	33–37	38–42
Number of people		3	6	7	5	4	

   (ii) Draw a histogram to represent the information in the frequency table.

(b) Of the 30 people questioned, 6 paid £2 each to see the football match, 8 paid £3 each, 4 paid £4 each, 10 paid £5 each and 2 paid £6 each.
   (i) Calculate the total amount paid by these 30 people.
   (ii) Calculate the mean amount paid by these 30 people.   (MEG)

272. In a survey 100 motorists were asked to record the petrol consumption of their cars in miles per gallon. Each figure was rounded to the nearest mile per gallon and the frequency distribution shown in the table was obtained.

Miles per gallon	26–30	31–35	36–40	41–45	46–50	51–55	56–60
Frequency	4	6	18	34	20	12	6

(a) (i) State the limits of the modal class of this distribution.
   (ii) Complete the 'less than' cumulative frequency table here.

Miles per gallon (less than)	30.5	35.5	40.5	45.5	50.5	55.5	60.5
Number of motorists	4	10					

   (iii) On graph paper draw the cumulative frequency curve (ogive) from your completed cumulative frequency table.

(b) Use your cumulative frequency curve to estimate:
   (i) the median of the distribution;
   (ii) the interquartile range.

A 'good' petrol consumption is one which lies beween 38 and 52 miles per gallon.

(c) Estimate the number of motorists whose petrol consumption was 'good'.   (NISEC)

273. In a survey, a number of employees were asked how far away they lived from their place of work.
Each employee ticked one of the following responses:

```
 0  km up to but not including 1 km,
 1  km up to but not including 5 km,
 5  km up to but not including 10 km,
10 km up to but not including 20 km,
20 km up to but not including 40 km,
40 km and over.
```

Exactly 100 ticked the "5 km up to but not including 10 km" response. No one ticked the "40 km and over" response.
The histogram shows the results of the survey.
Calculate the number of employees who took part in the survey. (LEAG)

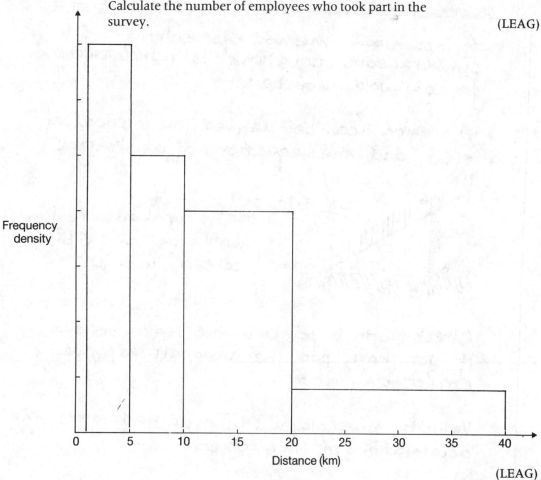

Distance (km)

(LEAG)

274. The weights of a number of potatoes were recorded as follows. **GRADE A***

Weight (grams)	Frequency
118–126	8
127–135	13
136–144	21
145–153	27
154–162	13
163–171	11
172–180	7

Calculate the standard deviation for the weights of the potatoes. (NEA)

275. 100 eggs are classified by mass in the following table.

	Mass (g)	Frequency
Extra small	40–42	1
Small	42–46	3
Medium	46–53	25
Standard	53–62	35
Large	62–75	36

(a) Draw a histogram to illustrate the data.
(b) Calculate estimates of the mean and the standard deviation of this sample.
(c) For a normal distribution it would be expected that more than 95% of the distribution would be contained in the interval mean ± 2 standard deviations. For this sample, using your answers to part (b), calculate the numerical limits of this interval and estimate the percentage of this sample which lies within this interval. (MEG)

3 Simultaneous equations, regions, more straight lines

A graphical method for solving simultaneous equations is advantageous for awkward numbers.

A region can be defined by inequality signs and the equation of a straight line.

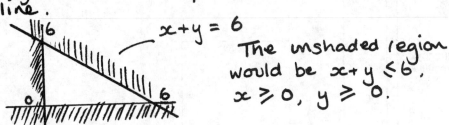

$x + y = 6$

The unshaded region would be $x + y \leq 6$, $x \geq 0$, $y \geq 0$.

Check with a point in the region to see if you have got the inequalities, the correct way round.

Velocity time graphs: The gradient gives the acceleration of the object.

The area under the graph gives the distance travelled. Make sure units on the axes are consistent.

Trapezium rule.   If an area is to be found under a curve, divide it into trapezia.

$$\text{area} = \frac{h}{2}\left[y_0 + 2(y_1 + y_2 + y_3 + y_4) + y_5\right]$$

this can be extended to any number.

Topic: simultaneous equations   ◀ GRADE C/D

WORKED EXAMPLE 141   Use a graphical method to solve the equations $4x + 3y = 5$; $17x + 8y = 9$. Give your answers to 1 d.p.

SOLUTION   The simplest way to draw the lines is as follows:

(i) $4x + 3y = 5$
    $x = 0$: $3y = 5$, so $y = 1.7$
    $y = 0$: $4x = 5$, so $x = 1.3$.

(ii) $17x + 8y = 9$
    $x = 0$: $8y = 9$, so $y = 1.1$
    $y = 0$: $17x = 9$, so $x = 0.5$.

The solution can be read from the graph as $x = -0.7$, $y = 2.6$.

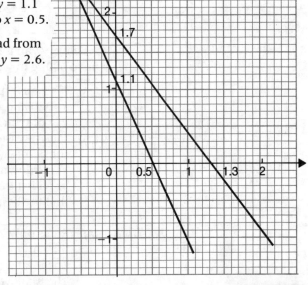

Topics: inequalities, locus   ◀ GRADE B

WORKED EXAMPLE 142   In the diagram, $ABCD$ is a square. P is a point which moves inside the square so that $PA \geq PB$, and $PC \leq PA$. Shade the region in which P must lie.

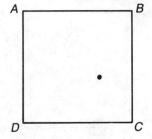

SOLUTION $PA \geq PB$ means that P is nearer to B than to A. This means that P lies in the shaded region shown in (a).
$PC \leq PA$ means that P is nearer to C than A. Hence P also lies in the shaded region shown in (b).

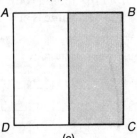
(a)

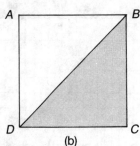
(b)

The region where these two areas overlap is shown in (c).

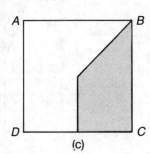
(c)

Topics: regions, linear programming

WORKED EXAMPLE 143 A depot for famine relief has 20 sacks of rice and 35 sacks of maize. The weight, volume and number of meal rations for each sack are shown in the table.

	Weight (kg)	Volume (m³)	No. of meals
Sack of rice	25	0.05	800
Sack of maize	10	0.05	160

A delivery van is to carry the largest possible number of meals. It can carry up to 600 kg in weight and 2 m³ in volume.

(a) If a load is made up of x sacks of rice and y sacks of maize, say why $x \leqslant 20$ and write down three other inequalities (other than $x \geqslant 0$, $y \geqslant 0$) which govern x and y.

(b) Illustrate these inequalities on a graph and indicate the area in which the point (x,y) must lie.

(c) Write down an expression for the number of meals that can be provided from x sacks of rice and y sacks of maize. Using the graph, find the best values to take for x and y.   (NISEC)

SOLUTION (a) Since only 20 sacks of rice are available, we must have $x \leqslant 20$.
Similarly, $y \leqslant 35$.
The total weight of rice is $25x$ kg.
The total weight of maize is $10y$ kg.
Since the lorry cannot carry more than 600 kg, it follows that
$25x + 10y \leqslant 600$.
$\div 5$: $5x + 2y \leqslant 120$.
The total volume of rice is $0.05x$ m³.
The total volume of maize is $0.05y$ m³.
Since the lorry cannot carry more than 2 m³, it follows that
$0.05x + 0.05y \leqslant 2$.
$\times 20$: $x + y \leqslant 40$.

(b) The region is shown in the graph. The points which will be needed can be found either by drawing or by simultaneous equations. They are
$A\ (0,35),\ B\ (5,35),\ C\ (\frac{40}{3},\frac{80}{3}),\ D\ (20,10)$ and $E\ (20,0)$.

(c) The number of meals is $800x + 160y = 160\ (5x + y)$.
This will be greatest when $5x + y$ is greatest. The values of $5x + y$ at the points found in (b) are $A\ (35),\ B\ (60),\ C\ (93\frac{1}{3})$, $D\ (110)$ and $E\ (100)$.
The best value is at D, i.e. $x = 20,\ y = 10$.

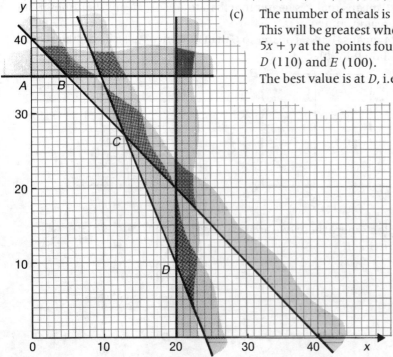

Topics: speed–time graphs, trapezium rule

WORKED EXAMPLE 144 The table below gives the speed (m/s) of a body measured every 2 seconds over a 10 s period. Using the fact that the distance travelled can be found from the area under the speed–time graph, find the approximate distance travelled in the 10 seconds by using the trapezium rule.

time	0	2	4	6	8	10
speed	0	3	7	15	24	20

SOLUTION The graph is first plotted, and found to be a curve. Divide the area into 5 trapezia (one is in fact a triangle in this case).

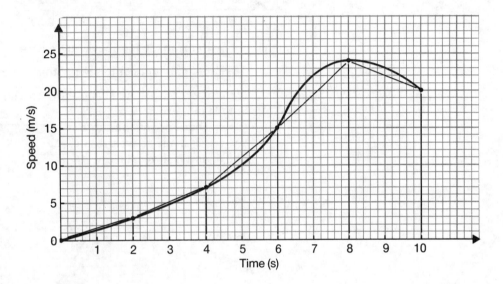

The width of each trapezium is 2, i.e. $h = 2$, $y_0 = 0$, $y_1 = 3$, $y_2 = 7$, $y_3 = 15$, $y_4 = 24$, $y_5 = 20$.

Using the formula, area $= \dfrac{2}{2}[0 + 2(3 + 7 + 15 + 24) + 20]$

$$= 118.$$

The distance travelled is approximately 118 m.

Topics: inequalities, regions   **GRADE A/B**

WORKED EXAMPLE 145 Draw a sketch to illustrate the regions
(a) $y \geqslant 1, x + y \leqslant 5, 3y - 2x < 6$;
(b) $y \geqslant x^2, y \leqslant x + 2$.

SOLUTION (a) We will generally operate the convention of shading the *unwanted* region.
Step 1 is to plot the lines without the inequalities, i.e. $y = 1, x + y = 5$, $3y - 2x = 6$.
The last will be drawn dotted because the inequality does not include the equal part.
$y \geqslant 1$ means shade below $y = 1$.

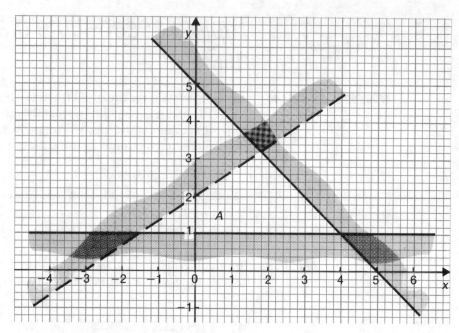

$x + y \leqslant 5$ means shade above line $x + y = 5$.

$3y - 2x < 6$: it is easier to rewrite this $y < \dfrac{2x}{3} + 2$

(careful with the sign); shade above this line.

(b)   Step 1: plot $y = x^2$, $y = x + 2$.
$y \geqslant x^2$, shade below the curve.
$y \leqslant x + 2$, shade above the line.
The region is shown below.

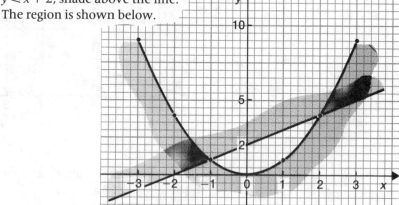

Topics: inequalities, errors

WORKED EXAMPLE 146 v, u, a and t are related by the equation $v = u + at$. If u, a and t cannot be measured exactly, then there is uncertainty in the value of v. If u, a and t can be guaranteed to the nearest whole number, what can be said about v when $u = 40$, $a = 4$ and $t = 15$?

SOLUTION   Since the values are only correct to the nearest whole number, then
$39.5 \leqslant u \leqslant 40.5$, $3.5 \leqslant a \leqslant 4.5$ and $14.5 \leqslant t \leqslant 15.5$.
Although 40.5 would be rounded up to 41, it is included to keep the working simple.
If the smallest values of u, a and t are taken, then
$v = 39.5 + 3.5 \times 14.5 = 90.25$.
If the largest values of u, a and t are taken, then
$v = 40.5 + 4.5 \times 15.5 = 110.25$.
Hence $90.25 \leqslant v \leqslant 110.25$.
Clearly, if this were a scientific experiment, we could be in trouble.

WORKED EXAMPLE 147   It is given that $H = \dfrac{4a}{2 + 4t}$, with a and t measured in centimetres to the nearest centimetre. If $a = 6$ and $t = 4$, find the range of possible values of H.

SOLUTION Since a and t are measured to the nearest whole number, a can be anywhere between 5.5 and 6.5,

i.e. $5.5 \leqslant a \leqslant 6.5$.

Similarly, $3.5 \leqslant t \leqslant 4.5$.

Strictly speaking, we should exclude 6.5, as this would normally be rounded up. But this leads to complications, and does not really affect the result.

Since H is a fraction, the largest value of H will have the largest numerator, and the smallest denominator. The smallest value of H will have the smallest numerator and the largest denominator.

Hence $\dfrac{4 \times 5.5}{2 + 4 \times 4.5} \leqslant H \leqslant \dfrac{4 \times 6.5}{2 + 4 \times 3.5}$

and hence $1.1 \leqslant H \leqslant 1.625$.

Topic: velocity–time graphs

WORKED EXAMPLE 148 A particle is moving with an initial speed of 4 m/s. In the next four seconds its speed increases uniformly to 10 m/s and then the speed decreases uniformly until the particle stops moving after a further eight seconds.

(a)   Show this information on a speed–time graph.

(b)   Find

(i)   the acceleration in the last eight seconds of the motion;

(ii)   the total distance travelled by the particle.   (LEAG)

SOLUTION (a)   The speed–time graph is shown below. Always label axes carefully.

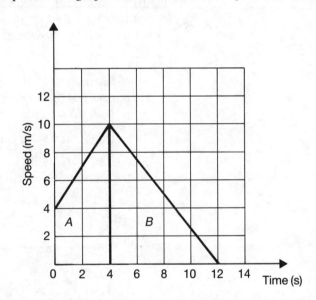

(b)   (i)   Since the particle is slowing down, the acceleration will be negative.

Hence acceleration = gradient of the line = $\dfrac{-10}{8}$

$= -1.25 \,\text{m/s}^2$.

(ii)   Distance travelled equals the area under the graph, which consists of a trapezium A and a triangle B.

Distance = area = $\tfrac{1}{2}(4 + 10) \times 4 + \tfrac{1}{2} \times 10 \times 8$

$= 28 + 40 = 68 \,\text{m}$.

WORKED EXAMPLE 149 The following diagram shows the speed–time graph for an underground train travelling between two stations. It starts from rest and accelerates at a constant rate for 10 seconds, then travels at constant speed for 30 seconds, and finally slows down at a constant rate. If the distance between the stations is 850 m, calculate:

(a)   the maximum speed;

(b)   the acceleration;

(c)   the time it takes to reach the half-way point.

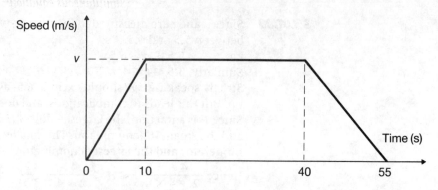

SOLUTION   Many questions on speed–time graphs can be solved on the basis that the area under the graph equals the distance travelled. Look out for triangles, trapeziums, etc.

(a)   Area of the trapezium $= \frac{1}{2}(55 + 30)v$

$$= \frac{85v}{2}.$$

But distance = area, so $\frac{85v}{2} = 850$;

this gives $v = 20$.
Maximum speed $= 20\,\text{m/s}$.

(b)   The acceleration equals the gradient of the line.

Acceleration $= \dfrac{20}{10} = 2\,\text{m/s}^2$.

(c)   To find how long it takes to reach the half-way point, we are trying to find the time T which divides the area under the graph into two equal parts; see the following graph. The shaded area must equal

$\dfrac{850}{2} = 425$.

Since the triangle Ⓐ has area $\frac{1}{2} \times 10 \times 20 = 100$,
then rectangle Ⓑ has area $425 - 100 = 325$;
$(T - 10) \times 20 = 325$.

$T - 10 = \dfrac{325}{20} = 16.25$; i.e. $T = 26.25$.

It takes 26.25 seconds.
Note: This is not one-half of 55 seconds.

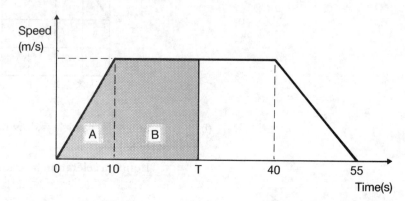

Questions to try

GRADE B

276.   Use a graphical method to solve the equations:

(i) $4x - 3y = 6$,
$2x + 7y = 11$.

(ii) $5x + 9y = 8$,
$6x + 4y = 11$.

(iii) $3x - 7y = 5$,
$9x + 11y = 4$.

277. The graph below shows the speed of a train on a narrow gauge railway as it travelled between two stations.

   (a)   How long did the train take to reach its maximum speed?

   (b)   What was the acceleration of the train over this period? Give your answer in m/s^2 (metres per second per second).

   (c)   How far, in kilometres, did the train travel between the two stations?

   (d)   What was the average speed of the train between the two stations? Give your answer in kilometres per hour.

                                        (WJEC)

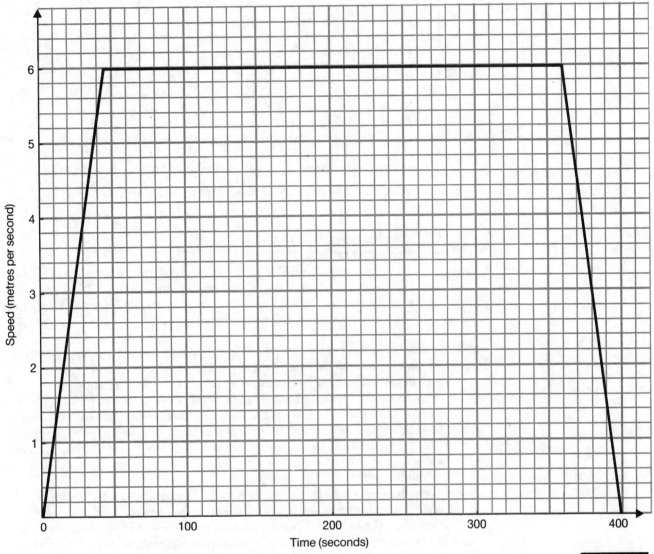

GRADE A*

278. A couple on holiday in Greece decide to bring back some 'duty free' drinks to England. They decide on two types of drink: wine, sold in $\frac{3}{4}$ litre bottles, costing 500 drachmas, and spirits, sold in 1 litre bottles, costing 900 drachmas. They are allowed to bring back only 6 litres between them, and have only 4500 drachmas to spend. They want to bring back at least one bottle of wine and one bottle of spirits.

Suppose that they bring back x bottles of wine and y bottles of spirits.

   (a)   Show that, because they only have 4500 drachmas between them, this leads to the inequality $5x + 9y \leqslant 45$.

   (b)   Write down three other inequalities which must be satisfied.

   (c)   On graph paper draw the necessary graphs and indicate the region in which all four inequalities are satisfied.

The couple decide that they want to bring back the greatest volume possible.

   (d)   State a combination of bottles of wine and spirits which the couple could bring back.

                                        (WEA)

279.

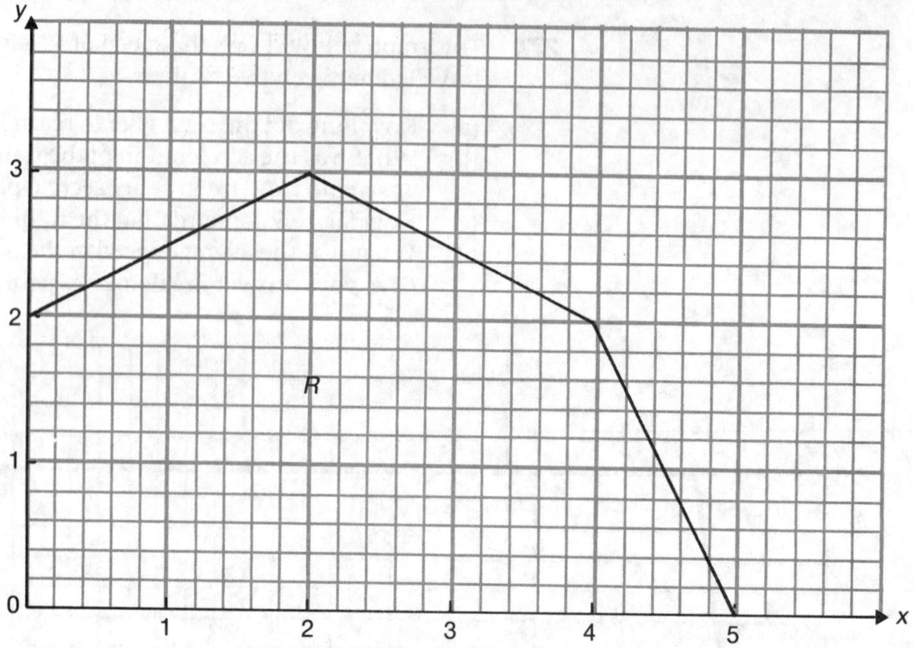

The region R as shown in the diagram is bounded by five straight lines.

(a) R is defined by five inequalities, three of which are

$$x \geqslant 0, \quad y \geqslant 0, \quad x + 2y \leqslant 8.$$

Find the other two inequalities.

(b)   For the points (x, y) in R find
  (i)   the greatest possible value of $x + y$ and the coordinates of the point at which this greatest possible value occurs,
  (ii)   the least possible value of $x - 2y$ and the coordinates of one point at which this least possible value occurs.   (MEG)

280.   A shopkeeper stocks two brands of drinks called Kula and Sundown, both of which are produced in cans of the same size. He wishes to order fresh supplies and finds that he has room for up to 1000 cans. He knows that Sundown is more popular and so proposes to order at least twice as many cans of Sundown as of Kula. He wishes, however, to have at least 100 cans of Kula and not more than 800 cans of Sundown. Taking x to be the number of cans of Kula and y to be the number of cans of Sundown which he orders, write down the four inequalities involving x and/or y which satisfy these conditions.

The point (x,y) represents x cans of Kula and y cans of Sundown. Using a scale of 1 cm to represent 100 cans on each axis, construct and indicate clearly, by shading the *unwanted* regions, the region in which (x,y) must lie. The profit on a can of Kula is 3p and on a can of Sundown is 2p. Use your graph to estimate the number of cans of each that the shopkeeper should order to give the maximum profits.

281.   A new book is to be published in both a hardback and a paperback edition. A bookseller agrees to purchase:

(a)   15 or more hardback copies;
(b)   more than 25 paperback copies;
(c)   at least 45, but fewer than 60, copies altogether.

Using h to represent the number of hardback copies and p to represent the number of paperback copies, write down the inequalities which represent these conditions.

The point (h,p) represents h hardback copies and p paperback copies. Using a scale of 2 cm to represent 10 books on each axis, construct, and indicate clearly by shading the *unwanted* regions, the region in which (h,p) must lie. Given that each hardback copy costs £5 and each paperback costs £2, calculate the number of each sort that the bookseller must buy if he is prepared to spend between £180 and £200 altogether and he has to buy each sort in packets of five.

282. Use the trapezium rule with 5 strips to find the area under the curve $y = x^2 + 1$ between $x = 1$ and $x = 2$.

283. The values in the table give the relationship between x and t:

t	0	1	2	3	4	5
x	0.8	1.3	1.8	2	1.4	0.8

Use the trapezium rule to find the area under the graph of x plotted against t.

284. The speed v m/s of an experimental trolley is measured running along a straight track after t seconds, and found to satisfy the equation $v = 16t - t^2$.

(a) Draw up a table of values for $0 \leqslant t \leqslant 16$ at intervals of 2 seconds.
(b) Using the scales of 1 cm to represent 5 m/s vertically and 1 cm to represent 2 seconds horizontally, draw the graph for $0 \leqslant t \leqslant 16$.
(c) Using your graph,
   (i) find the maximum speed of the trolley;
   (ii) find the acceleration of the trolley when $t = 4$ seconds;
   (iii) estimate the distance travelled in the 16 seconds, using the trapezium rule. Show your working clearly.

SHAPE AND SPACE

ATTAINMENT TARGET 4

13

1 Further mensuration and geometry problems

At the higher levels more ideas are brought into the problems.

Any mention of rate, means time is involved.

Take care that units are consistent.

You may need to rearrange a formula, e.g. If a cube has volume 80cm^3, find the length of the side

$$x^3 = 80, \quad \text{so} \quad x = \sqrt[3]{80}.$$

If involved in accurate drawing, make sure you have a complete set of drawing instruments. Look at page 234 for constructions.

If working with percentages, make sure quantities are all in the same units.
Do not give too many decimal places in an answer. Examination accuracy is usually 3 significant figures. But work with say 4 significant figures until the final answer.

WORDS TO LEARN

Locus = the path traced out by a moving point. Questions may involve geometrical constructions.

Topics: volume, percentages `GRADE C/D`

WORKED EXAMPLE 150   A firm sells Turkish Delight in cylindrical containers with radius 10 cm and height 5 cm.

(a)   Calculate the volume of the container.

There are 80 pieces in each box. Assuming each piece is a 2.5 cm cube, calculate:

(b)   (i)   the volume of one piece;
      (ii)   the volume occupied by the sweets expressed as a percentage of the volume of the box.

(c)   The Turkish Delight is also available in 'tubes' of length 40 cm and radius 4 cm. The weight of the contents of the first box is 250 g. If the same percentage of volume of the tube is occupied, find the weight contained in the tube.

SOLUTION   (a)   Using $\pi r^2 h$,
                     volume $= \pi \times 10^2 \times 5 = 1571 \, \text{cm}^3$.

(b)   (i) $2.5 \times 2.5 \times 2.5 = 15.625 \, \text{cm}^3$
      (ii) $80 \times 15.625 = 1250 \, \text{cm}^3$
      Hence the percentage $= \dfrac{1250}{1571} \times 100 = 79.6\%$

(c)   In the first box, 1250 cm³ weighs 250 g
      Hence 1 cm³ weighs $\dfrac{250}{1250} = 0.2 \, \text{g}$
      The volume of the tube $= \pi \times 4^2 \times 40$
      $= 2011 \, \text{cm}^3$
      79.6% of this $= 2011 \times 0.796 = 1600 \, \text{cm}^3$
      The weight $= 1600 \times 0.2 = 320 \, \text{g}$.

Geometrical constructions

In the following diagrams, points numbered ①, ② etc. show where and the order in which the compass point is placed and the corresponding arcs have the same numbers. Notes about restrictions on the radii are given at the side.

(a)   Bisecting a line *PQ* at right angles,

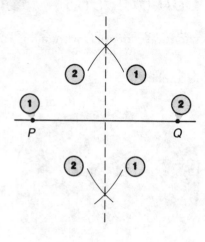

radius ① = radius ②, and must be
greater than half of *PQ*.

(b)   Bisecting an angle *ABC*,

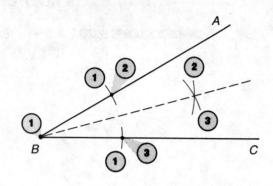

① any radius; radius ② = radius ③,
large enough for the arcs to meet.

(c)   Perpendicular from a point *P* to a line *AB*,

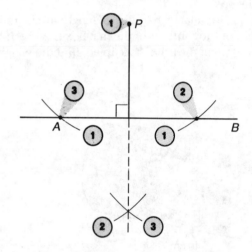

radii ①, ②, ③ equal, large enough
for ① to meet line *AB*.

(d)   Construction of 60° at a point *X* on *XY*.

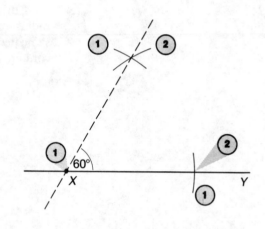

radius ① = radius ②.

(e)   Drawing a line through *P* parallel to *AB*,

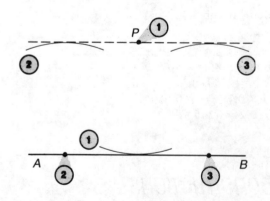

radii ①, ②, ③ equal, the arc ① just touches *AB*.

(f)   To construct an angle of 90° at *A* on *AB*,

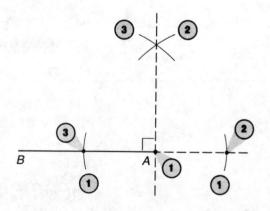

BA must be extended at *A*; radii ①, ②, ③ equal.

Topics: volume, rate

GRADE C/D

WORKED EXAMPLE 151

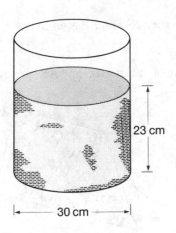

A gardener wishes to find out the time for which he needs to keep the water-hose turned on his garden so as to give the equivalent of 1 cm of rainfall.

(a) Firstly, he finds the rate of flow of water from his hose-pipe. To do this he runs water from the hose into a cylindrical tin which has a base *diameter* of 30 cm.
After 2 minutes he turns the water off and finds that the depth of water in the tin is 23 cm.
   (i) Calculate the volume of water in the tin.
   (ii) What volume of water comes out of the hose in one minute?

(b) The garden, *ABCD*, is in the shape of a trapezium *ABCE* and a triangle *ECD*. The edge, *AD*, is perpendicular to both *AB* and to *EC*. *AB* = 13 m; *EC* = 10 m; *AE* = 8 m; *ED* = 7 m.

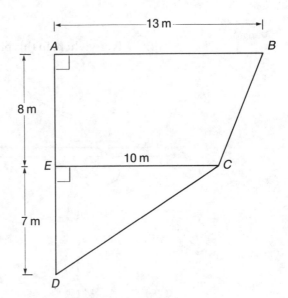

   (i) Calculate the area of the garden in m².
   (ii) What volume of water, in m³, falls on the garden when there is a rainfall of 1 cm?

(c) Use your answers to (a)(ii) and (b)(ii) to calculate the time for which the gardener would have to use the water-hose in order to achieve this depth of 1 cm.

SOLUTION

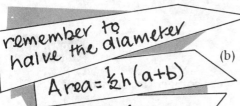

remember to halve the diameter

Area = ½h(a+b)

Change 1cm to 0·01m

(a) (i) Using $\pi r^2 h$,
volume $= \pi \times 15^2 \times 23$
$= 16258 \text{ cm}^3$.
   (ii) This is in 2 minutes, so divide by 2 = 8129 cm³/min.

(b) (i) Area of the trapezium $ABCE = \frac{1}{2}(13 + 10) \times 8 = 92 \text{ m}^2$.
Area of the triangle $ECD = \frac{1}{2} \times 10 \times 7 = 35 \text{ m}^2$.
The total area = 92 + 35 = 127 m².
   (ii) Treating it as a prism, the volume = 0.01 × 127 = 1.27 m³.

(c) To change m³ → cm³ you multiply by (100)³.
The volume of water = 1 270 000 cm³.
The time = 1 270 000 ÷ 8129
$= 156 \text{ minutes}$
$= 2 \text{ hours } 36 \text{ minutes}$.

Topic: *locus*

WORKED EXAMPLE 152   Describe as accurately as you can the locus of a point P that moves subject to the following conditions:

(i) $PA = 5$ cm where A is a point on a flat surface, and P lies on that surface.

(ii) $PA = PB$, where $AB = 12$ cm.

(iii) $PA + PB = 10$ cm, where A and B lie on a flat surface, and $AB = 6$ cm.

SOLUTION   (i)   A circle centre A, radius 5 cm

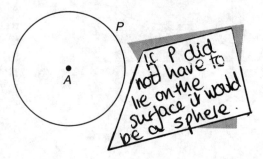

If P did not have to lie on the surface it would be a sphere.

(ii)   P is anywhere in this place

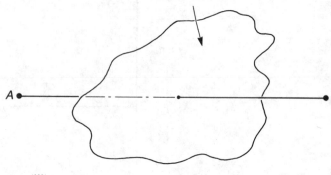

P lies in a plane at right angles to AB, passing through the centre of AB.

(iii)

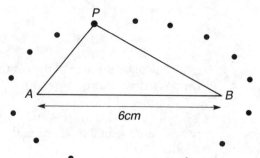

The diagram shows a number of positions for which $PA + PB = 10$. The set of points lies on an **ellipse**.

Questions to try

285.   **(In this question give all your answers correct to 3 significant figures.)**

(a)   A lead ball of radius 4 cm is melted and cast into small balls each of radius 0.25 cm.

    (i)   Calculate the volume, in cm^3, of the large lead ball.

    (ii)   Calculate the volume, in cm^3, of a single small lead ball.

    (iii)   How many small lead balls can be cast from the large ball?

(b)   A cylindrical can of radius 5 cm contains water to a depth of 6 cm. Four thousand lead balls, each of radius 0.25 cm, are dropped into the can. Calculate the rise, in cm, of the water level.

(c)   Lead in water is believed to poison water birds. A fisherman has 8 small lead balls on his line. He considers an alternative arrangement of the same volume of lead using a single lead ball in order to reduce the surface area.

(i)   Find the radius of this alternative lead ball.

(ii)   Find the surface area of this alternative lead ball.

(iii)   Calculate the surface area of a small lead ball of radius 0.25 cm.

(iv)   Copy and complete the following table to display all the evidence about the alternative balls.

	One small lead ball	8 small lead balls	One alternative lead ball
Radius	0.25 cm	0.25 cm	
Surface area			
Volume			

(LEAG)

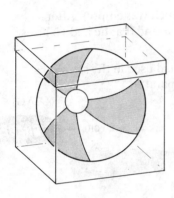

286.   A manufacturer of foam-filled beach balls packs each into a cuboid box of side 20 cm into which it will just fit.

(a)   Calculate the volume of:

(i)   the box;

(ii)   the ball;

(iii)   'wasted space', that is the volume of air inside the box not occupied by the ball. (You may use $\pi = 3.142$.)

(b)   The manufacturer later decides to use boxes of the same size to hold 8 smaller beach balls each of diameter 10 cm. Will there be more, less, or the same amount of 'wasted space'?   (MEG)

287.   Draw a line TQ, 20 cm long. Mark O on the line so that $TO = 5$ cm.

(a)   Draw a circle of radius 5 cm with its centre at O. On the same figure, mark a point P, on the line OQ, which is 13 cm from O.

(b)   Bisect line OP and mark the middle point M.

(c)   Draw a circle, centre M, with radius PM. The two circles meet in two points, A and B. Label these points.

(d)   Draw the lines OA and AP. Measure, and write down, the size of angle OAP.

(e)   Measure, and write down the length, in cm, of AP.

(f)   Using your measurement for AP, calculate the area of triangle OAP.

(g)   Describe clearly the locus of all points on the paper which are equidistant from A and B.   (LEAG)

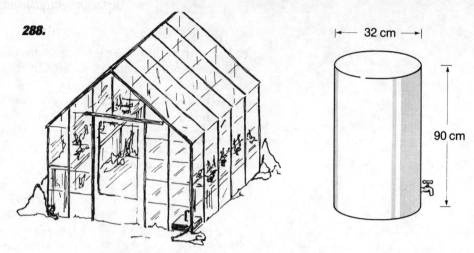

288.

Mr Jones warms his greenhouse with a paraffin heater. He stores the paraffin in a cylindrical tank. The internal height of the tank is 90 cm. The internal diameter of the tank is 32 cm.

(a)   Calculate the internal volume of the tank.
       Give your answer in cm³, to the nearest 100 cm³.
(b)   Write down the capacity, in litres to the nearest litre, of the tank.

Mr Jones put 70 litres of paraffin in the tank (which was empty). After 6 weeks he checked the level of the paraffin. He found that he had 12 litres left.

(c)   (i)   Calculate the amount of paraffin he had used in the six weeks.
       (ii)   Calculate the drop in the level of the paraffin.

(LEAG)

GRADE B

289.   A bucket can be considered as a truncated cone. If the radius of the base is 18 cm, the radius of the top is 21 cm, and the height of the bucket is 40 cm, find the volume of the bucket.
(Volume of a cone $= \frac{1}{3}\pi r^2 h$.)

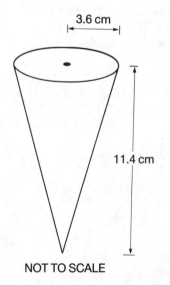

NOT TO SCALE

290.   (In this question, take π to be 3.142 and give each answer correct to three significant figures.)

(a)   The ice cream in a 'Conetti' is in the shape of a circular cone with base radius 3.6 cm and vertical height 11.4 cm. The curved surface is completely covered with wafer of negligible thickness.
       (i)   Calculate the volume of the ice cream.
       (ii)   Calculate the area of the wafer.
(b)

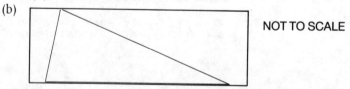

NOT TO SCALE

The 'Conettis' are packed in a rectangular box with their curved surfaces in contact with the base of the box. A vertical cross-section through the axis of one Conetti is shown in the diagram above. Calculate the least possible height of the box.
(c)   The ice cream is also sold in containers in which the ice cream has the shape of a circular cylinder of height 3.6 cm. The volume of ice cream in each container is the same as in one Conetti.
       Calculate the radius of the cylinder.

(MEG)

291. A hillside is in the form of a plane inclined at an angle of 25° to the horizontal. Nia walks from *A* to *B*, a distance of 200 metres down the slope by the steepest route.

(a) Find the distance *AD*, the amount by which Nia is below her starting point.

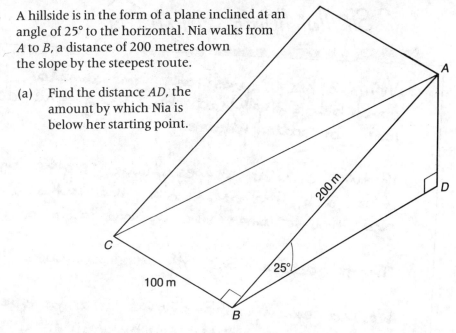

Stuart walks from *A* to *C* across the plane. He starts at the same place, *A*, as Nia and finishes at the same horizontal level, but 100 metres away from her, at *C*.

(b) How far has Stuart walked?

(c) Find the angle between Stuart's route and the horizontal plane.

(WJEC)

292. A cylindrical saucepan, diameter 19.8 cm and height 9 cm, contains water to a depth of 4.5 cm.

(a) Find the volume of water in the pan.

(b) A cylindrical can, diameter 8.5 cm and height 7.9 cm, is placed upright into the saucepan. The can does not float in water.

(i) Find the surface area of the water.

(ii) How far up the can does the water come?

(iii) How much more water would be required to just cover the can?

(WJEC)

2 Similar figures, mixtures

Very often, questions on similar figures can be simplified by using the ideas of ratio or scale factors.

If two similar shapes have lengths in the ratio $a:b$, the areas are the ratio $a^2:b^2$, and the volumes are in the ratio $a^3:b^3$.

Try to reduce one of the numbers to <u>one</u>.

Worked example 155 shows how a question can often be solved with very little working.

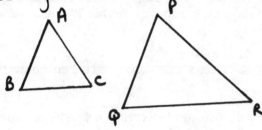

$$\frac{AB}{PQ} = \frac{AC}{PR} = \frac{BC}{QR}$$

Similar triangles

These occur in situations such as:

Here △ ABC is similar to △ ADE

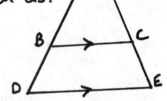

The letters must be in the correct order. These ideas are often met in cross sections of solids e.g. a truncated cone.

Topic: similar volumes

WORKED EXAMPLE 153   A sealed hollow cone with vertex downwards is partially filled with water. The volume of water is $200\,\text{cm}^3$ and the depth of the water is $50\,\text{mm}$. Find the volume of water which must be added to increase the depth to $70\,\text{mm}$.

(NISEC)

SOLUTION This is a question involving similar shapes. If the new depth of water is 70 mm, the ratio of the depths is $50 : 70 = 5 : 7$.

The scale factor $= 5 : 7$.

The ratio of the volumes $= 5^3 : 7^3$
$$= 125 : 343.$$

The smallest volume has to be made 200 cm.

$\div 5$: ratio $= 25 : \dfrac{343}{5}$;

$\times 8$: ratio $= 200 : \dfrac{343}{5} \times 8 = 548.8$.

Extra volume needed $= 548.8 - 200 \, \text{cm}^3 = 348.8 \, \text{cm}^3$.

Topic: similar figures

WORKED EXAMPLE 154 The diagram shows 2 *similar* bottles of lemonade. The small one holds 0.5 litres, and the area of the label on the large one is $40 \, \text{cm}^2$. Estimate:

(i)   the volume that the large bottle holds;
(ii) the area of the label on the small bottle.

SOLUTION Without accurate measurements, a reasonable guess would be that all lengths on the large bottle are twice the corresponding lengths on the small bottle. The scale factor is $\times 2$.

(i)   The ratio of volumes is $\times (2 \times 2 \times 2)$
i.e. $\times 8$.
The volume of the large bottle is $0.5 \times 8 = 4$ litres.

(ii) The ratio of areas is $\times (2 \times 2)$
i.e. $\times 4$.
The smaller area must be $40 \, \text{cm}^2 \div 4 = 10 \, \text{cm}^2$.

> Cube the scale factor for volume ratios
>
> Square the scale factor for area ratios

Topic: similar shapes

WORKED EXAMPLE 155 The diagram shows a parallelogram *PQRS*, and *T* is the mid-point of *PQ*. Find the following ratios:

(a) $\dfrac{\text{area of triangle } TQU}{\text{area of triangle } SUR}$;

(b) $\dfrac{\text{area of triangle } TQU}{\text{area of quadrilateral } PTUS}$.

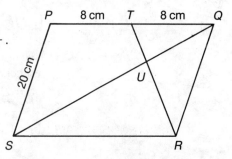

SOLUTION Since no angles are given, it is not possible to work out any of the individual areas. The methods of similar figures must be used.

(a) $\triangle SUR$ is an enlargement of $\triangle QUT$ centre *U* and scale factor -2
($SR = 16 \, \text{cm}$, $TQ = 8 \, \text{cm}$);
hence $\dfrac{\text{area } \triangle TQU}{\text{area } \triangle SUR} = \dfrac{1}{(-2)^2} = \tfrac{1}{4}$.

(b)   There is no direct enlargement from $\triangle TQU$ to the quadrilateral *PTUS*, hence a different technique must be used. Although the following method is not the only one, it has the advantage of being easily seen diagrammatically.

The area of $\triangle TQU$ is denoted by *A*. Hence the area of $\triangle SUR$ is 4*A*.

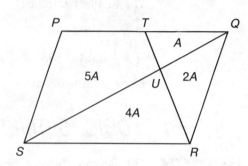

$UR = 2TU$, hence if you regard *TU* as the base of $\triangle TUQ$ and *UR* as the base of $\triangle URQ$, they have the same height, but the base has been doubled. Hence the area has been doubled. The area of $\triangle UQR$ is therefore 2*A*. Since the diagonal *SQ* divides the area of the parallelogram into two equal parts, the area of quadrilateral *PTUS* must be 5*A*.

Hence $\dfrac{\text{area } \triangle TQU}{\text{area } PTUS} = \dfrac{A}{5A} = \dfrac{1}{5}$.

Topic: mixtures

WORKED EXAMPLE 156   An Austrian bar sells 50 cl of beer for 35 schillings. It also sells 30 cl of lemonade for 12 schillings. Shandy is made up in the ratio 2 parts beer to 3 parts lemonade. How much should it charge for 50 cl of shandy?

SOLUTION   This type of question is a typical problem about *mixtures*.
Divide 50 cl in the ratio 2 : 3.
This gives 20 cl   : 30 cl
        beer   lemonade
50 cl beer costs 25 schillings
÷ 5   10 cl beer costs 5 schillings
× 2   20 cl beer costs 10 schillings.
We know that 30 cl lemonade costs 12 schillings.
Hence, the cost of the shandy is 10 schillings + 12 schillings = 22 schillings.

Try and find amounts of each part in the final mixture

Find the cost of each part.

Questions to try

GRADE B

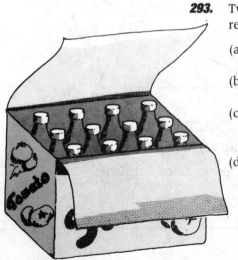

293.   Two bottles of sauce of circular cross-section are completely similar in every respect. One is 24 cm high, and the other is 36 cm.

(a)   Calculate the diameter of the outside base of the smaller bottle, given that the corresponding diameter of the larger is 6 cm.
(b)   The smaller bottle can hold 256 cm³ of sauce. Calculate the volume of sauce that the larger bottle can hold.
(c)   Twelve of the larger bottles are placed as four rows of three bottles in a rectangular box. If there is no room for the bottles to move in the box, calculate the area of cardboard needed to make a closed box.
(d)   What area is needed to make a smaller box for twelve small bottles packed in the same way?

(WJEC)

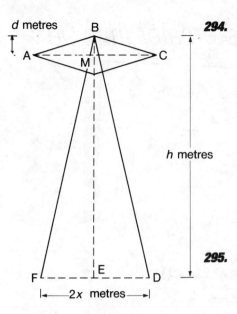

d metres

294. The figure represents the side view of a symmetrical electricity pylon standing on horizontal ground. The line AC is horizontal with the points A and C vertically above the points F and D, respectively. The vertical height BE is h metres, the distance BM is d metres and the distance FD is $2x$ metres. The triangles BMC and FEB are similar.

(a) Copy and complete the following equation:
$$\frac{BM}{FE} = \frac{MC}{}.$$

(b) Rewrite this equation:
    (i) using the letters d, h, x;
    (ii) with d as the subject.

(c) Calculate the height of A above F, given that $h = 12$ and $x = 3$.

(LEAG)

295. A rectangular block of ice cream measures 80 cm by 40 cm by 20 cm. It is to be cut into smaller blocks of the same shape as (i.e. similar to) the original block.
One possible cut is shown shaded, and the resulting block is $ABCDEFGH$.

(a) State the length of AB.
(b) State the number of blocks of this new size which can be produced from the original block.

These blocks are further divided into similar blocks each with a longest edge of 5 cm.

(c) State the other two dimensions of such a block.
(d) Calculate how many blocks of this size can be cut from the block 80 cm by 40 cm by 20 cm.

(NEA)

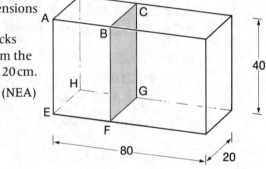

296.

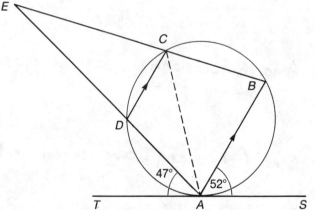

The figure shows a cyclic quadrilateral $ABCD$ with AB parallel to DC. The line TAS is the tangent to the circle at A. Angle $DAT = 47°$ and angle $BAS = 52°$.

(a) Find the size of:
    (i) $\angle ACB$; (ii) $\angle DCA$; (iii) $\angle CBA$.

The lines BC and AD are produced to meet at E.

(b) Show that triangle EBA is isosceles.

The triangles ECD and EBA are similar.
$EC : CB = 2 : 3$.

(c) Calculate the value of $\dfrac{\text{area of triangle } ECD}{\text{area of triangle } EBA}$.

(LEAG)

3 Non-right-angled triangles, angles greater than 90°

You cannot use Pythagoras's theorem in a non-right-angled triangle.

Sine rule:

$$\frac{a}{\sin A} = \frac{b}{\sin B} = \frac{c}{\sin C}$$

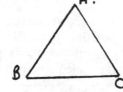

Use (i) 2 sides and 1 angle (not included)

(ii) 1 side and 2 angles.

Be careful when finding angles, because $\sin C = \sqrt{0.8}$ has two solutions. The obvious one is 53° but also 180° − 53° = 127°. This last one may not be possible.

Cosine Rule:

$$a^2 = b^2 + c^2 - 2bc \cos A$$

for angles $\cos A = \dfrac{b^2 + c^2 - a^2}{2bc}$

Use
(i) 3 angles
(ii) 2 sides and included angle.

Area of a triangle $= \frac{1}{2} ab \sin C \begin{bmatrix} \text{2 sides and} \\ \text{included angle} \end{bmatrix}$

Sine (or cosine) wave.

A calculator will give the correct sign for you.

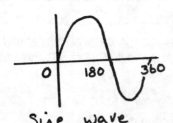

Sine wave

Cosine wave

Topic: area of a triangle

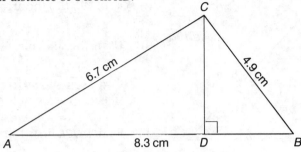

WORKED EXAMPLE 157   In triangle ABC, $AB = 8.3$ cm, $CB = 4.9$ cm and $AC = 6.7$ cm. Find the perpendicular distance of C from AB.

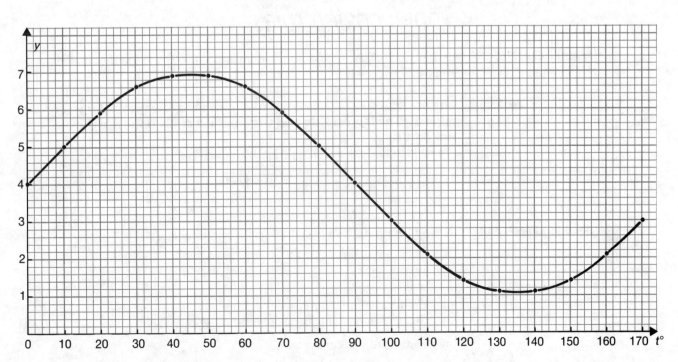

SOLUTION   Referring to the diagram, we are trying to find CD.
We begin by finding the area of the triangle using the formula

$$\text{area} = \sqrt{s(s-a)(s-b)(s-c)}$$
where $s = \frac{1}{2}(6.7+8.3+4.9) = 9.95$.
$\text{Area} = \sqrt{9.95 \times 5.05 \times 3.25 \times 1.65} = 16.42 \text{ cm}^2$.

Using $\frac{1}{2}$ base $\times$ height $=$ area, we get $\frac{1}{2} \times 8.3 \times CD = 16.42$.
$4.15CD = 16.42$, $CD = \dfrac{16.42}{4.15} = 3.96$ cm.

Topic: sine wave

WORKED EXAMPLE 158   Draw a graph of $y = 4 + 3 \sin 2t$ for values of t between 0 and 180° inclusive.

SOLUTION   Use t in steps of 10°. Remember to double t before using the sine.
So for $t = 10°$, $y = 4 + 3 \times \sin 20° = 5.0$
(You cannot plot more than 1 decimal place.)
The completed table is as follows:

t	0	10	20	30	40	50	60	70	80	90	100	110	120	130	140	150	160	170	180
y	4.0	5.0	5.9	6.6	7.0	7.0	6.6	5.9	5.0	4.0	3.0	2.1	1.4	1.1	1.1	1.4	2.1	3.0	4.0

The characteristic sine wave can now be plotted.

Topic: sine rule

WORKED EXAMPLE 159   In $\triangle PQR$, $\angle PQR = 63°$, $\angle PRQ = 48.4°$, and the side $PR = 8$ cm. Find:

(i) PQ; (ii) QR; (iii) the area of the triangle.

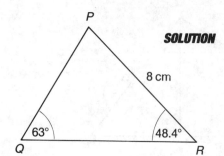

SOLUTION

(i)   Using the sine rule, $\dfrac{PQ}{\sin 48.4°} = \dfrac{8}{\sin 63°}$.

So $\dfrac{PQ}{0.7478} = \dfrac{8}{0.8910} = 8.979$.

Hence $PQ = 8.979 \times 0.7478$
$= 6.71$ cm.

(ii)   Find $\angle QPR$ first: $180° - 63° - 48.4° = 68.6°$.

Using the sine rule again, $\dfrac{QR}{\sin 68.6°} = \dfrac{8}{\sin 63°} = 8.979$.

Hence $QR = 0.9311 \times 8.979$
$= 8.36$ cm.

(iii)   Use area $= \frac{1}{2}ab \sin C$.
Area $= \frac{1}{2} \times 8 \times 8.36 \sin 48.4°$
$= 25$ cm^2.

Angles of a triangle add up to 180°

WORKED EXAMPLE 160   In triangle XYZ, $\angle XYZ = 30°$, $XY = 8$ cm, and $XZ = 5$ cm. Find the two possible values of XYZ and illustrate with a diagram.

SOLUTION   If you try to draw triangle XYZ, then the two possible triangles can be seen in XYZ_1 and XYZ_2.

$\dfrac{XY}{\sin Z} = \dfrac{XZ}{\sin Y}$, so $\dfrac{XY}{XZ} \sin Y = \sin Z$;

$\sin Z = \dfrac{8 \sin 30°}{5} = 0.8$.

Since $\sin Z$ is positive, Z could be between $0°$ and $90°$ or between $90°$ and $180°$.

Hence, $Z_1 = 53.1°$,
$Z_2 = 126.9°$.

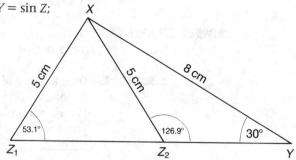

Topic: cosine rule

WORKED EXAMPLE 161   In triangle PQR, $PQ = 5$ cm, $QR = 6$ cm and $RP = 7$ cm. Find the smallest angle of the triangle.

SOLUTION   **The order of size of the angles of a triangle is always the largest angle opposite the largest side and the smallest angle opposite the smallest side.**

We need to find the angle opposite PQ, which is R.

So $\cos R = \dfrac{6^2 + 7^2 - 5^2}{2 \times 6 \times 7} = \dfrac{60}{84} = 0.7143$,

i.e. $\angle R = 44.4°$.

WORKED EXAMPLE 162   In the diagram ABC is a straight line, $CD = 6.4$ cm and $AB = 7.3$ cm. Calculate:

(a) BD;
(b) AD;
(c)   the area of triangle ABD;
(d)   the perpendicular distance of B from AD.

Give answers to 1 decimal place.

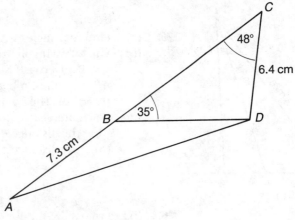

SOLUTION (a) $\dfrac{BD}{\sin 48°} = \dfrac{6.4}{\sin 35°} = 11.16.$

So $BD = 11.16 \times \sin 48° = 8.3\,\text{cm}.$

(b) Now $\angle ABD = 180° - 35° = 145°.$

So $(AD)^2 = 7.3^2 + 8.3^2 - 2 \times 7.3 \times 8.3 \cos 145$

$= 53.29 + 68.89 + 99.26 = 221.44.$

Hence $AD = \sqrt{221.44} = 14.9\,\text{cm}.$

(c) The area, using $\frac{1}{2}AB \times BD \sin ABD = \frac{1}{2} \times 7.3 \times 8.3 \sin 145°$

$= 17.4\,\text{cm}^2.$

(d) Using AD as the base of $\triangle ABD$,

the area of $\triangle ABD = \frac{1}{2} \times AD \times$ perpendicular distance of B from AD

$= \frac{1}{2} \times 14.9 \times h \text{ (say)}.$

But we know the area $= 17.4\,\text{cm}^2.$

So $7.45h = 17.4$

$h = 17.4 \div 7.45 = 2.3\,\text{cm}.$

Questions to try

GRADE C/D

297. A, B and C are three points on a map. $AB = 6.8\,\text{cm}$, $AC = 5.3\,\text{cm}$ and $\angle BAC = 44.6°.$

(a) Calculate the length of BC.

(b) Given that the actual distance represented by AB is 13.6 km, calculate the scale of the map in the form $1:n$, and the actual distance represented by BC in kilometres.

(c) Given that B is due East of A and that C is North of the line AB, calculate the bearing of C from A.

GRADE A

298. **Graph paper must be used for this question.**

The morning high-tide at Barport harbour on 15th November was at 5 a.m. The depth, h metres, of water in the harbour t hours later was given by the formula $h = 6 + 4 \cos (29t)°.$

(a) Copy and complete the following table, giving the values of h correct to 1 decimal place.

t	0	1	2	3	4	5	6
h	10				4.2		

(b) Using a scale of 2 centimetres to represent 1 unit on the horizontal t-axis and a scale of 1 centimetre to represent 1 unit on the vertical h-axis, draw a graph to show how h varied for values of t from 0 to 6.

(c) A ship requires a depth of water of 3 metres in order to leave harbour. Find from your graph the time by which the ship must have left harbour.

(d) Use your graph to help you find the rate, in centimetres per minute, at which the depth of water in Barport harbour was decreasing at 7 a.m. on 15th November.

(MEG)

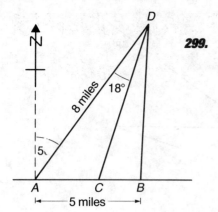

299. (a) Find two angles whose sine is 0.55.
    (b) The following figure, which is not drawn to scale, shows two points *A* and *B* on a coastline which runs from West to East where *AB* = 5 miles. A boat leaves *A* and sails 8 miles to *D* on a course 056° (N 56° E). The point *C* is between *A* and *B* such that ∠ *ADC* = 18°. Calculate:
    (i)   the distance *BD*;
    (ii) the distance *AC*.   (WJEC)

300. (i) From a lighthouse *L* a boat is seen at a point *A* which is due North of *L*, and 1.2 km away from it. The boat travels in a straight line, and 10 minutes later it is at a point *B* on a bearing of 105° from *L* and 1.8 km away from *L*. Calculate:
    (a)   the speed of the boat in km/h;
    (b)   the direction in which the boat is travelling;
    (c)   the shortest distance between the boat and the lighthouse.
    (ii) On a certain golf course, the distance from the tee *T* to the hole *H* is 350 m. A player drives his ball from *T* to a point *S*, where *TS* = 160 m and ∠ *STH* = 3°. Calculate, correct to 0.1 m, the distance *SH*.
        A second player drives his ball from *T* to a point *O*, such that ∠ *HTO* = 6° and ∠ *TOH* = 160°. Calculate, correct to 1 m, the distance to *TO*.
        A third player drives his ball a distance of 180 m from *T* to a point *P* which is 180 m from *H*. Calculate the angle *PTH*.

301. **(For this question, no marks will be awarded for answers obtained by scale drawing.)**

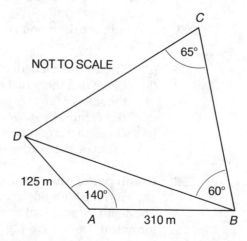

ABCD is a horizontal field. *AB* = 310 m, *DA* = 125 m, angle *A* = 140°, angle *C* = 65° and angle *DBC* = 60°.
Calculate the area, in hectares, of the field, giving your answer correct to 2 significant figures. (10 000 m² = 1 hectare.)   (MEG)

TRANSFORMATIONS
ATTAINMENT TARGET 4

14

1 Vectors

Remember : $\vec{AB}$ means A towards B

So $\vec{BA} = -\vec{AB}$

A vector can be written as a column $\begin{pmatrix} x \\ y \end{pmatrix}$

Addition $\begin{pmatrix} 2 \\ 8 \end{pmatrix} + \begin{pmatrix} 3 \\ 4 \end{pmatrix} = \begin{pmatrix} 5 \\ 12 \end{pmatrix}$

If using $\underset{\sim}{a}$, $\underset{\sim}{b}$, $\underset{\sim}{c}$ notation

(see worked example 166)

$\underset{\sim}{a} + \underset{\sim}{b} = \underset{\sim}{c}$ or

$\underset{\sim}{a} = \underset{\sim}{c} - \underset{\sim}{b}$

$\vec{AB} = \underset{\sim}{b} - \underset{\sim}{a}$ (B second - A first)

The length of a vector $|\vec{AB}|$ is sometimes called the modulus or magnitude.

If $\underset{\sim}{a}$ and $\underset{\sim}{b}$ are not parallel, and

$k\underset{\sim}{a} + h\underset{\sim}{b} = 0$ then both k and h must be zero

This idea is often used in vector geometry, see worked example 165.

Topic: vector algebra

WORKED EXAMPLE 163

If $3\begin{pmatrix} 2x \\ y \end{pmatrix} + \begin{pmatrix} -5 \\ 2x \end{pmatrix} = \begin{pmatrix} 1 \\ 6 \end{pmatrix}$, find x and y

SOLUTION

Simplify the left hand side

$$\begin{pmatrix} 6x - 5 \\ 3y + 2x \end{pmatrix} = \begin{pmatrix} 1 \\ 6 \end{pmatrix}$$

Hence $6x - 5 = 1 \therefore 6x = 6 \quad x = 1$

$3y + 2x = 6 \therefore 3y + 2 = 6$

i.e. $3y = 4$, so $y = 4/3$

WORKED EXAMPLE 164 ABC is a triangle. X is the midpoint of AB, and Y is the midpoint of BC. $\overrightarrow{XY}$ is produced to T so that $\overrightarrow{XY} = \overrightarrow{YT}$. Prove that $XBTC$ is a parallelogram.

SOLUTION   Referring to the figure, let $\overrightarrow{BX} = \mathbf{a}$, and $\overrightarrow{BY} = \mathbf{b}$. There are several other vectors that could have been used for $\mathbf{a}$ or $\mathbf{b}$. Try and choose those which give the simplest answers.

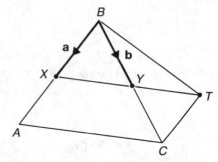

$\overrightarrow{XY} = -\mathbf{a} + \mathbf{b}, \overrightarrow{XT} = 2(-\mathbf{a} + \mathbf{b}) = -2\mathbf{a} + 2\mathbf{b}$.

$\overrightarrow{BC} = 2\mathbf{b}, \overrightarrow{XC} = -\mathbf{a} + 2\mathbf{b}$.

$\overrightarrow{TC} = \overrightarrow{TX} + \overrightarrow{XC} = -\overrightarrow{XT} + \overrightarrow{XC} = 2\mathbf{a} - 2\mathbf{b} - \mathbf{a} + 2\mathbf{b} = \mathbf{a}$.

Hence $\overrightarrow{TC} = \overrightarrow{BX}$. It follows that BX is parallel to TC and the same length.

$\overrightarrow{BT} = \overrightarrow{BC} + \overrightarrow{CT} = 2\mathbf{b} - \mathbf{a} = \overrightarrow{XC}$.

Hence BT is parallel to XC and of equal length.

So $XBTC$ is a parallelogram.

When trying to find an expression for, say, $\overrightarrow{XY}$, look at a route which takes you from X to Y, i.e. $X \to B \to Y$.

Hence $\overrightarrow{XY} = \overrightarrow{XB} + \overrightarrow{BY} = -\mathbf{a} + \mathbf{b}$.

WORKED EXAMPLE 165   In the triangle OAB, $\overrightarrow{OA} = \mathbf{a}$ and $\overrightarrow{OB} = \mathbf{b}$. L is a point on the side AB. M is a point on the side OB, and OL and AM meet at S. It is given that $AS = SM$ and $OS/OL = \frac{3}{4}$; also that $OM/OB = h$ and $AL/AB = k$.

(a)   express the vectors AM and OS in terms of $\mathbf{a}$, $\mathbf{b}$ and h;
(b)   express the vectors OL and OS in terms of $\mathbf{a}$, $\mathbf{b}$ and k.

Find h and k, and hence find the values of the ratios OM/MB and AL/LB.

SOLUTION   Referring to the figure,

Since $\dfrac{OS}{OL} = \frac{3}{4}$, $OS = \frac{3}{4}OL$.

$\dfrac{OM}{OB} = h$, hence $OM = hOB$.

$\dfrac{AL}{AB} = k$, hence $AL = kAB$.

Using vectors, therefore, $\overrightarrow{OM} = h\mathbf{b}$
also $\overrightarrow{AL} = k\overrightarrow{AB}$

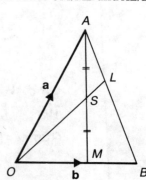

Now $\overrightarrow{AB} = -\mathbf{a} + \mathbf{b} = \mathbf{b} - \mathbf{a}$,

so $\overrightarrow{AL} = k(\mathbf{b} - \mathbf{a})$.

(a) $\overrightarrow{AM} = \overrightarrow{AO} + \overrightarrow{OM} = -\mathbf{a} + h\mathbf{b}$

$\overrightarrow{OS} = \overrightarrow{OA} + \overrightarrow{AS}$

$\qquad = \overrightarrow{OA} + \frac{1}{2}\overrightarrow{AM}$

$\qquad = \mathbf{a} + \frac{1}{2}(-\mathbf{a} + h\mathbf{b}) = \frac{1}{2}\mathbf{a} + \frac{1}{2}h\mathbf{b}$.

(b) $\overrightarrow{OL} = \overrightarrow{OA} + \overrightarrow{AL} = \mathbf{a} + k(\mathbf{b} - \mathbf{a})$

$\qquad\qquad\qquad\qquad\quad = \mathbf{a}(1 - k) + k\mathbf{b}$

Now $\overrightarrow{OS} = \frac{3}{4}\overrightarrow{OL} = \frac{3}{4}(1 - k)\mathbf{a} + \frac{3}{4}k\mathbf{b}$

Since both expressions for $\overrightarrow{OS}$ must be the same,

$\frac{3}{4}(1 - k) = \frac{1}{2}$, so $k = \frac{1}{3}$

$\frac{3}{4}k = \frac{1}{2}h$, so $h = \frac{1}{2}$

So $OM = MB$ and $\dfrac{OM}{MB} = 1$

$LB = 2AL$ and $\dfrac{AL}{LB} = \frac{1}{2}$

Topic: vector addition

WORKED EXAMPLE 166   A boat steers a course of 190° and travels at an average speed of 10 km/h. There is a current of 8 km/h flowing towards the west. By scale drawing, find the actual course the boat will travel on, and the resulting speed of the boat.

SOLUTION

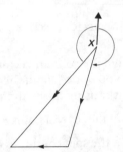

We need to add the two vectors together as shown in the diagram (notice the two single arrows follow each other).

The angle x is 135°

Hence the resulting course is 360° − 135° = 225°. The resulting speed is the length of the double arrowed line, this is 13.8 km/h.

Questions to try

GRADE A

302.   Find p and q given that

$$4\begin{pmatrix} 2q \\ 1 \end{pmatrix} - \begin{pmatrix} 11 \\ p \end{pmatrix} = \begin{pmatrix} q \\ p + 1 \end{pmatrix}$$

303. In a video game, a spot on the screen bounces off the four sides of a rectangular frame. The spot moves from *A* to *B* to *C* to *D*, as shown.

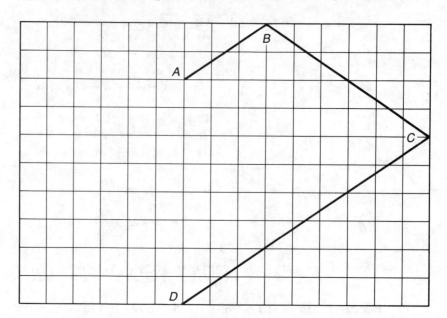

(a) What can you say about the angle at which the spot bounces off each side, compared with the angle at which it approached that side?

(b) The column vector describing the part **AB** of the movement is $\begin{pmatrix} 3 \\ 2 \end{pmatrix}$.

Write down the column vectors describing **BC** and **CD**.

(c) What do you notice about the parts of the path **AB** and **CD**? Justify your answer using the column vectors.

From *D*, the spot moves to a point *E* on the fourth side of the frame.

(d) Given that the spot continues in the same way, write down the vector **ED**.

(e) Given that the spot bounces off the fourth side at *E* and continues to move, describe its subsequent path.   (WJEC)

304. (a) Calculate the height of an equilateral triangle of side 1 unit in the form $p\sqrt{3}$, where p is a fraction in its lowest terms.

(b) A computer program, when run, moves a cursor on a screen according to the following instructions.

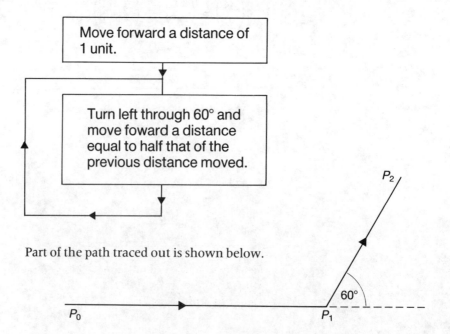

Part of the path traced out is shown below.

Continue the diagram to show the positions of P_3 and P_4.

(c)   Given that P_0 is (0,0) and P_1 is (1,0), calculate the coordinates of P_2 in the form $(a, b\sqrt{3})$, where a and b are rational numbers.   (NEA)

305.  A plane sets out on a bearing of 020°, travelling at an average speed of 200 km/h. The wind is blowing at 60 km/h from the west. Draw a vector diagram and find the actual bearing that the plane will fly on.

306.   This figure is NOT drawn to scale.

$OABC$ is a plane quadrilateral with $\overrightarrow{OA} = 4\mathbf{a}$, $\overrightarrow{OB} = 2\mathbf{a} + 2\mathbf{c}$, $\overrightarrow{OC} = 3\mathbf{c}$.

(a)   Express the vectors $\overrightarrow{CO}$, $\overrightarrow{CB}$ and $\overrightarrow{AB}$ in terms of $\mathbf{a}$ or $\mathbf{c}$, or $\mathbf{a}$ and $\mathbf{c}$.

The lines OA, OB and OC are produced to D, E and F, respectively, where $OC = CF$ and $OB : BE = OA : AD = 2 : 1$.

(b)   Find $\overrightarrow{FC}$, $\overrightarrow{BE}$, $\overrightarrow{FE}$ and $\overrightarrow{DE}$ in terms of $\mathbf{a}$ or $\mathbf{c}$, or $\mathbf{a}$ and $\mathbf{c}$.
(c)   Write down two geometrical facts about the points D, E and F.

    (LEAG)

307. OAD is a triangle with B and C on AD such that $\overrightarrow{AB} = \overrightarrow{BC} = \overrightarrow{CD} = \mathbf{y}$ and $\overrightarrow{OA} = \mathbf{x}$.

(a)   Find $\overrightarrow{AD}$ in terms of $\mathbf{y}$.
(b)   Find $\overrightarrow{OB}$ in terms of $\mathbf{x}$ and $\mathbf{y}$.

E and F are the midpoints of OB and OC, respectively.

(c)   Find $\overrightarrow{OE}$ and $\overrightarrow{OF}$ in terms of $\mathbf{x}$ and $\mathbf{y}$.
(d)   Find an expression for $\overrightarrow{EF}$ in terms of $\mathbf{x}$ or $\mathbf{y}$ or $\mathbf{x}$ and $\mathbf{y}$.
(e)   Write down two geometrical conclusions you can draw about the lines AD and EF.   (LEAG)

308.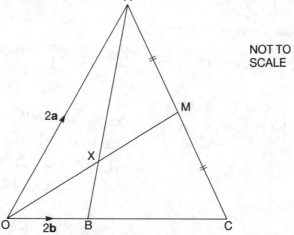

NOT TO SCALE

M is the midpoint of the side AC in a triangle OAC.
B lies on the side OC and $OC = 3\ OB$.
$\overrightarrow{OA} = 2\mathbf{a}$ and $\overrightarrow{OB} = 2\mathbf{b}$.

(a) Express in terms of **a** and/or **b**
   (i) $\overrightarrow{AB}$
   (ii) $\overrightarrow{OC}$
   (iii) $\overrightarrow{CA}$
   (iv) $\overrightarrow{OM}$

(b) *OM* and *AB* meet at *X*.
   (i)   Given that $\overrightarrow{AX} = k\overrightarrow{AB}$, write down $\overrightarrow{AX}$ in terms of k, **a** and **b**.
   (ii) Show that
   $$\overrightarrow{OX} = 2(1-k)\mathbf{a} + 2k\mathbf{b}.$$
   (iii) Given also that $\overrightarrow{OX} = h\overrightarrow{OM}$, express $\overrightarrow{OX}$ in terms of h, **a** and **b**.
   (iv) Use the two expressions for $\overrightarrow{OX}$ to find the value of h and the value of k.   (MEG)

309. In the triangle *OAB*,

$OC = \dfrac{2}{5}OB, \overrightarrow{OA} = \mathbf{a}, \overrightarrow{OB} = \mathbf{b}.$

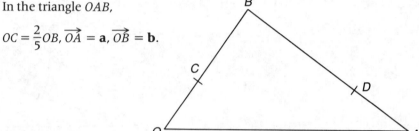

(a) Express the vectors $\overrightarrow{OC}, \overrightarrow{CB}$ and $\overrightarrow{BA}$ in terms of **a** or **b**, or **a** and **b**.
   The point *D* divides *BA* in the ratio 3 : 2.

(b) Find $\overrightarrow{BD}$ and $\overrightarrow{CD}$ in terms of **a** or **b**, or **a** and **b**.

(c) Give the special name of the quadrilateral *OCDA*.

(d) Calculate the value of $\dfrac{\text{area of triangle } OAB}{\text{area of triangle } CDB}$.

(e) Given that the area of the quadrilateral *OCDA* is 48 cm², find the area of the triangle *CBD*.   (LEAG)

310. Amin and Nathan are pulling a large trunk each with a force of 200 N by means of ropes making an angle of 10° with the direction of motion. What is the total force acting on the trunk?

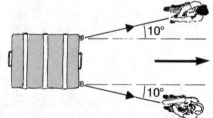

2 Matrices

A Matrix is a <u>store</u> of information.

$\begin{pmatrix} a & b & c & d \\ e & f & g & h \\ i & j & k & l \end{pmatrix}$ has 3 rows and 4 columns, it can be written a 3 × 4 matrix (called it's order).

<u>Addition</u> $\begin{pmatrix} a & b \\ c & d \end{pmatrix} + \begin{pmatrix} e & f \\ h & i \end{pmatrix} = \begin{pmatrix} a+e & f+b \\ c+h & d+i \end{pmatrix}$

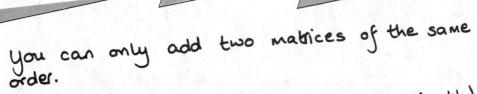

You can only add two matrices of the same order.

<u>Multiplying</u> $\begin{pmatrix} a & b \\ c & d \end{pmatrix}\begin{pmatrix} e & f \\ g & h \end{pmatrix} = \begin{pmatrix} ae+bg & af+bh \\ ce+dg & cf+dh \end{pmatrix}$

If multiplying $(m \times n)$ and $(p \times q)$ you must have $n = p$

The inverse of $\begin{pmatrix} a & b \\ c & d \end{pmatrix} = \dfrac{1}{ad-bc}\begin{pmatrix} d & -b \\ -c & a \end{pmatrix}$

$ad-bc$ is called the determinant of the matrix
Can be used in inverse transformations,
or simultaneous equations.
The inverse of A is written A^{-1}

Topics: matrix as an information store

WORKED EXAMPLE 167   The matrix, X, gives information about the number of chocolates of each kind in three different boxes:

	Nut	Soft centre	Hard centre	Toffee	Plain
Box A	3	5	4	2	3
$X =$ Box B	4	3	5	3	1
Box C	6	6	3	0	4

(a)   Multiply matrix X by the matrix $\begin{pmatrix} 1 \\ 1 \\ 1 \\ 1 \\ 1 \end{pmatrix}$ and state what information your answer gives.

(b)   Matrix Y gives information about the cost to the manufacturer of each type of chocolate and the number of calories in each type.

	Cost (pence)	Calories
Nut	4	30
Soft centre	3	25
$Y =$ Hard centre	2	30
Toffee	3	40
Plain	1	20

Evaluate the matrix product XY. Hence state the total number of calories in box A. What is the cost to the manufacturer of producing the chocolates in box C?

SOLUTION   (a)

$$
\begin{array}{c}
A \\ B \\ C
\end{array}
\left(
\begin{array}{ccccc}
3 & 5 & 4 & 2 & 3 \\
4 & 3 & 5 & 3 & 1 \\
6 & 6 & 3 & 0 & 4
\end{array}
\right)
\left(
\begin{array}{c}
1 \\ 1 \\ 1 \\ 1 \\ 1
\end{array}
\right)
=
\begin{array}{c}
A \\ B \\ C
\end{array}
\left(
\begin{array}{c}
17 \\ 16 \\ 19
\end{array}
\right)
$$

The answer gives the *total* number of chocolates in box A, box B and box C.

(b)

$$
XY =
\begin{array}{c}
A \\ B \\ C
\end{array}
\left(
\begin{array}{ccccc}
3 & 5 & 4 & 2 & 3 \\
4 & 3 & 5 & 3 & 1 \\
6 & 6 & 3 & 0 & 4
\end{array}
\right)
\begin{array}{c}
\text{Cost} \quad \text{Cal} \\
\left(
\begin{array}{cc}
4 & 30 \\
3 & 25 \\
2 & 30 \\
3 & 40 \\
1 & 20
\end{array}
\right)
\end{array}
=
\begin{array}{c}
\\ A \\ B \\ C
\end{array}
\begin{array}{c}
\text{Cost} \quad \text{Cal} \\
\left(
\begin{array}{cc}
44 & 475 \\
45 & 485 \\
52 & 500
\end{array}
\right)
\end{array}
$$

It should be noted that the headings for the columns in the first matrix are the same as the headings for the rows in the second matrix. The headings for the final matrix are the row headings from the first matrix and the column headings from the second. Providing care is taken, interpreting the answer should not be difficult.

Total number of calories in box A is 475.

Total cost of producing box C is 52p.

Topics: networks, matrices

WORKED EXAMPLE 168   The diagram shows a network consisting of 4 nodes, A, B, C and D, linked by seven arcs (1–7) which divide the plane into five regions (t, v, x, y, z) including the outside. Find:

(a)   the one-stage route matrix;
(b)   the two-stage route matrix;
(c)   the incidence matrix for arcs on nodes.

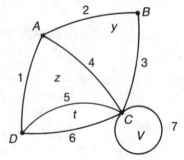

SOLUTION   (a)   A *one-stage* route between any two nodes is not allowed to pass through any of the other nodes. If R is the one-stage route matrix, then:

$$
R = \text{from}
\begin{array}{c}
A \\ B \\ C \\ D
\end{array}
\begin{array}{c}
\quad\text{to} \\
\begin{array}{cccc}
A & B & C & D
\end{array} \\
\left(
\begin{array}{cccc}
0 & 1 & 1 & 1 \\
1 & 0 & 1 & 0 \\
1 & 1 & 2 & 2 \\
1 & 0 & 2 & 0
\end{array}
\right)
\end{array}.
$$

Note that the matrix is *symmetrical* about the leading diagonal.

(b)   A *two-stage* route between two nodes passes through one other node on the way. The two-stage routes between A and C are shown below. It can be seen that there are five.

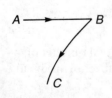 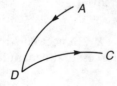 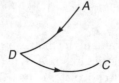 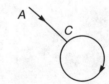

If you now evaluate R^2, you will find that:

$$R^2 = \begin{array}{c} \\ A \\ B \\ C \\ D \end{array} \begin{array}{cccc} A & B & C & D \\ \end{array}$$

$$R^2 = \begin{array}{c} A \\ B \\ C \\ D \end{array} \left(\begin{array}{cccc} 3 & 1 & 5 & 2 \\ 1 & 2 & 3 & 3 \\ 5 & 3 & 10 & 5 \\ 2 & 3 & 5 & 5 \end{array} \right)$$

five two-stage routes between A and C

This matrix gives the two-stage routes. You may like to try and justify ten for C to C. Similarly, R^3 gives the three-stage routes for the network.

(c) Node A lies on (is *incident* on) arcs 1, 2, 4. Node C is incident on 3, 4, 5, 6 and 7 (twice). The matrix N representing the incidence of nodes on arcs is given below:

$$N = \begin{array}{c} A \\ B \\ C \\ D \end{array} \left(\begin{array}{ccccccc} 1 & 2 & 3 & 4 & 5 & 6 & 7 \\ 1 & 1 & 0 & 1 & 0 & 0 & 0 \\ 0 & 1 & 1 & 0 & 0 & 0 & 0 \\ 0 & 0 & 1 & 1 & 1 & 1 & 2 \\ 1 & 0 & 0 & 0 & 1 & 1 & 0 \end{array} \right)$$

Topics: matrices, simultaneous equations

WORKED EXAMPLE 169   Use matrices to solve the equations $2x + 4y = 12$
$$3x - 7y = 5.$$

SOLUTION   These can be represented using matrices in the following way:

$$\begin{pmatrix} 2 & 4 \\ 3 & -7 \end{pmatrix} \begin{pmatrix} x \\ y \end{pmatrix} = \begin{pmatrix} 12 \\ 5 \end{pmatrix}$$

If $A = \begin{pmatrix} 2 & 4 \\ 3 & -7 \end{pmatrix}$, $B = \begin{pmatrix} 12 \\ 5 \end{pmatrix}$ and $C = \begin{pmatrix} x \\ y \end{pmatrix}$

then we have $AC = B$.

Now $A^{-1} = \begin{pmatrix} \frac{-7}{-26} & \frac{-4}{-26} \\ \frac{-3}{-26} & \frac{2}{-26} \end{pmatrix} = \begin{pmatrix} \frac{7}{26} & \frac{2}{13} \\ \frac{3}{26} & \frac{-1}{13} \end{pmatrix}$, and it can be shown that

$$\begin{pmatrix} x \\ y \end{pmatrix} = \begin{pmatrix} \frac{7}{26} & \frac{2}{13} \\ \frac{3}{26} & \frac{-1}{13} \end{pmatrix} \begin{pmatrix} 12 \\ 5 \end{pmatrix} = \begin{pmatrix} 4 \\ 1 \end{pmatrix};$$

the solution is $x = 4$, $y = 1$.

WORKED EXAMPLE 170   (a)   Find $\begin{pmatrix} 4 & 3 \\ -1 & 9 \end{pmatrix} \begin{pmatrix} 9 & -3 \\ 1 & 4 \end{pmatrix}$.

(b)   Use your answer to part (a) to solve the equations
$$4t + 3q = 31, \ 9q - t = 41.$$

SOLUTION   (a) $\begin{pmatrix} 4 & 3 \\ -1 & 9 \end{pmatrix} \begin{pmatrix} 9 & -3 \\ 1 & 4 \end{pmatrix} = \begin{pmatrix} 39 & 0 \\ 0 & 39 \end{pmatrix}$

(b)   The first part of the question in fact gives us straight away the determinant of the matrix as 39. Notice that the equations have been muddled up, and in fact are:
$$4t + 3q = 31,$$
$$-t + 9q = 41.$$

The relevance of the matrices can now be seen.

Find $\begin{pmatrix} 9 & -3 \\ 1 & 4 \end{pmatrix} \begin{pmatrix} 31 \\ 41 \end{pmatrix} = \begin{pmatrix} 156 \\ 195 \end{pmatrix}.$

This answer must be divided by 39.
Hence $t = 4$, $q = 5$.

Questions to try

GRADE A*

311. $A = \begin{pmatrix} 1 & 4 \\ -1 & 3 \end{pmatrix}$, $B = \begin{pmatrix} 2 & -2 \\ 4 & 1 \end{pmatrix}$, $C = \begin{pmatrix} 3 & -1 & -1 \\ 0 & 1 & 2 \end{pmatrix}$,

$D = \begin{pmatrix} 4 & 3 & 0 \\ -2 & -1 & 1 \end{pmatrix}$, $E = \begin{pmatrix} 2 & 1 \\ 4 & -2 \\ 3 & -5 \end{pmatrix}$, $F = \begin{pmatrix} 4 & 3 \\ -1 & 0 \\ 1 & 2 \end{pmatrix}$ and $G = \begin{pmatrix} 1 & -1 & -2 \\ 0 & 1 & 3 \\ 4 & 1 & 6 \end{pmatrix}$.

Evaluate if possible:
(a) $C + 2D$; (b) $3E - 2F$; (c) $A - 3B$; (d) $2D - 3E$; (e) $4G$; (f) $A + B + 2C$.

312.   Find the matrix M, given that:

$4M - \begin{pmatrix} 1 & 2 \\ -3 & 5 \end{pmatrix} = \begin{pmatrix} 6 & 1 \\ -1 & 4 \end{pmatrix}.$

313.   Find the matrix A if:

$\begin{pmatrix} 1 & 0 \\ 2 & -1 \end{pmatrix} - 3A = 2A + \begin{pmatrix} -1 & 0 \\ 1 & 2 \end{pmatrix}.$

314.   Find the inverse of the following matrices where possible:

(a) $\begin{pmatrix} 4 & 2 \\ 5 & 3 \end{pmatrix}$ (b) $\begin{pmatrix} 6 & -7 \\ -5 & 6 \end{pmatrix}$ (c) $\begin{pmatrix} 4 & 2 \\ -8 & -4 \end{pmatrix}$

(d) $\begin{pmatrix} 2 & 3 \\ -6 & 9 \end{pmatrix}$ (e) $\begin{pmatrix} 1 & 0 \\ 0 & -1 \end{pmatrix}$ (f) $\begin{pmatrix} 6 & -4 \\ 3 & 11 \end{pmatrix}$

315.   (a)   For the network shown write down:

(i)   the matrix X giving the number of arcs between any two nodes;
(ii)   the 3×7 incidence matrix T for arcs on nodes;
(iii)   the corresponding incidence matrix S showing the incidence of nodes on arcs.
(iv)   What is the relationship between S and T?

(b)   Evaluate (i) TS; (ii) $TS - X$. What does $TS - X$ represent?

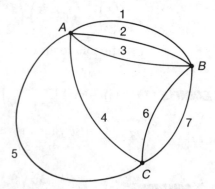

316.   The country of Albion has four local airstrips A, B, C, D, and two international airports G, H. Regular services exist or not between these, as shown by 1 or 0 in the matrix M. Flights from G and H to airports U, V, W in Gaul are given by matrix N.

$$\text{Matrix } M = \begin{array}{c} \\ A \\ B \\ C \\ D \end{array} \begin{array}{cc} G & H \\ \begin{pmatrix} 1 & 0 \\ 0 & 1 \\ 1 & 1 \\ 1 & 1 \end{pmatrix} \end{array} \qquad \text{Matrix } N = \begin{array}{c} \\ G \\ H \end{array} \begin{array}{ccc} U & V & W \\ \begin{pmatrix} 1 & 0 & 1 \\ 1 & 1 & 0 \end{pmatrix} \end{array}$$

Find the product matrix *MN* and interpret it. Local services in Gaul go from *U, V, W* to internal airports *X, Y, Z* as shown by matrix *P*.

$$\text{Matrix } P = \begin{array}{c} \\ U \\ V \\ W \end{array} \begin{array}{ccc} X & Y & Z \\ \begin{pmatrix} 1 & 0 & 1 \\ 1 & 1 & 0 \\ 0 & 0 & 1 \end{pmatrix} \end{array}.$$

A traveller wishes to travel by air between these countries. Find by any method

(a)   which of the journeys from A or B or C or D to X or Y or Z have no air route;

(b)   which of them are connected by more than one route.

3 Transformations

A transformation can often be written as a matrix (2 × 2).
See page 260 for a list of common ones.

To transform a point (x, y), by a matrix M, write the point as $\begin{pmatrix} x \\ y \end{pmatrix}$ and find $M \begin{pmatrix} x \\ y \end{pmatrix}$

A shape can often be represented by a single matrix.
Here   A (3.1) B $(2,5)$ C $(-1, 4)$ can be represented   by $\begin{pmatrix} 3 & 2 & -1 \\ 1 & 5 & 4 \end{pmatrix}$.

If M and N are two matrices, MN means N followed by M.

The inverse of a matrix gives the inverse transformation.

Remember, a reflection will be self-inverse.

USEFUL FACTS

A transformation can be represented by a 2×2 matrix.

(i)   Reflection

$\begin{pmatrix} 1 & 0 \\ 0 & -1 \end{pmatrix}$ represents reflection in the line $y = 0$.

$\begin{pmatrix} -1 & 0 \\ 0 & 1 \end{pmatrix}$ represents reflection in the line $x = 0$.

$\begin{pmatrix} 0 & 1 \\ 1 & 0 \end{pmatrix}$ represents reflection in $y = x$.

$\begin{pmatrix} 0 & -1 \\ -1 & 0 \end{pmatrix}$ represents reflection in $y = -x$.

$\begin{pmatrix} \cos 2\alpha° & \sin 2\alpha° \\ \sin 2\alpha° & -\cos 2\alpha° \end{pmatrix}$ is reflection in the line $y = x \tan \alpha$.

(ii)   Rotation

$\begin{pmatrix} 0 & 1 \\ -1 & 0 \end{pmatrix}$ represents a clockwise rotation of 90°.

$\begin{pmatrix} 0 & -1 \\ 1 & 0 \end{pmatrix}$ represents an anticlockwise rotation of 90°.

$\begin{pmatrix} -1 & 0 \\ 0 & -1 \end{pmatrix}$ represents a rotation of 180°.

$\begin{pmatrix} \cos \alpha° & -\sin \alpha° \\ \sin \alpha° & \cos \alpha° \end{pmatrix}$ represents a rotation of $\alpha°$ anticlockwise.

(iii)   Enlargement

$\begin{pmatrix} k & 0 \\ 0 & k \end{pmatrix}$ represents an enlargement scale factor k centre 0.

(iv)   Stretch

$\begin{pmatrix} k & 0 \\ 0 & 1 \end{pmatrix}$ is a stretch, scale factor k, parallel to the x-axis.

$\begin{pmatrix} 1 & 0 \\ 0 & k \end{pmatrix}$ is a stretch, scale factor k, parallel to the y-axis.

(v)   Shear

$\begin{pmatrix} 1 & k \\ 0 & 1 \end{pmatrix}$ is a shear, shear factor k, parallel to the x-axis.

$\begin{pmatrix} 1 & 0 \\ k & 1 \end{pmatrix}$ is a shear, shear factor k, parallel to the x-axis.

Topic: matrix transformations   **GRADE A***

WORKED EXAMPLE 171   (a)   Describe, in geometrical terms, the transformation given by:

$$\begin{pmatrix} x \\ y \end{pmatrix} \rightarrow \begin{pmatrix} 0 & 1 \\ 1 & 0 \end{pmatrix} \begin{pmatrix} x \\ y \end{pmatrix}$$

(b)   (i)   A square has vertices $P(1,-1)$, $Q(2,-1)$, $R(2,-2)$ and $S(1,-2)$.
Find the coordinates of the images P', Q', R' and S', respectively,
of the vertices under the transformation given in part (a).

(ii)   Draw and label the rectangles $PQRS$ and $P'Q'R'S'$ on graph paper.
Also draw the lines $y = x$ and $y = x + 3$.

(c) (i) What translation, following the transformation described in (a), results in the square *PQRS* being reflected in the line $y = x + 3$?

(ii) Hence, or otherwise, find the coordinates of the vertices of $P''Q''R''S''$, the reflection of *PQRS* in the line $y = x + 3$.

SOLUTION (a) $\begin{pmatrix} 0 & 1 \\ 1 & 0 \end{pmatrix} \begin{pmatrix} x \\ y \end{pmatrix} = \begin{pmatrix} y \\ x \end{pmatrix}$, so x and y have been interchanged.

Hence a shape is reflected in $y = x$.

(b) The shape and its reflection are plotted below. You must label the points.

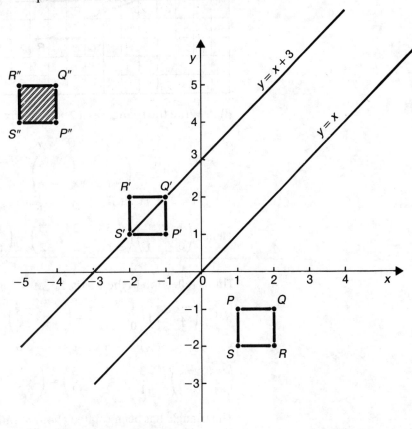

(c) (i) The square *PQRS* reflected in $y = x + 3$, becomes the shaded square labelled $P''Q''R''S''$. So, following (a), which is $P'Q'R'S'$, the translation that takes it to the shaded square is a simple slide.

As a vector, this is $\begin{pmatrix} -3 \\ 3 \end{pmatrix}$

(ii) The coordinates are $P''(-4,4)$, $Q''(-4,5)$, $R''(-5,5)$, $S''(-5,4)$.

WORKED EXAMPLE 172 Plot the triangle $P(3,-1)$, $Q(3,-2)$ and $R(5,-2)$ on graph paper.

(i) Find the image of *PQR* under the matrix $M = \begin{pmatrix} 1 & 0 \\ 0 & -1 \end{pmatrix}$.

Hence describe M.

(ii) If $N = \begin{pmatrix} -\frac{3}{5} & \frac{4}{5} \\ \frac{4}{5} & \frac{3}{5} \end{pmatrix}$, find NM and draw the image of $\triangle PQR$

under NM, and describe the transformation whose matrix is NM.

(iii) By finding the coordinates of the point (x,y) under the transformation whose matrix is N, show that the line $y = 2x$ is unchanged under the transformation, and describe the transformation whose matrix is N.

SOLUTION

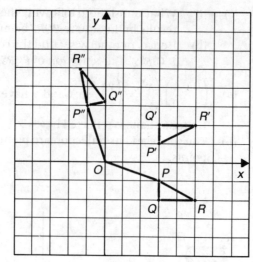

(i)   Write the triangle as a 2 × 3 matrix:

$$\begin{array}{ccc} P & Q & R \end{array}$$
$$\triangle = \begin{pmatrix} 3 & 3 & 5 \\ -1 & -2 & -2 \end{pmatrix}.$$

$$\begin{array}{cccccc} & P & Q & R & P' & Q' & R' \end{array}$$
Hence $\begin{pmatrix} 1 & 0 \\ 0 & -1 \end{pmatrix}\begin{pmatrix} 3 & 3 & 5 \\ -1 & -2 & -2 \end{pmatrix} = \begin{pmatrix} 3 & 3 & 5 \\ 1 & 2 & 2 \end{pmatrix}.$

This is reflection in the x-axis, i.e. M.

$$NM = \begin{pmatrix} -\frac{3}{5} & \frac{4}{5} \\ \frac{4}{5} & \frac{3}{5} \end{pmatrix}\begin{pmatrix} 1 & 0 \\ 0 & -1 \end{pmatrix} = \begin{pmatrix} -\frac{3}{5} & -\frac{4}{5} \\ \frac{4}{5} & -\frac{3}{5} \end{pmatrix},$$

$$\begin{array}{cccccc} & P & Q & R & P'' & Q'' & R'' \end{array}$$
$$\begin{pmatrix} -\frac{3}{5} & -\frac{4}{5} \\ \frac{4}{5} & -\frac{3}{5} \end{pmatrix}\begin{pmatrix} 3 & 3 & 5 \\ -1 & -2 & -2 \end{pmatrix} = \begin{pmatrix} -1 & -\frac{1}{5} & -\frac{7}{5} \\ 3 & \frac{18}{5} & \frac{26}{5} \end{pmatrix}.$$

The triangle has been rotated about O anticlockwise by an angle of 126.9°, hence NM is a rotation of 126.9° anticlockwise about O.

(iii)   Transforming (x,y) by N we have:

$$\begin{pmatrix} -\frac{3}{5} & \frac{4}{5} \\ \frac{4}{5} & \frac{3}{5} \end{pmatrix}\begin{pmatrix} x \\ y \end{pmatrix} = \begin{pmatrix} -\frac{3}{5}x + \frac{4}{5}y \\ \frac{4}{5}x + \frac{3}{5}y \end{pmatrix};$$

if $y = 2x$, the matrix on the right becomes

$$\begin{pmatrix} -\frac{3}{5}x + \frac{8}{5}x \\ \frac{4}{5}x + \frac{6}{5}x \end{pmatrix} = \begin{pmatrix} x \\ 2x \end{pmatrix}, \text{ hence } y \text{ is still } 2x$$

If a complete line is unaltered, unless some shearing has occurred, which the diagram shows it hasn't, the transformation N is a reflection in the line $y = 2x$.

Questions to try

317.   (a)   The vertices of a square A are $(0,0)$, $(4,0)$, $(4,4)$ and $(0,4)$.
Using x- and y-axes with values from 0 to 8, draw and label A.
(b)   Transformation S is defined by:

$$S: \begin{pmatrix} x \\ y \end{pmatrix} \rightarrow \begin{pmatrix} 1 & 1 \\ 0 & 1 \end{pmatrix}\begin{pmatrix} x \\ y \end{pmatrix}.$$

(i)   Draw the image of A under transformation S. Label it B.
(ii)   Describe the transformation S.

(c) Transformation T is 'reflection in the line $y = x$'.
  (i) Draw the image of B under transformation T. Label it C.
  (ii) Write down the matrix of transformation T.

(d) Transformation U is transformation S followed by transformation T. By evaluating a suitable matrix product, or otherwise, find the matrix of transformation U.

(e) Transformation V is defined by:

$$V: \begin{pmatrix} x \\ y \end{pmatrix} \rightarrow \begin{pmatrix} 1 & 0 \\ 1 & 1 \end{pmatrix} \begin{pmatrix} x \\ y \end{pmatrix}.$$

  (i) Draw the image of A under transformation V. Label it D.
  (ii) Explain why your answer to part (d) is not the same as the matrix for transformation V. (NEA)

318. R is the transformation with matrix $\begin{pmatrix} 0 & -1 \\ 1 & 0 \end{pmatrix}$.

S is the transformation with matrix $\begin{pmatrix} 0 & -1 \\ -1 & 0 \end{pmatrix}$.

A is the point $(1,0)$, B is the point $(3,0)$ and C is the point $(1,1)$.

(a) Find the coordinates of A_1, B_1, C_1, the images of A, B and C under R.

(b) Using scales of 2 cm for 1 unit on both axes, draw a diagram to show ABC and $A_1B_1C_1$. Label these points.

(c) (i) Find the coordinates of A_2, B_2 and C_2, the images of A_1, B_1 and C_1 under S.
  (ii) Add A_2, B_2 and C_2 to your diagram and label the points.

(d) (i) Calculate $\begin{pmatrix} 0 & -1 \\ -1 & 0 \end{pmatrix} \begin{pmatrix} 0 & -1 \\ 1 & 0 \end{pmatrix}$.

  (ii) Describe geometrically the transformation T which this represents.
  (iii) What is the relationship between R, S and T? (MEG)

319. (a) Plot the vertices of a rectangle $OABC$ whose coordinates are $O(0,0)$, $A(4,0)$, $B(4,1)$, $C(0,1)$.

(b) Join your points to form the rectangle $OABC$. Write down the area of the rectangle $OABC$.

(c) The matrix $\begin{pmatrix} 3 & -3 \\ 3 & 3 \end{pmatrix}$ represents a transformation T.

  Find the coordinates of the vertices of the image, $OA'B'C'$ of the rectangle under the transformation T.
  Draw the image $OA'B'C'$ and find the area of the quadrilateral $OA'B'C'$.

(d) The transformation T consists of an enlargement and a rotation. Describe fully this enlargement and this rotation, by using your results.

(e) The matrix $\begin{pmatrix} 0 & -1 \\ -1 & 0 \end{pmatrix}$ represents another transformation, S.

  Find the coordinates of the vertices of the image, $OA''B''C''$, of the quadrilateral $OA'B'C'$, under the transformation S.
  Draw the quadrilateral $OA''B''C''$. Describe fully in words the transformation S.

(f) Find a single matrix which represents the transformation T followed by the transformation S.

15

MENTAL ARITHMETIC AND AURAL TESTS

In the GCSE, you may be expected to sit a short mental arithmetic test as part of the final examination. Although the skills necessary to do well have been acquired over a number of years, there are still points to watch out for, as shown in the following examples. Study them first, and then try some of the practice papers. You will need a patient friend or relative to read the questions to you.

WORKED EXAMPLE 173   How many 17p stamps can you buy for £2?

SOLUTION   17 does not go exactly into £2 (200p). If you gave $200 \div 17 = 11.8$ as the answer, it would be marked wrong. The correct answer is 11.

WORKED EXAMPLE 174   Work out the area of a rectangle whose sides measure 3.5 m by 8 m.

SOLUTION 3.5×8 in your head is much easier if you do $3 \times 8 = 24$ and add $0.5 \times 8 = 4$. Hence the area is $28\,\text{m}^2$.

WORKED EXAMPLE 175   The diameter of a circle is 12 cm; estimate the circumference.

SOLUTION   The formula for the circumference of a circle is $2\pi r$ or πd. If you approximate $\pi = 3$, then the circumference $= 3 \times 12 = 36$ cm.

WORKED EXAMPLE 176   A square has a side of length 7 cm. What is the approximate length of the diagonal?

SOLUTION   Using Pythagoras' theorem to find the length D of the diagonal, we have
$D^2 = 7^2 + 7^2 = 98$.
Hence $D^2 \approx 100$ ($\approx$ means approximately equals).
So D is approximately 10 cm.

WORKED EXAMPLE 177   Estimate the size of the angle p.

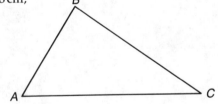

SOLUTION   When the examiners ask you to estimate an angle, they are expecting reasonable accuracy.
Clearly, p is between $180°$ and $270°$.
It probably isn't as large as $225°$ (i.e. half-way).
So guess $p = 210°$.

WORKED EXAMPLE 178   In the diagram, the length of AC is 8 cm, find the area of the triangle.

SOLUTION   Remember you will not have a ruler. The height of the triangle is about half of AC.
Hence: base $= 8$ cm
           height $= 4$ cm (approximately)
The area $= \frac{1}{2} \times 8 \times 4 = 16\,\text{cm}^2$ (approximately).

WORKED EXAMPLE 179   Find $12\frac{1}{2}\%$ of £96.

SOLUTION   It is worth knowing certain percentages as fractions.
$12\frac{1}{2}\%$ is one eighth.
£96 $\div$ 8 = £12.

WORKED EXAMPLE 180   Add together $23 + 45 + 15 + 7$.

SOLUTION   It is much quicker if you add $23 + 7 = 30$ and $45 + 15 = 60$ and then $30 + 60 = 90$.

You are now in a position to try one of the following tests. Try to find somewhere quiet, and the person reading the questions to you should read each question *twice*, give you enough time to write down each answer, and then move on to the next question. Try to complete the test in the allocated time.

Mental Arithmetic Test 1 (time 20 minutes)

1. How many twenty two pence stamps can you buy for one pound?
2. What is the approximate value of forty-one multiplied by thirty-nine?
3. How many posts spaced half a metre apart would be needed in fencing a length of six metres?
4. A train service runs every twenty minutes. If one train leaves at nine forty-seven, what time will the next train leave?
5. What is the smallest number that six and eight divide into exactly?
6. What is the cost of four reels of cotton at twenty-nine pence each?
7. If today, Monday, is the twenty-eighth of January, what is the date on Tuesday next week?
8. What time p.m. is sixteen thirty-eight on the twenty-four hour clock?
9. How many tiles fifty centimetres by fifty centimetres are needed to cover an area of floor which measures two metres by one metre?
10. Jane normally earns one pound eighty an hour. On Saturdays, she is paid time-and-a-half. How much an hour does she earn on Saturday?
11. Write down in figures one hundred and twenty eight thousand eight hundred and five.
12. Two angles of a triangle are fifty-four degrees and thirty-seven degrees. What is the third angle?
13. Jason is playing darts. With his three darts he scores eight, double five and treble twenty. What is his total for that throw?
14. The train fare to London is seven pounds. If fares are increased by four per cent, what is the new fare?
15. It costs twenty-five pounds a day to hire a Ford Sierra. You get a twenty per cent reduction if you hire the car for a week. How much does it cost to hire the car for one week?
16. The average weight of three parcels is twelve kilograms. If the average weight of two of the parcels is fourteen kilograms, how much does the third parcel weigh?
17. A car travels at an average speed of thirty-five miles per hour. How far does it travel in two and a half hours?
18. A committee is made up from four men and two women. A chairperson is selected from the six. What is the probability that it is a woman?
19. The mortgage rate is increased by one and three quarters per cent from ten and a half per cent. What is the new interest rate?
20. David was sent to the shops to buy ninety bolts. Unfortunately, they were only sold in bubble packs of twelve, which cost twenty pence. How much did he have to pay to get the bolts he required?

Mental Arithmetic Test 2 (time 20 minutes)

1. Tickets to see a pop concert cost £10.50 each. How much did Jill and her three friends pay altogether to see the concert?

2. Eight glasses of wine can be poured from one bottle of wine. How many glasses can be poured from six bottles?

3. A tin of emulsion covers ten square metres. How many tins are needed to paint a wall which measures nine metres by eight metres?

4. The sides of a rectangle measure six metres and three metres. Estimate the length of the diagonal.

5. A batsman scored eight, twenty-three and fifty in three innings. What was his average score?

6. Ann and Bill went picking peas. Ann picked twice as many peas as Bill, and altogether they picked seven and a half pounds. How many peas did Ann pick?

7. Write down the cube root of 125.

8. How many vertices has a cuboid?

9. The radius of a circle is 8 cm. Estimate the area of the circle.

10. David bought half a pound of tea at forty-five pence a quarter and two cut loaves which cost thirty-five pence each. How much did he spend?

11. Rashid just missed the 14.15 train. If the service is every fifty minutes, what is the earliest train he can catch next?

12. Simplify as far as possible four x multiplied by two x.

13. A car averages seventy miles an hour on a motorway. How long does it take to travel one hundred and seventy-five miles?

14. A piece of glass has an area of twelve hundred square millimetres. Express this area in square centimetres.

15. Write down any fraction that lies between two-thirds and five-sixths.

16. Two angles of a triangle are eighty degrees and thirty-five degrees. What is the third angle?

17. Peter's radio-controlled car can travel at twenty miles an hour. How many minutes would it take to drive around a quarter-mile course?

18. The number of customers attending the first day of a sale was twenty-eight thousand, seven hundred and nine. Write this correct to two significant figures.

19. The surface area of a box is four square centimetres. The surface area of a similar box is sixteen square centimetres. If the volume of the smaller box is one point five cubic centimetres, what is the volume of the larger box?

20. What time p.m. is twenty-one twenty-one on the twenty-four hour clock?

Mental Arithmetic Test 3
(time 15 minutes)

1. A rectangle measures three point five centimetres by eight centimetres. What is its area?
2. What is the largest prime number less than forty?
3. All goods in a shop are reduced by ten per cent in a sale. If the sale price of a washing machine is one hundred and eighty pounds, how much was it before the sale?
4. I buy four pens costing sixty-five pence each. How much change should I get from a five-pound note?
5. Write down in full, the number one hundred and five thousand and eight.
6. The Battle of Hastings was fought in ten sixty-six. How long ago was this?
7. The temperature overnight fell from twelve degrees Celsius to minus nine degrees Celsius. How much did the temperature fall by?
8. What is the perimeter of a square which has an area of sixty-four square centimetres?

For the rest of the questions, you will need a copy of the information sheet which comes after Test 4.

9. How far is it from Cambridge to Norwich?
10. The parallelogram is drawn to scale. The length of the longest side is six centimetres. What is the approximate area of the parallelogram?
11. How many kilometres an hour is thirty-four miles an hour?
12. Estimate the size of angle *x*.
13. How long does the return journey from Honiton to Worthing take on a Saturday?
14. How much would it cost to have two films, each with twenty-four pictures, developed in a matt finish including postage?
15. How much would it cost to send an airletter weighing thirty grams to India?

Mental Arithmetic Test 4 (time 15 minutes)

1. How many seconds are there in one hour?
2. What is the cost of twenty-two pens at twelve pence each?
3. What is the volume of a box whose dimensions are eight centimetres by five centimetres by six centimetres?
4. The height of a horse is measured in hands. One hand is four inches. How high is a horse measuring fifteen hands?
5. A photograph has an area of twenty-four square centimetres. If it is enlarged by a scale factor of two, what is the area of the new picture?
6. Write down the fraction that lies half-way between one-eighth and one-quarter.
7. A large tube of gum contains two hundred millilitres. What area in square centimetres would it cover if spread to a depth of two millimetres?
8. A night storage heater normally costing one hundred and twenty pounds is offered at a twenty per cent discount. What is the reduced price?

For the rest of the questions, you will need a copy of the information sheet which comes after this test.

9. How far is it from York to Cambridge?
10. The parallelogram is drawn to scale, and the largest side is six centimetres. Estimate the length of the longest diagonal.
11. What is ninety kilometres per hour in miles per hour approximately?
12. Estimate the size of angle y.
13. I wish to travel from Axminster to Plymouth on Saturday, September the twentieth. What time does my train depart?
14. How much, including postage, would it cost to have a fifteen-exposure disc developed, including a duplicate set of prints?
15. A letter to Japan costs sixty-four pence to post. What is the heaviest that the letter could weigh?

INFORMATION SHEET

9.

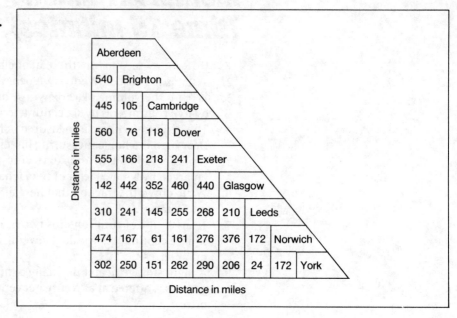

10.

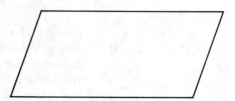

11.

Miles per hour (A) to kilometres per hour (B)					
A	B	A	B	A	B
1	1.6	7	11.3	25	40.2
2	3.2	8	12.9	30	48.3
3	4.8	9	14.5	50	80.5
4	6.4	10	16.1	75	120.7
5	8.0	15	24.1	90	144.8
6	9.7	20	32.2	100	160.9

12.

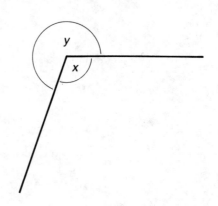

13.

TO PLYMOUTH and PENZANCE & BACK

	FRIDAYS OUTWARD		SATURDAYS OUTWARD		RETURN	
BRIGHTON	dep	11 11	dep	09 13	arr	18 13
WORTHING	dep	11 26	dep	09 27	arr	17 58
BARNHAM	dep	11 42	dep	09 44	arr	17 42
CHICHESTER	dep	11 52	dep	09 54	arr	17 33
HAVANT	dep	12 06	dep	10 06	arr	17 21
COSHAM	dep	12 19	dep	10 19	dep	–
FAREHAM	dep	12 29	dep	10 29	dep	17 05
SOUTHAMPTON	dep	12 52	dep	10 53	dep	16 42
SALISBURY	dep	13 23	dep	11 25	dep	16 09
YEOVIL JUNCTION	dep	14 07	dep	12 07	dep	15 21
AXMINSTER	dep	14 31	dep	12 36*	dep	14 56
HONITON	dep	14 50	dep	12 51*	dep	14 44
EXETER (CENTRAL)	arr	15 08	arr	13 10*	dep	14 21
EXETER (ST DAVIDS)	arr	15 13	arr	13 15*	dep	14 17
NEWTON ABBOT	arr	15 43	arr	13 53	dep	13 39
PLYMOUTH	arr	16 26	arr	14 40	dep	1300

CALLS CERTAIN STATIONS BETWEEN PLYMOUTH AND PENZANCE

TRURO	arr	18 03	arr	16 02	dep	11 34
PENZANCE	arr	18 50	arr	16 48	dep	10 50

Notes: *–Until 28 June and from 13 September departs Axminster 12 30, Honiton 12 45, and arrives Exeter Central 13 07 and Exeter St Davids 13 13.

14.

SUPERB GLOSSY OR MATT PRINTS

TICK A BOX TO MAKE YOUR CHOICE

GLOSSY . . . A shiny finish for extra sharpness. Ideal for albums. ☐   **MATT** . . . A lustrous finish, attractive but durable, resistant to marking. ☐

24 EXPOSURES FOR ONLY £2.09 + P&P

NUMBER OF EXPOSURES	OUR PRICE	NO. OF FILMS SENT	WRITE AMOUNT HERE
12 OR 15 (DISC)	£1.89		£ ~.
24	£2.09		£ .
36	£2.69		£ .
Add 35p per film for postage and packing			£ . Add P&P
A duplicate set of prints only £1.40 more per film			£ .
TOTAL			£ .

15.

Inland Letters
United Kingdom, Channel Islands, Isle of Man and Irish Republic.

	60g	100g	150g	200g
1st class	17p	24p	31p	38p
2nd class	12p	18p	22p	28p

The rates shown here are effective from November 1985.

Please use the postcode

Overseas Air Letters

	10g	Each extra 10g
Zone A	29p	11p
Zone B	31p	14p
Zone C	34p	15p

Postcards 26p
Aerogramme 26p
Europe Surface rates apply

Overseas Surface Letters and Postcards

	20g	60g	100g
All countries	22p	37p	53p

Zone A
N Africa
Middle East

Zone B
Americas
Africa
India
SE Asia

Zone C
Australasia
Japan
China

PROGRESS TEST 1

1. Shade as many squares as you think necessary so as to represent the fraction $\frac{5}{9}$.

2. From the following list of numbers,

    (i)   put a ring round the prime numbers;
    (ii) put a cross through any multiples of 3.

    3   5   12   23   42   49   60   61

3. The following sum is correct, but the brackets have been missed out.
    Insert brackets where necessary to make it correct.

    $(4 + 3) \times (6 - 2) = 28$.

4. (i)   Write down three numbers of which 4 is the highest common factor.

         16
    ....

    (ii) Write down two numbers of which 40 is the lowest common multiple.

    ....

5.

    (i)   Find the cost in the sale of a jug normally priced at £8.

    £ 6.400

    (ii) A tea set has been reduced by £16.80. How much did the tea set cost
          before the sale?

                    16.80

    £..........................

6. The radius of a circle is 5 cm (to the nearest cm). What is the smallest value
    that the circumference could have?

7. Jean enters a number into her calculator, and then presses the following buttons:

$\boxed{\times}$ 6.4 $\boxed{+}$ 12 $\boxed{\div}$ 10 $\boxed{=}$

The number obtained was 135.6. What number did she start with?

....

8. Peter was set some homework on correcting numbers to 2 significant figures. His answers are shown alongside. Mark Peter's homework with a ✓ or a ✗ (right or wrong). Write any corrections alongside.

Question	Answer
867	87
5.86	5.9
0.1032	0.11
99.9	100
1.065	1.07
102.3	100

9.

There are two routes to travel between the villages of Avalon and Buckfast. The distance along the ring road is 5.5 km, and the distance through the town centre is 2.25 km. Express the difference in these distances as a percentage of the shorter distance, giving your answer to 1 decimal place.

.... %

10.

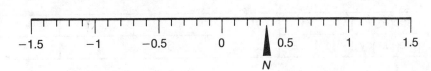

(i) Mark on the number line as accurately as you can the number -1.05.
(ii) Express the value of N in standard form.

11. Solve the equation $x^3 = 16$, by using a trial and improvement method. Give your answer correct to 1 decimal place.

12. Find an expression for the n'th term of the sequence 2, 7, 12, 17, . . .

13. A wine glass holds about 60 cm³ of wine. How many glasses can you fill from a ½ litre bottle of wine?

14. The dimensions of a cuboid, are 4 × 3 × 2. If one of the vertices is (2,2,0), find the possible coordinates of another vertex.

15. Jodi has just bought a new typewriter. The price she paid was £141 including V.A.T. Because her business is V.A.T. registered, she is able to claim the V.A.T. back. How much of the purchase price is V.A.T.?

16. The test scores of a class of 25 pupils were summarised by the teacher in the following way.

score	0–9	10–19	20–29	30–39	40–49
frequency	4	7	6	7	1

Find an estimate for the average test score for the class.

PROGRESS TEST 2

1. A square field has an area of $9500\,\text{m}^2$. Find the length of one side of the field, giving your answer to the nearest metre.

2. A tray of 12 plants costs a garden centre £7 to produce. The plants are sold at 95p each. Calculate the percentage profit made.
(Give your answer to 1 decimal place.)

3. Solve the equations:

(i) $4x + 15 = 7x + 3$; (ii) $4 - 3x = 5$.

4. A set of books entitled *The World of Science* can be bought cash for £98.95 or by paying in 8 equal monthly instalments of £13.20. How much is saved by paying cash?

5. Anne works in an office and earns £135 per week. She is allowed to earn £52 a week before paying tax at 25p in the £. How much money is she left with after paying tax?

6. A supermarket sells potatoes in 3 lb bags at 55p per bag, in 5 lb packs at 86p and in 20 lb sacks at £3.60. Which is the best buy? Give a reason.

7. Tina went on holiday to the U.S.A. Her air fare was £228 and she spent $800 while there. If the exchange rate was £1 = $1.60, calculate the total cost of the holiday to the nearest £1.

8. Factorise completely

(i) $4x + 8y$; (ii) $4x^2y^3 - 6xy^2$

9.

Janna wants to mount two pictures so that they are similar rectangles in shape. The smaller mount has width 22 cm and height 29.5 cm. If she wants the larger mount to have width 35 cm, what should its height be? (Give your answer to the nearest 0.1 cm.)

10. A chicken stock 'cube' measures 2 cm × 1 cm × ½ cm. They can be bought in a catering size box with measurements 10 cm by 8 cm by 4 cm. How many 'cubes' can be packed into a box?

11. At 10.00 a.m. George set out from home to ride his cycle to a friend's home 12 km away. He rode at a steady speed of 18 km/h but, after 20 minutes, one of his tyres was punctured. After spending 5 minutes trying to repair it, George walked the rest of the way at 6 km/h.

(a) Using a scale of 2 cm to represent 10 minutes on the time axis and 2 cm to represent 2 km on the distance axis, draw a distance–time graph for George's journey.

(b) Find the time at which George arrived at his friend's home.

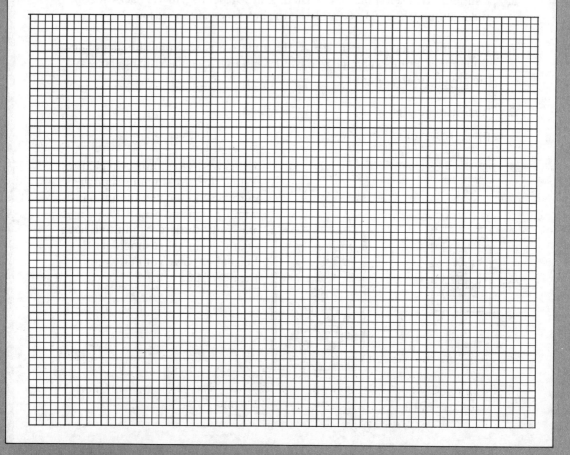

12. A spinner with 6 sides is numbered 1, 2, 3, 1, 2, 3, as shown in the diagram. The spinner is spun twice.

    (i)   Complete the tree diagram to show the probabilities.

    (ii)   What is the probability that the spinner shows a three on both occasions?

    (iii)   What is the probability that the spinner shows a different number on each occasion?

    (ii)   _____

    (iii)   _____

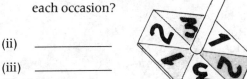
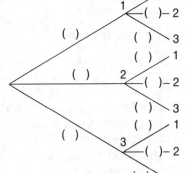

13. In the diagram, $AB = 5\,\text{cm}$, $BC = 12\,\text{cm}$, $\angle ABC = 90°$ and $AC = CD$. Find $\angle ADC = x°$.

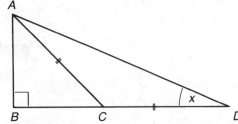

14. Referring to the diagram alongside, write down

    (i)   the coordinates of A; ____43____

    (ii)   the gradient of AB; _____

    (iii)   the equation of the line AB; $y =$ _____

    (iv)   the coordinates of the point where the line AB intersects the line $x = -3$.

       _____

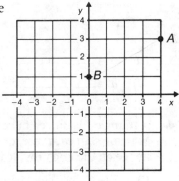

15. Solve the equations

    (i) $4(x + 1) = 3 - x$;

       $x =$ _____

    (ii) $\dfrac{5}{x + 6} = 3$

       $x =$ _____

16. From the top of a cliff which is 80 m high, Enka looks directly out to sea and sees a windsurfer at an angle of depression of 18°. She also observes a swimmer at an angle of depression of 26°. Given that Enka, the swimmer and the windsurfer are in the same vertical plane, what is the distance between the swimmer and the windsurfer:

PROGRESS TEST 3

1. (a) Write, in full, the number shown on a calculator as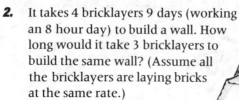

_____

(b) Write the number 69 800 000 using standard index form.

_____

2. It takes 4 bricklayers 9 days (working an 8 hour day) to build a wall. How long would it take 3 bricklayers to build the same wall? (Assume all the bricklayers are laying bricks at the same rate.)

_____ days

3. The formula for finding the total surface area of a cylinder A is given by $A = 2\pi r^2 + 2\pi rh$. Find:

(i) A if $r = 3$ cm and $h = 5$ cm;
(ii) h if $r = 2$ cm and $A = 40$ cm^2.

(i) $A =$ _____ cm^2

(ii) $h =$ _____ cm

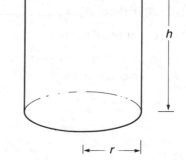

4. A triangle T is moved in various ways as follows. In each case, draw the final image on the grid provided.

(i) $T \rightarrow T_1$ by a clockwise rotation of 90° about A.
(ii) $T \rightarrow T_2$ by an enlargement centre A, scale factor 2.
(iii) $T \rightarrow T_3$ by a clockwise rotation of 90° about B.
(iv) Describe the transformation that takes $T_3 \rightarrow T_1$.

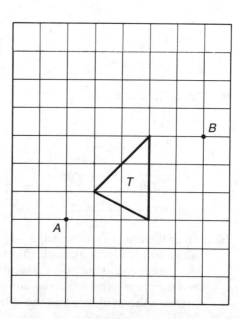

5. Write down an irrational number that lies between 20 and 30.

6. A parcel measuring 25 cm by 15 cm by 8 cm is tied with string as shown. If 20 cm is allowed for the knot, how long is the piece of string?

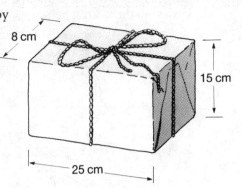

7. A coach service leaves Alwick at 9.30 a.m. to travel to Burpham, a distance of 20 miles. The coach travels at an average speed of 30 miles an hour, and makes one fifteen minute stop at a service station half-way between the two towns.
Part of the travel graph has been drawn below. Complete the diagram, and state what time the coach arrives at Burpham.

....

At 9.00 a.m., an athlete sets out to run from Burpham to Alwick. His journey is shown on the same diagram.

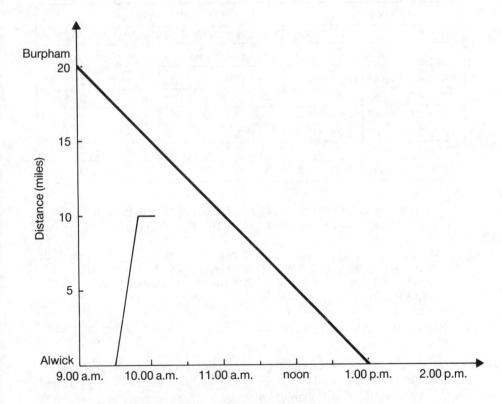

    (i)   What is the average speed of the athlete? ....

    (ii)   What time does the coach pass the athlete? ....

8. A plate is priced at £9.45 which includes V.A.T. (charged at 17.5%). How much is the V.A.T.? (Answer to the nearest penny)

9.

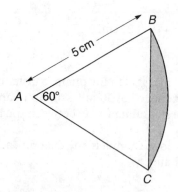

In the diagram, *ABC* is a sector of a circle of radius 5 cm. Find the area which is shaded.

10. The table gives the number of rolls of wallpaper needed for various dimensions of rooms.

Height of room		Length of walls								
feet		28'0"	32'0"	36'0"	40'0"	44'0"	48'0"	52'0"	56'0"	60'0"
metres		8.53	9.75	10.97	12.19	13.41	14.63	15.85	17.07	18.29
7'0" to 7'6"	2.13 to 2.29	4	4	5	5	6	6	7	7	8
7'7" to 8'0"	2.30 to 2.44	4	4	5	5	6	6	7	8	8
8'1" to 8'6"	2.45 to 2.59	4	5	5	6	6	7	7	8	8
8'7" to 9'0"	2.60 to 2.74	4	5	5	6	6	7	8	8	9
9'1" to 9'6"	2.75 to 2.90	4	5	6	6	7	7	8	9	9
9'7" to 10'0"	2.91 to 3.05	5	5	6	7	7	8	9	9	10

(i) How many rolls of paper will be needed to paper a room which measures 8'6" by 15' with a drop of 8'10" (ignore doors and windows)?

_____ rolls.

(ii) How many rolls of paper will be needed to paper a room which measures 4.6 m by 2.8 m and is 2.8 m high (ignore doors and windows)?

_____ rolls

11. Tanya was answering a multiple choice test which contained 3 questions. Each question had 4 possible answers *A*, *B*, *C* and *D*. If she randomly guessed the answers, what is the probability that she will get two questions correct?

12. Complete the table below for the graph of $y = 3 - 2x^2$.

x	-3	-2	-1	$-\frac{1}{2}$	0	1	2	3
y	-15					1		

(a)   On the grid provided, plot the graph. Use your graph to find

(i) y when $x = 0.8$;

(ii) x when $y = -10$.

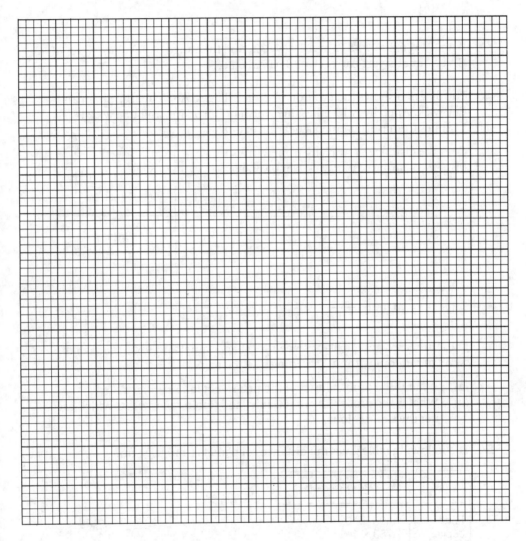

(b)   By drawing a suitable straight line on your graph, solve the equation

$$x = 2 - 2x^2$$

PROGRESS TEST 4

1. A cuboid has an edge from $A(2,0.0)$ to $B(6,0,0)$. Another edge is from A to E $(2,7,0)$ and a third edge is from A to D $(2,0,k)$. The face $ABCD$ is a square. Find (i) k; (ii) the coordinates of the points F, G and H of the other face $EFGH$.

2. E is related to H, x and y, by the formula

$$E = \frac{H}{x - y}$$

If $4 \leqslant H \leqslant 6$, $7 \leqslant x \leqslant 12$ and $1 \leqslant y \leqslant 2$, find the range of possible values of E. Give your answers correct to 1 decimal place.

3. The diagram shows the position of three villages, Appleby, Burpham and Cattwick. Appleby is 15 miles due North of Burpham, and Cattwick is 11 miles from Burpham on a bearing of 048°.

(i) the distance of Appleby from Cattwick;
(ii) the bearing of Cattwick from Appleby.

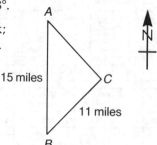

4. Solve the equation $\dfrac{14}{x + 2} = \dfrac{3}{5}$.

5. There are 6 red and 14 black sweets in a bag. Daniel and Robin each take a sweet at random without returning it to the bag.

(a) What is the probability that the first sweet taken is black?
(b) What is the probability that Daniel and Robin take sweets which are not the same colour?

6. The following table gives the distances of planets from the Sun.

Planet	Distance in kilometres
Earth	1.496×10^8
Jupiter	7.783×10^8
Mars	2.279×10^8
Mercury	5.791×10^7
Neptune	4.498×10^9
Pluto	5.900×10^9
Saturn	1.427×10^9
Uranus	2.869×10^9
Venus	1.082×10^8

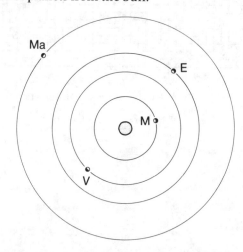

(i) Roughly how many hundreds of times greater is the distance of Pluto from the Sun than Mercury from the Sun?
(ii) Roughly how far apart are the Earth and Neptune when closest together? Give your answer in standard form.

7. In the diagram, $ABCDA'B'C'D'$ is a cube of side 6 cm. M is the midpoint of CC'. Find:

   (i)   the angle between AM and the plane $BB'C'C$;

   (ii)   the angle between the planes ABM and $ABCD$.

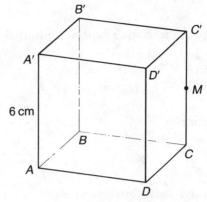

8. In the diagram, AOC is the diameter of a circle centre O, and ABC is an isosceles triangle. PT is a tangent to the circle and $\angle OPT = 38°$.

   (a)   Find (i) x; (ii) y, giving clear reasons for your answers.

   (b)   If AB is perpendicular to PT, find z.

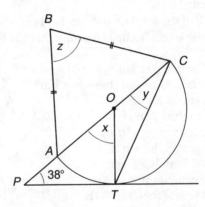

9. In the diagram, $ABCD$ and $SPQR$ are identical rectangles.

   (a)   (i)   Show, with an explanation using words or a diagram, that the area A square metres of the T-shape is given by the formula $A = b(2l - b)$.

         (ii)   Rearrange this formula to express l in terms of A and b.

   (b)   Find the formula for the perimeter of the T-shape in its simplest form.

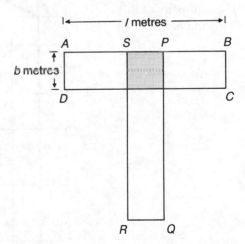

10. Use your calculator to find

$$\frac{6.29 \times \sqrt{8.06}}{16.2^2 - 14.3^2}$$

(i) showing all figures; (ii) rounding your answer to 3 significant figures.

11. Evaluate

(i) $8^{-\frac{2}{3}}$; (ii) $(6x^2)^{-2} \times (2x)^4$.

12. Simplify

$$\frac{1}{(x+2)} + \frac{2}{(x+1)}$$

13. Solve the inequality

$$5x - 13 < 3x + 4 < 6x - 11,$$

given that x is an integer.

14. A bottle holds $120\,\text{cm}^3$ of liquid. A similar bottle holds $200\,\text{cm}^3$ of liquid. If the height of the smaller bottle is $20\,\text{cm}$, find the height of the larger bottle (1 decimal place).
If the area of the label on the smaller bottle is $10\,\text{cm}^2$, what is the area of the label on the larger bottle? (Assume that the labels are also similar.)

15. Pete and Sean are running a race around a 400 m track. They start together, but Sean can run at a speed about 2 m/s faster than Pete, who can run a lap in 90 s. If they started together, how many laps would Sean have to run before he caught up with Pete again? (Assume they are both running at a constant speed.)

16. In the triangle ABC, $\angle BAC = 80°$, $AB = 5\,\text{cm}$ and $AC = 8\,\text{cm}$. M is the mid-point of BC. Find AM.

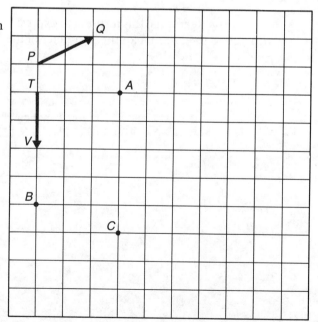

17. Draw clearly on question 16's grid vectors which represent:

 (a)   the vector $\overrightarrow{AX}$ equal to $\overrightarrow{PQ} + \overrightarrow{TV}$;

 (b)   the vector $\overrightarrow{BY}$ equal to $\overrightarrow{PQ} - \overrightarrow{TV}$;

 (c)   the vector $\overrightarrow{CZ}$ equal to $3\overrightarrow{PQ}$.

18. A sample of caterpillars was measured and the lengths were as follows.

$$1.8\,cm, 0.9\,cm, 1.3\,cm, 1.4\,cm, 1.9\,cm, 0.7\,cm.$$

Find the standard deviation of the lengths of this sample.

ANSWERS TO PROGRESS TEST 1

Award marks as shown. If your method is correct but the answer wrong, award 1 mark where 2 have been allowed. Add up the marks, and then look at the comments given at the end.

1. Since $\frac{5}{9} = \frac{10}{18}$,
shade any 10 squares.

1 mark

2. (i) all ringed correct,   1 mark
(ii) all crossed correct. 1 mark

3. $(4 + 3) \times (6 - 2) = 28$. 1 mark
Only one possibility.

4. (i) e.g. 12, 20, 28. 1 mark
Many possibilities.
(ii) 5 and 8 for example. 1 mark

5. (i) 20% of £8 is $0.2 \times 8 = £1.60$
Sale price = $£8 - £1.60 = £6.40$. 2 marks
(ii) 20% = £16.80. 1 mark
100% = $£16.80 \times 5 = £84.00$
Original price = £84.00. 1 mark

6. $2 \times \pi \times 4.5 = 28.3$ cm. 2 marks

7. 21. 1 mark
Easy to get 210, but remember the calculator does
$12 \div 10 = 1.2$ first, i.e. $21 \times 6.4 + 1.2 = 135.6$.

8. 87 should be 870. 1.07 should be 1.1. 2 marks
0.11 should be 0.10.
Subtract 1 mark for any extra found wrong.

9. Difference = 3.25 km
Hence % = $\frac{3.25}{2.25} \times 100 = 144.4\%$. 2 marks

10. (i)

$$-1.5 \quad\quad -1 \quad\quad -0.5 \quad\quad 0$$

1 mark

(ii) 3.5×10^{-1}. 1 mark

11. 2.5. 2 marks

12. $5n - 3$. 1 mark

13. $\frac{1}{2}$ litre = 500 cm³
$500 \div 60 = 8.3$
8 glasses. 2 marks

14. (6,5,2). 2 marks

15. $(£141 \div 117.5) \times 100$
= £120. 2 marks

16. $(4 \times 4.5 + 7 \times 14.5 + 6 \times 24.5$
$+ 7 \times 34.5 + 1 \times 44.5) \div 25$
= 22.1 2 marks

How to interpret your scores

22–30 Grade C/D: (a good start).
15–21 Grade E: check mistakes carefully.
8–14 Grade F: a lot of work ahead.
0–7 Grade G: only just registering on the GCSE scale.

ANSWERS TO PROGRESS TEST 2

1. $\sqrt{9500} = 97\,\text{m}$ (to the nearest m). **1 mark**

2. $12 \times 95\text{p} = £11.40$. Profit $= £11.40 - £7.00 = £4.40$. **1 mark**

% Profit $= \dfrac{£4.40}{£7.00} \times 100 = 62.9\%$. **2 marks**

3. (i) $15 - 3 = 7x - 4x$, so $12 = 3x$, $x = 4$. **1 mark**
(ii) $4 - 5 = 3x$, $-1 = 3x$, $x = -\frac{1}{3}$. **2 marks**

4. $8 \times £13.20 = £105.60$. **1 mark**
Saving $= £105.60 - £98.95 = £6.65$. **1 mark**

5. Taxable earnings $= £135 - £52 = £83$. **1 mark**
Tax $= 83 \times £0.25 = £20.75$. **1 mark**
Take home pay $= £135 - £20.75 = £114.25$. **1 mark**

6. Work out the cost of 1 lb in each case.
$55\text{p} \div 3 = 18.3\text{p}$, $86\text{p} \div 5 = 17.2\text{p}$, $£3.60 \div 20 = 18\text{p}$. **1 mark**

The 5 lb pack is the best buy. **1 mark**

7. $\$800 = £\dfrac{800}{1.6} = £500$. **1 mark**
The total cost $= £228 + £500$
$= £728$. **1 mark**

8. (i) $4(x + 2y)$ **1 mark**
(ii) $2xy^2(2xy - 3)$ **1 mark**

9. Scale factor $= \dfrac{35}{22}$ **1 mark**

new height $= 29.5 \times \dfrac{35}{22} = 46.9\,\text{cm}$ **1 mark**

10. $(10 \times 8 \times 4) \div (2 \times 1 \times 0.5) = 320$ **1 mark**

11. (a) See graph.

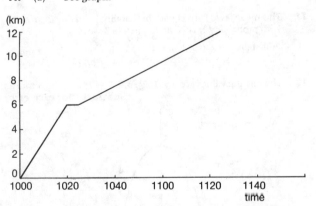

(b) Arrival time = 11.25 am. **1 mark**
1 mark } each
1 mark } line
1 mark

Notes:
(i) 18 km/h for 20 mins covers 6 km.
(ii) 5 mins on the scale is $\frac{1}{2}$ cm.
(iii) Remaining 6 km must take 1 hour.

12. (i) All probabilities are $\frac{1}{3}$. **2 marks**
(ii) $\dfrac{1}{3} \times \dfrac{1}{3} = \dfrac{1}{9}$. **2 marks**

(iii) Easier to do (1 – probability both the same)
$= 1 - \dfrac{1}{9} - \dfrac{1}{9} - \dfrac{1}{9} = \dfrac{2}{3}$. **2 marks**

13. Find $\angle ACB$ first, $\tan ACB = \dfrac{5}{12} = 0.4167$, hence $ACB = 22.6°$.
So $\angle\,ACD = 180° - 22.6° = 157.4°$. **2 marks**
$\triangle\,ADC$ is isosceles, so $x = \frac{1}{2}(180 - 157.4°) = 11.3°$. **1 mark**
(There are other methods.)

14. (i) $(4,3)$. **1 mark**
(ii) $\frac{1}{2}$. **1 mark**
(iii) $y = \frac{1}{2}x + 1$. **1 mark**
(iv) put $x = -3$ in equation (iii), $y = \frac{1}{2} \times -3 + 1 = -\frac{1}{2}$. **1 mark**
The point is $(-3, -\frac{1}{2})$.

15. (i) $4x + 4 = 3 - x$,
$4x + x = 3 - 4 = -1$,
$5x = -1$,
$x = -\frac{1}{5}$. **2 marks**
(ii) $5 = 3(x + 6) = 3x + 18$,
so $5 - 18 = 3x$,
$-13 = 3x$, $x = \dfrac{-13}{3}$. **2 marks**

16. Note: it is easier to put the angles of depression in as angles of elevation.

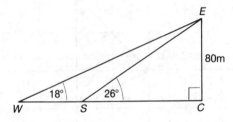

In triangle ECS, $\tan 26° = \dfrac{80}{SC}$,

so $SC = \dfrac{80}{\tan 26°} = 164\,\text{m}$.

Similarly in triangle ECW, $WC = \dfrac{80}{\tan 18°} = 246\,\text{m}$.
The distance between the swimmer and windsurfer
$= 246 - 164 = 82\,\text{m}$. **3 marks**

How to interpret your scores

36–45 Grade B: well done.
28–35 Grade C/D: check carefully topics not correctly answered.
20–27 Grade E: thorough revision needed.
10–19 Grade F: do not do the next paper before redoing this one.
0–9 Grade G: only just registering on the GCSE scale.

ANSWERS TO PROGRESS TEST 3

1. (a) 0.000682. **1 mark**
(b) 6.98×10^7. **1 mark**

2. $4 \times 9 = 36$ days for 1 bricklayer,
$36 \div 3 = 12$ days for 3 bricklayers. **1 mark**

3. (i) $A = (2 \times \pi \times 9) + (2 \times \pi \times 3 \times 5)$
$= 18\pi + 30\pi = 48\pi$
$= 150.8\,cm^2$ (1 decimal place). **2 marks**
(ii) This requires rearrangement of the formula
$40 = (2 \times \pi \times 4) + (2 \times \pi \times 2 \times h)$
$40 = 8\pi + 4\pi h, \, 40 - 25.13 = 12.57h$
$14.87 = 12.57h, \, h = \dfrac{14.87}{12.57} = 1.18\,cm$. **2 marks**

4. (iv) translation $= \begin{pmatrix} -2 \\ -8 \end{pmatrix}$ **1 mark**

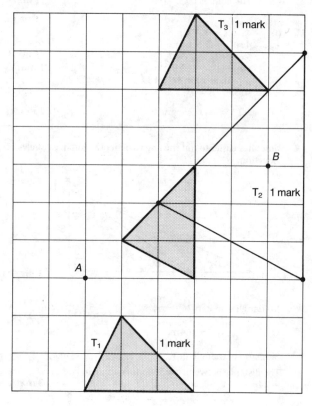

T₃ 1 mark
T₂ 1 mark
B
A
T₁ 1 mark

5. $\sqrt{21}, \sqrt{22}$ etc. **1 mark**

6. $(25 \times 2 + 8 \times 2 + 15 \times 4)$
$+ 20 = 146\,cm$ **2 marks**

7. 10.25 a.m. (It takes 40 mins + 15 min stop). **1 mark**

(i) $\dfrac{20}{4} = 5\,m.p.h.$ **2 marks**

(ii) approximately 10.15 a.m. **1 mark**

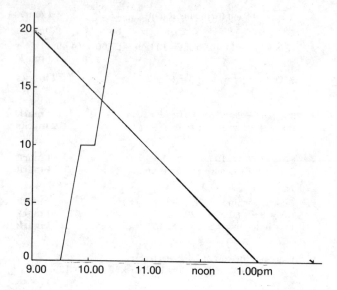

8. $(9.45 \div 117.5) \times 17.5$
$= £1.41$ **2 marks**

9. Sector − triangle
$= \pi \times 5^2 \times \dfrac{60}{360} - \dfrac{1}{2} \times 5^2 s \text{ in } 60°$ **1 mark**
$= 2.26\,cm^2$

10. (i) Length of walls $= 2 \times 8'6'' + 2 \times 15'$
$= 17' + 30' = 47'$.
Look at the column headed 48' and height 8'7'' to 9'0''.
This gives 7 rolls. **1 mark**
(ii) Length of walls $= 2 \times 4.6 + 2 \times 2.8\,m$
$= 9.2 + 5.6 = 14.8\,m$.
Look at the column headed 15.85 m and height 2.75 to 2.90 m.
This gives 8 rolls. **1 mark**

11. This means two correct with probability $\frac{1}{4}$ and one incorrect with probability $\frac{3}{4}$. This can happen in 3 ways.
Probability $= 3 \times \dfrac{1}{4} \times \dfrac{1}{4} \times \dfrac{3}{4} = \dfrac{9}{64}$ **2 marks**

12. The missing values are $-5, 1, 2\frac{1}{2}, 3, -5, -15$. **3 marks**
Subtract 1 for each error

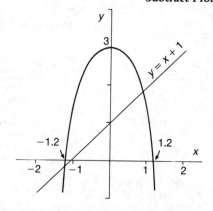

(a) (i) $-1.7 \, (\pm 0.1)$. **1 mark**
(ii) 2.5 (± 0.1). **1 mark**
(b) $x = 2 - 2x^2$
add one to each side
$x + 1 = 3 - 2x^2$
the required line is
$y = x + 1$ **1 mark**
The solutions are
$x = 0.8$ or -1.3 **2 marks**

How to interpret your scores

28–34 Grade A: very good.
23–27 Grade B: a good standard for GCSE.
16–22 Grade C/D: not good enough for the higher tier.
8–15 Grade E: more work needed to reach Grade C standard.
0–7 below Grade E standard.

ANSWERS TO PROGRESS TEST 4

1.   (i) $k = 4$ (the length of the side of the square).   **1 mark**

    (ii)   (2,7,4) (6,7,4) (6,7,0) in the order you have labelled it.   **2 marks**

2.   To make E as large as possible, take $H = 6$, and $x - y = 7 - 2 = 5$.

$\therefore E = \dfrac{6}{5} = 1.2.$ **1 mark**

To make E as small as possible, take $H = 4$, and $x - y = 12 - 1 = 11$.

$\therefore E = \dfrac{4}{11} = 0.4.$ **1 mark**

3.   (b)   (i) 11.2 miles,

      ± 0.1 **2 marks**

      ± 0.2 **only 1 mark**

      (ii) 133°,

      $\pm 1°$ **2 marks**

      $\pm 2°$ **only 1 mark**

4. $14 \times 5 = 3(x + 2)$,

$70 = 3x + 6.$ **1 mark**

$64 = 3x.$

$x = 21\frac{1}{3}.$ **1 mark**

5.   (a) $\dfrac{14}{20}$ or $\dfrac{7}{10}.$ **1 mark**

    (b)   Black followed by red or red followed by black is:

$\dfrac{7}{10} \times \dfrac{6}{19} + \dfrac{3}{10} \times \dfrac{14}{19} = \dfrac{42}{95}.$ **2 marks**

6.   (i) $5.9 \times 10^9 \div 5.791 \times 10^7$ is approximately 100.   **1 mark**

    (ii) $4.498 \times 10^9 - 1.496 \times 10^8 = 4.35 \times 10^9$ km.   **2 marks**

7.   This is a difficult question.

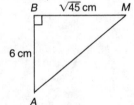

    (i)   angle AMB is required.

      Find BM by Pythagoras.

      $BM^2 = 6^2 + 3^2 = 45$. So $BM = \sqrt{45}$ cm.

      Hence $\tan AMB = \dfrac{6}{\sqrt{45}} = 0.8944$, so $AMB = 41.8°$.   **2 marks**

    (ii)   Angle MBC is required.

      $\tan MBC = \dfrac{3}{6} = 0.5$, so $MBC = 26.6°$.   **2 marks**

8.   (a)   (i)   Angle $OTP = 90°$ (angle between tangent and radius).

        So $x = 180° - 90° - 38° = 52°$.   **2 marks**

      (ii) $OC = OT$ (radii), so ΔOCT is isosceles.

        $\angle TOC = 180° - 52° = 128°$.

        Hence $y = \frac{1}{2}(180° - 128°) = 26°$.   **2 marks**

    (b) BA must be parallel to OT, so $\angle BAC = \angle BCA = x = 52°$.

      Hence $z = 180° - 104° = 76°$.   **2 marks**

9.   (a)   (i)   There are two rectangles $= 2 \times l \times b = 2lb$.   **1 mark**

      The overlap b^2 is counted twice, so subtract b^2.

      The area of the 'T' shape $= 2lb - b^2 = b(2l - b)$.   **1 mark**

      (ii) $A = 2lb - b^2$, so $A + b^2 = 2lb$.

        Hence $l = \dfrac{A + b^2}{2b}$.   **1 mark**

    (b)   Perimeter $l + 2b + (l - b) + (l - b) + (l - b) + b = 4l$.   **2 marks**

10.   (i)   0.308151812.   **1 mark**

    (ii)   0.308.   **1 mark**

11.   (i) $\frac{1}{4}$ (or 0.25).   **1 mark**

    (ii) $\dfrac{1}{36x^4} \times 16x^4$.   **1 mark**

      $= \dfrac{16}{36} = \dfrac{4}{9}.$ **1 mark**

12. $\dfrac{(x + 1) + 2(x + 2)}{(x + 2)(x + 1)}.$ **1 mark**

    $= \dfrac{x + 1 + 2x + 4}{(x + 2)(x + 1)}.$ **1 mark**

    $= \dfrac{3x + 5}{(x + 2)(x + 1)}.$ **1 mark**

13. $5x - 13 < 3x + 4$.

$2x < 17.$

$x < 8.5.$ **1 mark**

$3x + 4 < 6x - 11.$

$15 < 3x.$

$5 < x.$ **1 mark**

So $5 < x < 8.5$.

But x is an integer, so

$x = 6, 7, 8.$ **1 mark**

14.   Ratio of volumes is $120:200 = 3:5 = 1:1\frac{2}{3}$.

So ratio of lengths is $1 : \sqrt[3]{1\frac{2}{3}} = 1 : 1.186$.

Height of larger bottle $= 20 \times 1.186 = 23.7$ cm.   **2 marks**

Ratio of areas $= 1 : (1.186)^2 = 1 : 1.407$.

The area of the larger label $= 10 \times 1.407 = 14.07$ cm^2.   **2 marks**

15.   Sean has to make up 400 m to catch Pete up again.

This takes $\dfrac{400}{2} = 200$ seconds.

In this time, Pete has run $\dfrac{200}{90} = 2\frac{2}{9}$ laps.

Hence Sean has run $3\frac{2}{9}$ laps.   **2 marks**

16.   The question involves more work than at first sight.

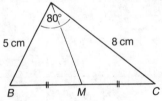

Find BC first using the cosine rule:

$BC^2 = 5^2 + 8^2 - 2 \times 5 \times 8 \cos 80 = 75.11$.

Hence $BC = 8.67$ cm.   **2 marks**

So $BM = 8.67 \div 2 = 4.335$ cm.

Now find angle B using the sine rule:

$\dfrac{\sin B}{8} = \dfrac{\sin 80}{8.67}$. Hence $B = 65.32°$.   **2 marks**

Now use the cosine rule in triangle BAM:

$AM^2 = 5^2 + 4.335^2 - 2 \times 5 \times 4.335 \cos 65.32 = 25.69$.

So $AM = 5.07$ cm.   **2 marks**

17.   (a) $\begin{pmatrix} 2 \\ -1 \end{pmatrix}$ (b) $\begin{pmatrix} 2 \\ 3 \end{pmatrix}$ (c) $\begin{pmatrix} 6 \\ 3 \end{pmatrix}$

    starting at A **1 mark**

    starting at B **1 mark**

    starting at C **1 mark**

18.   Using $\text{SD} = \sqrt{\dfrac{\Sigma x^2}{n} - \left(\dfrac{\Sigma x}{n}\right)^2}$

    $= \sqrt{\dfrac{11.80}{6} - \left(\dfrac{8}{6}\right)^2}$

$$= 1.96 - 1.77$$

$$= .43$$

How to interpret your scores

50–60   Grade A*: an excellent result.
40–49   Grade A: a high standard.
30–39   Grade B: perhaps still more work to do.
20–29   Grade C/D: only just on the highter tier.
 0–19   Below Grade D certainly not good enough for the higher tier.

ANSWERS AND SOME HINTS TO QUESTIONS TO TRY

1. (a) 36. (b) No, the answer should be an exact whole number. (c) 19.

2. (i) 8532. (ii) 5832 for example. (iii) 35 and 82.

3. 60

4. (a) 31. (b) 17. (c) O. (d) R, U.

5. (i)

1	12	14	7
4	15	9	6
13	2	8	11
16	5	3	10

(ii) for example 1 + 4 + 13 + 16,
1 + 3 + 14 + 16.

6. (i) 17. (ii) 175. (iii) 57 and 81. (iv) 175 (any number ending in 75 and using these digits).

7. (i) 847 cm. (ii) 8856 gm. (iii) 9000. (iv) 6. (v) 8.8. (vi) 880 000.

8. (i) 8812. (ii) 8800.

9. (a) (i) 19. (ii) 8500. (iii) 1000. (iv) 8.0. (v) 92. (vi) 85 000. (vii) 9.0. (viii) 85. (b) (i) 8.7. (ii) 9.0. (iii) 8.1. (iv) 19.0. (v) 9.1. (vi) 8.9. (vii) 10.0. (viii) 4.9.

10. (i) 37 809. (ii) 38 000. (iii) 40 000.

11. (i) $\frac{4}{7}$. (ii) 0.049. (iii) 0.52.

12. Change each fraction to a decimal; (i) $\frac{6}{11}$. (ii) $\frac{8}{9}$. (iii) $\frac{13}{18}$ and $\frac{19}{12}$.

13. Start with 3.5 which is between $\sqrt{9}$ and $\sqrt{16}$: 3.4.

14. $4\frac{3}{10}$.

15. (a) $\frac{5}{8}$. (b) $\frac{3}{8}$.

16. (i) $42\frac{1}{4}$. (ii) £3.80.

17. (a) (iv), (vi), (vii), (ix), (x). b) $\sqrt{2}$ and $\sqrt{8}$ would give $\sqrt{2} \div \sqrt{8} = \sqrt{0.25} = 0.5$

18. (a) $\frac{5}{8}$. (d) $\frac{7}{10}$. (e) $\frac{7}{2}$.

19. nothing about $\frac{1}{17}$ and $\frac{1}{19}$; $\frac{1}{18} = 0.0\dot{5}$, $\frac{1}{21} = 0.0476190$.

20. 6°C.

21. (i) 7°C. (ii) still 7°C.

22. (i) 255. (ii) 120.

23. (i) 7, 12. (ii) 18, 12. (iii) 24, 7.

24. (i) 105. (ii) $13\frac{1}{8}$. (iii) (£10.25 ÷ 25) × 60 = £24.60. (iv) £24.60 ÷ $13\frac{1}{8}$ = £1.87.

25. (a) (1.8 ÷ 9) × 2 = 0.4 tonnes. (b) 8.

26. (a) Aberdeen. (b) Aberdeen. (c) not really, temperature differences are roughly equal, but perhaps Swansea is on average slightly warmer.

27. £1.

28. (i) 28 kg. (ii) 41.7%.

29. (i) 3 km is 300 000 cm : ÷ 20 000 to give 15 cm. (ii) On the map 1 cm = 20 000 cm = 0.2 km. ∴ 1 cm² on the map = 0.2 × 0.2 = 0.04 km². ∴ 10 cm² is 10 × 0.04 = 0.4 km².

30. (a) 4. (b) 30 and 120 for example. (c) Number on large wheel = 4 × Number on small wheel.

31. (a) 60 km/h. (b) 3 hours 18 minutes.

32. (i) 0.556. (ii) 18.2%. (iii) 5.73.

33. 8 × 4 − 7 = 25.

34. (i) 9856. (ii) 29.77. (iii) 4.39 (2 dec. pl.).

35. (i) 8.64×10^4. (ii) 9.57×10^2. (iii) 2×10^{-3}. (iv) 4.06×10^{-2}. (v) 1.8×10^4. (vi) 1.6×10^{-2}.

36. (i) 6000. (ii) 6. (iii) 1. (iv) 2000. (v) 6000.

37. (i) 4.22×10^6. (ii) 3.36×10^6. (iii) 4.6×10^{-2}. (iv) 1.2×10^6. (v) 3.6×10^{13}. (vi) 1.25×10^{-1}.

38. (i) 0.167. (ii) 3.833 (iii) 1.688.

39. (i) $\frac{3}{20}$. (ii) £76.50.

40. (a) 33.2%. (b) 19. (c) 114 700.

41. £19 350.

42. 275 ml.

43. (i) 85p. (ii) 70p. (iii) £1.30.

44. 15%.

45. £80.

46. £84 000.

47. 32.25%.

48. (i) 65 km/h. (ii) 128 km/h.

49. (i) 150°C.   (ii) 28 km/h.   (iii) 108 mg.

50. (a) 60.   (b) 96.   (c) About $\frac{5}{8}$.

51. (a) 1.1 kg.   (b) £1.90.   (c) £2.75.   (d) £2.95.
(e) £1.70.

52. (a) £4.70.   (b) £4.15.   (c) (i) £172.   (ii) £11.40.
(iii) £215.50.

53. (a) 10.12 p.   (b) 60.72 p.   (c) 35.42 p.

54. (a) + 10%.   (b) 1.3 hatchback.

55. (a) Seven hundred and thirty three thousand three hundred
and forty two.   (b) 158 000.   (c) Robbery.
(d) Criminal damage.

56. (i) 62 cm.   (ii) 250 000.   (iii) 5×10^6 mg.
(iv) 0.8 l.

57. (a) (i) 42.   (ii) £7.60.   (b) £7.10   (c) £6.

58. (i) 5.556.   (ii) 0.6875.   (iii) 6.350.   (iv) $\frac{11}{16}$.

59. (i) 6400.   (ii) about £3.10.   (iii) £12 500.

60. (a) 3.   (b) Queen Victoria.

61. 7 min 56 s.

62. (i) 8 h 58 min.   (ii) 8.26 p.m.   (iii) 15.
(iv) 575.   (v) 39.   (vi) 8784.

63. (a) 0.51s.   (b) 2 min 02.49s.

64. (i) Monday.   (ii) Friday.   (iii) November 19th.

65. (a) 2.   (b) D. Maragh A, F. Jones B, J. Smith B.

66. (a) 2.50 p.m.   (b) 374°F.

67. (a) 0839.   (b) 52 m.p.h.   (c) 13.50.   (d) 25%.

68. (a) 20 03.   (b) 2 h 39 min.   (c) 1 h 34 min.
(d) 58.4 km/h.

69. (a) 08.50.   (b) 10 min.   (c) (i) 30 min.
(ii) 40 km/h.   (d) (i) 12.30.   (e) (ii) 13.48.

71. (i) 83 miles.   (ii) 1 h 40 min.

72. (a) 16 hours.   (b) £40.

73. (i) 125.   (ii) 128.75.   (iii) £52.79.   (iv) £62.59.

74. (i) $6\frac{3}{4}$ h.   (ii) 35.   (iii) £556.80.

75. £2057.08.

76. (a) (i) £150.   (ii) £600.   (b) £108.27.

77. (a) £146.80.   (b) 21.   (c) £633.10.   (d) £12.57.

78. (a) £17.95.   (b) 1222.   (c) £53.77.   (d) £0.84.
(e) £72.56.   (f) £10.88.   (g) £83.44.

79. 14.

80. £2.72: $8 \times 19 + 8 \times 15$;
£1.90: 10×19;
85p: $2 \times 15 + 3 \times 19$ (= 87).

81. The letter Hannah sent.

82. 43.4 miles/gallon.

83. (a) £248.   (b) £342.   (c) June 8th.   (d) (i) £203.
(ii) £162.40.   (iii) £730.80.

84. (a) £415.   (b) (i) £790.   (ii) 1080 francs.
(iii) £100.

85. (a) £35.40.   (b) £42.32.   (c) £7.72.

86. (i) 2791.8.   (ii) 2821.50.
(iii) No, it depends on how much is changed.

87. (i) 49p.   (ii) 20 750 yen.   (iii) 108.2 rand.
(iv) 4958 lire.

88. (i) £3.10.   (ii) No, if you cannot eat them all before they
go rotten.

89. Large bag most economic but party size would give more
variety.

90. (a) (i) £85.   (ii) 2.30 a.m.   (b) (i) £8.   (ii) £15.

91. (i) 231 km.   (ii) 48 litres.

92. 13 litres; 3 tokens; 27 weeks.

93. (a) 300.   (b) £25 320.

94. £24 392.

95. £200; £166.50.

96. £63.50.

97. (i) £309.60, £92.40.   (ii) £17 640, £1270.08.

98. (a) £190.   (b) (i) 33%.   (ii) £381.71.   (c) 24.
(d) (i)£400, £280, £240, £200, £160.
(ii) Better off by £55 if he does not claim.

99. £4176.

100. (i) 17.   (ii) − 5.   (iii) 17.

101. $n + p + 2$.

102. $10F + 200$.

103. (i) £$(E + 52e)$.   (ii) £$\left(e + \dfrac{E}{52}\right)$.

104. 39.2 m, 0.784 m too much.

105. (a) 122.   (b) (i) $x + y$.   (ii) $\frac{1}{2}x + y$.

106. (i) $7x^2$.   (ii) $12x^2$.   (iii) $9x^2$ $(3x \times 3x)$.
(iv) $36x^2 \div 4x^2 = 9$.

107. (i) $(4x + 1) + (2x - 3) = 6x - 2$.
(ii) $(x + 10) - (x + 6) = 4$.
(iii) $\frac{1}{2}[(6x - 5) + (2x + 9)] = \frac{1}{2}(8x + 4) = 4x + 2$.

108. (i) $1\frac{1}{2}$. (ii) $3\frac{1}{2}$. (iii) $1\frac{1}{5}$. (iv) 3. (v) 12.
(vi) 12.

109. $(3x + 2) + (x + 10) + (x + 1) = 5x + 13$.
(i) $5x + 13 = 63$ gives $x = 10$.
(ii) Yes; $3x + 2 = x + 10$ gives $x = 4$.

110. (i) $3x$. (ii) $3x + 10$. (iii) $3x + 10 = 2(x + 10)$
(Remember Daniel will be 10 years older). Hence $x = 10$, so at present, Daniel is 10, Peter is 30.

111. (i) 138. (ii) $x, x - 1, x + 7, x + 8$. (iv) 26.
(v) x would not be a whole number.

112. (a) 137. (b) $x, x - 9, x - 17, x - 18, x - 19$. (c) 70, 61, 53, 52, 51. (d) (i) not whole numbers, (ii) based on 36 which is not all in the square.

113. (i) $-1.11°$C. (ii) $9C = 5(C - 32)$, Hence $C = F = -40°$C. (iii) $F = \dfrac{9C + 160}{5}$

114. (i) 10. (ii) $\dfrac{V - q}{4}$. (iii) 4.

115. (i) $x = \dfrac{(y - 2t)}{k}$
(ii) $x = \dfrac{(y - ak)}{a}$. (iii) $x = ty^2$. (iv) $x = \dfrac{1}{y} - 1$.
(v) $x = \dfrac{2t}{3(y - a)}$

116. (a) multiply by 2. (b) 31.

117. (a) 1, 8, 27, 64. (b) 1000 (cube numbers).

118. (a) 8.5. (b) 8.75. (c) No; numbers are always less than 8, in the first sequence they are more than 8.

119. (a) 5, 7, 9, 11, 13, 15.
(b) line 20 PRINT NUMBER * NUMBER.

120. (a) 81,729, 6561, 59049. (b) 9 (odd power).

121. (a) (i) 1 6 15 20 15 6 1. (ii) 1 7 21 35 35 21 7 1.
(iii) 64. (iv) 1024 ($= 2^{10}$). (b) (i) 13. (ii) 21.
(iii) 89.

122. (a) 35, 5×7; 35, $5^2 + 2 \times 5$.
(b) $n \times (n + 2)$, $n^2 + 2 \times n$ (note they are the same).

123. (a) (i) 7, 9, 11, 41. (ii) $a = 2n + 1$. (iii) $n = \dfrac{a - 1}{2}$.
(b) (i) 16, 20, 24, 84. (ii) $p = 4n + 4$. (iii) $n = \dfrac{p - 4}{4}$.
(iv) 19.

124. (a) 10 joins. (b) 15 joins. (c) 21 joins. (d) 1, 3, 6, 10, 15, 21, 28, 36 : difference increases by 1 each time.
(e) $\frac{1}{2}n(n - 1)$ triangular numbers.

125. (i) 14.5. (ii) 15. (iii) 13.75.

126. (a) 11.4m. (b) 10. (c) 3 hours.
(d) (i) 1500 kg. (ii) 1.5 tonnes. (e) £69.60.

127. (a) 20 m. (b) 23.2 m². (c) 23.5 m.

128. (i) 6. (ii) 5.

129. (a) 699 yards. (b) 69 yards. (c) 18.5 yards.
(d) 805 yards.

130. (a) 6, 3. (b) 5, 1, 4.

131. (a) P. (b) 588 cm². (c) 24.

132. (a) C, E, G.
(b) (i) rotational order 4, also 4 axes of symmetry.
(ii) rotational order 4, also 4 planes of symmetry.
(c) 5, 8, 5.
(d) a square.

133. (a) (i) 36 000 cm³. (ii) 36 litres. (b) (i) 40 cm.
(ii) 125.

134. (a) 1.92 m². (b) 2 m. (c) 6 m². (d) 5.76 m³.

135. (a) 1.2 m². (b) 3 m³. (c) 1630 cm³.
(d) 2.625 kg. (e) 10.075 kg.

136. (a) 2 cm. (b) 24 cm. (c) 101 cm³.
(e) 326.7 cm². (f) 416 cm². (g) (i) 24. (ii) 48.

137. 4.07 cm³.

138. (a) (i) $\frac{1}{6}\pi d^3 + \frac{1}{4}\pi d^2 h$.
(ii) each part has 3 lengths multiplied together.
(b) $\pi d^2 + \pi dh$.

139. (i) 110.7 g, 3.44 cm³. (ii) 9×10^{-5} g/cm³.

140. (ii) approx. 2260 cm². (iii) 490 cm.

141. (i) 68°, 112°. (ii) 36°, 108°, 72°.

142. (a) (i) v. (ii) q. (b) (i) 180°. (ii) 360°.
(iii) 720°. (c) 4.7 cm. (d) 1.71 cm. (e) 10.42 cm.

143. (b) (i) 9.7 cm. (ii) 485 m. (c) (i) 41°.
(ii) 121°. (iii) 301°. (d) 416 m.

144. (a) (i) 37°. (ii) 53°. (iii) 106°. (iv) 74.
(b) (i) $f = 180 - 2x$. (ii) $g = 2x$. (iii) all values.

145. (a) (i) 140 km. (ii) 175 km. (b) (i) 60°. (ii) 320°.

146. (i) 108°, 36°, 72°. (ii) $\angle$ DEA + $\angle$ EAC = 108° + 72° = 180°.

147. (a) (i) 30°, 60°. (ii) equilateral. (b) $1\frac{1}{4}$.
(c) 812 rev/min.

148. (i) 1.2 km. (ii) 40 cm. (iii) 125 cm².

149. (a) Kite. (b) Right angled. (c) *EFGH* and *KLMJ*.
(d) 54°.

150. 450.

151. (b) (i) front. (ii) 37 front, 36 back.

152. (a) $y = 0$. (b) $(0, -2)$. (c) $(-1, 1), (-1, 2)$, $(-1.5, 1)$.

153. (a) (i) 90°. (ii) 120°. (iii) 150°. (b) (ii) 12.

154. (a) 4 and 3.   (b) 4 and 3, 3 and 2, 5 and 3.
(c) The numbers do not have a common factor.
(d) Divide the numbers by the common factor.

155. (i) 60°.   (ii) 20°, 70°, 50°.   (iii) 140°.   (iv) 70°.
(v) 65°, 50°.   (vi) 144°, 36°.

156. 90°, 40°, 40°.

157. (i) 60°.   (ii) 240°.   (iii) 30°.

158. (i) 64°.   (ii) 107°.

159. 140°.

160. (a) 90°.   (b) (i) 12 cm.   (ii) 5 cm (Use Pythagoras).

161. (a) (i) 30°.   (ii) 30°.   (iii) 90°.   (iv) 30°.
(b) (ii) a diameter.

162. 140°, 80°, 40°.

163. 38°, 58°.

164. (a) $90 - x$.   (b) $2x$.   (c) $2x - 90$.

165. (i) 3.10 cm.   (ii) 17.36 cm².

166. (i) 56.4°.   (ii) 49.3°, 3.49 cm.   (iii) 40.0°, 9.01 cm.
(iv) 26.8°, 8.39 cm.   (v) 7.61 cm, 3.55 cm.
(vi) 53°, 6.95 cm.

167. (a) 5 m.   (b) 29°.   (c) 102 m².

168. 36.9°, 2.76 m.

169. 58.2 m.

170. (i) 12 ft.   (ii) 73.7°.

171. (a) 25.1 m.   (b) 65°.

172. (i) 45.8°.   (ii) 40 cm².

173. (a) (i) $\frac{1}{6}\pi R^2$.   (b) (i) $R - r$.   (ii) $\frac{\pi(R - r)^2}{4}$.

174. (a) (i) 17.3 cm.   (ii) 73.9°.
(b) (i) $73.9° \div 2 = 36.95°$.   (ii) 3.76 cm.

175. (i) 3.05 cm.   (ii) 14.3 cm².   (iii) 85.8 cm³.

176. 2.62 m².

177. (i) (a) 173.7 m.   (b) 337°.   (ii) 086°, 1.25 km approx.

178. (a) 14°.   (b) 4.8 m.

179. (i) 18.1 km.   (ii) 128.7°.   (iii) 3.7°.

180. (b) (i) 440 m.   (ii) 245°.   (c) 1200 hours.
(d) 333 m.

181. (a) 4.05 cm.   (b) 135 cm³.   (c) 6.43 cm.
(d) 8.15 cm.   (e) 75.7°.

182. (a) 10 cm.   (b) 200 cm³.

183. (a) 7.10 m.   (b) 61.4 m².   (c) 410.

184. (a) 50, 80.   (b) 35, 55, 75, 95.   (e) 150 km.
(f) (i) D.I.Y.   (ii) £3.   (g) $C = 0.2x + 35$.

185. (b) (i) £76.   (ii) 47.   (iii) £25.   (c) (i) 36.
(ii) £9.

186. (a) (i) $12\frac{1}{2}$.   (ii) $100 \div 35 = 2.86$ galls.
(b) 33.5 miles per gallon.
(c) No, because it depends on the speed.

187. (a) 10.20.   (b) 10 km.   (c) (i) Stop.   (ii) begin
return journey.   (d) 30 km.   (e) 60 km/h.
(f) (i) No.   (g) 5 mins.

188. (i) (4, 12).   (ii) isosceles.   (iii) (4, −12).
(iv) $y = -3x$.

189. (a) 90, 180, 210.   (c) 220 km.   (d) $C = 0.6x + 60$.

190. (b) (i) 42.   (ii) 2.   (c) $\frac{1}{3}$.   (d) $y = \frac{1}{3}x + 31.5$.

191. (a) $y = 3x$.   (b) $y = 3^x$.   (c) $y = \frac{3}{x}$.

192. (a) 16   (b)

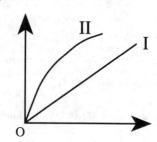

193. (a) 2.5 m.   (b) (i) 0, 4, 16, 49.   (iii) (a) 9 m³.
(b) 2.5 m.

194. (a) 100, 200, 400, 800, 1600, 3200, 6400.
(ii) 3 h 20 mins.   (c) 2.62×10^7.

195. (a) $4xh + 2x^2 = 72$, hence $h = \frac{36 - x^2}{2x}$.
(b) $V = x^2 \times \frac{(36 - x^2)}{2x} = 18x - \frac{1}{2}x^3$.
(c) 17.5, 32, 27.5.   (e) $x = 1.8 - 1.9$ cm,
$h = 8.5 - 9.1$ cm.

196. (a) 240 ft.   (b) 28 m.p.h.   (c) 250 ft.

197. (c) Remember $x = 0$ is the y-axis.   (d) $\begin{pmatrix} 3 \\ -2 \end{pmatrix}$.

199. (a) (i) 24 cm².   (ii) 22 cm.   (b) (i) translation so that
AD is on top of CB.   (ii) rotation of 180° about E.
(c) (i) 20 cm.
(ii) 24 cm.

200. (4, 0, 2), (4, 5, 0), (1, 5, 2), (4, 5, 2).

201. (a) (i) (15, 4, 12), (3, 16, 12), (3, − 8, 12) for example.
(ii) Sphere centre Q, radius 12.
(b) (i) $\sqrt{3^2 + 4^2 + 12^2} = 13$.   (ii) (0, 0, 24).
(iii) 135°.

202. $BA-$, $B - A$, $- AB$, $- BA$.

203. $\frac{1}{2}$.

204. (i) $1 - \frac{1}{4} = \frac{3}{4}$. (ii) $\frac{3}{4} \div 5 = \dfrac{3}{20}$. (iii) $\dfrac{3}{20} + \dfrac{1}{4} = \dfrac{2}{5}$.

205. (a) 9. (b) $\frac{7}{9}$.

206. $\frac{2}{3}$, 32.5 mins.

207. (a) $\frac{3}{20}$. (b) $\frac{3}{40}$.
(c) $\frac{1}{2} \times \frac{1}{4} \times \frac{3}{5} + \frac{1}{2} \times \frac{3}{4} \times \frac{3}{5} + \frac{1}{2} \times \frac{1}{4} \times \frac{2}{5} = \frac{7}{20}$.

208. (b) $\dfrac{24}{125}$. (c) $\dfrac{58}{125}$.
(d) a delay of more than 5 minutes is $\dfrac{19}{125}$.

209. (i) $\frac{4}{5}$. (ii) $\frac{2}{3}$. (iii) $1 - \frac{2}{3} = \frac{1}{3}$.

210. (a) $\frac{1}{3}$. (b) $\frac{2}{5}$. (c) $\frac{11}{15}$. (d) $\frac{2}{21}$.
(e) $\frac{10}{21}$. (f) $\frac{4}{105}$, $\frac{67}{91}$.

211. (a) $50 - 44 = 6$. (b) (i) 49. (ii) 48.
(c) $2388 \div 50 = 47.76$. (d) Yes to the nearest whole number. (e) $\frac{20}{50} = 0.4$.

212. (a) 2.
(b) $(1 \times 17 + 2 \times 31 + 3 \times 24 + 4 \times 28) \div 100 = 2.63$.

213. (a) $(2 \times 12.99 + 7 \times 13.99 + 23 \times 14.99 + 20 \times 15.99 + 17 \times 16.99) \div 69 = £15.61$. (b) 35th value is £15.99. (c) £14.99. (d) (i) mean.
(e) Total number sold $\times$ mean $=$ takings.

214. (a) (i) 38 days. (ii) £2.80. (b) (i) 145.
(ii) £33.55. (iii) 23p.

215. (a) frequencies are 6, 2, 5, 4, 4, 3, 1.
(b) 13th value is 252. (c) (i) $\frac{2}{25}$. (ii) $\frac{12}{25}$.

216. $(3 \times 14 + 7 \times 20) \div 10 = 18.2$.

217. $(6 \times 1.8 + 9 \times 1.5) \div 15 = 1.62$ m.

218. Total must be $8 \times 13 = 104$, hence the extra value is 27.

219. $39 + x = 45$ hence $x = 6$.

220. (b) (i) The sample might not fully reflect everybody's opinion.
(ii) Ask a certain number from each class in the school.

221. (i) $1 + 1 + 1 = 3$. (ii) $2 + 6 + 1 + 1 + 1 = 11$.

222. Second year wrong, seems to make no difference. Fourth year wrong, better test result from those nearer the back.

223. $111°$.

224. (i) mode $= 3$, median $= 2$. (ii) 108. (iii) 2.16.
(iv) $\frac{9}{10}$.

225. (a) (i) 1440. (ii) 3760. (b) 20%.

226. (a) 570 approx. (b) £3300 approx. (c) £5.80.
(d) Thursday.

227. (a) 8. (b) 30. (c) 81. (d) 2.7.

228. (a) $80°, 140°, 28°, 24°, 36°$. (c) (i) $6\frac{2}{3}\%$. (ii) $22.5°$.
(iii) £78.75.

229. $y = \frac{1}{2}x + 5$.

230. (c) about 37. (d) Physics : 15 : Mathematics.
(e) D is higher than expected.

231. (i) 2^5. (ii) 3^2. (iii) 2^4. (iv) 3^8. (v) 2^6.
(vi) 4^{12}.

232. (i) $5x + 8$. (ii) $8t - 2$. (iii) $9k - 9$. (iv) 8.
(v) $3ab + 2a + b$.

233. (i) 5, 2. (ii) $-2, -5$. (iii) 2, 4. (iv) 1.1, 0.3.
(v) $6, -\frac{1}{2}$.

234. (a) $\frac{1}{2}a^2$. (b) $\frac{1}{4}a^2$. (c) $A_n = a^2 \div 2^{n-1}$.

235. (a) 1.6. (b) 0.6 or -1.6.

236. (a) 3^3 is less than 50, 4^3 is more than 50. (b) 3.7.
(c) 3.68.

237. (i) $4(x + 2y)$. (ii) $x(x + y)$. (iii) $2x(2y - t)$.
(iv) $3x(x + 3)$. (v) $5(5x - 3y)$. (vi) $pq(q + p)$.

238. $a + b = 8.7$ and $2a = a + 2b$ hence $a = 2b$, simultaneous equations give $b = 2.9$, $a = 5.8$, $p = 11.6$.

239. $F + T = 35$, $5F + 20T = 445$, hence $F = 17$, $T = 18$.

240. (a) 1.41 cm. (b) 8 cm^2. (c) 16 cm^2.
(d) 2048 cm^2. (e) $4 \times 2^{n-1} = 2^{n+1}$.

241. (a) 9, 14, 20. (b) (i) 54. (ii) 11. (c) $d = \frac{1}{2}n^2 - \frac{3}{2}n$.

242. (a) 503. (b) (i) $(x - 10), (x + 1)$.
(ii) $(x - 10)(x + 1) + x = x^2 - 8x - 10$. (c) 36.

243. (a) $180 - x$. (b) $\dfrac{360}{x}$. (c) $\dfrac{360}{x}$. (d) $\dfrac{360}{x}$.

244. (a) (i) 40, 50, 35, 45. (ii) $10n$, $10n - 5$, 9.
(b) (i) 90 cm. (iii) 4.

245. (i) 100. (ii) 9. (iii) 0.3. (iv) $\frac{1}{25}$. (v) $\frac{1}{3}$.
(vi) 4. (vii) 1. (viii) 7. (ix) 4. (x) $\frac{1}{25}$.
(xi) $2x^3$. (xii) $\dfrac{5p^{-8}}{4}$. (xiii) $12x^{-6}$.
(xiv) -27 m^3. (xv) $3x^2$. (xvi) $5y^8$.
(xvii) $4q^{4/3}$. (xviii) y. (xix) $9y^4$. (xx) $\frac{8}{27}$.

246. (i) $y(a + 4y)$. (ii) $t(3t^2 + 2t + 5)$.
(iii) $p^2q^2(q - p)$. (iv) $4(p - 2)$.
(v) $(p + q)(y - z)$. (vi) $(r - p)(q + s)$.
(vii) $(t - 3)(t - p)$. (viii) $(x - y)(a + b + c)$.
(ix) $(x - 3)(x - 8)$. (x) $(x + 3)(x - 1)$.
(xi) $(x + 13)(x - 2)$. (xii) Impossible.
(xiii) $(2x + 3)(x + 5)$. (xiv) $(2x + 1)(2x + 3)$.
(xv) $(3x - 1)(2x - 1)$. (xvi) $(9x + 2)(x - 1)$.
(xvii) $(4x^2 + 1)(x - 1)(x + 1)$.
(xviii) $(2x - 5)(2x + 5)$. (xix) $(1 - x)(1 + x)$.
(xx) $\pi(R - r)(R + r)$. (xxi) $x(x - 6)$.
(xxii) $(11xy - 2)(11xy + 2)$. (xxiii) $(2x - 3y)^2$.
(xxiv) $(5x - y)^2$. (xxv) $(5 - b)^2$.

247. (i) $\dfrac{x+1}{x^2}$.   (ii) $\dfrac{2b+3}{ab}$.   (iii) $\dfrac{13x}{12}$.   (iv) $\dfrac{25}{3y}$.

(v) $\dfrac{4x^2+1}{x}$.   (vi) $\dfrac{7a+12b}{8}$.   (vii) $\dfrac{2x-1}{6}$.

(viii) 2.   (ix) pt.   (x) $\dfrac{2a}{b}$.   (xi) $\dfrac{b^2}{c^2}$.   (xii) $\dfrac{8x}{5y}$.

(xiii) $\dfrac{2q}{3}$.

248. (i) $3, -1$.   (ii) $2, 8$.   (iii) $\frac{1}{2}, -1$.   (iv) $\frac{1}{3}, 3$.
(v) $1.85, -4.85$.   (vi) $1.82, 0.18$.

249. (a) $8x$.   (b) $2y/x^2$.   (c) x^3.   (d) x^{-2}.
(e) $\dfrac{(2x+1)-2x}{2x(2x+1)} = \dfrac{1}{2x(2x+1)}$

250. (b) (ii) 2.   (c) $2.73, -0.73$.

251. (a) $175, 315$.   (d) 46 m.p.h.   (e) 30 m.p.h.

252.

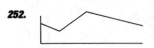

253. (a) £4.   (b) £7.50.   (c) $nc = 60$.   (d) B.
(e) straight line through the origin.

254. (a) $4 = 2a + \frac{1}{2}b, 1 = 4a + \frac{1}{4}b$.   (b) $a = -\frac{1}{3}, b = \frac{28}{3}$.
(d) $x^2 + 12x - 28 = 0$.   (e) $x = -14$.

255. (a) multiplies by -1.   (b) (i) -7.   (ii) -7.
(iii) -7.   (c) multiplies by -1.

256. (a) 5.   (b) (i) -1.   (ii) 9.   (iii) 14.   (v) 6.2.
(c) {positive integers > 3}.

257. (a) $1 + 2 + 4 + \ldots + t$.   (b) (ii) $1 + p + p^2$.
(iii) $1 + p + p^2 + \ldots + p^n$.

258. (a) $(x-3)(x-2)$.   (b) $x = 3, 2$.   (c) (0,6), (2,0),
(3,0);.   (d) $-4, -5$.

259. (a) $(x-1)^2 + 2$ ($a = 1, b = 2$).

260. (i) 25.   (ii) $-1.5, 2.5$.

261. (i) 20 litres/min hot, 32 litres/min cold.
(ii) 3 mins 5 seconds.

262. (i) $1\frac{1}{8}$.   (ii) $\frac{4}{9}$.   (iii) 121.5.

263. (a) 2160 g/cm^2.   (b) 10 cm.

264. (a) $-\frac{1}{2}$.   (b) $\frac{4}{3}$.   (c) $\frac{4}{25}$.   (d) $x = 64y^{-2}$.

265. 62.

266. (a) 19.   (b) 32.

267. (a) 34%.   (b) (ii) 24.   (iii) 3.

268. (a) $0, 1, 3, 6, 10$.   (b) $1, 2, 3, 4$.   (c) n.   (e) 99.

269. (a) (i) 4.   (ii) 49.   (iii) 484.

270. (a) (i) 2.29.   (ii) $x^3 = 12$. Second method converges quicker.

271. (a) 3, 2.   (b) (i) £114.   (ii) £3.80.

272. (a) (i) $40.5 - 45.5$.   (ii) $28, 62, 82, 94, 100$.
(b) (i) 43.5.   (ii) 8.   (c) 70.

273. 278.

274. 14.6.

275. (b) $58.9, 8.11$.   (c) 58.9 ± 16.22 gives a range $42.68 - 75.12$ appears to include 99%.

276. (i) $2.21, 0.94$.   (ii) $1.97, -0.21$.   (iii) $0.86, -0.34$.

277. (a) 45 s.   (b) 0.13 ms^{-2}.   (c) 2.145 km.
(d) 19.3 km/h.

278. (b) $x \geq 1, y \geq 1, \frac{3}{4}x + y \leq 6$.   (d) 3 wine, 3 spirits.

279. (a) $y \leq \frac{1}{2}x + 2, y + 2x \leq 10$.
(b) (i) 6 at (4,2).   (ii) -4 at (2,3).

280. $x + y \leq 1000, y \geq 2x, x \geq 100, y \leq 800, 333, 667$.

281. (a) $h \geq 15$.   (b) $p > 25$.   (c) $45 \leq h + p < 60; 25, 30$.

282. 3.34 units^2.

283. 7.3.

284. (a) $0, 28, 48, 60, 64, 60, 48, 28, 0$.   (c) (i) 64 m/s.
(ii) 8 ms^{-2}.   (iii) 672 m.

285. (a) (i) 268 cm^3.   (ii) 0.0654 cm^3.   (iii) 4096.
(b) 3.33 cm.   (c) (i) 0.5 cm.   (ii) 3.14 cm^2.
(iii) 0.785 cm^2.

286. (a) (i) 8000 cm^3.   (ii) 4189 cm^3.   (iii) 3811 cm^3.
(b) Same amount.

287. (d) 90°.   (e) 12 cm.   (f) 30 cm^2.
(g) the line TQ.

288. (a) 72 400 cm^3.   (b) 72 litres.   (c) (i) 58 litres.
(ii) 72.1 cm.

289. 33 200 cm^3.

290. (a) (i) 155 cm^3.   (ii) 135 cm^3.   (b) 6.87 cm.
(c) 3.7 cm.

291. (a) 84.5 m.   (b) 224 m.   (c) 22.2°.

292. (a) 1390 cm^3.   (b) (i) 251 cm^2.   (ii) 5.51 cm.
(iii) 600 cm^3.

293. (a) 4 cm.   (b) 864 cm^3.   (c) 3888 cm^2.
(d) 1728 cm^2.

294. (a) BE.   (b) (i) $\dfrac{d}{x} = \dfrac{x}{h}$.   (ii) $d = \dfrac{x^2}{h}$.   (c) $11\frac{1}{4}$ m.

295. (a) 10 cm.   (b) 8.   (c) 2.5 cm, 1.25 cm.   (d) 4096.

296. (a) (i) 52°.　(ii) 47°.　(iii) 81°.　(iv) 4/25.

297. (a) 4.8 cm.　(b) 9.6 km.　(c) 45.4°.

298. (a) 9.5, 8.1, 6.2, 2.7, 2.0.　(c) After 4 hours 45 mins.
(d) 2.9 cm/min.

299. (a) 33.4°, 146.6°.　(b) (i) 4.76 miles.　(ii) 3.14 miles.

300. (i) (a) 14.4.　(b) 133.8°.　(c) 0.87 km.　(ii) 190.4 m,
248 m, 13.5°.

301. 7.9 ha.

302. $p = \frac{3}{2}$, $q = \frac{11}{7}$.

303. (a) Equal.　(b) $\begin{pmatrix} 6 \\ -4 \end{pmatrix}$ $\begin{pmatrix} -9 \\ -6 \end{pmatrix}$.　(d) $\begin{pmatrix} 6 \\ -4 \end{pmatrix}$.
(e) Returns to A.

304. (a) $\frac{1}{2}\sqrt{3}$.　(c) $(1\frac{1}{4}, \frac{1}{4}\sqrt{3})$.

305. 034.3°.

306. (a) $-3\mathbf{c}$, $2\mathbf{a} - \mathbf{c}$, $2\mathbf{c} - 2\mathbf{a}$.　(b) $-3\mathbf{c}$, $\mathbf{a} + \mathbf{c}$, $3\mathbf{a} - 3\mathbf{c}$,
$-3\mathbf{a} + 3\mathbf{c}$.　(c) *DEF* is a straight line, *DE = EF*.

307. (a) $3\mathbf{y}$.　(b) $\mathbf{x} + \mathbf{y}$.　(c) $\frac{1}{2}\mathbf{x} + \frac{1}{2}\mathbf{y}$, $\frac{1}{2}\mathbf{x} + \mathbf{y}$.　(d) $\frac{1}{2}\mathbf{y}$.
(e) parallel, $EF = \frac{1}{6}AD$.

308. (a) (i) $2\mathbf{b} - 2\mathbf{a}$.　(ii) $6\mathbf{b}$.　(iii) $2\mathbf{a} - 6\mathbf{b}$.
(iv) $\mathbf{a} + 3\mathbf{b}$.
(b) (i) $2k\mathbf{b} - 2k\mathbf{a}$.　(iii) $h\mathbf{a} + 3h\mathbf{b}$.　(iv) Must have
$h = 2(1 - k)$ and $3h = 2k$. Solve as simultaneous equations
to give $h = \frac{1}{2}$, $k = \frac{3}{4}$.

309. (a) $\frac{2}{3}\mathbf{b}$, $\frac{2}{3}\mathbf{b}$, $-\mathbf{b} + \mathbf{a}$.　(b) $\frac{2}{3}(\mathbf{a} - \mathbf{b})$, $\frac{2}{3}\mathbf{a}$.
(c) Trapezium.　(d) $\frac{2}{3}$.　(e) 27 cm².

310. $2 \times 200\cos 10° = 394$N.

311. (a) $\begin{pmatrix} 11 & 5 & -1 \\ -4 & -1 & 4 \end{pmatrix}$.　(b) $\begin{pmatrix} -2 & -3 \\ 14 & -6 \\ 7 & -19 \end{pmatrix}$.

(c) $\begin{pmatrix} -5 & 10 \\ -13 & 0 \end{pmatrix}$.　(d) Impossible.

(e) $\begin{pmatrix} 4 & -4 & -8 \\ 0 & 4 & 12 \\ 16 & 4 & 24 \end{pmatrix}$.
(f) Impossible.

312. $\begin{pmatrix} \frac{7}{4} & \frac{3}{4} \\ -1 & \frac{9}{4} \end{pmatrix}$.

313. $\begin{pmatrix} \frac{2}{5} & 0 \\ \frac{1}{5} & -\frac{3}{5} \end{pmatrix}$.

314. (a) $\frac{1}{2}\begin{pmatrix} 3 & -2 \\ -5 & 4 \end{pmatrix}$.　(b) $\begin{pmatrix} 6 & 7 \\ 5 & 6 \end{pmatrix}$.　(c) Impossible.

(d) $\frac{1}{36}\begin{pmatrix} 9 & -3 \\ 6 & 2 \end{pmatrix}$.　(e) $\begin{pmatrix} 1 & 0 \\ 0 & -1 \end{pmatrix}$.

(f) $\frac{1}{78}\begin{pmatrix} 11 & 4 \\ -3 & 6 \end{pmatrix}$.

315. (a) (i) $\begin{pmatrix} 0 & 3 & 2 \\ 3 & 0 & 2 \\ 2 & 2 & 0 \end{pmatrix}$.　(ii) $\begin{pmatrix} 1 & 1 & 1 & 1 & 1 & 0 & 0 \\ 1 & 1 & 1 & 0 & 0 & 1 & 1 \\ 0 & 0 & 0 & 1 & 1 & 1 & 1 \end{pmatrix}$.

(iv) $S = T^T$ (transpose).　(b) (iii) $\begin{pmatrix} 5 & 0 & 0 \\ 0 & 5 & 0 \\ 0 & 0 & 4 \end{pmatrix}$.

316. (a) *A* to *Y*.
(b) *A* to *Z*(2), *B* to *X*(2), *C* to *X*(3), *C* to *Z*(3), *D* to *X*(3),
D to *Z*(3).

317. (b) (ii) A shear.　(c) (iii) $\begin{pmatrix} 0 & 1 \\ 1 & 0 \end{pmatrix}$.

(d) $\begin{pmatrix} 0 & 1 \\ 1 & 1 \end{pmatrix}$.

318. (c) (i) $(-1,0)$, $(-3,0)$, $(-1,1)$.　(ii)　(d) (ii) reflection
in *y* axis.　(iii) $T = SR$.

319. (b) 4 units².　(c) 72 units².
(d) Enlargement by $\sqrt{18}$, 45° anticlockwise.
(e) Reflection in $y = -x$.
(f) $\begin{pmatrix} -3 & -3 \\ -3 & 3 \end{pmatrix}$.

ANSWERS TO MENTAL ARITHMETIC TEST 1

1. 4.

2. 1600.

3. 13.

4. 10.07.

5. 24.

6. £1.16.

7. 5 February.

8. 4.38 p.m.

9. 8.

10. £2.70.

11. 128 805.

12. 89.

13. 78.

14. £7.28.

15. £140.

16. 8 kg.

17. 87.5 miles.

18. $\frac{1}{3}$.

19. $12\frac{1}{4}$%.

20. £1.60.

ANSWERS TO MENTAL ARITHMETIC TEST 2

1. £42.

2. 48.

3. 8.

4. 6.5–7 m.

5. 27.

6. 5 lb.

7. 5.

8. 8.

9. 192 cm².

10. £1.60.

11. 15.05.

12. $8x^2$.

13. $2\frac{1}{2}$ h.

14. 12 cm².

15. $\frac{3}{4}$.

16. 65°.

17. 45 s.

18. 29 000.

19. 12 cm³.

20. 9.21 p.m.

ANSWERS TO MENTAL ARITHMETIC TEST 3

1. 28 cm².
2. 37.
3. £200.
4. £2.40.
5. 105 008.
6.
7. 21°C.
8. 32 cm.
9. 61 miles.
10. 18 cm².
11. 54.7.
12. 110°.
13. 3h 14min.
14. £4.88.
15. 59p.

ANSWERS TO MENTAL ARITHMETIC TEST 4

1. 3600.
2. £2.64.
3. 240 cm³.
4. 5 ft.
5. 96 cm².
6. $\frac{3}{16}$.
7. 1000 cm³.
8. £96.
9. 151 miles.
10. 8 cm.
11. 56.
12. 250°.
13. 12.30.
14. £3.64.
15. 30 g.

INDEX

First published 1986 by
THE MACMILLAN PRESS LTD
Houndmills, Basingstoke, Hampshire RG21 2XS
and London
Companies and representatives throughout the world

ISBN 0–333–59704–4

A catalogue record for this book is available
from the British Library

Printed in Great Britain by
Unwin Brothers Ltd, The Gresham Press,
Old Woking, Surrey.
A member of the Martins Printing Group.

First edition reprinted three times
Second edition 1987
Reprinted twice
Third edition 1991
10 9 8 7 6 5 4 3 2 1
02 01 00 99 98 97 96 95 94 93